Handbook for
Family Analysis

Handbook for Family Analysis

Gordon Shipman
University of Wisconsin,
Stevens Point

LexingtonBooks
D.C. Heath and Company
Lexington, Massachusetts
Toronto

Library of Congress Cataloging in Publication Data

Shipman, Gordon.
  Handbook for family analysis.

  Includes index.
  1. Family—United States. I. Title.
HQ728.S523   1982   306.8'5'0973   82-47579
ISBN 0-669-05548-4   AACR2

Published simultaneously in Canada

Printed in the United States of America

Casebound International Standard Book Number: 0-669-05548-4

Paperbound International Standard Book Number: 0-669-05549-2

Library of Congress Catalog Card Number: 82-47579

To all my former students

This book is really not mine to dedicate for it is the collective effort of thousands of students. I simply put the pieces together. The general attitude of the students when they returned their papers to me was epitomized by one who said, "If my story will be of help to others, then here it is." Those whose bits of autobiographical material were not summarized or quoted can rest assured that their contributions simmered in my subconscious to affect my theories.

Contents

Chapter 6   **Dyads**   67

                 Two Boys   69
                 Two Girls   76
                 Older Brother/Younger Sister   80
                 Older Sister/Younger Brother   88

Chapter 7   **Male Triads**   97

Chapter 8   **Female Triads**   101

Chapter 9   **Mixed Triads**   107

                 Boy and Two Girls   107
                 Girl and Two Boys   111
                 Girl, Boy, Girl   118
                 Boy, Girl, Boy   122
                 Two Girls and a Boy   125
                 Two Boys and a Girl   127

Chapter 10   **Fours and Fives**   131

                 Contrasting Character Development between
                     Older and Younger Sibs   135
                 All-Boy Families   138
                 All-Girl Families   140
                 Only Boy Oldest among Sisters   142
                 Only Boy in the Midst of Sisters   144
                 Only Boy with Older Sisters   147
                 Two Boys and Two Girls   150
                 Reverse Leadership   152
                 Violation of Generational Role Boundaries   154
                 What Do Women Really Want?   156

Chapter 11   **Large Family Systems**   157

Part III   *Family Patterns*   169

Chapter 12   **Family Rituals**   171

                 Periodic Rituals   172
                 Seasonal and Recreational Rituals   175
                 Strategic Rituals   176
                 Spontaneous Idiomatic Rituals   181
                 Rituals in the Family Life Cycle   182
                 Summary   184

Figures

Tables

Preface and Acknowledgments

For many years I gave students in my marriage and family classes a special assignment, inviting them to analyze their families of origin with the assistance of an outline (appendix A.) I expected them to utilize all appropriate concepts from their social-science courses. The assignment was voluntary, and all papers were returned with comments. When I deemed it inadvisable for certain students to write a family analysis, I gave them an alternate project. It takes great courage for a student from a very bad family to come to grips with the unpleasant realities of his family life. Many such men and women came to my office with their problems, and I spent many hours listening to them. On occasion, I referred a student to the counseling office.

When a paper revealed special insight or illustrated a concept, I asked for a copy for my files. All names in the book are fictitious. For each excerpt, there were dozens, even hundreds, of others that had similar themes or circumstances.

During a twenty-year period, I read nearly 5,000 papers and collected some 1,200. The vast majority of my students considered the writing of their analyses so valuable to them in so many ways that I thought their personal reports would be helpful to others. It is quite possible that my rapport with students was influenced by my experience, during an earlier period, as a state probation-parole agent.

Certain people have been most helpful in my writing. My daughter, Anne Pasch, and Dr. Pamela Kemp read each chapter as it was finished. Dr. Ruth Jewson, Dr. Dennis Elsenrath, and Mary Croft read much of the manuscript and made valuable comments. From beginning to end, my wife, Agnes, played the roles of typist, proofreader, editor, and consultant.

Part I
Preparation for
Family Analysis

1 Family Quality in Search of a Term

As a rule, people get married and start a family without a blueprint for a good family. They depend entirely upon impressions acquired from their families of origin, without really analyzing the strengths and weaknesses of that family. They also do not analyze systematically and objectively their spouse's family. Occasionally, a young person will become acquainted with a family of unusual quality that may constitute a model to be studied. However, most couples are without guidelines that not only could prevent subsequent unfortunate family difficulties but also could lead to greater satisfactions. Of course, we do have an abundance of moralistic platitudes but no social consensus on what a family of high quality should be like. The process of defining what we want seems to be facilitated by delineating what we do not want, and family experts are no exception. It is therefore appropriate to review briefly what scholars have done in this connection over the past half century.

When scholars began to study the family systematically, they were concerned about the quality of marriage although they rarely used the term *quality*. They became preoccupied with defining, measuring, and developing instruments to predict marital success. They used terms such as *happy-unhappy, stable-unstable, adjusted-maladjusted, successful-unsuccessful*—all of which have been criticized. When it became apparent that predictive instruments were not very useful, they began to focus their attention on the family as a whole, and some of them considered it as a system. However, those who studied the family had the same problems: What words and concepts could be used to designate variations in quality? What was meant by quality? Those who had a constructive stance toward families used terms such as *normal, successful, healthy, wellness,* and *competent*. It was not clear to what end families should be normal, successful, or competent. They described with brilliance the characteristics of such families in terms of love, security, awareness, vitality, self-esteem, satisfaction of needs, ability to communicate, and possession of a network of friend-families; but the essence of a model family, an excellent family, or a family of highest quality was not clarified.[1]

By 1970s, marriage counselors had developed the concept of relationship therapy in which a relationship is an entity distinct from the parties

3

thereto and is the focus of treatment. Since relationships in counseling practice included children, marriage counseling became marriage and family counseling. Two related ideas are expressed or implied in this literature: (1) There are universal values, applicable to all human beings, centering around growth in all its aspects; and (2) human beings, like all other organisms, have an innate urge to grow and to complete their life cycle. A recent book by two family therapists puts it this way:

> [T]he desire to expand, to develop himself, and to experience life is instinctive and innate. That desire can be trampled on, brutalized, put under unbelievable pressure, and it may be twisted into destructive pathways, but never destroyed.[2]

Carl Rogers, Abraham Maslow, and the humanists were concerned about values. Maslow coined the term *self-actualization.* He stressed the meeting of needs of people so that they could develop all their potential completely. He and others stressed health and wellness as a function of growth. One is in a state of wellness if growth prevails and in a state of illness if growth has stopped.[3]

During the 1960s and 1970s, a variety of church-sponsored encounter groups developed more or less independently of each other. The largest of these was the Catholic Marriage Encounter Group. Its primary concern is to allow married couples to experience genuine interpersonal communication with their spouses.

Under the leadership of David Mace, various programs, both lay and religious, developed enough common concerns to be called family enrichment programs.[4] This movement focuses on reasonably healthy couples who have no need for therapy but who desire to improve their marriages and their families. The goals of the programs are described in terms of marital growth, marital potential, and marital health. Mace discarded both the educational and the therapeutic approaches for an experiential one that involves active communication among group members under the stimulation of the group leaders.[5]

In my opinion, the most significant of recent studies dealing with quality in families is that of a research team led by Lewis and Beavers.[6] They used expressions such as *healthy, well-functioning, competent, optimal,* and *global family health.* They also developed a series of five scales to measure family competence. These scales were used while judging the quality of families by viewing family interaction with videotapes. This research demonstrated that raters could agree, with high reliability, in evaluating the health of families. They also found that individual members of a family made estimates of their family's health that corresponded with the rating of the researchers. This suggests that it is practical to develop a self-rating instrument that family members can use to evaluate the quality of their own family (see chapter 19).

We still have the problem of defining a high-quality family and the problem of delineating in simple terms those patterns of family behavior that move the family in either direction on the high-and-low-quality spectrum.

Why was it that experts in the family field over a period of decades could describe all the desired qualities of families but could coin neither a suitable term for a family that encompassed most or all of them nor an antonym that encompassed few or none of them? One explanation for this is the emphasis on cultural relativity. Ten years ago, when I suggested to a colleague that we proceed to define and measure quality in family living, he objected strongly and said it could not be done because we have so many subcultures in our society that we could never agree on what we mean by quality. Another explanation is that family sociologists, just like everybody else, are immersed in the pathological bias of our culture. In medicine and in the social sciences, we have developed a vast literature on pathologies and personal and social disorganization but a paucity of materials on health and health models. This is reflected in our vocabulary. I quote from Sisson:

> [T]here are more words for forces inimical to man, the forces of calamity, evil, destruction, war, fear, and the like, than for those of peace and general well-being. For example, there are in this book 64 words for "evil," 76 for "brutal," 111 for "cruel," and 465 words or expressions for "bad," but only 150 words for "good." There are 124 for "attack" and 67 for "calamity," but only 28 for "peace."[7]

From the history of ideas regarding quality in family living, I combine two concepts for my definition of the model family. This model would be a family in which the patterns of family behavior are conducive to the maximum growth of all family members in an aura of altruism. The latter phrase is used in a broad sense so that the love and devotion that family members have for each other radiate outward to relatives, friends, the community, and society. This definition rules out families who develop their talents for antisocial purposes. In this ideal family, the responsibility of every member is to stimulate the growth of every other member. This means that each spouse would improve the growth potential of the other and of all the children and that each child would encourage the growth potential of his siblings and that of the parents. Not only does growth have a beneficial impact on the family but so does the good feeling family members experience toward those who facilitate their growth. People love their mentors. The dynamics of such a family would be defined, not in terms of success but of quality. With this idea in mind I searched for a term. It was supplied by

Professor Panos Bardis of Toledo University, who said the word I wanted was *pantrophic* from the Greek. *Trophic* means "fostering, rearing, nourishing," and the prefix *pan* means "all."

Various authorities have said that at the present stage of our culture most people develop only a small fraction of their potential. If the term *pantrophic* is to be practical, we shall have to apply it short of the ideal. I shall, therefore, use it in the following pages to designate families that seem to be far superior to others in promoting the potential of family members. We also need a term for a family system in which the patterns of family behavior stymie the development of potential. For this purpose, Professor Bardis suggested the antonym of pantrophic, *dystrophic*. Dystrophic, therefore, is the adjective for any feature of a family that checks or retards the cultivation of talents or skills. Many such behaviors seem minor and thus are neglected. For example, a father, pretending concern lest his son become egotistical, made it a point to downgrade any idea or opinion the boy expressed. When the lad got to school, he could not respond to the teacher's questions because his self-expression was retarded and his self-esteem diminished.

Most families have a mixture of pantrophic and dystrophic elements. If we had a family in which the pantrophic and dystrophic elements canceled out each other, we should have point zero on our scale; those on the plus side would be increasingly pantrophic; those on the minus side would be increasingly dystrophic. Some day we shall have an instrument to score families on such a scale. In chapter 19, I present two lists of indicators that are associated with either a pantrophic family or a dystrophic one.

I think the pantrophic-dystrophic model is superior to the success model that was applied to the quality of marriage in an earlier period. In those studies, success was defined partly in terms of the absence of something harmful like conflict. In my model, positive and negative patterns are differentiated and go by different names.

The idea in the pantrophic-dystrophic model is not to appraise what is good or bad about family members but to improve relationships and to change patterns of behavior that stymie growth to patterns that promote growth. For example, the firstborn of either sex usually becomes an achiever and acquires a fine academic record, while the secondborn withdraws from competition and refuses to study even though his potential is just as good or better. Parents and teachers, with the best intentions, say things to the secondborn that make him backfire; this situation is dealt with in chapters 6 and 7. I shall also quote what some parents have said to stimulate the secondborn to do his best.

Some years ago two psychiatrists wrote a book called *The Happy Family*.[8] I was not impressed with its value for persons desiring to reach its limited goal, but the title was so alluring to the public that the book went through several printings in a short time. The word *happy* is not dynamic and may be confused with contentment. A family whose members sit around smoking marijuana might consider themselves quite happy. The term *pantrophic* implies growth, the acquisition of personal identity, the improvement of skills and self-esteem, stimulation of relationships, a zest for life, compelling interests, attainment of maturity, and a sense of social responsibility.

During infancy and early childhood, growth in several dimensions takes place rapidly within the family context. However, as the child progresses in school, more and more of his intellectual growth takes place in a school context, and more of his social growth takes place in a peer context. It has been said that educational institutions are encroaching upon the socialization function of the family, but those who take this position are neglecting a salient function of parents—that is, the orientation of children to the outer world in such a manner that they will be motivated to take advantage of growth opportunities in school and college as well as in museums, art galleries, recreational facilities, and music, religious, and social organizations. To make the most of such opportunities requires the acquisition of judgment, self-discipline, and skill in allocating one's time, energy, and money among options. There is no substitute for parents in such orientation. In parts II and III, my students reveal some common mistakes made by parents and teachers in this area.

Another kind of orientation takes place within the family—namely, the orientation to love, sex, and marriage. In pantrophic families wherein the children have experienced love and affection, positive and healthy attitudes toward the opposite sex and marriage are developed. Thus, pantrophic features are carried over to the family of procreation. In dystrophic families wherein conflict is the rule, the children develop negative attitudes toward marriage and, sometimes, the opposite sex. They also may lose confidence in themselves for playing the marital role. A girl who is abandoned by her father and discriminated against by her family in favor of her brother may spend the rest of her life getting even with men at considerable cost to herself. Later chapters illustrate this problem. The orientation to love and sex of one kind or another takes place in every family. Great variations on this theme are covered in chapter 16.

When one examines the life histories of many people, he is impressed with the idiosyncratic nature of each family. However, one also is impressed with that elusive but potent element that seems to come from between the lines. It is something that cannot be captured in an excerpt; it comes from the total family experience. I refer to the prevailing mood of a family. As most geographic regions have prevailing winds, so do families have prevailing moods. The family mood may ebb and flow like the wind and tide, but it tends to prevail as an entity for varying periods throughout the life cycle. The following expressions give examples of the nature of prevailing moods:

> In our house there is lots of laughter.
>
> In our house the word *love* is used frequently.
>
> We lived in dread because we never knew when father would come home drunk and start a fight.

The prevailing mood of a family is influenced by personal temperaments, family rituals, and the physical and artistic features of the home. In a healthy family, the central core of a positive prevailing mood is unique; it has an aura of cohesiveness, solidarity, pride, security, love, and continuity. These feelings radiate outward from the nuclear unit to relatives. In some families, all of this is missing. One student described his family as merely a group of people, each pursuing his own way but living under the same roof. Another student said his father followed an army career for several years, coming home rarely and only for a day or so. When the father came home to stay, the student said, "I didn't pay any more attention to him that if he were a roomer." Another student said, "When Christmas time comes around, I always make it a point not to go home." A female student had a family whose members made her feel that she could never do anything right. Their attitudes and behavior made her depressed. However, she was bright and her teachers encouraged her. When she entered the university, she had neither moral nor financial help from her family. A brother offered to loan her money, but on such conditions that she rejected his offer. When she wrote her family analysis, she said she "cried a million tears" because she realized that, to preserve her health, she would have to reject her family and never go home again.

The unhealthy elements in this young woman's family were undoubtedly reflected in its prevailing mood. A healthy prevailing mood fosters personality development. I asked a colleague, Dr. L. Baird Callicott, University of Wisconsin at Stevens Point, to suggest a term. He said the mood should be called *hestia,* the ancient Greek word for "hearth." Primitive man had difficulty procuring fire and maintaining it. When an ancient Greek left the home of his parents to establish a new household, he carried with him embers from his father's hearth. This continuity of fire in the hearth symbolized the continuity of the family. When towns were established, there was a public *hestia* and eventually a fire deity, the goddess Hestia. In the course of time, the word *hestia* came to have four meanings: (1) the shrine of the household gods, (2) the house itself, (3) a family, and (4) an altar or shrine.[9] For the Greeks, *hestia* had the connotation of home and the ceremonies and rituals of family life. If there is an absence of *hestia,* there is a void that handicaps growth. You will not find the term employed in the excerpts from the student papers because I sought for this term after having worked with them. A family that has a genuine *hestia* has no delinquency, mental breakdown, or suicide; instead, it has creative activity conducive to growth. When one makes an analysis of his family he will, among other things, think about its *hestia* and consider ways to make it something to cherish.

A certain family therapist went into the room where a client family was waiting for him; he suddenly felt depressed. When no member of the family spoke, the therapist told them he felt depressed and asked for their explanation. The father began to cry and then admitted to an episode in his recent life for which he was ashamed. It transpired that all family members knew about it but had ignored it.

Now suppose the receptionist in this center for family therapy played a trick on the same therapist. Instead of scheduling a family in need of therapy, she scheduled a wholesome family whose members were privy to the trick. How long would it take the nonverbal cues of the pantrophic family with its fine *hestia* to make the therapist inquire why they were so happy?

Let us contrast the *hestia* of an imaginary felon in his cell with that of a college student from a happy family. Each is about to go home—the first one on parole, the second for Christmas recess. The first is thinking of home in terms of brown walls with broken plaster, a slovenly wife working in a disordered living room, caring for a baby he did not father, and a dirty window with a view of a red brick wall beyond the noisy railroad tracks. The student is thinking of her welcome at home. She anticipates the joyous greetings of family members and the scramble to give her hugs and kisses. She sees herself in a delightful, spacious livingroom engaged in festive activities with her siblings. She knows exactly what the family routine will be during the holidays, even to the menu on Christmas day. She thinks about their gathering around the fireplace where some will sing Christmas carols accompanied by others playing musical instruments. On Christmas morning they will open their presents before the picture window that overlooks trees and the river beyond the meadow.

In summary, the pantrophic family possesses family patterns conducive to growth on an equitable basis for all family members in which devotion with adequate nurturance is combined with a *hestia* that permits family members to relax in an aura of well-being and cohesiveness. In families of high quality, the *hestia* is most evident during family rituals. Whether the ritual involves a quiet sense of love and security or spontaneous laughter and gaiety, the underlying spirit of the family remains. In families of low quality, the rituals are either missing or few and artificial. Family rituals are discussed in chapter 12.

Following are quotations by college students that contrast a pantrophic family with a dystrophic one. Persons in dystrophic families seem to have more to say than others. Although the first has but two paragraphs, every sentence illustrates pantrophic trends—trends that are reinforced in the rest of her paper.

My parents are very affectionate; they have never had a major fight. There has never been any favoritism in our family, and my brother and I were treated equally well. My father and I are very close. He has a good sense of humor and is very affectionate. My friends (of both sexes) have always liked my dad a lot as he makes them very comfortable when they come to our home. Mom is more like a sister in some ways. We talk a lot about everything and anything and have always been very close. She, too, is very affectionate and has a fantastic sense of humor.

My brother and I are very close. He confides in me and I have been of help to him. As far as cooperation goes, everyone does his share and there is rarely any argument about it. We were taught the importance of saving and were included in decisions when major items were purchased. My parents have always believed that each individual is different and should be allowed to live his life in the way it best suits him. I have always had a wholesome attitude about sex as everything was explained to me in full by my parents. Given this responsibility, I had the opportunity to make my own decisions and it helped me to reason for myself. The family rituals are always the same and bring us many happy memories. We have always enjoyed doing things together, and because of these shared experiences, we are a very close family. We have never had any trouble with communication at our house. There is no one dominant person in our family. We all have equal say in decisions and have hardly any trouble compromising. We are a very emotionally stable family.[10]

My family of orientation is not a healthy one; it has a sickness that has spread and infected each member. My father is alcoholic. Although my brother idolized me, I couldn't stand him. I could not love him. We became best of enemies. There was a poor level of communication between my parents and us kids, and my father yelled a lot.

My brother was not informed in matters concerning sex. At age eleven, he started becoming very insecure and confused. He was a big troublemaker at school and around the neighborhood.

There was a distinct communication gap between myself and my family. From the beginning, my father drank excessively. His family became the scapegoat for his frustrations, and the bottle became his refuge.

My mother had emotional breakdowns. Their level of communication had reached the child level with his constant yelling and her defensiveness. While my mother was in the hospital, it was pure hell at home. I was really scared of my father. He blamed Mom's breakdown on my brother and me and it hurt badly. I wanted to establish a strong relationship with her because of the guilt feelings I had concerning her breakdown.

My boyfriend and three of his friends came over to visit me one night. I challenged my father when he began to say derogatory remarks about the guys. He became furious and called me a tramp. He said the only reason the guys came over to see me was because I was loose and gave them what they wanted. I felt such deep pain. My whole world was shattered. My boyfriend and his friends got into a bitter argument with my father and were thrown out. I cried. The hurt was so excruciating that I began to build a wall between us so that I would never feel such pain again. I learned to turn off my feelings whenever he would cut my values for me. I was not the only one affected by my father's drinking. Almost every night my brother and Dad would end up shouting at each other.

Mother's reactions varied. Occasionally she would fight with Dad; at other times she would shut her mouth and hold the tensions inside. My father felt insecure most of his life. He was never happy with his line of work. His instability made our family unstable, and each member felt an overpowering amount of turbulence within.

I had hardened. I took on the role as the rock of the family. My family became quite dependent on me. I suffered a lot from role confusion for I was no longer a daughter. I was a companion to my mother, a mother to my brother, and an alien to my father, although I realized that he, too, needed me. Dad was really proud of me. It made me feel good when he approved of my high school achievements, yet there was a wall between us.

I had immense guilt feelings for shutting my father off, especially since I believed that I might have been able to help him. I tortured myself with these thoughts and began to hate the hard person I had become. My boyfriend wanted to become engaged at Christmas and it scared me. I didn't want anything to do with marriage because I felt that I could not become involved in something that had destroyed four people. So I broke up with him. This really maximized my feelings of destructiveness, for now I had hurt not only father and mother but my boyfriend as well. [Daughter left home to go to college.]

In my study of families, two things stand out with great clarity. One is the idiosyncratic nature of each family; the other is the wide differences in the quality of family living within classes or groups, however defined. I am positive, from my case-history material, that the differences in family quality within each class or group are far greater than the differences between such classes or groups. Certain kinds of statements about families should not be made unless the researcher indicates what kinds of families he is talking about. For example, a statement that is valid for many families may apply neither to families high on the pantrophic scale nor to families low on the dystrophic scale.

How many families are in the pantrophic range, and how many are in the dystrophic range? This depends on time and place and on the social exigencies of war and depression. My student analyses are from two universities in the Midwest during the 1950s, 1960s, and early 1970s. Most of them

Table 1-1
Student Ratings of Happiness of Parents' Marriage by Size of University and Combined Totals, 1960 and 1968

Happiness of Parents' Marriage	Metropolitan University		Small City University		Combined Totals	
	Number	Percent	Number	Percent	Number	Percent
Extraordinarily happy	32	12	13	8	45	10.3
Happy	116	33	79	47	195	44.6
Average	90	43	51	30.5	141	32.2
Unhappy and extremely unhappy	32	12	24	14	56	12.8
Totals	270	100	167	99.5	437	99.9

Source: Modified from Gordon Shipman, "Speech Thresholds and Voice Tolerance in Marital Interaction," *Marriage and Family Living* 22 (1960):206–208. Copyrighted © 1960 by the National Council on Family Relations. Reprinted by permission.

Note: The ratings were made at midwestern universities during the 1960s.

were middle class, a few were upper class, while others had been clients of relief agencies. In connection with a research project dealing with families, I asked the students to fill out a questionnaire in which they rated the quality of their parents' marriage (see table 1-1). Sometimes the only good thing about a bad family is the marital relationship, but on the whole, the quality of the marriage is related to the quality of the family.

From the table, we could guess that in the Midwest, during the 1960s, about 12 percent of families rated very high on the pantrophic scale, about 12 percent rated very low on the dystrophic range, and the remainder were in between.[11]

We are now ready to examine the interface between the family and the settings of family members beyond the family. This interface involves rhythms of dispersion and convergence. The nature of these rhythms and how family members handle their settings have much to do with the quality of family living.

Notes

1. Carle C. Zimmerman and Lucius F. Cervantes, *Successful American Families* (New York: Pageant Press, 1960). See also William Westley and Nathan B. Epstein, "Family Structure and Emotional Health: A Case

Study Approach," *Marriage and Family Living* (February 1960); and Herbert A. Otto, "Criteria for Assessing Family Strength," *Family Process* 2 (September 1963):329–338.

2. Shirley Luthman and Martin Kirschenbaum, *The Dynamic Family* (Palo Alto, Calif.: Science and Behavior Books, 1970). Chapter 1 deals with the growth model.

3. Abraham Maslow, *Motivation and Personality* (New York: Harper & Row, 1954).

4. Ronald R. Regula, "Marriage Encounter: What Makes it Work," *Family Coordinator* 24 (1975):153. See also Rebecca M. Smith, Sarah M. Shoffner, and Jean P. Scott, "Marriage and Family Enrichment," *Family Coordinator* 28 (1979):87–93.

5. David and Vera Mace, "Marriage Enrichment—Wave of the Future," *Family Coordinator* 24 (1975):131–135. Six other articles in this issue are on the marriage-enrichment movement.

6. Jerry M. Lewis, W. Robert Beavers, John T. Gossett, and Virginia Austin Phillips, *No Single Thread: Psychological Health in Family Systems* (New York: Brunner/Mazel, 1976).

7. A.F. Sisson, *Sisson's Synonyms: An Unabridged Synonym and Related-Terms Locater* (West Nyack, N.J.: Parker Publishing Co., 1969).

8. John Levy and Ruth Monroe, *The Happy Family* (New York: Alfred A. Knopf, 1938).

9. Leddell and Scott, *Greek English Lexicon* (New York: Oxford University Press, 1889), p. 319.

10. For an entire book on a real family that was pantrophic in spite of incredible difficulties, see Ruth Engelmann, *Leaf House—Days of Remembering* (New York: Harper & Row, 1982).

11. For the real-life story of a black girl who grew up in a poverty-stricken dystrophic family in rural North Carolina, see Mary E. Mebane, *Mary* (New York: The Viking Press, 1981).

2 The Family and its Various Settings

The following pages hold accounts of children from pantrophic families who suffered from devastating (dystrophic) experiences beyond the family settings such as playground and school. Conversely, also included are accounts from persons whose home life was dystrophic but who were sustained by pantrophic influences in playground, school, and friend-families.

The term *setting* requires some explanation. For example, the parents go to a work setting that has its special place and a particular set of colleagues, coworkers, customers, clients, pupils, or patients. Each child attends his particular class in a school and romps on his particular playground with a succession of peers, classmates, and teachers. If the mother is a homemaker, her daily schedule is in the house setting from which she goes to various outside settings. Adolescents and young adults also may go out for evening activities with their peers.

The family develops a daily rhythm of comings and goings. This rhythm varies for each family according to different circumstances. Family interaction for the whole family usually is limited to mealtimes, evenings, weekends, holidays, and vacations. Family rituals take place during these periods, and family members sense their solidarity and experience the activities and emotional tone of family living—their *hestia*—during such times.

While experience in the home setting is usually stable and predictable, experience in the individual settings beyond the home is changeable and not so predictable. The settings for a grade-school child change every time the youngster is promoted to the next grade, moves on to a new school, or when his or her family moves to a new neighborhood. High mobility makes these settings kaleidoscopic in nature. As there is a particular experience for each person in his family life cycle, there is also, for each a life cycle, experience in his changing settings.

It is difficult for researchers to organize material so that one can study simultaneously the impact of family setting and outside environmental settings on a person over a period of time. This, however, is what my students often did. Although the subject of the assignment had to do with the impact of students' families on their developing personalities, they integrated their family experiences with their other setting experiences, and this blending of closely related experiences makes their chronicles more valuable.

The types of settings may be divided roughly into educational, work, and kin-friend settings. This larger circle of friends and relatives with whom the central family interacts is extremely important, as we see in later chapters. If a family depicted in our study was so isolated that it had no such circle, it was both dysfunctional and dystrophic.

Relation of Quality to the Settings

I suggest that there are four aspects in the relationship of the family to its settings that determine its pantrophic or dystrophic character: balance, integration, mobility, and visibility. In his discussion on the quality of life, Gerson dwelt upon a person's commitment of resources—money, time, skill, and sentiment—to his various settings.[1] Each setting, which may be formal or informal, provides gratifications to its members, but also imposes demands and restraints. Gerson said that the way in which the individual negotiates the simultaneous distribution of resources among his many settings is related to the quality of life. It has more significance to the quality of family life. This principle of balance was violated by a selfish father who spent a large share of his limited income drinking with cronies at his yacht club, which cut into the family budget and deprived the family of his presence. It takes cooperation, leadership, fairness, and good judgment on the part of the husband-wife team to allocate family resources to the settings of family members. As the children mature they must take increasing responsibility for the allocation of their personal resources.

Integration

Integration of settings deals with the extent family members participate in the same setting. For example, family members may constitute a family orchestra or be involved in family camping, family reunions, family work projects, and church activities. Such integration often involves family rituals that improve the *hestia* and family cohesion.

Mobility

The rate of geographic mobility may have pantrophic or dystrophic implications with respect to settings. Some students in families with moderate mobility (moving every four to six years) found moving to be exciting and challenging. High mobility, however, was usually dystrophic because it destroyed the roots of friendships, made it difficult to maintain kinship ties, and involved trauma due to sudden change. The effect of mobility on a given family must be analyzed in terms of the transition of settings for each family member. For example, the move for the father may involve a promotion in which his vocational setting is challenging and enjoyable, while for the children the move may involve a change from a happy to an unhappy setting. Each move for the family uproots, for each member, personal friendship and confronts each with the task of establishing new ones. For some members it is easy and exciting, for others it is difficult and dismaying.

A nineteen-year-old girl described the journey of her family from Eastern Europe in the early 1960s to Paris where they lived for one year to New York City for a stay of six months to a small Midwestern city for ten months and, finally, to a large Midwestern city where they hoped to settle down. The father was a professional man.

Since our family was alone among strangers for long periods of time and, in the beginning; without knowledge of the language of the new country, we all found refuge in one another, and we felt that we were very strong being together. We all know that if anything goes wrong with us, the first thing we ought to do is to discuss it at the supper table. I am sure our travels had an influence on the development of this closeness and ease of communication.

Another advantage is that members of the family had a chance to learn a new language. The most difficult hours in my life were the first few days in the new country without knowing the language and not even being able to ask for a glass of water or a piece of bread. I will never forget the first few days I spent in a French school and those in an American school in New York. In France, people who do not speak French fluently are called *étrangers,* which was the first French word I learned. The first day when I walked in the classroom, I did not understand too much what was going on. I could not talk to others, and when they realized I did not know French, they were not willing to spend their time trying to make themselves understood. Because I was an *étrangère,* they left me alone. I learned the language quite well during the first three months by studying it ten to twelve hours a day. It was very difficult for me to understand why they were so nationalistic. During the first three months, I was disappointed and disillusioned. I hated school, and when it was over in the afternoon, I was very glad to go home where I was understood, respected, loved, and felt to be somebody.

My experience in learning English was very different, although I was quite frightened and not very willing to start learning a new language again. My first day in class in New York City was different from my first day of school in Paris. It was a small school and everybody was very nice. Every day, each girl in my class wrote a word on a card and drew a picture for what it meant. Thus, daily, with their help in pronunciation and spelling, I learned thirty new words. I will always remember how I started to learn English, and the previous feeling of being a stranger never occurred to me again. I think our moving experiences made us children more broad minded and maturer than persons of similar age. A disadvantage in moving from one city to another that is very hard is the separation from good friends.

The loss of old friends is often followed by the rebuff of cliques in a new school. The newcomer is grist for the mill by groups whose maintenance is based on exclusiveness. "I had a difficult time because I was never completely in or out of the groups. Most of the time I played alone because I hated the snobbery of the cliques."

The degree of trauma from moving is determined to some extent by the pull or push of the old home in contrast to the attractive or distasteful features of the new home and neighborhood. One girl reminisced, after moving, about her longing for the beautiful old home in a wooded area on a lake, with plenty of friends of both sexes and in close proximity to loving grandparents. One boy described his loneliness after his family moved to a rural area in which he had not a single playmate of either sex. A number of students said that difficulties in making a place for themselves in a new neighborhood tended to make them shy and insecure.

The timing of the move and the rate of moving are important variables with respect to emotional consequences. Moving prior to school age and after high school has a minor effect, but especially disturbing for a youth is moving just before graduating from grade school or high school. If the rate of moving is moderate, the children may take change in stride and find it stimulating and challenging. This is more likely the case when the family is stable, and this factor is another variable to consider when estimating the effects of moving.

I think all the moving around affected me in various ways. First of all, I am more at ease with people, I am not afraid to meet new people, and I love to travel. However, it affected me psychologically in that I now long for a deep sense of security. I'm not afraid to meet new people as long as I have a group of established friends and a home base to fall back on.

I had no role in peer groups in the neighborhood, school, or church. We moved so often I barely got acquainted with anyone. I attended nine different elementary schools in eight years. I had but one childhood friend. I always had a hard time in school trying to keep my grades up. With all my duties I had no time to play. It seems as though I hardly had an ego or personality. I only remember being anxious, nervous, shy, and timid.

Families of breadwinners who are in the military service should be considered in a special category because, for them, moving is an accepted feature of their way of life. Nevertheless, these family members also suffer from frequent moving. Like others, it can give them a sense of family cohesion. They develop, however, a sense that they live in a world apart and that they have a subculture of their own.

One girl whose father was a colonel in the air force mentioned the difficulty of establishing consistent family rituals because, in each new family setting, the customs were different. She also explained how moving affects one's self-concept:

> The most disconcerting aspect of moving so often is that one finds it impossible to evaluate oneself. When one's roles are radically changed from one place to another, when one is popular in one place and left out in the next, what conclusions can be drawn? And it always seemed that just when life was beginning to become stabilized, when I had developed friendships and gotten into a few activities, it was time to go again. My father's status brought us into the highest social level wherever we went so that I joined in school and other activities, occasionally holding an office. But I developed a strong self-consciousness from being the new girl on trial so many times.

One girl whose father's occupation required the family to move frequently wrote that each move broke up budding friendships. Finally, the family seemed to have settled down, and the girl made friends, adjusted well in school, and was selected by the teachers to play the principal role in a pageant. She worked with diligence on her costume and, in great excitement, wore it on the day of the dress rehearsal. As she carried her costume home from school that day, she saw the moving van in front of the house. In rage and despair, she tore her costume to shreds.

Each family member has his own dynamic social network involving a sequence of settings. When a child moves beyond the parameters of his family, he begins the history of his social network in variable settings. As time goes on, this history becomes more important for his health and growth.

In our culture, there is great concern for the disruption of families but scarcely any for the disruption of friendships. However, there is little curiosity about the relationship between the two. Each family member makes a positive or negative contribution to his social setting, and he also brings back to his family the positive or negative impact of his social setting.

Visibility

Visibility means the extent to which the settings of family members are known to other family members. Integration of settings increases their visibility.

Children may know much or nothing about their fathers' and mothers' occupations and their roles in them. Likewise, the children may know much or nothing about their parents' social or recreational activities. The same is true for wives and husbands and for parents, regarding children.

In rural communities, occupational visibility is usually high because children are in close proximity to the parents' occupations and may play an active role themselves, for example, in farming, feed mills, general stores, small garages, gasoline stations, and taverns. In small towns, such businesses are family affairs, and any member of the family may answer the telephone, serve customers, or keep the books. In these small retail establishments as well as on farms, age grading is less than in urban settings. In rural communities one may see persons representing three generations working together. On occasion they may play together in recreational activities such as hunting, fishing, dancing, snowmobiling, and in the celebration of weddings, family reunions, and religious services.

It seems reasonable to speculate that visibility of occupational settings within the family is greater in rural areas than in urban areas, but I would not speculate the same way regarding visibility in the social activities. Regardless of the rural-urban dimension, a vast difference exists among families regarding the visibility of children's social settings for their parents. Such visibility increases when parents attend school and recreational activities wherein their children perform. Such attendance not only increases visibility but also satisfies the craving of children for the praise of parents.

For example, a college basketball player from a pantrophic family told me how his mother attended the basketball games and cheered his team as loudly as the cheerleaders. In another case, a high school boy, who was slight of build, went out for football. The coach realized he did not have the build for football, but he coached the boy specifically on one play. During the football season the boy begged his father to attend the games, to no avail. Finally after much persuasion, the father agreed to attend the last game of the season, which would decide the championship. Near the end of the fourth period, the score was tied. The coach then sent in this lad to play his one play. He caught the forward pass, made the winning touchdown, and then ran to the stands to greet his father—only to learn that his father had gone home at halftime.

There is also a great difference in the extent to which parents know something about the dating partners and social activities of their adolescents. By the same token, there is a vast difference among families about the extent to which children know and appreciate the occupational successes, failures, gratifications, and dissatisfactions of their parents, as well as the ups and downs of their social activities beyond the family.

Visibility of settings is affected by the degree of trust within the family and trust as related to respect for privacy. Chapter 13 deals with family patterns associated with both trust and privacy and how both are related to pantrophic influences.

Let us now consider a family that, in the beginning, had reasonable balance (good allocation of time, money, and energy for the various settings), low mobility, and high visibility. In the course of time, it became out of balance and developed high mobility and low visibility of settings. The father was a professional man of modest means whose family enjoyed camping trips, rituals, and other activities. The father bought a house and, with the help of the son, remodeled it. Later the father sold the house and bought another that again was remodeled, improved, and sold at a profit. This pattern of buying, improving, selling, and moving occurred with increasing tempo so that, by the time the son had reached late adolescence, the family had moved thirteen times within the metropolitan area. As the father became more affluent, he became more extravagant and spent less time with his children:

> During my early high school days I didn't mind it (the buying and remodeling) because I thought the home was for the whole family to enjoy, but later I found out that when the home was completed we would move. I developed the attitude of not caring to help any more because we never enjoyed the homes anyway.

As things became worse, the father made a common mistake that cuts down visibility of the son for the father:

> My father would constantly kid me about girls, and this made me very embarrassed. I had a fear my father would razz me to no end if I did take out a girl. This turned out to be true. He did exactly that, and I soon learned to keep my mouth shut and not tell him where I was going. Those were the years when he should have known exactly what I was doing, but since he teased me, I didn't confide in him, and he didn't know when I went out on a date or what I was doing on them. My parents became crosser and crosser and I did likewise. As the situation worsened, we tended to do less and less together, as though complete strangers were living under the same roof. The few pleasant rituals we did have ceased to exist. The cohesiveness of the family became very weak. Hostility grew to such an alarming degree that I finally broke with my parents and was asked to leave home. A few weeks ago my older sister, too, was asked to leave home.

This case illustrates that when a wholesome family changes (1) from low mobility to high mobility, (2) from integrated activities to separate activities, (3) from balanced to unbalanced distribution of time and resources, and (4) from high to low visibility, the family becomes dystrophic.

Both pantrophic and dystrophic influences exist in the course of one's experience in changing settings. On occasion, a student from an unhappy home will find within his peer setting a pantrophic home that has tremendous impact. I recall a girl whose parents experienced chronic conflict and who later divorced. One day she visited in the home of her boyfriend and was enthralled with its delightful *hestia* and with the gracious treatment she received from the boy's parents. She was nurtured and instructed better in this family than she was in her own home. On Sunday morning, she would watch at the window until this family drove by on their way to church. If she arrived at church first, she would eagerly watch for them to arrive and file into their pew. She finally decided that she was in love not with her boyfriend but with his family. A colleague of mine suggested that if this girl fantasized this boy's parents as her own, then the incest taboo would rule him out as a possible husband. Such families not only radiate emotion and provide a *hestia* that builds up the self-image of a hurting child but also provide models for spousal and parental roles for a later period. The illustrations in this book alert the reader never to underestimate what this kindness can do for the child next door. Even a superficial contact with a model family might save a child in a distressful situation.

The following case describes how continuing contact with good families can have a beneficial effect on traumatized children. Recently, while cleaning out her attic, a woman found a copy of a paper she had written years before in my class. This paper had detailed the tragic events of her early life after her alcoholic father died. The family moved to a distant state where her mother began to drink heavily and was drowned in a boating accident. The brother was arrested and brought into juvenile court. The children were separated and went to live with various nurturant relatives. After finding her paper, this woman wrote me a letter, saying that she was now happily married and had two healthy children. The brother who had been delinquent was now doing fine as were all the other siblings.

In contrast, another case illustrates what happens when there is no sustaining home setting and when the relatives will not provide one. It involves a teenaged lad in a rural community whom I, as a probation agent, was taking to the county jail in my car. As we drove down the highway he started to cry. Between sobs he said, "I never had a chance. My mother died when I was a baby and my father was a drunk. In the spring of the year when there was a lot of work, my relatives took me in; when the fall work was done and winter came, they wanted me out."

The next case involves a student whose bitterness against his parents was as great as any I ever heard from a parolee. He came to my office to say he could not write about his family. It was so bad he became distraught even to think about it—so bad that he should never get married. He related how his father had met him at the airport with no show of affection when he returned from Vietnam. His father's indifference and unconcern about him as a human being were such that he was overwhelmed with negative feelings. His relationship to his mother was even worse. He said, "If my mother should die right in front of my eyes I wouldn't give a shit." During his teens, he left home and worked on a farm a few miles away where he was treated as a member of the family. He described this home as a good one. All the children in this family went on to college. After his outburst in my office, he calmed down and later wrote a paper for me. He did well in his studies. The family he lived with for a short time undoubtedly had much to do in redirecting his life. Thus, when a person from a bad home environment does well and when a person from a good home does poorly, we may find some explanation by examining how a person is sustained or buffeted by his changing sea of setting complexities.

Another complication has to do with the way the forces in a setting impinge upon a personality. The effect of a force on an object depends upon the shape and position of the object. Figure 2-1 shows that two forces (F and F_1) of equal strength each impinge upon an object of the same mass, size, and shape: A and B. A, however, has turned so that the force F strikes it a glancing blow on its convex side that sidetracks A but slightly. A similar force F_1 strikes B in the center of its concave surface and pushes B far to the right.

Although personalities do not come in shapes and sizes, they do vary in their constituent makeup and, thus, in their sensitivity to adverse pressures. The turning of the objects in figure 2-1 is comparable to the developmental process in children who become more susceptible to trauma of certain kinds at certain stages of development. If the forces are pantrophic, they will have maximum effect at the critical period. Fairy tales may be more beneficial in early childhood than in the teens. The moral support of the mother given at the time of menarche has greater value to the daughter than when given a year before or after the event. The dystrophic reaction of a fourteen-year-old daughter to an inadequate stepfather may be quite different from the reaction of a four-year-old daughter.

In conclusion, I suggest that whether a person becomes a credit to his family or to society depends upon the overall impact of pantrophic and dystrophic influences in all his settings. Whichever is greater determines the outcome.

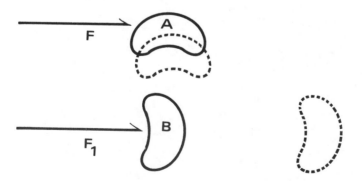

Figure 2-1. Result of Force according to Shape of Object

Note

Elihu M. Gerson, "On 'Quality of Life'," *American Sociological Review* 41 (October 1976):793–806.

Part II
The Family Constellation and Sibling Relationships

3

Charting the Family Constellation

Figure 3-1 is a chart of the constellation of a mythical family. Triangles are symbols for males, circles for females. The parental generation is the top configuration; the children, below. The line for each generation is a broken one, each segment of which represents one year, with time moving from left to right.

In 1960, J and R each leaves the parental home and marries, he at age 24 and she at age 22. In 1962, son A is born, followed by B (1966), C (1968), and daughter D (1971). We see at a glance that the father J is the oldest of three brothers born two years apart. Throughout his life, his position as the oldest of three brothers with the two-year intervals will influence the way he treats his wife, his children, and his co-workers. Likewise, mother R will be influenced by her position as the youngest of three sisters, three years apart, in the way she relates to her husband, children, friends, and coworkers. On the bottom line we list the four children, A, B, C, and D. They will reflect throughout their lives the effects of their positions in the family constellation in all sorts of ways, including work patterns.

If these children were to write a family analysis, each would do so from the perspective of his or her respective position, and each would be somewhat different. We must therefore indicate who is making the analysis. In

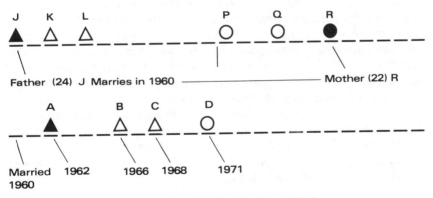

Figure 3-1. Sample Family Constellation

27

this case, A is the student who is writing the hypothetical paper. His triangle is identified by shading. J's triangle is shaded to indicate he is the father of A, B, C, and D. R's circle is also shaded to indicate she is the mother of A, B, C, and D.

A has been an only child for four years before his next brother B is born. For four years he has had the special attention from his parents that firstborns usually receive. This special attention stimulates him so that he gets a good start in school. When he plays with his younger siblings, he selects the game, gives the rules, and assigns the roles. This develops his capacity for leadership. When he is older, his parents will explain that he should be a model of good behavior because the others will copy him. When the parents leave the house for several hours, they will put him in charge and hold him responsible for what happens during their absence. When his younger siblings are attacked by outsiders, he will come to their rescue.

When the children are together, questions will arise and decisions must be made. The younger children will then look to A for the answers and the decisions. This expectation for answers and decisions also applies to the oldest sister of sisters so that the firstborn is pushed into the role of leader and decision maker. These few inferences, based upon case-history material, illustrate the significance of position in the family constellation. Before examining constellations, let us get a bit of perspective on how scholars have approached the problem.

The Work of Walter Toman

Some researchers have said that science forges ahead when the right questions are asked and that it lags when the wrong questions are asked. For many decades past, a common question was: How does birth order affect achievement or personality? I submit that this was a poor question. Until a few years ago, the results of such research were confusing and contradictory. In 1961, Walter Toman wrote a book called *Family Constellation,* in which the implied question was vastly different.[1] It was something like this: If we know the ordinal position of all the siblings and the ordinal arrangement of each of the parents in their sib systems, along with age and sex differences in both generations, can we then predict traits of the children?

On the basis of clinical experience, Toman answered this question by boldly setting forth certain characteristics of people who had the following positions in the family constellation:

Only child,	Youngest brother of sisters,
Twins,	Youngest sister of sisters,

Oldest brother of brothers,   Oldest sister of brothers,

Youngest brother of brothers,   Youngest sister of brothers,

Oldest brother of sisters,   Oldest sister of sisters.

Toman did not deal very much either with mixtures such as oldest brother of brothers and sisters or with characteristics of middle children except to say that they might acquire a blend of traits of both the youngest and the oldest. He pointed out that his predictions were not applicable if age differences reached six or seven years or more.

From his first edition, I mimeographed what Toman said about the traits of persons as listed in these ten positions and distributed this material to my students before they wrote their family analyses (see appendix B). (In later editions, Toman portrays the characteristics for the various positions differently).

Throughout part II, I examine what my students have said about how Toman's alleged traits for various positions fit or do not fit themselves or their siblings. Toman's ideas were stimulating to the students, and most of them had something to say about how their positions (and those of certain siblings) affected work and leadership patterns and relationships with parents, friends, lovers, and spouses.

Is there any validity to Toman's allocations of traits based on position in the family constellation? My case histories give considerable support to the characteristics he attributed to the oldest child of either sex in terms of achievement, leadership, sense of responsibility, and capability, even including a middle child who happens to be the oldest of a subgroup. However, support for Toman's characteristics of the youngest in various categories was not so clear.

A number of studies in the past fifteen years have given support to the greater achievement of the oldest child.[2] However, greater achievement does not mean greater intelligence.

In my opinion, predictions regarding the development of personality traits should be based not on position but on a set of certain circumstances. In reviewing their cases, various writers have come vaguely to associate these peculiar circumstances with a given position and then jump to a generalization about the importance of the position. The important thing in family analysis is to examine for these sets of circumstances. They may or may not go with the position of a given child, and if they do not, then the generalization about traits for the position will not apply. Another advantage for examining the circumstances is to emphasize that parents can, to some degree, alter the circumstances so that a child can take full advantage of growth opportunities in his position and thus avoid the disadvantages of that position.

In the literature, little attention is given to cases in which the expected traits for a given position fail to develop or to cases in which traits develop contrary to position. An analysis of the circumstances explains both. Many factors alter circumstances, such as the effects of accident, illness, genetics, intelligence, and physical attributes. One more circumstance is paramount—namely, the nature of the peer-group setting. For example, the oldest brother of brothers is supposed to have an advantage in the development of leadership. Suppose, however, that all his younger brothers are very much younger and that all the neighborhood peers are older, stronger, and more dexterous. The nature of the children's settings and how the child fits into the setting, as well as parental visibility, are also important. Although Toman neglected the settings, we should give him credit for being the first to get away from a narrow conception of birth order and to emphasize the total family constellation that encompasses several generations and that discriminates on sex and spacing.

Toman had another idea that deals with marriage adjustment and how it is affected by partners coming from different positions in their own families. For example, figure 3-1 shows that J had no sisters and that R had no brothers. Toman claims that people who never had siblings of the opposite sex are likely to have conflict in marriage because they never had an opportunity to understand the opposite sex when growing up. He also suggested that we may expect conflict due to rank order when the oldest brother of brothers marries the oldest sister of sisters. Both would be in the habit of making decisions and taking the lead and thus might clash or irritate each other. We might also have difficulty (but of a different kind) when the youngest brother of brothers marries the youngest sister of sisters. Each might expect the other to take the lead or to make decisions. The best combination would be for the oldest brother of sisters to marry the youngest sister of brothers. In this case, there would be neither rank nor sex conflict. At the end of appendix B, I have set forth groups of paired combinations from bad to excellent, according to the amount of sex and rank conflict.

Toman did some research on families in Germany that supported his thesis,[3] but a recent U.S. study did not.[4] Several other investigators like Smith and Mendelson found support for Toman's ideas.[5] The reader should notice the considerable extent to which my students testified to the validity of his theories. Toman suggests that daughters with no brothers could absorb insights on how to deal with men from a mother who had brothers. We can speculate that an understanding father who gives his daughters some attention might also be important.

In charting one's family constellation, one should include relatives who live in the same household, noting time of entry and departure. Sometimes it is important to make a three-tier chart to include material on grandparents. We might have fathers in three generations having the same positions or alternating positions. Sometimes information on grandparents throws light on the development of crippled personalities like when the only or youngest son is babied by a bevy of women in two or three generations. Toman has emphasized rightfully that when a child loses a parent through death or divorce without adequate mourning and comfort from substitute parent figures, he may become a problem parent who jeopardizes the success of his own family. It is therefore helpful when charting the constellation to give data on death, divorce, remarriage, and the ages of children when the crisis occurred.

One thing to watch for as one views a chart is the matter of identification between parent and child when each has the same position in his respective set of sibs. In figure 3-1, we notice that both the father J and his son A are the oldest of three brothers. We can imagine that J would understand the feelings of A when A is remonstrating brother B for not doing his work. Identification, however, does not guarantee a smooth relationship and is not to be confused with interaction. The roots of friction may be present when two people work together, both of whom are in the habit of making quick decisions and taking the lead. Friction due to rank order may take place between parent and child as well as between spouses.

After one has completed a chart for a family constellation, he should look for what I call psychosexual imbalance. This arises from three different circumstances: one in which there is an all-boy or all-girl set of siblings, a second in which a child is devoid of a parent of the same sex and is surrounded by persons of the opposite sex, or a third in which several children of one sex are devoid of a parent of the opposite sex.

Students from all-boy or all-girl families said they were handicapped in relating to the opposite sex. As to whether this handicap prevails at the time of marriage, the students were unable to say because most of them were still single. For obscure reasons, we have few references to this handicap unless the sib system has three or more children of the same sex.

The other types of psychosexual imbalance may have greater consequences. For example, I received on probation a youth who lived with his mother, aunt, and grandmother. The father was working in another city, and the mother was considering a divorce. This boy committed a burglary that led to his being placed on probation. Two weeks later he committed another burglary. When I went to the jail to see him, his mother was there. I admired the way this woman handled herself, although she was obviously distraught. She wondered whether her son was suffering from a brain injury since his head had been injured severely in a recent automobile accident. A medical examination revealed no injury to the central nervous system, but a psychiatrist at the hospital recommended that the boy be taken from his family for a time. This was done and my probationer was later discharged from probation without further violation. This was not the only case of its kind in my experience. Thus, being an only son without a father and surrounded by women seems to be a risky situation.

I am not saying that a family analysis should be done only via the constellation model, but I do say that such an analysis should begin with the constellation model. The constellation chart serves as a map to facilitate the identification of subgroups and the analysis of relationships.

When a student came to my office troubled about family problems, I found myself reaching for a blank chart for him to fill out. Charting the family constellation first was a method of establishing rapport and also a way of comprehending quickly the essence of the family problem, readying my questions, and determining whether the student should be referred to the counseling office. It was equally beneficial to the student in evoking insight and in clarifying his problem.

Notes

1. Walter Toman, *Family Constellation: Its Effects on Personality and Social Behavior,* 3rd ed. (New York: Springer Publishing Co., 1976). Copyright © 1976 by Springer Publishing Company, Inc., New York. Used by permission. See also Lucille K. Forer, *The Birth Order Factor* (New York: David McKay Co., 1976).

2. Jane M. Pfouts, "Birth Order, Sibling I.Q. Differences, and Family Relations" (Paper read before National Council of Family Relations, Philadelphia, October 1978), contains an excellent bibliography in this field.

3. Walter Toman, "Family Constellations of Divorced and Married Couples," *Journal of Individual Psychology* 18 (1962b):48-51. See also Walter Toman and B. Gray, "Family Constellations of 'Normal' and 'Disturbed' Marriages: An Empirical Study," *Journal of Individual Psychology* 17 (1961):93-95.

4. George Levinger and Maurice Sonnheim, "Complementarity in Marital Adjustment: Reconsidering Toman's Family Constellation Hypothesis," *Journal of Individual Psychology* 27 (1965).

5. M.E. Smith, "Birth Order Compatibility and Same Sex Dyads," *Journal of Social Psychology* 99 (1976):291-292. See also M.B. Mendelson, "Heterosexual Pairing and Sibling Configuration," *Journal of Individual Psychology* 30 (1974):202-210.

4 Singletons

The only child, or singleton, is not the only one to be treated as such. The oldest child in any family is treated as an only until the arrival of the second-born. Likewise, the lastborn may be treated somewhat as an only child if the next older sibling is very much older. Characteristics due to rank order of the older and the younger do not seem to apply if the difference in age is six or seven years or more. The younger child in such a case is merely a little brother or little sister whom the older one may be required to babysit. Of course, this protective role may promote skill in caring for children and a sense of responsibility.

The structure of the family of a singleton has the rigidity of a triangle. When his parents marry, they constitute a twosome, or dyad, with one relationship. When the first child arrives, the family becomes a triangle, or triad, with three relationships: husband-wife, mother-child, and father-child. The equation for the number of relationships is $Y^2 - Y/2$, in which Y is the number of persons in the family. The birth of the secondborn increases the number of relationships to six and the number of possible triads to four. The formula for the number of potential triangles in a family is $Tn = n(n - 1)(n - 2)/6$, in which n is the number of persons in the family. This increase in complexity is given in table 4-1.

The only child functions in a family having but three relationships

Table 4-1
Increasing Complexity of Family Relationships according to Size

Number of Persons	Number of Relationships	Number of Triads
1	0	0
2	1	0
3	3	1
4	6	4
5	10	10
6	15	20

encompassed in a single triad. This is in contrast to larger families having many relationships in which each parent can act as a pivot for separate triads and in which the children may form triads among themselves. The triad is important because it involves the ever-changing phenomenon of two against one as in confrontations and tattling.

Forty-five student papers were written by singletons, of which seven were adopted children. Sixteen (35 percent) mentioned difficulties with parents on a triangular basis. The only child is likely to be more vulnerable when the parents take sides against him or when each solicits him as an ally against the other. He has no chance to secure allies among siblings or to point up his argument regarding his siblings, and the pressure to solicit him as a parental ally is not lessened as it might be in the presence of other children: "All my life I have been between my parents. In any argument that arises, each one wants me to take his side against the other." If an only child should be tempted to seek an alliance with one parent against the other, he may sense the danger of triggering a conflict that undermines his own security and produces feelings of guilt.

Single-child families have less overt conflict than large families because animosities arising from parental favoritism are absent, as well as the quarreling and fighting among siblings. However, if parents become abusive, the only child has no recourse to sibling allies. When parents become abusive in large families, children may forget their own quarrels and unite against a common enemy.

In a larger family, a child may torment a sibling within the home but fiercely defend him against an outsider. A child might find comfort in a sibling about his problems in the peer group. We shall presently see how older sisters advise brothers on dating problems and how older brothers alert sisters about undesirable boyfriends.

Characteristics of the Only Child

Imagine how the singletons in my classes must have felt when they read in the first page of appendix B the following list of traits that Toman attributed to them in 1961:

Remains a child long after adulthood,

Wants to be the center of attention,

Will not mind making a fool of himself as long as he is the center of attention,

Takes all material things for granted,

Would subject mate to continual humiliation,

Is never ready for a peer relationship,

Finds work a nuisance.

In his third edition, Toman did not reprint this list but gave a brilliant description of the behavioral tendencies of both male and female singletons as he observed them among his clientele.[1] He also stressed the more-adultlike behavior of the only child. His clients in therapy would be somewhat different from the run-of-the-mill college students.

Let us consider some cases illustrating the seven points listed by Toman for the only child, although several of the excerpts unavoidably involve more than one idea. The first item deals with any dystrophic impact of parents on the child to impair his growth to maturity.

Remains a Child Long after Adulthood

In the previous chapter, I referred to the dystrophic influence upon an only boy when his father is absent and he is surrounded by several females including sisters, aunts, and grandmothers. In the only-child families, the dystrophic risk from overprotection and domination is likely to be greater than in multichild families. The damage will be greater still if the mother (or father) has personality defects. Both overprotection and domination (which are hard to disentangle) should be viewed within the rigid confines of the triangle, although in pantrophic families, the parents take pains to foster flexibility, spontaneity, and creativity.[2]

In one analysis, the mother was described as being high strung, critical, scolding all the time in a voice loud and shrill, and very dominating with her daughter. In outbursts of anger she called her daughter foul names. The daughter's friends would not come to her home because the mother was so openly critical of them.

This daughter resented the mother's hold on her, "but I can't break out of it." She had conflict with her boyfriend because she could not follow through on his advice to stand up against her mother. She had an affectionate relationship with the father, which the mother resented. As a child, this girl suffered from separation anxiety. On an overnight visit to the home of a friend she had to be taken home in the middle of the night. "Even now, at age 20, I am less independent than many of the freshmen."

When a mother with a single male child loses her husband early in the child's life, that boy is high risk for delayed maturity unless male adults in the extended family or in the neighborhood are available to model appropriate roles. This kind of psychosexual imbalance with excessive mothering was much more noticeable in my probation experience than in my teaching experience. I sensed that my probationers whose growth had been stymied by overprotection harbored deep-seated resentments against their mothers. The following paper illustrates the dystrophic developments in a mother-son dyad:

I was born one year after my parents were married, and because of my father's untimely death, I have no brothers or sisters.

My mother was always overaffectionate and overly domineering with respect to me and my growing up. She loved me very much, and still does, and in my estimation accorded me all the love she had for my deceased father, along with the love she had foreseen for all her children. It is probably due to this that she is dominant and overaffectionate. I think that she simply did not want something to happen to me so that she would be alone in the world. For example, when I was in grade school, I was forbidden to play football lest I get hurt. I soon began to participate behind her back in everything that seemed enjoyable to me, no matter how rough and forbidden it was by her. She resented this, and I rejected her because of it.

Any girl, no matter how popular or beautiful she seemed, was no concern of mine if she displayed dominance and overaffection. However, I did experience the joys of fulfilling relationships with girls, but only until they became overly dominant.

Oftentimes religion was used by my mother as an excuse for why she didn't think I should go out with a particular girl. This was her way of telling me that she didn't want to lose her little boy to another woman. And if this religion idea was not effective, she would always give me reasons why a particular girl was not the right one to take out. After a while I began to ignore these statements, and many times I would continue dating a girl just to spite my mother.

After a while I began thinking of the marriage possibility and would reject any girl who exhibited traits of my mother and would look for traits that seemed most to parallel those of Bill's mother. She was always treating me extra special and I have never forgotten it. [Bill was a pal whose family he admired.] In short, Bill's mother treated me like a human being, one who had to make up his mind and rationalize things for himself, while my mother thought I was incapable of such acts and was thus making up my mind for me. Because of this, I rejected my mother and all of her characteristics and anyone who exemplified these traits to any extent.

Through interactions with my mother, she instilled the idea that the world was threatening and dangerous, contradictory and unpredictable, and that I should be constantly on my guard against manipulators who are out only to better themselves without regard for others like myself. She also told me to come to her whenever I had a problem. Unfortunately, I did go to her for the most part of my younger years, and this restricted my drive for independence and self-esteem. However, I later learned that personal accomplishment makes for the growth of self-esteem, and I restricted my seeking help from her.

My mother only punished me verbally, but she did so to the point that I was afraid to express my views on relevant topics such as whom I was dating and what I should or should not be able to do. When I performed opposite to her expectations in regard to these conflicting areas of concern, I was criticized and threatened with the loss of her love. In response to these circumstances, I would become very anxious and would apologize for my actions, whether or not I viewed them as right.

Growing out of this anxiety was a sense of paranoia. I continually felt my mother was prying into my personal life, my letters, belongings, and my life in general. I felt as though she was always watching, always manipulating, and always controlling me and my life. As a result, I tended to acquire the characteristics of a humble and modest individual, one who listens and learns.

The small family of which I am a member is definitely a case of instability. Unfortunately, the love and affection and seeming concern exhibited by my mother have driven us our separate ways. I am now in college, and she is finally beginning to realize that her little boy has grown up. I telephone her irregularly and ask how everything is, but a distance other than miles separates us. It is a cognitive distance produced through too much conflict. I feel I am so much maturer now that I have experienced and almost completed college; and I also feel that my mother is realizing my maturity.

The writing of this analysis has exposed some very interesting points of view of mine. For example, how much love is too much? I have realized through this study that both parents are very important for the full satisfaction of family life.

Although this man represents a special type of overprotection, accentuated by the absence of the father-husband, about 70 percent of my sample of singletons indicates some overprotection by parents. Overprotection is not a discrete entity. Its nature is hard to pinpoint, its degree is hard to measure, and it may impinge on any child with sibs but especially to the only son. Overprotection tends to frustrate the decision-making process in the recipient. Freedom to make appropriate decisions and to take responsibility for those decisions is important in the development of judgment, and judgment is an important aspect of maturity.

I alluded earlier to the idea that a child ultimately may be saved from certain dystrophic parental behaviors by appropriate rebellious action. This was illustrated by a boy who rejected his father's assertion he could not succeed in college. That case and this one are similar because both used rejection to good advantage and both went to college.

Wants Center of Attention

Two items on Toman's list of traits for the only child deal with the desire to be the center of attention. Such a child is in a family triangle in which he is the recipient of parental watchfulness. He has no sibling competitor for parental attention, and if that attention is gratifying, he will yearn for it wherever he goes.

> I do enjoy being the center of attention and would not mind making a fool of myself to do so. This was evident when I had to parade through the student union as a pledge in a fraternity.

I tried to sift through the forty-five papers written by singletons to see to what extent they admitted or denied the traits that Toman ascribed to them. Since they were not called upon to do this, their comments can only be considered as voluntary and spontaneous expressions about themselves; 27 percent admitted to a craving for attention.

Takes Material Things for Granted

The economic advantage of having only one child makes it easier to meet the child's needs without hesitation. A number of students appreciated this advantage and admitted to this expectation.

> I do take material things for granted to a certain extent. Although I don't believe I'm spoiled, I usually have been given what I asked for.

The term *spoiled* is not precise. Sometimes it seems to mean indulgence, and sometimes it seems to mean excessive permissiveness regarding behavior. About 35 percent admitted that they tended to take material things for granted, and 45 percent admitted to being indulged or spoiled.

Would Subject Spouse to Continual Humiliation

The phrase regarding continual humiliation was not repeated in Toman's third edition, and the rationale for it is obscure. I recall only one instance in which a student referred to it, and he did so in a way that made no sense to me.

Is Never Ready for a Peer Relationship

Toman says that the only child is not well prepared for contacts with peers. "He learns how a man and a woman relate to each other by observing par-

ents, but he has little opportunity to practice it with other children. . . .
There are no other children to identify with. An only child behaves toward
his father the way his mother does, and vice versa. . . . On the average we
can say that only children have been more poorly prepared for contacts with
peers than children with any other sibling position.''[3] This idea was given
support by one student who wrote, ''I don't feel I will ever be ready for a
peer group.''

About 35 percent of my singletons mentioned difficulties in peer relationships, but there is nothing inevitable about the alleged traits. Parents of
singletons are more concerned than other parents about the availability of
neighborhood children, playgrounds, cousins, nursery schools, and kinder-
gartens. If such parents have pantrophic inclinations they may influence
their child to be assertive. Some researchers have found many singletons to
be leaders.

Finds Work a Nuisance

There was practically no support from students on the last item, regarding
work. There were more objections to it than to any other. Only two boys
admitted that work was a nuisance. One might speculate that, since housekeeping chores are fewer in a one-child family compared to larger families,
parents would be less inclined to teach the only child to do household
chores. If an only child should be lackadaisical about work, it likely has less
to do with his status as an only child and more to do with the lackadaisical
attitudes of the parents in teaching him how to work.

Of Toman's seven traits for the only child, I would strike the two
regarding mates and work. Whether the others apply to any appreciable
extent depends on whether the family is pantrophic of dystrophic. General-
izing about the traits of the only child is futile unless one takes into consideration the quality of the family in which the child lives. In pantrophic families, the parents seem to be aware of the disadvantages of the single status
and to make sure that the child make the best of his advantages. The illustrations point up the alertness of parents in such families to provide for the
special needs of singletons such as opportunities for wholesome group activities with age-mates, special training in learning to share, curtailment of
parental tendency to indulge the child, and attention to behaviors that promote autonomy.

In many one-child families, the parents tend to be indifferent or
unaware of the child's difficulties with loneliness, being a pawn in the family triangle, feelings of inadequacy in social situations, a tendency to be self-
centered, parental indulgence, and settings beyond the home.

Other Characteristics

Eleven percent of my sample admitted to selfishness or being unable to share, and 29 percent mentioned their loneliness in childhood. The contrast in the attitudes of students regarding their one-child status varied considerably and is evident in the following two quotations:

> As a child I was sensitive to the disappointment of my parents in having only one child and I, too, felt cheated out of having brothers and sisters.

> I find it almost impossible to imagine my friends as having lived in families with other children. The idea seems strange to me that a child would have to worry about one of his siblings breaking his toy or taking it from where he left it.

In the following excerpt, the student longed for siblings, but she described a number of positive factors about her family that may be considered as upward indicators on the pantrophic scale:

> I'm a singleton. Being an only child means enjoying certain superior advantages and opportunities, particularly insofar as individual care, praise, and attention, as well as the economic resources involved; but there are disadvantages too. For one thing, I missed a great deal in the way of companionship. One of my closest friends whom I have known since childhood is also a singleton. We did many activities together and often stayed at one another's house overnight. Each of us constituted a sibling for the other. Although both of us have acquired many acquaintances, we still maintain a close friendship and feel like sisters. In spite of this close friend along with many other playmates, I nevertheless feel this has not made up for my lack of siblings because we were not together all the time under the same roof.

> In addition, it's comfortable to have people around, besides parents, with whom you feel you really belong. You can sometimes talk things over with a brother or a sister in a way that is impossible even with your closest friend. Because they're close to you, they know a great deal about you and you don't feel so alone. Often when I disagree with my parents, I feel that I'm the only one against two, that I have no one on my side to help me. In my imagination I thought that a large family provided a partylike atmosphere that adds sparkle and vitality that isn's as easy to achieve in a small family.

> The position of being an only child has influenced my ideas and feelings in three areas. First, I don't like being alone but enjoy people. Second, I have decided to become a teacher. When I was a youngster in the primary grades, I always missed being able to talk about or show off my new baby brother or sister. My mother says that I talked about being a teacher and having thirty little children all to myself when I was in the second grade, and I have never changed my mind since. Finally, I want to have at least three children so they can enjoy companionship, closeness, and the partylike atmosphere that comes only with a family of more than one child.

The interpersonal relations between my parents and myself consist of love and affection. This is essentially true because I am the only child; therefore, they consider me their pride and joy. My parents, especially my mother, are quick to express words of advice, comfort, encouragement, or consolation as well as praise, admiration, and appreciation. For this reason, I feel extremely close to my mother and tell her all of my problems. If things go wrong and I feel tense, nervous, and irritable, I can open up my heart, knowing she can assess my feelings and motives correctly and put herself in my position. When I come home, whether it be from school, work, or a date, she is concerned about my having had a good time and what I did. She does this in such a manner that I gain a sense of importance and concern rather than feeling like a participant in a quiz program. This sense of being loved and trusted and feeling that I am a companion of my parents means more to me than being showered with numerous and expensive possessions.

My parents have influenced my dating through their encouragement of my bringing home friends—both girls and boys. Because of their hospitality, I have always felt proud to invite friends or have them drop in unexpectedly. When a group of friends and I get together, we usually meet at my house; in fact, it often is called Grand Central Station. At such times my parents are always friendly, and almost always my mother brings out cookies and cake.

All in all, one of the finest gifts my parents have given to me is a feeling that I am a credit to the family, that they like me and are proud of me. The circumstances that have brought this out are happiness of my parents, lack of conflict between my parents and myself, and a home atmosphere that is firm yet consisting of love and understanding. I hope to establish these main patterns in my own family of procreation.

Failure in Three Settings

The hazards to any child should be examined in three settings: family, playground, and school. Not one of the writers on family constellation deals with settings.

An unsatisfactory playground setting of the only child is not mitigated by the protection of siblings. Thus, he is more susceptible to uncongenial peer groups and more affected by absence of peers of the same or opposite sex, by peers too young or too old, or by peers that attack or ridicule.

The following case involves parents who had a good relationship between themselves and, in some ways, a good relationship with their only son but who failed to perceive the predicament of their son in his settings. Their visibility for his suffering in the three settings seemed to be nil, and his nonperceiving teacher had even less comprehension of his situation.

I turned out to be the only child of my family, which I consider to be a misfortune. I believe this was not due to any failure on the part of my parents, however, because I experienced all the parental love and affection a child could want.

In the early period of my life, I strongly identified with my father. To me he seemed a superman, strong but at the same time hostile, one to be feared. During the age of five to eight, I remember only the bad moments when my father yelled at me or physically punished me. I know that he loved me, that we did have great times together, but still there were times when I disappointed him or hurt him by doing something wrong like lying and came into physical conflict with him. The things I was most bitter about were those incidents for which I was not responsible but still was punished.

I remember making up fantastic stories and telling them to my classmates. During this time I took dares and lied about everything under the sun. Many a time my parents were victims of my fantasizing. These things, in combination with other incidents, caused me anxiety and fear of punishment.

When I was six, my family moved into a neighborhood of girls. For me, between the ages of six and twelve, this was terrifying. I made very few friends. Now, instead of misbehaving for attention I became a goody-two-shoes. If there is one way to keep from getting friends in grade school, it is to be too good. At this point in my education, my parents failed to notice that I lacked self-confidence, a knowledge of the opposite sex, and friends. The worst years of my life occurred as I approached puberty. Loneliness may be the key to much of my maladjustment during those critical years. I had no one to talk to or confide in. I became different from everyone else, though I knew not why. I was not accepted and my teacher did little to help. She used my acute lack of self-confidence to make an example of me. When I failed to think for myself, she made a mockery of me. She probably thought that by hurting me she would make me try harder, but I began to withdraw, to forget things, and to make more errors. When I failed, the kids seemed to feel more superior to me.

Home at this time was a place of refuge. My parents did not hurt me because of my grades. They only said, "Do your best."

During junior high school I felt this loneliness most acutely since I was reaching early adolescence and had a deep yearning for friendship. I was a joke to those whom I wanted for friends, and I heard their laughs. I hated myself and those who joked at my expense.

At home, my loneliness was growing all the time. I had anxieties and problems that my parents never knew about. I remember one time in particular when I was looking forward to my mother's coming home so I could talk and maybe play a game or something. When she did come, a friend called and asked her to go out and relax for a while. She asked if I'd mind and I said, "No," so she left and I've never felt more alone than at that moment. I cried for hours because I hurt with deep pain; I just wanted someone, anyone.

This boy's problems were exacerbated by lack of sexual knowledge and consequent sexual anxieties. By the time he reached college, he had improved considerably, although he was not without problems:

I have been dating a girl for about two years now, and I find myself reluctant to express my feelings or emotions toward her, and I have an even worse time accepting her intimate personal affection for me.

There is no doubt that this lad was suffering, but we have no inkling as to what his mother and teacher would have said about him. The case, however, should alert parents and teachers to look for symptoms of maladjustment and to consult each other as well as playground directors.

We may speculate, since Toman's traits for the various positions were gleaned from clients in therapy, that many of these clients came from dystrophic families. Generalizations about families should never be made unless the researcher indicates how his sample of families rates on a quality scale. My case-history material suggests that singletons from pantrophic families have few of the negative traits Toman allocates for singletons. Some researchers like Feldman found that singletons are often competent, reliable, assertive persons who may have a flair for leadership.[4] In pantrophic families, the parents seem to be aware of the hazards of the singleton status and take special pains to overcome them, as in the following case:

The child raising of my parents was geared to the needs of an only child. They tried to compensate by having my cousins stay with us frequently. I began day camp at age five and continued attending until age ten. When I was seven years old, they sent me to overnight camp, and I went every year until my sixteenth birthday. I loved camp. My camping days were some of the most valuable, since I gained self-assurance and independence. I learned the meaning of sharing and cooperative living, which of course I had minimally at home. Instead of resentment in not being the center of attention, I experienced great joy and satisfaction, and camping actually compensated for what I thought life with sisters would be like.

Camping also widened my interest in many activities such as sports, nature, and crafts. In fact, this was one of my parents' motives for sending me to camp. They felt if a child had acquired varied interests and skills, he would be better able to relate to other youngsters. I am grateful for their foresight, because I derive pleasure from varied activities, and today life holds much meaning for me. One further factor must be attributed to camp life. I developed a broad outlook and democratic feeling toward all types of people—not barring classes and races. Not believing in the so-called exclusive, expensive private camps, my parents sent me to Girl Scout camps and YMCA camps, where I had invaluable opportunity to live with other types of people at an early age.

I always excelled in school and liked it. Peer acceptance was very important to me and I had many friends.

Though they could well afford to, my parents deliberately did not make me into the stereotypical spoiled child. In fact, I rarely asked for material things because they were unimportant to me. However, I was spoiled with love. [I assured this girl that no one can be spoiled by love; but one could be spoiled by someone who fakes love.]

When my mother was hospitalized for several weeks, I became a very self-sufficient girl, cooking full-course meals for my dad and me, keeping up the house, and even washing occasionally. My girlfriends and boyfriends were very sympathetic, and they often came home with me after school to help me cook. Their concern and those days of cooking together brightened my outlook. Fortunately, to bolster my morale, I had become a leader and was considered one of the popular girls at school. Since that time, I have always cherished the warmth, security, and companionship of my friends during periods when I feel, as I did then, very much alone and frightened.

Learning to Work

An important feature in the growth of children is the acquisition of skills related to work. The learning and performance of work skills gives children joy and improves their self-image and self-confidence. It also provides an opportunity for developing the traits of leadership, responsibility, dependability and cooperation. The earliest development of such skills takes place in the milieu of household tasks.

In a large family, the pressure of things to be done is great, and plenty of opportunity exists to learn skills related to such activity. However, the pressure of chores to be done is minimal in one-child, affluent urban families, so the parents of an only child may do well to give some thought to providing work-related opportunities for the growth of their single offspring. Sometimes parents find it much easier to do the tasks themselves.

An acquaintance related the following experience. She had two children and became pregnant again. When the doctor announced that she was going to have twins, she became obsessed with the idea that she would die, although she was perfectly healthy. With her demise in mind, she hastened to teach her son and daughter how to do all sorts of household tasks so that after her death they would be self-sufficient. She delivered the twins normally and had no trouble. When relating her experience to her friends she said, "It was the best thing that ever happened to me. The children were a big help in the housework and with the babies."

In the following account, the impending death of the mother was real, but the results on character development were similar:

My parents moved away from the city and ran a small store, a business my mother ran mostly by herself since my father retained his old blue-collar job. This was crucial because my mother had less time at home, my father likewise because of travel time to and from his job, and I was put to work. All this did not hurt my relationship with Mother because, even though I was only nine years old, I spent considerable time in the store. I think this helped me learn how to accept responsibility and kept me from becoming a spoiled child. It taught me at a tender age that there are many different types of people in the world, each having his own traits and characteristics. I know that working in the store taught me to stand up for my beliefs and not to take any mistreatment from people.

I feel that two of Toman's ideas on only children do not apply to me: I don't feel that work is a nuisance, and I was taught early not to take material things for granted and to respect the value of money. I do enjoy being the center of attention. However, I feel that Toman is wrong when he says I will remain a child long after adulthood. There are circumstances to negate this point. My mother spent a lot of time teaching me how to perform household tasks such as cooking, cleaning, washing, and ironing. When I was thirteen I learned the reason for this. She told me she had a bad heart and would die before I was very old. She must have been trying to prepare me and to soften what was eventually going to come. She died when I was fifteen, and it hit me very hard. Prior to her death, my mother had tried to make me more sociable, for I had always been in a shell, not caring whether I socialized or not. After her death I promised myself that I would try as hard as I could to make a good name for myself and to lead my life as she would like it. I have become more outgoing, accepted a great deal more responsibility for our home, and become much more competitive. I always strove to be the leader in whatever group I participated in: sports, scholastics, fraternity activities.

A Composite of Traits

In the following cases the students have described a composite of the traits that Toman listed. These cases have been selected because they illustrate how traits may be combined, as well as what parents have done to accentuate the advantages and to curtail the disadvantages of single-child status. For example, one case warns against the use of folklore clichés that downgrade children. Another discusses the identification of parent and child when they have the same position in the family constellation.

The following case is that of a girl whose father was a successful farmer. He was the youngest of three children, having both a brother and a sister. The mother was a singleton. The daughter preferred doing chores with her father over housework and admired his strength, talents, and ability to make decisions. She went fishing and played ball with her father. Her mother was active in various organizations. From the daughter's description, I would judge her family to be pantrophic.

With her parents' encouragement she joined a 4H club when she was ten and became active and successful in a great variety of projects. She was active in photography, sewing, conservation, knitting, music, forensic events, and junior leadership.

I have heard the old cliche that only children are spoiled and get everything they want. Well, that was not the story in my case. My parents have given me only the very essential items and very few of the so-called luxury items. My parents gave me an allowance, and I learned the value of a dollar from my father. If there was anything big I wanted to buy, I had to save for weeks for it because they would not buy it for me. My parents always let me be very independent. They never forced anything on me; they always let me make personal decisions. There were times when my parents disagreed with me, and I would be a little rebellious and mad, but after a while all that would go away.

My position in the family constellation probably had the following effects on my personality: I always wanted to do things myself and do them well because I was the only one around to show my parents my work. I like to do things for other people too, more than I want to do them for myself. This I seem to have gotten from Mother because she is always helping a friend with problems. My parents are very easygoing and have a sense of humor.

In the following case, the daughter had a father who was a singleton and a mother who had siblings:

I soon realized that being the only child was an important factor in my personality development. I was constantly asking my mother for a baby brother or sister. I never enjoyed being alone. Although I don't recall having had any problems meeting my peers in kindergarten through high school, I have found it unreasonably difficult to meet people in college because I was totally unprepared.

I do take material things for granted to a certain extent. Although I don't believe I'm spoiled, I usually have been given what I asked for. I was never really bothered whether or not I got it, though.

I don't feel I will ever be ready for a peer group, except for my high school class. On Toman's final point, I disagree. I don't feel that work is ever a nuisance. I have always done my share of work around the house, and the summer I was sixteen, and the four following summers, I worked in a factory. I expect to pay for my own education by working, and I do enjoy being busy. I get irritable and bored when I have nothing to do.

I believe my father and I are very much alike, and my mother has often told me so. We are both only children and expect a lot of attention. All in all, I do believe my father identifies with me because we are in the same position in the family constellation.

The loneliness of a singleton may be compounded by circumstances such as a working mother, inadequate babysitters, or marital conflict.

I don't believe it was such a good idea for my mother to teach while I was growing up. I was the only child and can remember coming home to hired girls whom I detested. When I started school there was one in particular whom I hated. In the fourth grade, I would come home and find the house empty. It caused me to feel lonely, and perhaps a bit neglected, though my mother would be home within two hours or so.

As an only child I was rather dominated by my parents, particularly my mother. My mother was so pleased-when everyone said I was such a good girl. My mother expected too much of me while I was young.

My father was never domineering, but he allowed Mother to do whatever she wanted with me. When things got bad, he would side with me and then my parents would argue, and I would be relieved of pressure for at least a time. In high school I became quite rebellious. I can't say I was spoiled, although I received many things that other children my age didn't have. Our family was always quite close though sometimes it seemed as though there were two against me.

In one case of a singleton whose parents both came from large families, the child once heard her father say, "Little girls are to be seen and not heard." The girl attributed to this one sentence her shyness in self-expression and a complete inability to respond to a teacher's question. Patterns of parental behavior that encourage or discourage self-expression impinge with great force upon all children. A similar case is mentioned in chapter 1 in which parental downgrading of the son's ideas stymied the boy's capacity to answer his teacher's questions.

In the absence of siblings some parents believe that an only child needs special training in sharing. One student wrote:

I had a very poor concept of sharing, I must admit. I never had to share anything with anyone, so I didn't know what it was to share. I remember one day my Dad gave me a stick of gum and asked if I wouldn't share it with him and Mom. I broke the gum in half, and Dad said there were three people and only two pieces of gum; so I broke one of the halves in half again, put the first half in my mouth, and gave a quarter of it to Mom and the other quarter to Dad. My parents proceeded to tell me that what I did wasn't very nice. They told me I should share equally, not keep the most for myself. I felt very bad about it, but I guess I learned a good lesson. Even now it is still hard for me to share material things as well as share myself with others.

Impact of Grandparents and Friends

I would like the reader to notice in the following material the benign impact of persons beyond the nuclear family who succored children suffering from family conflict, divorce, brutality, or rejection. Such help may involve grandparents or other relatives, neighbors, friends, and teachers. The help to such unfortunate children is sometimes indirect, such as providing a parent surrogate, a parental model, or a family model. Sometimes it is positive stroking (transactional-analysis term for social reinforcement) or simple human kindness. I am convinced that such people who assuage the hurt of damaged children often are unaware of or underestimate the good they have done.

In the following account, the grandmother's influence was paramount.

Joanna's father died shortly after her birth, and she lived with her grandparents until she was eight. At that time her mother remarried, and Joanna came back to live with her mother and stepfather. This was difficult because she had accepted the grandparents as natural parents. After three years, the mother divorced her husband and then mother and daughter went back to live with the grandparents. A great-aunt was in the household so Joanna had three mothers who clashed over issues in child training. When Joanna was twelve her grandfather died, and she took his death very hard. His death brought the family into even more psychosexual imbalance. Joanna wrote:

I always considered my grandmother as my true mother because, whenever I had a problem or question, I always went to her rather than to my mother.

My family happiness, during this three-mother period, wasn't really bad, now that I think back. The four of us had some really wonderful times together. I can remember how we'd all go out to eat together on days like Mother's Day or Easter. Or my grandmother and I would spend a whole day in the kitchen with her showing me how to bake cakes and cookies.

Despite the fact that there was much confusion having three mothers, I guess I was much luckier than most girls. All their attention was showered on me, and most of the time I got the things I asked for. Both my aunt and my grandmother sewed, and so I never had to worry about clothes. Also, when I was younger, I got an allowance from all three of them for helping with the housework, which amounted to something like $6.00 a week.

My grandma had always taught me the importance of being independent and of handling money correctly and saving as much as I could. That's why, when I got my first job at the age of fifteen, she was so pleased. It was only a job at the neighborhood grocery store that paid $10.00 a week, but it was a good start. Through my grandma's teaching, I managed my money and was able to pay my way through a Catholic high school and pay for all my clothes. That is one fact I'm very proud of.

My job also taught me how to shoulder responsibility. After I was there about a year, my boss placed the care of the store more and more in my hands. He would let me do all the buying and pay all the bills when they came in. He also used to go on all-day trips, allowing me to open the store at eight in the morning, tend it all day alone, and close up at nine in the evening. That was a long day for anyone to work, but it really taught me a lot and I'm very thankful for it.

Upon my graduation from high school, I got a job at a summer ranch resort, doing waitress work. My whole family was glad because they felt it would teach me how to be on my own. Two weeks before I left for the ranch, however, my aunt had a heart attack and died. It was very sudden and left an empty feeling in me. I hadn't always been as good as I could have been to her, and now I felt it was too late. However, I'll always be grateful to her for her kindness to me.

I left for my job at the end of June, and at this place I discovered how wonderful it is to be part of a real family. There were eight other girls besides me at the ranch and about the same number of boys. As the weeks passed, we all became as close as real brothers and sisters. Our boss, Jeanne, and her husband, Bill, were just like a mother and father to us and to me in particular. I became very attached to them and they treated me just like their own daughter. I don't think I was ever happier in my whole life than that summer at the ranch. I had always wanted a mother, father, and brothers and sisters and now I had them, in a sense. I really hated to leave and actually broke down and cried when the time came. I also got homesick for them during the winter, something I hadn't felt for my own home and family.

That fall I started college, and this helped me grow up quite a bit. I began to realize how good my grandmother and my mother were to me and that I should try to appreciate them more. I really tried, and at the end of my first year, I had a better understanding and interaction with my grandmother than ever before. I was also beginning to understand my mother much better.

Last June I went back to the ranch. I was really happy that I could. It was just like going home. In July my mother and grandmother came up to the ranch for a week's vacation. It was the first real vacation my grandmother had ever had and she really enjoyed herself. Everyone loved her and kept telling me what a wonderful grandmother I had. I guess it was then I first realized what a remarkable woman she really was. I made up my mind that, when I got home, I was really going to start doing things for her. Then, two weeks after she left the ranch, I got a phone call—she had died of a heart attack. The same thing had taken my aunt (her sister) last summer. I doubt if I could put into words what I felt. I only know that I didn't want to come home again because it just wouldn't be the same without her. Then Jeanne told me that my mother needed me more than ever, and I now realize that she was right.

When I came home, there were many adjustments to make. As I said before, my interaction with my mother was almost nil. It now is a little better but not much. It's hard to talk to someone and confide in her when you never have before. Then, too, my mother hadn't had to make any decisions in such a long time that she couldn't do it any more. Now, whenever anything big comes up, she comes to me, and most of the time I make the final decision. Our relationship is more one of sisters than one of mother and daughter. Sometimes I feel that the relationship is almost reversed, with her taking the daughter role and my taking the mother role. I truly wish things could be different, but I doubt if they will change in the near future. My mother has always been dependent upon someone, and she won't be able to change overnight.

I also feel that my strange family situation—that of having three mother figures and no father figure for so many years—has affected my attitude toward men. While I'm not exactly afraid of men, I distrust most of them to a very great extent. I realize that this isn't a normal, healthy attitude for a girl my age, and I'm trying my best to overcome this feeling. I have to some extent, but it's going to take time.

Impressions from my experience with parolees and students lead me to feel that singletons suffer more than other children when the family gets out of balance psychosexually. The girl in this case seemed to be happy until her grandfather died. Then she became aware of her three-mother period. She had an upsurge at the ranch where Jeanne and Bill were like a mother and father. In the end, she expresses the emotional residue from psychosexual imbalance by referring to her fear and distrust of men.

Parental Control

The girl in the following case was subject to the influence of four adults. The father's method of control became a model for the others.

> Being the only child in the family has presented many problems. Our family consists of my parents and my mother's parents. My mother has worked ever since I was eight years old. Thus, my grandmother influenced me during the day and my mother at night. I was an overprotected and spoiled child. There were always conflicts as to what I should wear and eat and where I could go. This overprotection and spoiling did not carry over into my middle teens. The family could see that I resented it and soon stopped treating me as a child.

> Every family punishes the child in one way or another. I was very seldom punished by a beating. In fact, I can remember only one instance of being hit. Most of my punishment was verbal. My grandfather never punished me at all. My grandmother would tell me how bad I was, but this did not have much of an effect on me. The one that really got to me was my father. He never beat me or threatened me but simply took me aside and told what I was doing wrong and why I should not do it. He was firm, exact, and to the point. I never had a chance to talk my way out. When the rest of the family saw that I respected his authority, they began using him as an example and I soon straightened out.

The following case illustrates what happens when both parents are inadequate and turn against the only child, a girl. Does a dystrophic family have greater impact on an only child because of the triangle and because the child is easier to isolate? Note that when the father attacked the daughter, the mother came to the defense of the daughter but that when the father withdrew, the mother attacked the daughter.

My mother put me first before my father in everything. She would rarely leave me with a babysitter and go out with my father. On the few times that they did go out, it was usually with my aunt and uncle. On one of these occasions, I woke up and discovered my mother gone. The sitter couldn't get me calmed down or back to sleep, and I sat up crying until my mother returned. For weeks after this, I'd wake up in the night calling for her. When it didn't stop after the first few times, my father became very angry. I remember that he came into the bedroom instead of my mother one night. I don't remember what happened, but even as I write this I feel a terrible fear as if something is going to happen. As I look back on my childhood, the one thing that stands out is a terrible fear of my father that turned to hatred in later years.

This girl continued to live in fear of her father and to suffer from the downgrading of her mother after each attack by the father. She said the daughter was bad, was ruining her marriage, and was ungrateful for all the mother had done for her. The daughter felt more and more rejected as conflicts at mealtime continued, with the father furious about the daughter's eating habits.

The daughter described her loneliness at every holiday, especially Christmas. Her parents would socialize with adult relatives, completely ignoring her loneliness as she sat isolated. "As I look back, I can't remember one happy Christmas. Each one seemed more terrible and lonely than the one before."

The parents substituted presents for love. One Christmas the father gave his daughter a television set but conditioned its use upon her behavior. This was the turning point at which hatred of her father broke out in open rebellion. "Every time he attacked me he had a full-scale war on his hands." The mother began to drink heavily and became more antagonistic and vindictive. Then the father died and the mother became jealous of the daughter's boyfriend. She clung to her daughter and tried to break up the love affair. The daughter ends her remarks: "I have a horrible feeling that the future will bring more trouble between my mother and myself."

Transactional analysis says that participants in a triangle rotate themselves around the triangle, each taking his turn at being the prosecutor, the victim, and the rescuer. For example, when the father railed at the child for eating too slowly and the mother tried to protect her daughter, he was the prosecutor, the daughter the victim, and the mother the rescuer. Moments later the father withdrew (presumably with disgust and self-pity), the mother as prosecutor now attacked the child, and the daughter suffered again as the victim. Then the mother indulged in self-pity and was the victim. If we had a videotape of these scenes, the missing roles in the rotating sequence might be discovered.

In the nomenclature of transactional analysis, both parents gave this daughter the injunction she was no good. The daughter's counterattack against the father likely saved her; but the father died and the mother became alcoholic. We can imagine the despairing isolation of the mother as, toward the end, she both reviled the daughter and yet clung to her by rejecting the boyfriend.

One might suggest from this account that parents of singletons should take special pains to diminish the risk of their child's loneliness, especially at holiday times. Any child, however, can be lonely during a holiday when neglected.

Divorce in a One-Child Family

I have alluded to subtle repercussions due to the triangularity of the one-child family system. Do the effects of divorce in such a rigid system have a different impact on family members than in a larger family? I am not sure about the legitimacy of the question and less sure about its answer. The following is an abbreviated account of a girl who explained what happened when her parents divorced while she was very young. She ends by stating what she wants in her own family of procreation.

> Before my mother returned to work, she spent much time with me, reading and teaching me much that I was supposed to learn in school. As a result, I was always ahead of the class in the primary grades. The longer my mother continued to work, the less time she had to spend with me. My mother and I grew farther apart, and I became a very quiet and timid girl.

> I was never aware of any open hostility between my parents, although now I realize their personalities are very different.

> Before my father remarried, we saw each other every weekend and remained very close. My mother resented my looking forward to seeing him and would often say anything to make my father look bad in my eyes. In turn, I resented her for doing this and was extremely hurt to see my mother turn against me and my feelings for my father. Consequently, I stood up for him and refused to believe anything she said. When my father remarried, I was afraid to tell my mother for fear of what she would say against him and his new wife. Little lies became big ones, and of course you can imagine the mess and embarrassment when everyone realized what had happened. From then on, I couldn't understand why my mother would always question me so much about my father when she no longer loved him, and this I resented even more.

> My relationship with my father since his remarriage has been one of steady decline. I loved my father very much and still do. His wife is extremely different from my mother and we get along quite well, but I always have the feeling that she resents me at times. Their daughter is a wonderful and charming little girl, and whenever I can, I enjoy taking her to the zoo or

just visiting with her. I see my father less each year, and we seem to be living entirely different lives.

There are many patterns in my family of orientation that I would change in establishing my own family of procreation and a few that I would not. If possible, I hope to have several children and do not wish to work while they are young. I would like to settle down in one house while raising my children, and it will be open to their friends whenever they wish to come over. I want my children to be able to talk to me about anything and never be afraid of me. Most of all, I hope that my husband and I will never have to get a divorce. These are all things that I did not have in my family of orientation. However, I hope that I will be able to let my children make their own decisions just as my mother has let me make mine. I hope that Christmas and holidays will be family affairs as they have been in my present family. I also hope that I can teach my children to respect their grandparents as my mother has taught me to respect my grandmother. Most of all I hope my children will be able to love their parents in spite of their faults as I do mine.

The following case illustrates the importance of a father in countermanding the overprotectiveness of the mother as analyzed by the son. The principle of balance has many facets, one of which is identification. The father in this case urged his son to accept the responsibility for his own behavior. This theme recurs throughout the book and is considered a requisite for any pantrophic family.

Many times it's very lonely to be an only child, and I remember when I was young, I always wanted a brother or sister. The thing I missed most about not having any siblings was not being able to take anyone into my confidence. Little secrets were shared by me alone. I have quite a few friends, but no one I could really call a very close friend. I think this is due in part to the fact I never had anyone my own age I ever felt really close to. I was always big for my age, and I was usually respected and looked up to by other kids my age, but I still wasn't very close to them in a brotherly sort of role.

My father was always very strict, fair but strict. I always gave my father plenty of things to be strict about. When I first started high school, I associated with older boys and I was in trouble several times during my first couple of years of high school. I could never lean on my father, so I had to depend on myself. When I got into small scrapes, my father would tell me to fight my own battles, but when something big would happen, he'd always do his best to get me out of trouble. My mother didn't play as important a role in my life as my father. She was always trying to be overprotective. This meant mama was always trying to protect me, and Dad would always say, "He should have known better." When I was younger, I had a tendency to lean on my mother and to hate my father because he'd never give me any sympathy. This background made me love authority; I like people to depend on me, and I like to tell them what to do.

The role of the father in the United States in countermanding the over-protective stance of the mother is well recognized. This role is especially important in cases of the only son, the lastborn son, the favorite son, or the handicapped son. This role should not involve the inculcation of toughness, but it should involve the imperative that boys mature and accept responsibility for their behavior.

Adopted Singletons and Foster Children

Adopted children have special problems, several of which focus on the way they learn of their adoptive status, their yen to know something about their biological parents, and the nature of their contacts with such parents if and when they are located. Unfortunately, only a few of the students spelled out exactly how they were told of their adoptive status, although several implied that they learned of it very early and were not especially disturbed about the learning process. The following case involves an adopted child who had a natural-born sibling and who suffered from rejection by the adoptive parents:

> My brother and I were separated by nearly twelve years. He was born when my parents were young, and he was a natural child. I was adopted at the age of two months when my parents were much older. Our differential status caused an immediate conflict, but not between us as much as within myself. I was jealous of him, and my jealousy and rivalry were helped considerably by my mother, who often reminded me of my status or compared me, unfavorably, to my brother. When she was angry, she would call me the devil's child or say that I had bad blood. Later she taunted me by saying she knew what my real mother was—a prostitute.

> My brother reaped the benefits of young parents. They did many things together. The family unit was cohesive. I suppose I could say that I reaped the benefits of older parents—the financial benefits, at least. However, when I was young, the family was no longer a cohesive unit. My mother had a job and her clubs; my father had his job; my brother was in the navy. Rather than a family unit, I dealt with three autonomous individuals who happened to live at the same address. I never, consequently, knew my father, my mother, or my brother well. In fact, I felt like an outcast. First, I was not even a real member of the family, as I was often told. Second, I had no real family unit to cling to. I, too, was supposed to be autonomous.

> If I felt like an outcast in my family, I probably felt more so among my peers. I had few friends, and they were children whom no one else liked.

> Shortly after my father's death, I went, in my mother's words, completely berserk. I had always been a disciplinary problem for my parents, but after my father's death I became worse, and my mother became less capable of coping with me.

Although my father left my mother fairly well off, my mother continued to work. She didn't want to die, but she feared living so long that she would run out of funds. And she felt that I was a financial burden.

Apparently, I was also a psychological burden to her. My father had a heart condition, and when he died my mother placed the blame on me. She felt that I had caused undue stress and that the stress caused his last heart attack. I could never convince my mother that I had not killed my father.

Nevertheless, after my father died, my mother did not want to, and could not, cope with a fifteen-year-old daughter. I stayed out late at night or overnight. I made friends with the city's beatnik element, and like them, I drank, partied, drank, and partied. Because I needed money to support my binges, I forged a number of checks on my mother's account.

It took a while before I was discovered, but when I was—well, my brother stepped into the situation, and together with my mother, they had me placed in the detention home. I stayed there for a month before going to court. The court took me out of my mother's custody and placed me in a school for delinquent girls.

This girl got to college in spite of the strikes against her.

The next histories illustrate some of the problems associated with adoption, including the manner of revealing to the child his adoptive status. The first case involves a pantrophic family in which the mother, a professional woman, had two sisters and an adopted brother.

I was told about adoption—what it is and why it is done—before I was told that I was adopted. I realized that this was a wonderful thing for a baby, since the new parents who couldn't have children of their own have a lot of love to give to the child who might not otherwise be given love. When I was told (at seven) that I was adopted, I was the happiest child around. I felt very loved, wanted, and needed. The psychological approach to telling the child something as important as this means a lot to the future development of the child. I was ready for this since I knew exactly what it meant.

This case involves a dystrophic family.

Everything went smoothly for about the first eight years of my life, even though I was aware that my parents were more rigid and somewhat different from other parents. After being informed that Santa Claus was a myth, I was casually informed that I was an adopted son and was shown my adoption papers. Needless to say, this was traumatic. I felt I had been purchased as one would purchase a piece of furniture. The seeds of hostility and rebellion were planted.

I never witnessed any display of affection between my foster parents. I never confided in either parent since our relationship prevented any feeling of closeness or understanding.

I gradually became ashamed of my foster parents and of our poor living conditions. I never invited any friends to my home. Instead of identifying with my foster family, I identified with one of my friend's parents who seemed to understand and accept me. I envied my friend for having parents who were younger than mine and who shared many things with him. I can remember going to places like the supermarket with my friend and his parents and pretending that they were my parents. I used to wish that I had brothers and sisters and parents that I could enjoy.

Some of the most discouraging cases I observed during my experience with parolees involved children who had lived in a series of foster homes interspersed with periods in penal institutions. I marvel that one such case got to college, and I include it here because he was able to articulate his feelings. If the reader dislikes what this man says about his distrust of women and his negative attitude toward marriage, his dreamlike description of the kind of woman he might marry, and his loss of hope for attempting marraige, keep in mind that he never experienced any genuine parental affection of any kind during infancy; that he never witnessed in any of his foster homes an exchange of spousal affection or had a single model of a father or mother figure; and that, in these foster homes, the wife dominated and downgraded her husband in a milieu of ignorance and fanaticism.

I am forced to approach my autobiographical analysis a little bit differently from other college students. I cannot point to one man and woman and say, "These are the parents with whom I was brought up, with whom I've learned so much, and have so many experiences with. Rather, I've had the unique experience of being brought up in three institutions, five foster homes, and several jails.

My mother was already married, and without getting a divorce, she married my father. They lived together two years before I was born. When I was twenty months old, it was discovered that my mother was a bigamist. At this time society blew the whistle, called a halt to the affair, and stepped in to arrange everything into a neat and logical order. Society got my father fired from his job. It stripped my mother of both her husbands, admonished her publicly, and sent her to jail. It changed my name from my father's to my mother's and sent me to a county children's home. This, so far as the society was concerned, settled the matter. Unfortunately, I grew up despite myself.

I remained in the county home among other social outcasts. Here we grew, played, laughed, giggled, romped, stole, lied, and giggled and romped and grew some more. None of us knew the world we were to face outside, while those who were older and wiser didn't quite know how to break the news to us. It seemed that the whole world watched breathlessly while we giggled and played for they felt we should be humble, subdued, respectful, fearful and thankful and that we should worship society in our unfortunate predicament. We as children made our own evaluations and lived our own lives. We didn't judge our friends by what family they came from, how much money the family had, what part of town they came from, how much education they had, or who the kids knew. Rather, we judged all friends by how well they could kick the can, how smart they were when they hid, how fast they could run, how much they laughed and giggled, and whether they could keep a secret better than others.

The adult world to us was far removed, cold, and impersonal. The matrons who took care of us were professional but patient, crisp but friendly, and businesslike but warm. The matrons couldn't be mothers to all of us for there were too many children and not enough mothers to go around. Therefore, my impression of a mother image is vague in some areas, while in other areas it is completely blind. We couldn't run to the matron with our troubles. We couldn't seek her help, her warmth, or affection because there was none.

When I was nine, I was placed in my first foster home. I recall being asked if I wanted to live in that foster home. I really didn't want to go there, but I couldn't put my feelings into words. I went because all the other kids talked me into it. They thought it would be great for me to get out of the county home. I wish I could have been able to disagree in clear terms. Looking back on it now, I recall that I was quite content in the county home. I had a simple and routine life, I could bury myself in the crowd of children when I wanted to, or I could excel and become unique when I wanted to be recognized. I was enjoying myself thoroughly and would have been content to stay there until I was old enough to go into the army.

The foster family was from a middle-class family that still felt the cold hand of the Depression close behind them. Their religion was fundamentalist Protestant, their education was high school level, and their house was clean, neat, and precisely similar to the neighbors' houses up and down the block. Their outlook on events in society was: "It's either all black, or it is all white. It is either good, or it is bad. It is either an instrument of the devil, or it is sent directly from God. I will either go to heaven, or I will go to hell."

The mother was the tallest person in the family—she towered a foot over her husband. She was the leader since the little man sensed the superiority of his wife's strength; therefore, he sensed the superiority of his wife's ideas. The other child in our "warm" family of four was a girl about my age. She had been adopted by these people when she was one year old.

Our happy family had a happy routine of physical chores we had to perform good naturedly. However, the high point of the evening was our family reading of the Bible. We each read six paragraphs, and we would discuss each segment as we went along. At certain points I might disagree with the interpretation as advanced by my parents. I was then informed that their true son, who had died, *never* disagreed with his parents and that the bad boy from the county home had always disagreed. It was clearly implied that I wouldn't want to disagree for I would only end up in a reform school.

As it was turning out, I was getting the long end of a short stick. My relationship with the family was slowly being undermined. I couldn't meet the image set up by the deceased legal son. I continued to fit the pattern of the boy in the reform school according to their standards. The girl and I never got along too well because she felt insecure in the family and told stories behind my back to make her own position securer. I began to be fearful and apprehensive of their religion. I could not play any musical instrument as their deceased son had been able to do. I could not accept either adult as my parent, for I began to fear them and mistrust them, and I couldn't fit into any of their ideas as to what a boy should be.

I never saw or experienced real sympathy, affection, love, or happiness in that home. I never saw the father kiss the mother with real love or affection. When he came home from work, their lips would meet in a short pop and each would gently look away and start talking about the weather, the car, or the job. I never knew either of the parents to show any tenderness, concern, or love to the other.

I usually went to bed at 9 P.M. One night I went to say goodnight to my foster parents, and the father said, "Sit down, I want to talk to you." I sat down and got a three-hour lecture on the evils of sin. Then I was allowed to go to bed. I got the same treatment the next night and the next and the next until several months had gone by. What was happening was that I was having wet dreams without my knowledge. They thought I was masturbating. Since the parents thought that masturbation was sinful, evil, and likely to make me insane, they tried to stop this by keeping me up till I was exhausted. They had me circumcised several months later; they made me go to church every night to ask for forgiveness of my sins; they threatened to call the police, put me in jail, or put me in a mental institution. I began to think they were crazy because I couldn't understand what they were driving at. They never told me about masturbation or wet dreams. When they asked if I was playing with myself and I told them I wasn't, they thought I was a liar. One night they called the children's home and told them I was to leave that night or they would call the police and have me spend the night in jail. They told the social worker they couldn't stand having me in their house another hour.

It wasn't until a year later, in another foster home on a farm in another part of the state, that I discovered masturbation. It took another few months for me to realize what the first foster-home parents had been driving at all the time. Soon my relationship deteriorated with the second foster home and I ran away. I was caught several days later and spent a week or so in jail until the paper work was cleared so I could return. I then was placed in an institution for boys but ran away once a month. From that time until I entered the air force, I was in and out of foster homes, in and out of jail, and in and out of one institution after another.

In most of the foster homes, I discovered that the wife was dominant and the husband was insignificant. I never knew any of them to have a sense of humor. The only time they laughed was when someone else looked ridiculous, be it actor, friend, foster child, or each other. The wife usually said what she wanted, when she wanted to, while the husband said little or nothing. No person in all the homes I've been in could really place himself in another person's shoes. All of the foster parents seemed incapable of understanding someone else's problem. When they criticized, they did so with a loud voice and with righteous indignation. I never knew any one of the husbands openly to express words of praise, admiration, or appreciation about his wife or found a woman who praised her husband. Seldom did I hear a man criticize his wife but frequently heard the wife ridicule her husband behind his back.

I have seldom dated because I don't trust women. I cannot confide in them and cannot understand them. My relationships with women since the first matron in the county home to the last foster mother have been poor. For this reason, I make no effort to date, be around women, confide in them, cultivate their friendships, or attempt to understand their ways. I've also come to hold their method for getting men in contempt. I've discovered that I will be better off as a bachelor. I feel that if I were to marry, we would both be unhappy.

I doubt if there is a woman in the world who would understand my complex, difficult, and emotionally torn background. Even if she were to understand, I doubt if she could ever be careful enough not to corner me, threaten me, interrogate me, or attempt to humiliate me, for if she even implied that she were going to do any of these things, I would react swiftly and decisively and our love would be destroyed.

I realize it is impossible to find the woman I'm looking for, but I would like to state what she must be. She must be a few years younger than myself, have a college degree, be a paragon of diplomacy, have a pleasing voice, a warm and friendly personality, a sincere desire to make me happy, a deep desire to love me. She must trust me, forgive my mistakes and weaknesses, never attempt to humiliate me, never pressure me, want no more than three children, be economical, content, and happy with her family. She must never holler or raise her voice. She must try to appreciate the things I can do, praise my efforts, show her affection to me, be able to communicate when she feels unhappy so we can work it out; must not drink, smoke, or eat to excess; and must be willing to sacrifice her own wants for the happiness of the family.

I, in turn, would offer her a bachelor of science, a master's degree, and perhaps a doctorate. I would try to be careful what I say and when I say it. I would attempt to make her happy and give her a happy life. I would be willing to build a home with my hands to our specifications. I would work and strive to be an above-average provider and would try to make her warm, comfortable, and content with her life. I would be a good father to the children and love them, respect them, and need them as much as they need me. I would trust her, I would not be extravagant, and I would be moderate in drinking, smoking, and eating. I would try never to holler—I seldom do anyway. I would recognize her value and worth and would show appreciation for the things she does. I would be willing to play down my own desires in order to keep a cohesive family unit.

My impressions of the family units I've lived with leave me to believe that most men and women are not happy with marriage. By the time they are forty years old, they seem to tolerate each other, but beyond that time, there is a wide gulf of misunderstandings and thwarted dreams. I realize that there must be warm and happy marriages, but I have never seen any. Therefore, no matter how I wish to get married, I must look to the hard realities of the marriages I've seen and count myself out. The woman I look for is a dream that is unlikely to come true. For a time it seemed almost unbearable to realize that I would never marry. Now, as each month goes by, I have less desire to get married, and I know that the time will come when I'm content to be a bachelor.

This man in all his life had never experienced the *hestia* of a pantrophic family. From the matron in the county home to the last foster home, not a single adult had played the role of a concerned and loving parent. It is amazing that he succeeded in college. In trying to account for this, I am reminded of Harlow's experiment in which baby monkeys who were isolated from their parents and permitted to romp with peers turned out to be relatively happy. The only suggestion of happy times in this case were the times he romped with peers in the county home until he was nine.

What kind of therapy would be helpful in a case like this? I would prescribe several months of living with a model pantrophic family, paying for his board and room. I would select a family in which the husband is taller than the wife and who has an edge on decision making, a family in which orthodoxy is minimal, the *hestia* has a aura of love and concern, the children romp with laughter, and cohesion obtains while each member retains his unique separateness and autonomy.

Summary

From the material in this chapter, one can appreciate certain advantages and disadvantages of the only child. How can parents maximize the advantages and minimize or counteract the disadvantages of the singleton status? In order to achieve these aims, it is necessary for both parents to play their parental roles to the fullest and with balance; but it seems that this balance is even more important for the only child than for children with several siblings. In our culture, this means that a father must take genuine responsibility, not only to counteract overmaternalism but also to play positive and constructive paternal roles. He should always keep in mind that how his son relates to the opposite sex and to his future wife will be influenced by the way the father treats his wife from day to day. The same is true for the wife with respect to her daughter. The behavior of both parents will also influence the kind of partner their child selects for marriage. More of this follows in chapter 16. Even if the parenting process is balanced, the parents should be careful not to make the child feel he is trapped in a triangle and the pawn of a powerful and arbitrary coalition.

The necessity for providing suitable peer groups for the only child is well understood, but it may not be so well understood that the loneliness of an only child may find no overt expression to alert the parents. The clamor for a brother or sister may be symptomatic of loneliness, but nothing can substitute for careful observation by a sensitive parent. One way to provide contact with peers for any child is to make the home a favorite rendezvous for the neighborhood children. This makes any child happy, and when he cannot bring his friends home or when they are loath to come to his home, he is unhappy. The degree of popularity of a child's home by his friends is one criterion by which to evaluate the quality of parenting that the child receives.

Some of these cases have suggested that the only child is entitled to some special lessons regarding selfish and unselfish behavior, although excellent character traits possessed by the parents in this dimension may suffice.

Several of our singleton students have mentioned their difficulties relating to peers when they got to college. This difficulty is supposed to be due to lack of experience in relating to siblings, but some of it could be due to the expectation of being waited on, to self-centered preoccupation, and to having less self-reliance and a bit of immaturity. Some of these traits are found in other children like the youngest brother of sisters, but parents of singletons might do well to take some pains to train their child as related in the pantrophic families described here.

In this training process, the parents might imagine that their child will have, as dormitory or fraternity mates in college, persons who have had plenty of experience in fighting with siblings over space, clothes, and chores. Those future college mates will be quick to identify individuals who are overly dependent and self-centered and who fail to do their share of the chores.

Parents of adopted children have the special problem of deciding when and how to tell the child about his adoptive status. During my experience in parole work, I believed that an adopted child should be told about his status so early in life that he could not remember a time when he was unaware of it. To cover up the adoptive status or to delay it so that the child learns about it from other sources has disastrous and traumatic consequences. I recall a case in which a teenager learned of his adoptive status from the hired man. He became obsessed with a desire to secure his birth certificate and the circumstances of his background. When depressed, he would get a little drunk and perform a harmless burglary. I was positive that his delinquency was a response to the way his adoption was handled and to his frustration in not being able to learn more about his background. A key element in successful adoption, however, is the warmth and security that adoptive parents provide. In one of the mentioned happy cases, the parents first explained the nature of adoption and then told the daughter that she was adopted when she was seven. The adoption process had been described as something wonderful for a baby, and the little girl was quite happy with adoptive status.

Notes

1. Walter Toman, *Family Constellation: Its Effect on Personality and Social Behavior,* 3rd ed. (New York: Springer, 1976).

2. In my probation work, I was so impressed with the dystrophic influence of a mother upon the only son, the sickly son, the last son, and the failing son that I wrote a satirical article entitled "How to Make Your Son a Misfit," published in *American Mercury,* March 1938, pp. 283–288. I featured the prevalence of the mother-son complex in the genesis of delinquent behavior.

3. Toman, *Family Constellation.*

4. G. Feldman, "Only Child as a Separate Identity: Differences between Only Females and Other First Borns," *Psychological Report* 42 (February 1978):107–110.

5 Twins

Identical Twins

Identical twins are a novelty, and novelties attract public attention. A family, therefore, can get attention by displaying twins in a manner that focuses public attention on the thing that makes them novel—namely, their sameness. To get attention for the family novelty, one may increase the sameness by giving them similar names, dressing them in identical clothes, and keeping them in the same class and circle of friends. This produces a clucking of tongues in comparing them—an activity, incidentally, that the twins may like when they are very young but that they dislike as they get older.

The main problem for twins is to achieve their separateness, personal identity, individuality, independence, and autonomy. Genetic similarities may start them off with compatible interaction, and family and social pressures may keep them together. However, they need interaction with diverse personalities in peer groups in order to facilitate the breakaway so necessary for the achievement of identity.

> From the day we were born, I lived with a shadow, a girl so much like me in looks, in stature, in temperament, and in personality that I was never considered an individual child. I was always half of someone else, never a whole child, an entity by myself. Without doubt this has affected both our lives quite drastically. My sister has been the most influential person upon my life and I upon hers. Until this day I have never completely attained my identity apart from her. Until we came to college, we dressed exactly alike and did everything possible together. We were sent to the same grade school and high school, so consequently we were never separated for any considerable length of time. My parents, especially my mother, encouraged us to look and act as much alike as possible. We were called twin rather than our names. Consequently, people refused to think of us as two separate girls, and we became extremely dependent upon each other. I used to dread doing anything by myself. I always felt that there was something missing. In fact, I can remember the time we entered high school and were separated in one class. Throughout the class in which we were separated I had to keep myself from crying. After our classes were over, we would run to see each other. I never felt secure or comfortable unless she was with me. Worry over her constantly filled my thoughts. Most of the time I was more concerned over her welfare and well-being than my own.

63

The following twins did not achieve a breakaway until they entered college:

> We were identical twins. When we were very young, people oh'd and ah'd over us. We never really minded this because we, too, felt this way. We always did things together and felt we were just half of a team. We had very few friends outside of each other and hated doing anything alone or with anyone except each other. Many people still think of us as one. During our last year or so in high school, we began to wake up to this. We realized that we were much too close for our own good. Now that we are in the university, we refuse to believe any longer that we are just one person. We have chosen similar but different professions, are making our own friends, and are finding our own place in the world.

The difficulties arising from the mutual dependency of male twins may be compounded by maternal overprotection:

> I resented more and more Mother's possessive, overprotectiveness, which I felt to be emotionally crippling and emasculating. This need for indisputable masculinity resulted from lack of a strong father figure.

All children need the help of parents in achieving identity as unique human beings, but more strategies are required in the case of twins. Some parents make much of one twin being the firstborn because he arrived some minutes before the other. Family members then assign the role of firstborn to one and the role of secondborn to the other. In the case of fraternal twins, one may outshine the other in physical and/or mental development; thus identity is easier to achieve. Some parents of twins take pains to emphasize or encourage differentiation with respect to names, dress, task roles, friends, teachers, and even schools. As with all children, invidious comparisons should be avoided and the expectation of uniqueness for each child should be stressed. (This will be discussed further in chapter 6.)

The following excerpts indicate the extent to which students were aware of identity and autonomy problems of twins and they describe some appropriate strategies employed by their parents.

> Andy and I are very dependent upon each other. Almost everything we do is done together. My mother, being a twin herself, foresees the future danger of too much dependency. She made sure when we first began school that we were placed in separate classrooms. She hopes in this way we will learn to perform separately and to make our own friends. She also hopes this would prevent other people from constantly comparing us. Although still pretty close, we have adjusted quite well to the separate classroom situations.

Fraternal Twins

Such problems are not so great when twins are fraternal, not identical, especially when they are of different sex. This is what one girl from a pantrophic family wrote about herself and her opposite-sex twin:

> The firstborn was a boy and then a girl, myself, was born six minutes later. I am the youngest of the family. There is little rivalry and little favoritism. There are periods when we stick together for something and other times when we divide. My brother and I are quite different. He is very mechanically minded and I am studious. As freshmen in high school, we were mistaken for steadies. The biggest mistake I felt my parents made (and they realized it when we reached seventh grade) was not separating us in grade school. This caused my brother to take a lax attitude toward schoolwork, figuring that if I got it, he'd get it. After the separation we both did better. I tend to be shy and less talkative. Now we have gone our separate ways more or less; I feel more independent also because of this. Also I know he is more independent, and we don't feel each is watching over the other.

Since twins are so much alike, we should expect parents to treat them alike, meaning—among other things—no favoritism. My data seemed to bear this out. However, what happens when favortism is showered on one twin and the other feels rejected? Does favoritism do more damage in a situation when siblings are close in age like twins?

One mother of twins (a boy and a girl) had married her boyfriend on the West Coast just before he embarked for overseas duty in World War II. Their parents, who lived in the Midwest, were not informed of the wedding until later. The young mother gave birth to the twins in isolation and loneliness, without the presence of husband or relatives, and suffered a nervous breakdown. She was hospitalized for a time before her relatives brought her back home to live with her parents-in-law. Her father was dead and her mother had thirteen children. Contrary to her physician's advice, she had three more children including a daughter, Cindy, who wrote the family analysis featuring the twins, Tom and Anna:

$$
\begin{array}{c}
\triangle \\
---\bigcirc-\triangle-\bullet--------\triangle------- \quad (5.1)
\end{array}
$$

Tom And Anna   Cindy

> They were opposite babies. Tom was quiet and passive while Anna was curious and mischievous. Since our mother was a nervous, impatient sort of person, very sensitive to noise, she tended to favor Tom who was more obedient and quiet, and she tended to yell more at Anna for getting into

trouble. Anna was blamed for everything that was broken, while Tom was not. Thus, in Anna's eyes, Tom represented the angel who could do no wrong.

As a result of this favoritism, my sister developed a serious complex; she developed a negative attitude toward boys in general so that she would not date in high school or in college. She became competitive with Tom at school and in sports. She graduated with a 3.9 grade point and secured a master's degree in physical education. Tom did not go to college.

Anna was the only girl in the family until I was born seven years later. She was jealous of me and fearful that I would take away her father's love for her. Her jealousy likely increased because I was a fussy baby and got a lot of attention from Mother. Her jealousy got worse and she tattled on me. My popular social life (which was the opposite of Anna's) intensified her jealousy, and she tried to ruin my social life in all sorts of ways. I turned to my brothers for help; I confided in them and trusted them. I get along very well with boys, but I feel uneasy around girls.

Two women in one of my classes were fraternal twins with no other sibs, and each wrote a family analysis. Both mentioned by name the one who was born six minutes ahead of the other, but this did not seem to have any later significance. In different words, the two girls said the same things about their pantrophic family. The forebears were Greek. The relationships between the parents, between the parents and the twins, and between the twins were excellent. In this family there was a balance between the time and energy the father devoted to his occupation and the time and attention he gave to his wife and daughters. There seemed to be good visibility since husband and wife carried out recreational and social activities together and planned many activities for the whole family, especially for the children. Communication was excellent in all relationships, and an aura of love, trust, and security pervaded not only the numerous family rituals but also daily living. This family would rate high on all the other family patterns to be mentioned later in this book.

Nothing in the report of either twin throws light on how the twins achieved their identities except that, although they were similar in some ways, "We have developed individual tastes as we have grown older."

Summary

The achievement of separate identities for twins is their main problem; as we have seen, it has been encouraged by various strategies like enrolling the twins in separate classes or schools and by the encouragement of individuality and independence.

6 Dyads

This chapter deals with four combinations of sibling dyads: (1) two brothers, (2) two sisters, (3) older brother/younger sister, and (4) older sister/ younger brother. The narrator is sometimes the younger, sometimes the older, which gives us eight points of view on dyadic reaction and its influence on personality development. Does the influence of position impinge as much on a child who has only one sibling as compared to several? I do not think so, but it is amazing how many students who have only one sibling attribute Toman's traits to either or both of them. The oldest brother of three brothers will find his leadership more challenging than when there is one brother. The youngest brother of five sisters will develop more strongly the expectation that women are to wait on him than when there is one older sister.

My students were familiar with two of Toman's ideas: identification and complementarity in family relationships. Identification takes place when a son in a given position with his sibs takes on the characteristics of his father who has the same position with his sibs.[1] The oldest brother of brothers assumes the leadership of his younger brothers like his father does with his brothers or coworkers. This father will identify with this son as he observes him using the same strategies in leadership that he did. Another twist to the father's identification with the son occurs when the father is so proud of his son's accomplishments that he perceives the son as an extension of himself.

Complementarity in family relationships has to do with the matching of lovers and married couples according to sex and rank factors in the sib constellations of each as described in chapter 3 and appendix B.

Toman rightly makes the distinction between identification between parent and child and the relationship of the two. The nature of the relationship between the child and his cross-sex parent is different from that with the same-sex parent. This difference has been treated by psychologists and novelists for centuries. When dealing with cross-sex relationships, students are more apt to use terms such as *partial, fond, close, favorite,* and *protective.* Recognition of this difference is given by sociologists when they refer to expressive roles being learned from the cross-sex parent and task roles from the same-sex parent.[2]

A good relationship is characterized by satisfying emotional overtones, but this is not necessarily the case with identification. Suppose the father, the oldest brother of brothers, inducts his son into the leadership role over his younger brothers. Father and son will have similar habits in making quick decisions in the presence of peers and in carrying out their decisions by directing others. However, suppose the son learns only too well how to be proficient, to make decisions quickly, and to take the lead. When father and son are working together, their ingrained habits and attitudes may clash and lead to friction. If there is a great disparity between the skill and experiences of father and son relative to the task at hand, the oldest son will accept and defend his father's status and leadership. Friction that develops between any two family members because of similar positions is not likely to occur except when the parties are engaged in some kind of task or the resolution of a decision.

In his third edition, Toman applied the concept of complementarity of sex and rank to the parent-child relationship. My students assumed the significance of cross-sex relationships, but they did not consciously apply the idea of complementarity of rank to the parent-child relationship; they used complementarity of both sex and rank only to boy-girl and husband-wife relationships.

Identification between parent and child because of similar position in their respective sib configurations may or may not involve a warm emotional relationship. The nature of such a relationship will be determined by similarity in temperament, interest, and mutual trust more than by similarity or complementarity of position.

I think my students made two significant contributions to personality development in the group process: They pointed up the necessity of combining simultaneous experience within the sib group with experience in the peer group, emphasizing the dialectical mesh of life in the family setting with that of their settings beyond the home. There can be an absence or a proliferation of persons of one sex in the peer group just as we can have it in the sib group. The advantage or disadvantage of age in the sib group can be nullified or reversed by the ages of peers.

Besides the factor of age, we have variations in personal resources (many of them genetic in origin) such as height, weight, intelligence, strength, dexterity, balance, quickness, and so forth that sometimes reverse or nullify sib rank according to age or even to sex. In the analysis of their families, my students also pointed up the significance of sex roles and how they could reverse leadership based on age.

Another contribution is the suggestion that the dystrophic or pantrophic features of a family can nullify the effects of position and of identification and can mute or nullify complementarity or noncomplementarity. The effect of the family system and its *hestia* is the background upon which the factors of rank and sex operate, and these will operate differentially according to the nature of the system.

In spite of exceptions to Toman's generalizations, his concepts dealing with personality development within the family configuration and how they affect later social relationships are significant and useful. My students have given his concepts a great deal of support. We can expand our horizons through the study of exceptions.

No parental thrill is quite like the birth of the firstborn who will, indeed, get a great deal of stimulation from excited parents. This stimulation gives the older child some advantage in developing aptitudes that will be helpful when he goes to school. For example, in the case of two brothers, the mother will employ strategies to induce the older brother to take a helpful and protective stance toward the younger one. Because of this process, the older child is more likely to make decisions when the two are playing by themselves. The habit of decision making propels the older one into a more assertive role. The older child will more often be expected to answer questions when the mother is not around.[3] If the older boy or girl is uncertain about the answer he may put up a bluff for some kind of an answer. Since the younger one is not often in a position to challenge the answer, the older one is vindicated and becomes bolder in making assertions.

The parents of an only child may compare him or her with other children of the same age. When they have twins, there is much ado about their sameness. When we have two siblings, the focus of attention may be on their sameness and differences. Talk and attitude about such differences by parents and teachers have much to do with promoting or stultifying growth. Invidious comparisons of children should be outlawed. Such comparisons are found in two-child families and seem to rise to a peak in three-child families, then decline so that they are absent in very large families. When parents come from large families, they make few invidious comparisons and put less pressure on a child to achieve like an older one.

After making an invidious comparison, a parent or teacher may put pressure on the lesser achiever to do as well as the other sib. The pressured one then withdraws from competition and does more poorly than before. Even though parents and teacher say not a word, a child may sense that he can never catch up with an older sibling in a given field. He may then withdraw from that field and concentrate his efforts in another activity. We shall now consider cases in which withdrawal of competition is complicated by identification with fathers who have two sons.

Two Boys

Because my brother was five years older and so much smarter in math and the sciences, I knew I couldn't compete with his outstanding performance. But in the subjects in which he was the weakest, I studied the hardest and excelled. So it could be said that I did display behavior known as withdrawal from competition by switching fields of interest.

I think my father slightly favored me over my older brother, not only because we were both the youngest in our respective families but also because I excelled in athletics and my brother didn't because of lack of interest. My father always emphasized sports and spent all his extra time playing with us. So when I became captain of the high school hockey team and made the city team, he became immensely proud of me.

In this case, identification due to rank was reinforced by common interests. In another case, the younger of two brothers was much quicker than the older:

Father identified with this quality in me. My brother, Don, however, was always very slow and methodical and was criticized severely by my father because of this. A deep inferiority complex developed in my brother and was not erased until his early twenties. While I held the quick aggressive qualities that put a twinkle in my father's eyes, Don held the sensitive, aesthetic, coordinated mental qualities that took years for my father to understand. About the only time jealousy emanated from my brother was when Father compared us on the subject of quickness. In such instances, especially in group activities, Don would withdraw to his bedroom and remain there until the activities were over. Now, Dad admires Don very much—he feels very remorseful over his past criticism.

In another case, the parents did not pressure their sons to compete in sports. However, the older one became a track star, and everyone in school expected the younger one to do likewise; therefore, he withdrew from sports and devoted his attention to his studies.

A number of constellations throw light on factors that reduce risk of withdrawal and illustrate the processes of identification, complementarity, and traits for positions in dyads. The first involves the narrator, the younger of two sons:

Since there was less than a two-year difference between my brother and me, we were generally treated as equals. We were usually assigned the same duties around the house, got similar allowances, and had about the same hours in which we were allowed to stay out. Therefore, I don't think I was actually thought of as the younger or baby brother. This was probably a carry-over from my parents' treatment as children. Both of my parents came from large families where they had brothers or sisters of the same sex who were approximately the same ages as my brother and I. My parents had a close relationship with their brothers and sisters and were treated as equals in their families. My parents also were shown no favoritism in their families and, as a result, showed none to either of us.

I would say that I was never jealous of my brother. We received equal attention at home, we both got about the same grades in school, and we were pretty equal in sports, which were very important to my brother and me. The only possible thing I may have resented was that I received a lot of hand-me-downs from my brother. However, my parents took care of this problem by buying me new things such as sports equipment and a bike of my own plus some clothes, and since these were the kinds of things that were important to me.

As far as withdrawal from competition, I don't think I ever did withdraw. My brother and I were of about equal abilities, and so he never really set any high standards that I felt I had to live up to or that I felt I wasn't capable of attaining. Even though my brother got higher grades in school, I usually didn't try any harder because of it. The reason for this was that my parents neither pressed me to do as well as my brother nor told me to try to be like him. They simply stressed doing the best I could and not worrying about what my brother got for grades. Most of the competition between my brother and me was in sports and that wasn't on a serious level.

In constellation 6.1, the father identified with the older son because each was the older of two brothers, but he also identified with the younger son because of his talents. However, the second son experienced difficulty in identifying with his father because of the father's absence from home. The mother was not only the bossy oldest sister of sisters but also the older sister of one brother. The two sons reacted quite differently to her big-sister mothering.

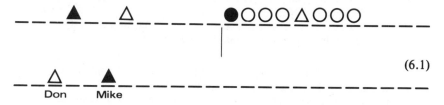

(6.1)

Don   Mike

In Toman's family constellation, I fit the position of the youngest brother of brothers. Many of my personality traits do follow the patterns suggested by Toman. For example, I have always admired my brother, and many times I have played bellboy for him. This might have marred my incentive to be a leader, but I feel I could handle the position if the need arose.

Also, I see myself as somewhat capricious—I feel I'm more of a romanticist than a realist—but rather than annoying elders, I tend to feel uncomfortable around them.

The older brother assumed a leadership role because of paternal admonitions such as:

"Now be sure and take care of Mom and Mike while I'm gone"—I floundered in my attempt to achieve a proper identification with my father. The only source available for identification came through my brother, and that's possibly why I was so subservient to him when I was younger. Now we fight a lot—I have an extreme temper when I get wrought up.

Not to flatter myself, but I do think I'm soft with women and also am a gentleman. I haven't arrived at these conclusions myself but have been told so by most of my dates. In analyzing my behavior with women, I have gained some insight as to why I behave the way I do with them. First of all, I have no sisters. This single fact makes me put myself out to a greater extent on a date than a person who, let's say, had sisters in his family and thus was aware of their moods and knew to some extent what women's intuition meant and about the other intrinsic qualities that girls possess.

My mother is the oldest sister of sisters. Although she is subservient to my dominant father, she takes efficient control of household tasks and is effective in serving people. Because she can't express a dominant role over my father, she passive/aggressively achieves her own authority by overwaiting on people. The members of my family have become habitually used to this. On taking a candid view of the scene, it can be said she controls it. Mother came from a family of seven girls and one boy, and since she was the oldest, she had to assume more responsibility than the other children and learned her role as a future wife very early.

Mother's overprotective nature affected my brother first. I have only come to be annoyed by it recently. It may sound trite, but I was quite shocked by the disparity between the degree to which Mother waited on me at home and the degree to which people waited on me outside of home, but it was so easy to give in to the services of one so warm and loving. *Don rejected Mother's overpampering, whereas I gave in to it.* There might be some favoritism shown by my mother because of this. It should be noted, however, that when my dad criticized Don for anything, he ran straight to Mother for comforting support. During these years he was much closer to Mom than I.

I suppose all kids fight among themselves. I know Don and I did our share, but whenever Dad caught us at it, he would make us clasp our hands and promise always to stick together. Whether the sentimental nature of this act still lingers in our minds, or whether we grew more aware of the meaning of such a little ritual as the hand clasping, remains a question. The fact is, we do feel very close on serious matters; and although we differ markedly in our personalities, Don and I would not hesitate to go out of our way for each other if the need arose.

Don was a good leader and well liked. Of course, I ran most of his errands and envied him the most for his abilities in this scene. In later years, Don assumed the role of my big brother, especially when I first entered pubescence. He showed me the ropes for getting along in varied social situations, and he admired my knack for picking things up quickly.

Parents tend to be more uptight in raising the firstborn and more relaxed with the second one. This differential treatment, like relaxed discipline, may lead to complications. This case also illustrates the common phenomenon of escaping from parental restraints and blossoming upon entrance to college.

In the next excerpt, the narrator, Tom, has a brother, Jim, who is two years older. The father has an older brother two years older and three younger sisters. The mother had a sister two years older.

> We always played together when we were small. Jim would bring his friends home and I would play with them also. My mother forced Jim to play with me, which led to resentment and conflict, and Jim would get punished. In school I was known as Jim's little brother. My parents pressured me to follow in Jim's footsteps. This had an adverse effect on me in that I rarely had a chance to make my own decisions until later in high school.

Tom implies that the parents were unsure of themselves in raising the firstborn. They restricted Jim a great deal, and he had to beg hard for each new privilege. They punished him for each infraction, but when Tom went through the same stages in high school, he was treated more leniently. Jim noticed this and his resentment led to conflict with both parents and with Tom. The more-relaxed and better relationship between parents and Tom embarrassed Tom in his relationship with Jim.

> After I started college my attitudes changed completely. I think of myself as a completely different person now, being able to express myself and to develop my personality the way I wish, with little family hindrance. I was always perturbed throughout high school that I didn't have a distinct personality and did not have the opportunity to let it blossom.

The second son in the following case, in spite of his age handicap, persisted in competition with the older brother, and the latter admitted the leadership capacities of the younger one. Note also that the constellation position of the father is not conducive to leadership, but unusual circumstances in his family setting plus leadership opportunities in his occupational setting generated such qualities.

> My position in the family constellation is the older of two brothers who are five years apart. My brother Harry was constantly pushed around and doing tasks that I was supposed to be doing. To a certain extent he was even put down by my parents. For example, I remember hearing my parents tell him, "You'll never be like your brother." Now I realize those comments could have harmed him, *but he never withdrew from competition.* For some strange reason he always wanted to compete with me though he always got the short end of the deal. Because of the constant competition between us, he didn't develop into Toman's analysis of a younger brother. He seems to be a good leader (from observing him in his peer group), and he also seems to be a good worker.
>
> My father could be classified as the youngest brother of sisters. He follows most of Toman's qualifications in that he expects my mother to wait on him hand and foot, and he gives little gratification in return. There is one point in which he does not follow the classification—leadership. The

youngest brother of sisters isn't supposed to be a good leader. On the contrary, my father is an excellent leader. Besides his occupation, he is a union official and loves being one. His leadership quality does stray from Toman's pattern, but it could be attributed to his early family experience. His father drank quite heavily and wasn't around much, so much of the family responsibilities fell upon my father. Consequently, this became embedded in him as a personality trait.

My mother is the younger sister of a brother. One point Toman brought out about her type was that she should be able to take orders from men. This is one reason why our family is stable. My mother can take orders that are given her quite regularly by her husband.

A second son may rebel against both his older brother and his father. In one family, the rebellion of the second son against the father (older brother of two sisters) had little or nothing to do with position but everything to do with the manner of exercising authority. The father was almost brutal in his physical punishment of the second son and would not tolerate the slightest opinion his two boys might venture on family affairs. The second son alleged that the father favored the older brother, but the thing that left its mark on the secondborn was the hostile tone of voice the father used in giving orders.

It is quite interesting to look at Toman's family constellation. In connection with my older brother, the characteristics listed by Toman thoroughly cover his personality, and the description seems perfect. Relative to my position as a younger brother, my analysis is exactly the same as my older brother with the exception of one point. To look at my position from an objective point of view, I have concluded that I have much trouble accepting authority from anyone who presents it in a hostile manner. I feel a sudden impulse to rebel, often get extremely worked up about it, and become completely stubborn to any requests. Any order put in a pleasant tone of voice, either a task or a favor, I feel honored to perform. To analyze this point, it can probably be related back to my childhood when the presence of my father was prevalent. His dominating authority continuously being presented in a hostile fashion has undoubtedly left its mark. My case presents a classic example of inability to accept demonstrative authority, not as a result of an older brother giving orders to his younger brother, but as a result of a parent constantly punishing and being hostile with a child of tender age.

My data indicate that, unless the family is very dystrophic, the jealousies, resentments, and conflicts among young siblings are usually transformed into cooperation when they reach late adolescence. Entering college often becomes a turning point. This time element is featured in the following:

My older brother Emil assumed a position of leadership and superiority over me whenever any conflict arose between the two of us. My feeling in this regard has, however, decreased noticeably in the last few years as both of us approached adulthood and maturity.

My feelings, as the baby of the family, were full of inferiority and jealousy, and I thought I was getting the worst end of everything that came along. Now as I look back at it, however, it becomes apparent to me that my parents were very fair and equal in raising my brother and myself.

My father, who was the older child in his family, tends to identify with my older brother, and my mother, the secondborn in her family, tends to identify more with me. For example, when a conflict arises between my brother and me, my father seems prejudiced toward the idea of the older as leader, while my mother is more understanding toward the inequality of the younger.

When sibs of either sex are more than six years apart, each of them is treated essentially like an only child, and they take on the characteristics of such. In the following case, however, the two sons were born years apart but did not get the usual parental treatment accorded to the first or only child. When children do not get loving attention from parents, they seek and find it in each other. The following was written by a student from a dystrophic family who had a much younger brother:

My father always beat me, at my mother's directions. She completely discouraged the neighborhood children from playing at our home, and I was forced to go out and seek my own friends because they would never come to my home.

I received high grades in school and enjoyed many of the activities, especially the associations with people of my own age. My parents never complimented me or encouraged me in my schoolwork, much to my disappointment. They never gave me any affectionate embraces or told me that they loved me. I have never seen my mother or father kiss each other. This lack of affection at home, also lack of encouragement, has brought about an attitude of unconcern for my parents. Their indifference to me has caused me to be indifferent to them. I assume an attitude of independence, but my house is not my home [emphasis added].

When my brother Dick was born twelve years later than I, parental attention, such as it was, was shifted to him. He and I became great pals. He is a very mischievous boy who looks up to me as his big brother. He much prefers the company of my fiancée and me to that of our parents; he seems to see us as the kind of parents he'd like to have—young and fun loving. Because I have become so independent, my parents are trying harder to keep Dick under their guidance and protection. My fiancée and I enjoy taking him to church, but my parents rarely let him go, insisting he is their son and should go to church with them. They seem to feel I'm taking his affections away from them.

Boys without sisters and girls without brothers are sometimes handicapped in relating to peers of the opposite sex, and they may fumble more in the precourtship period. When such children come from prudish families, the opposite sex has a mystique about it that may make a youngster shy, baffled, and uncertain.

> Having had no sisters, I was often uneasy around girls. Throughout high school I shied away from girls because, unfortunately, I did not know how to act around them. Many girls interpreted my actions as being stuck up, when in reality I possessed feelings of inferiority.

> Dealing with the opposite sex was intriguing to me. Since I had no sisters, this delightful strangeness enthralled me.

Two Girls

The following lists Toman's first four attributes of the oldest sister of sisters (see appendix B):

1. Can take care of others and boss them effectively,
2. Says things with certainty and finality,
3. Pretends to be surer of herself than she really is,
4. May cut people short who know more about the subject.

I am inclined to believe, however, that these characteristics of the older (oldest) sister are more pronounced when there are three or more sisters in a series than when there are only two.

Any sudden change in the parents due to ill health or accident will impinge upon two brothers or two sisters differently according to their age level. The same is true with divorce and the acquisition of a stepparent. If one or both parents are severely and chronically handicapped in the parental role, the expected traits and relationships of siblings may not develop.

The quality of parenting received by children reflects the quality of parenting by the grandparents. More important, it will be adversely affected by the premature death of a grandparent or the divorce of grandparents. Toman has emphasized this point, especially the premature demise of grandparents when the parents themselves were young children. Much of my data sustain Toman's stand on this. No family analysis is complete unless it covers two or more generations.

The aggressive-leadership role versus submissive-followership role also may be reversed if the older child is physically or mentally handicapped.

Constellation 6.2 supports Toman's ideas on the absence of rank and sex conflict in the good marriage of the student's parents because her father is the youngest brother of a sister and brother while her mother is the oldest sister of brothers.

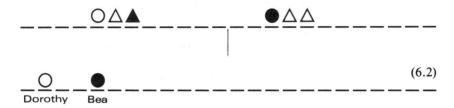

(6.2)

Dorothy   Bea

> My parents have a smooth relationship. My mother has always been the leader in the home and likes to give advice to all family members. Mother is our only disciplinarian since my father never wanted to take part in raising us, although he is urged to do so by my mother. My father has almost complete authority on farm matters and important financial decisions. Father never played with us or encouraged us to help him on the farm. Mother helps him in human relations connected with the farm since he lacks a good sense for communication.

> Mother and I have good communication. I probably talk to my mother as I would to a friend. I feel free to discuss problems about my boyfriends and school. My mother has a way of making me feel good when I come to her with a problem.

> My father and I have an easygoing relationship, since it is casual and no discipline is involved. Father has never been a disciplinarian. In this sense he is like another person in the family, not a strict father image. I admire his sense of humor. We would always have a good time laughing. He hated to see me cry and he could always bring me out of a bad mood; but he and I communicate very little.

> When younger I was shy and quiet. I hated my shyness, and when I began living away from Dorothy, I began opening up to live my own kind of life. Since high school I have changed so much, and now I really can say I enjoy life. I guess I blame Dorothy for implanting this trait of shyness upon me.

> My mother and I get along because I am obedient and usually cooperate with her. If I rebelled at all it was because I did not like to see Dorothy get out of doing things. I was easier to reason with and to persuade to do what was right.

The social handicap of not having a sib of the opposite sex is greater when a girl has a slight or poor relationship with her father and when a boy has a slight or poor relationship with his mother. These handicaps are accentuated when a boy suffers an interval without a mother or has a mother who is woefully inadequate or when a girl suffers an interval with no father or a cruel or neglectful father.

> Since I grew up with no brothers and little communication with my father, I did have a difficult time relating to boys. I sometimes feel rejected if a guy

does not ask me out again. I blame myself for not being able to keep up a conversation. After a data I would often say to myself, "He doesn't like me." I have a poor image of myself because I lacked a loving father.

In eleven cases of female dyads, scarcely a case among them completely contradicted Toman's thesis about the predicted traits according to rank position and sex. Most of them also agreed with his ideas on the mesh or conflict of personalities of couples due to similarity and difference in position.

In four cases, the differential in age of the two daughters was over six years, and all of them alleged that some of the traits of the only child obtained. In four cases the student compared the two girls with respect to academic and artistic achievement, and in all four showed that the older one did better, while the younger compensated by excelling in social and/or athletic activities. Some rivalry, jealousy, and conflict were common when the children were young, but these diminished as they grew older. Nearly all were good friends by the time the first one entered college.

When a father yearns for a son and is frustrated by a succession of daughters, he will develop a special rapport for the daughter who is the tomboy, usually the secondborn. In the following story, the narrator is the younger daughter by three years:

> I was Daddy's little girl. I think my dad wanted a son, and when I showed tomboyish tendencies, we became great pals. My sister was anything but a tomboy, and she got her satisfaction from ballet lessons and classical music. I don't think my mother favored either of us to any large extent, but she and I shared a similar sense of humor, and I didn't have my sister's tendency to have tantrums. I could usually manage to get what I wanted by going to my father, while Cindy didn't get along with him very well. My mother would usually stick up for her, and with my sibling jealousy, I'd side with my dad.

> When my sister and I grew older and could respect each other for abilities that we did have, we sometimes formed a coalition against our parents when one of us talked the other into wanting something. There was still competition for grades and honors in high school. I continued to be athletically inclined and remained in my father's good graces more than my sister, who was more interested in fashions and flirting than appeasing my dad, who really can be a bear to live with sometimes.

Sometimes we have a situation in which the younger of two children fails to do as well as the older one in some area of competence and in which the parents are careful not to make invidious comparisons but instead to encourage the younger one with praise when accomplishment is still mediocre. In one such case, the older child with an excellent record felt slighted because there was no praise coming her way when she did the better of the two. In another case two girls who were four years apart had considerable conflict. The older one, A, reasoned that the conflict was due to competition for grades in which the younger one, B, did less well. The mother praised B for each little improvement, but in private, she explained to A that while she did not praise her in front of B she was very proud of A's fine record. All this reinforces what has been mentioned before about the two elements in the *hestia* of a family that tend to eliminate jealousy, withdrawal from competition, and conflict: first;, the prevalence of the idea that each family member is expected to be unique and different from all the rest so that all comparisons are invidious and, second, the idea that each family member is proud of all the others. When these conditions prevail, the family is more likely to be pantrophic.

When two sisters are two to four years apart, the older one tends to take on the characteristics of the oldest sister of sisters. For example:

I have one sister two years younger, and I fit Toman's ideas remarkably well. I can stand on my own feet, take care of others, and boss them effectively. I am a dominating person and feel best when I assume this role. I have always been a leader even when I was very young. [She then describes a succession of elections to leadership roles in social and job positions.] Even today at my part-time job I assume responsibility beyond that of my co-workers. Toman says, "She will tend to identify with her superior, especially if he is a man." This is very true of me. I identify with my father. He and I have always been very close. Toman may be right in saying that she is a "self-righteous Queen accepting orders only from her King Father." Along with this Toman says that I despite official female figures above me and this, too, I will have to agree with. It seems that Toman's family constellation sums up well how my position in the family has affected my personality.

When sisters are wide apart in age it makes a difference:

My sister and I were thirteen years apart, so that each of us was like an only child. We each possess the traits of the only child; but in addition, she has some of the traits of the oldest sister of sisters, and I have some traits of the youngest sister of sisters. I think our respective positions were somewhat disadvantageous to our personality growth. Another thing, my sister and I both tend to have one close friend rather than a number of friends. Maybe we were looking for a sister image.

When two children are wide apart, then one or both may take on the traits of an only child:

I feel that I have many of the characteristics of the youngest sister of sisters. For example, I like adventure, entertainment, and change; am rather submissive; and tend to be a poor leader. The one characteristic of a youngest sister of sisters that I feel does not apply to me is competitiveness. I dislike competing and, in many cases, even try to avoid it.

Characteristics of an only child that seem to fit me include: feeling that work is a nuisance and wanting to be the center of attention. Also I sometimes question my maturity, for I tend to act impulsively and, consequently, often rather childishly.

My sister Judy, being six years older than myself, made it seem for quite a few years as if I were an only child. Naturally, because of the age difference, Judy was the leader and I generally did what I was told. Hence, I failed to develop leadership qualities and learned the role of submissiveness.

I cannot account for my liking of adventure, entertainment, and change, unless possibly I feel dominated and therefore the idea of freedom and change appealed to me. I would be interested in knowing Toman's explanation for that characteristic.

My dislike of work, I believe, stems from the fact that I was somewhat spoiled at home. My mother would ask me to do work around the house, but if I didn't do it right away, she would do it for me, and so I came to rely on her. I feel I have become more self-reliant since I have been away from home.

My sister Judy has good leadership qualities, there is a certainty and finality in what she says, and she does pretend to be surer of herself than she actually is. Some of the other characteristics defined by Toman don't seem quite so applicable. Her leadership qualities no doubt result from the fact that she was the oldest and had to assume responsibility.

Older Brother/Younger Sister

The cases that follow show that the influence of differences in rank and sex begins early in life. Children in boy-girl combination may learn earlier than the children in same-sex combinations about sex differences. The little boy is likely to be scripted by his parents to protect his little sister, and he may get his cue from the way his father treats his mother. As his father is rewarded by affection from the mother, so too the little boy may be rewarded by affection from his sister. His advantage in age makes him the decision maker and the leader. The big advantage for both children is getting an early start in life in understanding the psychic and physical nuances of the other sex. This early start in experience with a sibling of the other sex seems to predispose children to take more interest in persons of the other sex beyond the family, and this is admitted to in the writings of many students.

It should be kept in mind that an examination of the family constellation was only a part of the students' analyses. They had in their possession

Toman's list of traits. Students involved in the brother-sister combination would read, from Toman, the oldest brother of sisters and the youngest sister of brothers sections (see appendix B).

The two children in the following case start out as Toman would predict, but the domination of the older brother combined with the mother's open favoritism of him made the younger daughter rebellious, which led to closer attachment to girlfriends and a defensive attitude toward boys as revealed in the last two paragraphs. The daughter was four years younger than her brother Dickie.

My brother played with me when I was a toddler, but I was usually the guinea pig for the games he would fabricate.

I felt very much left out when my brother formed a close childhood relationship with my cousin Joyce. She was an only child, lived across the street, and she and Dickie were only six months apart. They constantly excluded me from their games because I was too little. A few years later we all played together, and still later Dickie was excluded from our girl games.

After we moved to a new neighborhood, Dickie assumed a position of superiority, being older and masculine. He became the rule maker and decision maker.

I went along with Dickie's ideas because I admired him and had good times with him. We did, however, quarrel often as I began to grow resentful of his air of superiority. Mother acted as arbiter, and I thought she generally favored my brother. I began to resent this and felt sorry for myself as a victim of injustice. I was often very jealous and hurt by my mother's favoritism of my brother. I often felt convinced that she had an inferior love for me. I concluded that the cause of which was because I was adopted (which I really wasn't).

I was the apple of my father's eye, and my mother wanted to make sure that Dickie wouldn't be disturbed by this. My father had been the youngest child and so he sympathized with me. My mother, however, came in the middle of a large family and was expected to care for her younger siblings.

Competition for academic achievement was quite strong between my brother and myself. I am grateful that we both had more or less an equal ability for achievement. This prevented injured egos and withdrawal from competition. The dominance of my brother teamed with my mother's favoritism for him caused me to become rebellious rather than submissive.

I form very close ties with girlfriends and confide in them frequently. This may be due to my early success with peer-group relationships in grade school and attendance at an all-girl high school. My sense of humor has become sarcastic, and I am sometimes on the defensive with boys, using my sarcasm as a crutch.

The next girl discounts sibling position because she and her brother are close in age. Although she and her father both are secondborn, and the brother and mother both are firstborn, she attributes identity in the two cases more in terms of similarity of temperament than to similarity of position. The similarities between mother and daughter improved the relationship, but similarities between father and daughter did not.

There are two children in our family: my brother Lloyd who is now 21 and myself, now 20. As to how my position as secondborn has affected my personality, I don't believe it has. I have a dominant personality, and I have always enjoyed holding positions of leadership and authority. I find this in direct conflict with Toman's theories that the younger sister of brothers is the best person to work under somebody's guidance. I have never enjoyed being supervised and my parents have always granted me this privilege, realizing that each person is an individual.

My brother also has a dominant personality; however, the two of us have never come into direct conflict as our interests lie in different categories. For instance, I have always enjoyed excelling with good grades while he has always gotten good grades but never placed any emphasis on them.

I believe the reason my family position has not affected me is that my brother and I are so very close in age. This might have presented problems if we had both been of the same sex, but as it was, we both knew our positions and soon learned to let each other go in his own direction. Perhaps my mother always telling me to act like a lady and my brother like a gentlemen helped us to discern our different roles very soon.

My brother and I have always been extremely close to each other. Even though we are so close in age, I still consider him a true big brother to whom I can turn in an emergency for reassurance.

As we grew up we each had our own friends and never entered into vigorous competition. There was always a lot of good-natured kidding and teasing between us, but it was founded on a deep appreciation for each other.

The idea of role identity between parents and children is very well illustrated within our family. My mother and brother identify closely, probably due more to the fact that their personality makeup is almost identical rather than their holding a similar position of the oldest child. I feel my mother can understand my brother more easily than me as they both are even-tempered, reserved, and always seem to be in control of the situation.

My father and I also hold the same position of second oldest in our respective families, and we are of the same temperamental composition. Both of us have hot tempers, find it easy to carry a grudge, and are very emotional. Where a likeness between my mother and brother has seemed to help their relationship, it has interfered considerably with my father and me. I think we both read each other's reactions much faster than others can, and we also spot weakness in the other that we see in ourselves. Instead of creating a feeling of empathy, this has served to build a wall between us.

My parents have always showed a great deal of love and affection toward us. This is not manifest in open physical action but rather through subtler means. There were absolutely no signs of hostility or rejection ever shown to us. My parents never struck either my brother or myself and always preferred to talk things over sensibly with us, even at an early age.

My mother was completely impartial in her dealings with both of us. However, my dad has always been very partial to me. He has always been kind to Lloyd, but sometimes he gives the impression that Lloyd will never measure up to his expectations.

I have always been very independent toward my parents. I never felt I should be forced to come around to their way of thinking just because they were my parents.

Constellation 6.3 illustrates the importance of probing the childhood of parents to understand their behavior better. The mother in this constellation, who had teased her younger sister, was now permitting her favored son to tease his younger sister. The father, who had seen his drunken father beat his mother, was now enraged when his son beat his younger sister.

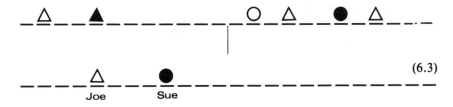

(6.3)

When Joe was four years old, I was born. He was suddenly not the center of attention, and be became very jealous. As far back as I can remember, he teased me. I never felt safe because I never knew when he would descend upon me. If I did not react to his teasing, he would hit me or hurt me in some way. He was really unmerciful, and I came to hate him. As I look back on it I can understand that he just wanted attention.

When I was twelve, a turning point came in our relationship. At this time he was on crutches because he had some difficulty with his feet. I grew my nails long and sharp. One day I threw a butcher knife against the wall about four yards away from him in order to frighten him. He thought the knife was meant for him and thus developed a new respect for me. When Joe entered college we became good friends, and gradually he gained my confidence. He worried about me and came to see me.

As a child I can remember running from Joe and clinging to my mother's skirt. My mother would scold Joe, but she would never stop him. Many times she would laugh at him.

My grandmother told me that, as a child, my mother was always the noisiest and naughtiest. She teased her little brother. I came to realize my mother identified with my brother. I felt my mother loved my brother best. This was confirmed by my grandmother and aunt. I started to cry because it was a relief to find out it was not just my imagination and because it was something I was emotionally involved in. My mother and I were never very close and did not understand each other. My father and I were pals and did understand each other. There was a good basis for this attachment. The only time I felt safe from Joe was when my father came home from work. He would not allow Joe to plague me. In fact, the only time he ever lost control of himself was when Joe hurt me. He punished Joe severely and blackened his face. My father used to give my brother lectures about not hurting me, but Joe would not stop. I really think one of the reasons why Dad got so upset was his memories of his drunken father beating his mother. Dad hated this. When Joe hurt me, Dad transferred this hatred to Joe.

In constellation 6.4, the student admits to practically all of Toman's traits for his position; likewise the traits for his younger sister. He then describes how the father engaged in a four-sided controversy (the quadrangle) with all family members, siding with the son against the mother and daughter; in a three-sided (triangular) controversy, siding with son against mother. On occasion the mother sided with the daughter against the son. The student analyzes parental bias in such controversies in terms of parental position, identification, and childhood experience.

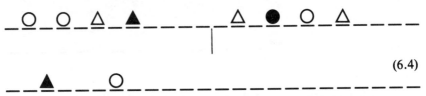

(6.4)

In the light of Toman's ideas concerning family constellations, I feel that my position in my family constellation did have an appreciable effect on my personality development. I have developed many of the traits of an older brother of sisters. Although my family constellation is small and I have only one sister, I still possess the characteristics of an older brother of sisters that one might expect to develop in a larger family.

Love is my most important concern. I have a romantic viewpoint of love. I feel that love is the most important aspect of life, that it makes all other activities possible, and that love makes life in general a truly wonderful thing. I also enjoy working with women, and I work most efficiently with female co-workers. I like women who need help (or pretend to) and strongly detest women who are bossy. This is possibly an illustration of a rank conflict.

I am basically a loner and definitely not a gang man. I dislike going out with the boys and enjoy far more greatly the company of a woman.

My sister has also developed Toman's attributes of a youngest sister of brothers. She is an excellent worker and attracts men very readily. She is also very feminine. She is the baby of the family, and this could have been one of the factors that caused me to develop an early independence.

My father, being the youngest in his family, has identified with my younger sister, I feel. Possibly this could be because of their similar positions in their family constellations. He usually sides with her against Mother and myself. Father also sides with me against my mother in most arguments. This could be comparable to his resentment of bossy sisters in his youth. Mother also sides with my sister against me in arguments. This could be comparable to her resentment of her bossy older brother in her childhood.

Parents should be alert not to permit a child to downgrade a sibling in a manner that has a dystrophic impact upon the sibling's growth in self-expression in any context. In one family, the younger sister had plenty of verve with playmates but was shy with adults because of her brother's ridicule.

In another family, the father insisted on the same rules for the two children in spite of a four-year age difference. The resulting rebellion of the older boy was exacerbated by the father's outright rejection of his son. There was also cross-sex parental favoritism. In this case the son feared he might become like his father. Mothers in similar cases should be alert to such a dread and should learn how to handle it. The father treated both children similarly in spite of the age difference.

> We both had the same privileges, and they were at my sister's level. When I was twelve and she was eight, we both had to go to bed at the same time— early. I've always had to fight Father for things all my friends were granted without question. This made be a social isolate. I've rebelled against my father since I can remember.
>
> Father favored my sister; my mother favored me. When I was younger, I felt resentment toward my sister because Father only permitted me to do what he considered proper for her to do.
>
> My father hurt me badly. He yelled at me constantly and often told me he wished I were dead, that I was stupid, and so forth. He had a bad temper, and I have never confided in him. The one thing I dread is that I might someday become like him. He feels inferior to me intellectually and tries to prove his worth by putting me down. I hate everything he stands for. My father's capacity to have fun has been drained from him by his overdominating mother. I can talk to my mother, but not to my father. Because of my dad's rejection I became a lone wolf.

The pathos seen in the following excerpt stems from loneliness because the narrator's brother was six years older and she had no playmates (rural setting). Note also the narrator's reasons for explaining why she does not relate to children or women but has a talent for relating to older men. Notice the contrast between the key expressions describing her maternal relationship and her paternal relationship: on the one hand, "overprotective," "forbade," "never at ease," "never communicate," "screaming," "punisher"; on the other hand, "easygoing and kind," "never punished," "lots to talk about," "praised me all the time."

Personnel experts might save time and do a better job if they began interviews with applicants by charting the family constellation and followed through with pertinent questions. It might be useful to store such data in a computer. Note how the VISTA social workers figured out in this case that this girl would work best with male patients.

Father is the youngest of eight children. Mother is the oldest of three sisters. Toman is correct in saying a good match is between the youngest of brothers and the oldest of sisters. I think this is correct when I consider my parents. Father is easygoing and kind. Mother stands on her feet and bosses my father effectively. She is the leader in our family and Father is dominated by her. He hardly rebels.

My brother is six years older than myself, and sometimes it seems he is not a part of the family because when I was in high school he was in the service, and when he came home I was gone. He is my mother's favorite; he will talk to my mother but never to my father. My father and brother never did anything together. I really don't know my brother. I have always been proud of him and we never fought. I've always liked him.

Even though my brother is my mother's favorite, it has never bothered me. I'm my father's favorite. It evens out. My brother is so much older than myself that I sometimes feel I grew up as an only child because, in a way, I have an empty feeling of not having been close to anyone when I was young. This has affected my personality in such a manner that I do not relate well to children. I feel I missed something by being so far apart from my brother. Although I feel like an only child, I wasn't spoiled. My mother controlled the money, and she wasn't about to waste a penny.

Because Mother played the dominant role in my family, I have always felt rejection and became indifferent to her. We never communicated and we still can't. First of all, she was overly protective of me. When I started dating in high school, Mother would worry, and if I came home one minute late, she would just scream. I cannot recall that she ever asked if I had had a nice time; I can only remember her screaming for my coming home late. Her worry while I was out made me feel guilty and this affected my personality. I could never feel at ease.

My mother was my punisher; she hit me and forbade me to do things. I reacted with hostility. My father never punished me. My attitude toward him was the opposite. My father and I have communication and cooperation. *I have the habit of telling my mother what I'm going to do and asking my father what I should do. This has affected my personality in that I can relate much better to older men than to women and children* [emphasis added]. I proved this to myself when I worked in VISTA. I was bad with women and children, but the social workers told me how much the male patients at the hospital liked me and how well I could work with them.

On the farm I spent all my free time doing chores right next to my father. My brother was gone so I was my father's only help. Father praised me all the time. We had a lot to talk about, and it made me feel a part of the family. Mother hardly had a chance to notice my accomplishments because she never had a chance to teach me anything. I was always with my father.

I had happy experiences in my peer group in high school and was involved in many activities. I didn't stay home much, and when I did, I would help my father. To this day I don't enjoy housework or cooking.

Friends and neighbors are often mystified when, in a two-child family, one succeeds and the other fails. Family therapists can explain such results best because the answers are, indeed, complex. The following summary does not give a complete picture of this family, but the timing of the father's heavy drinking impinged more upon the son and he was subjected to scapegoating—one of the most potent of dystrophic influences. Out of the turmoil of this family, one child became stronger, the other weaker.

Both parents were singletons. When the son, Bill, was growing up, the father's drinking was at its worst, and during this time the father scapegoated his son and favored his daughter, which of course led to sibling jealousy. Another complication was a great age discrepancy between the father and his children. The father's occupation kept him away from home for weeks at a time, and when he returned he was too tired or too drunk to play with his son. Any attention he gave to his son was confined to criticizing or scapegoating. This was also the period when the father engaged in such violent arguments with the mother that she contemplated divorce.

The mother, whose family had suffered hardship due to an accidental economic reversal, was excellent in her role as mother. The daughter had a good relationship with both parents; the son, only with the mother.

The son, soon after marriage, deserted his wife and children. He was said to be quite mixed up and in need of psychiatric attention.

Some parents scapegoat a child even when sober, but the combination of alcoholism and scapegoating is more destructive. How did the father get that way? He, too, had suffered in childhood. When he was seven, his own father died a tragic death, and at the age of twelve, he left home to fend for himself because of a cruel stepfather.

The sequel to all this is interesting. The father, on his own volition, stopped drinking, and the daughter entered the university. In the meantime, she came to understand the origin of her brother's difficulty. Their former jealousies were forgotten, and they gave each other psychological support. At the end of her paper, the daughter wrote:

I was not as openly affected by our family instability as my brother. But I have gone through a lot of fights, silence periods between my parents, lack of display of affection, and many more aspects of family living. In a way I am glad I have seen what an unhappy family can be like because now I have a conception of the type of marriage and family I want.

Because of the fine things my parents have given to me, I want my children to have the same chance I did to do something with their own lives. At the same time, because of the hardships my mother endured, I want a man who can be a real father to our children and who will accept responsibility when it comes. After hearing arguments all my life, I am definitely not going to argue in front of the children when I am married. Believe me, this has a very adverse effect on children. Because of my brother, I do not want my children to grow up confused and feeling that they have wasted their lives. I know I have written a lot of things that I expect to happen when I am married—and perhaps it won't work out that way—but I am going to try my best to make my family of procreation happy and stable.

As I look back and examine my family of orientation, I see love, hardships, disasters, misery, affection, and many other things. In spite of everything, we are still a family and do love each other—only sometimes we don't show it.

I have enjoyed analyzing my family, and I can see the relationships between all family members more clearly. Most of all, I can understand myself and the role I play in the family.

Older Sister/Younger Brother

In the older sister/younger brother combination, the same trend applies regarding continuing interest in members of the opposite sex. The sister becomes decision maker and protector of her brother. Vis-à-vis men, she gets an early start in developing patterns of solicitude and helpfulness. If fortuitous circumstances do not impair a good relationship to her father or her brothers, the oldest sister of brothers will often become a confidante of men. This role can develop whether the brothers are older or younger.

The younger brother is the focus of solicitude by both mother and older sister. He enjoys female helpfulness and comes to expect it from women for the rest of his life. He may develop great skill in dealing with women, but his motives are geared to his own comfort. As we shall see in later cases, he may achieve independence by rebelling against female oversolicitude.

From my material on dyads, sibling jealousy, arising only from circumstances of sex and ordinal position, apparently is mitigated by stressing the personal worth of each child as a unique and separate human being, by equal treatment and fairness, by appealing to the protective qualities of older children, by a fair and adequate distribution of parental attention, and by positive stroking. When this obtains, the family becomes cohesive, competition is healthy, and every member is proud of everyone else. There is mention of pride in the last paragraph of the next case.

The narrator, Liz, was a year older than her brother. In portions of her paper, she indicated that the father is the lastborn son many years younger than his siblings. She intimated that her father was handicapped in playing the father role because he was dominated and overprotected by his mother, whose behavior encouraged snobbish jealousy among all her children. Liz felt, however, that her mother, is spite of suffering tragic events in childhood, was excellent in playing the maternal role:

Because of my mother's wonderful personality, thoughtfulness, and religious values, she made her marriage work during those first difficult years and is still doing the same thing today. My father is a good provider, but his personality traits are similar to those of his mother. He is a very difficult person to live with.

According to Toman's family constellation, the following unique characteristics are evident because of my position as older sister of a brother: (1) A helper of men. They are important to me; I am impelled to retain the one I have or to find new ones or win back an old one. (2) Men like her. They tend to confide in her. She has an ear for them and is a good sport. She does not compete with men, but rather assists them as a big wise sister. (3) Knows how to handle a belligerent man. Generally tactful. I can hardly believe it, but those three characteristics of my position are 100 percent correct.

Besides this, my position has had other effects on my personality. Being the older child more or less forced me to be a leader. My parents usually placed responsibility on me before they would on my younger brother. However, this did not bother Tom because he depended on me to tell him what to do. The leadership role I played in high school and now college is due to the responsibilities given to me during my childhood.

I enjoy being one of the important persons in any activity I undertake. It gives me great pleasure and a feeling of security to have people depend on me. However, I would not say that I am completely domineering. And, although my nature is not a rebellious one, if I am in the minority group, I am not afraid to state my opinion or defend it. Very seldom do I ever become angry.

She goes on to describe relationships in her family:

Father-Son: Their relationship has been a distant one because Dad never knew how to be a real father. They never could talk to each other about anything. Tom was a typical little boy who loved to hunt, fish, and be active in sports, but Dad would never do any of this with him.

Father-Daughter: Our relationship has been somewhat closer than that with his son, but it still has lacked many qualities. Dad is not very understanding, so I seldom approached him with any of my problems. I suppose the reason that I am the apple of his eye is because of my musical talent. You see, Dad's outside activities are completely centered around his love of music.

Mother-Daughter: Our interpersonal relationship has been a wonderful one, one that I hope to experience some day with my own daughter. Although Mother seldom talks of her childhood, I have a feeling of empathy with her. She wanted to be a good mother because she never had one. I want to be extremely close to her so she can substitute many of the joys and happiness we have that she never experienced with her own mother. I love my mother very deeply and would never do anything to make her sad. Mother and I can talk very freely with each other. We do many things together and always have a good time doing them. I have many wonderful memories of our relationship that I will cherish the rest of my life.

Mother-Son: Because of the great distance between my father and brother, Mother practically played a dual role as both a mother and a father. She was never partial to either of us; everything was always equal. Tom confided in her sometimes but not all the time. Their relationship was not as close as our mother-daughter relationship.

Brother-Sister: Our relationship has been a cooperative one. Of course, during our childhood, we had many arguments and fights, but that was only natural. We were rather competitive scholastically in high school, but it was a healthy type of competition. He ranked third highest in his graduating class, and I was second in mine. During my high school and college years, I have received many honors; these have not created jealousy but have made him very proud and has caused a deep respect for me. Likewise, he also has had honors, and I have the same pride and respect for him that he has for me. We have a very close relationship that contains much love for the other.

Sometimes a child conceives of himself in an unfavorable light by comparison with other family members. When his lowered self-esteem in the family setting is accentuated by real or imagined failure in the peer setting, we have the kind of problem set forth in the following case.

This case should alert parents to the sensitivities of early adolescence and to any symptoms that might indicate the harboring of suppressed feelings that need ventilation. Sometimes feelings of jealousy and inadequacy are blown out of proportion to realities as perceived by adults.

My parents are the same age. Being the only daughter, my father is very protective of me. This has caused some problems in his limiting my activities just because he thought of me as his little girl. It is very hard for him to let go of me, and consequently, I have rebelled to this attitude, yet not by any drastic means.

The closeness in age has not been detrimental to Joe's and my relationship except during our early years. I, of course, was the jealous, selfish sister. One incident comes to mind: My parents had to chain his crib to the wall so that I wouldn't knock him over. Undoubtedly, I grew out of this jealousy, but it was substituted with a feeling that my parents favored Joe. I had myself believing that I couldn't measure up to his outgoing and vivacious personality. At one point (thirteen) I felt as though I was the family failure, mostly because I wasn't in activities like Joe or a cheerleader and in plays like Mother. I was obsessed with the notion that I was the family's black sheep. Also, I was struggling through the typical high school problems such as being accepted, getting good grades, and finding a boyfriend. In essence, it was a period of insecurity.

My parents could sense that something was wrong, so one night when I was very upset, the entire story came into the open. As for the feeling of favoritism, they assured me in a very loving way that both Joe and I meant the world to them, that in no way could they love or care for one of us more. They assured me that they loved me for me and that nowhere was there anyone else like Annie. I was failing to remember all that my parents had done for me—they were always interested in what I was involved in. They encouraged dancing lessons and had birthday parties, Mom was the Brownie leader, Dad took the whole troop flying.

Thus, feelings of insecurity and favoritism were so resolved. In my mind I was no longer competing with Joe for recognition, but I enjoyed his achievements as he did mine. Similarly, it didn't make me greater because I was smarter; he turned and asked me for help in his studies. In turn, I knew I didn't have to be anyone else but myself to make my parents and others happy.

The next girl likes her brother, and she likes men:

In Toman's constellation, I would best fit the oldest sister of brothers. I consider myself a helper of men. They are very important to me, not because they are of the opposite sex but because I enjoy the company of men—not necessarily one man but a group of men. I enjoy the more-honest exchange of experience and the frankness of opinion. I enjoy the practical, active, dynamic thinking. Generally, I would say men like me. Some of my best and oldest friends are men, who on occasion do confide in me. I do not actually compete with them on their exact plane but rather on a distinct parallel plane—close, very close, not one where I would infringe on what I consider male virtues and areas of power. I have my capabilities and they have theirs. Working constantly with men, I would say that I know how to handle them. It is a necessity in radio work. If you do not get along, you do not have a show.

My brother and I get along well—in fact, so well that I took him along every time I went out of town for a few days during the summer and also when I went on vacation, just because I think he is a good egg. I am constantly on the go and have nearly forgotten how to relax, but in just the past year or so I have noticed that, when my brother is around, we can have fun because he is very relaxed and he makes me relax.

My brother and I play the role of the stereotypical brother and sister, outwardly fighting and seemingly writing off the ideas of the other, while actually we are fiercely loyal and respect and follow each other's advice.

The following is from a fatherless boy whose mother was nearly worn out by trying to earn a living and rearing two youngsters. The sister is four years older. For such a boy the peer setting is critical. In this case, the boy's unbalanced home was counterbalanced by a healthy peer group in which he became a star athlete:

> I am told that I relied on my sister for protection. There was a boy in the neighborhood who was bigger than I. I would constantly tease him, and when he tried to catch me, I would run to my sister. When he saw my sister, he would step cold in his tracks. My sister was the tyrant of the neighborhood, and no one dared cross swords with her. Thus, I took considerable advantage of my sister's position.
>
> My sister, during these years, was a contributing force to my mother's constant verbal explosions at night. My sister has a domineering type of personality, and she would stand toe to toe with my mother and battle things out verbally. This just further agitated my mother, and she would have more to complain about. I was submissive at this time and would mostly be seen and not heard.
>
> The relationship between my sister and me after the first couple of years at school was not too close. She had her friends and I had mine, and the four-year difference in age made a difference in interests. We did confide in each other to a certain extent, but just lately we have gotten to be the best of friends. The only place I could express myself was with my peer group.

The next analysis illustrates the parents' awareness of the possibility of their son's withdrawal from competition with the brighter older sister and how their foresight and skill paid off. This was a two-career pantrophic family with plenty of rituals. Notice also how the parents nurtured the self-esteem of the children, encouraged their growth, and gave them an awareness of their separate uniqueness, which improved the cohesion of the family.

> I was never rewarded as such for desired behavior. I knew what my parents expected of me and always wanted to do the best I could. They never pushed me for grades, although they knew I was capable of always keeping my grades up. I managed to maintain a 4.0 grade point all through high school, but I received much more praise from outsiders than from my parents. Even when I was valedictorian of my graduating class and received a number of honor scholarships, my parents never really made much of a fuss over me. I knew they were proud of me; it was just their way not to express themselves openly. Part of the reason for not talking about my grades was because my brother never did as well as I did in school. They did not want him to feel like he had to live up to my standards; Jon and I got the same reaction when I brought home all As and he brought home all Cs. Jon never felt there was any real competition between us. He did not withdraw from competition; he was instead encouraged to develop his talents.

Jon and I have always been treated as important members of the family and as persons worth listening to. When matters of interest to the entire family came up, everyone was able to give an opinion and have it considered with equal weight. Jon and I were treated as a source of pleasure for our parents. They loved us for our individuality and because we were people—not just their children.

I think the most important aspect of the communication in my family is that Jon and I were encouraged to be independent and autonomous. My parents put their trust in us and treated us like adults long before our peers were considered adults by their parents. Instead of being pushed into adulthood, Jon and I accepted the challenge and grew as a result of it.

I tended to identify with my father, while Jon identified more closely with my mother. That goes along with the idea that fathers usually teach their daughters expressive roles and mothers teach their sons expressive roles. Jon and I learned task roles from the parent of the same sex. This was done not by mere instruction but by involvement in the actual task. Mom always let me bake (something she had been denied as child), even when it took twice as long and made twice the mess for her to clean up.

If I ever needed anything, I knew I would get it if I asked my dad. He and I are a lot alike emotionally, too. We tend to take things in stride and are more easygoing. Mom and Jon are the ones who worry about almost everything all of the time. They get upset more easily over little things than either Dad or I.

The advantages of the older sister from her position, in the next excerpt, were nullified by dystrophic overtones in the family, by the mistakes of the parents, and by the hostilities between the children. The younger boy's potential was hindered by these same factors. The father was preoccupied in a successful business, but his relationship to the children was superficial, and the marital relationship was poor.

I was the only girl child in my family, which would indicate, according to Toman, that I would be at ease around men and be someone in whom men would confide. However, I do not find this to be the case with me. I feel that the relationship between my brother and me was, much of the time, one of hostility that evolved, as we grew older, into a relationship that is probably best described as tolerant. When I started school, I received good grades that my parents assumed my brother would receive also. However, when he started school, he did not receive these grades and was given much criticism in return. I feel that my brother almost withdrew from competition but not entirely. I feel that my parents judged my brother unfairly on the basis of my performance in school. At first, I enjoyed the attention of my parents, but as I grew older, I realized that my brother should have been encouraged instead of discouraged. This behavior, though, did not have an extremely damaging effect on my brother because now that he is maturer he is getting more conscientious in his schoolwork and receiving better grades.

When I was older, my mother told me that my father really wanted me to be a boy instead of a girl. I think it would help if my father would show an interest in the achievements of my brother. My mother is trying to do this, but my father still finds fault with whatever he does and fails to encourage or praise him.

In the next family, we have again a bright older girl, the narrator; and a younger boy who is an underachiever. The family is dystrophic. The mother is overprotective, and the father is rigid. Conflict and hostility exist between the parents, and manifestations of affection are absent. The partiality of the mother for the son made her blind to the mistakes she made with him.

Jim has always found schoolwork difficult. As a result, when he was in grade school, my mother began assisting him with his homework. After a while he became dependent upon her help more and more, relying less upon his own abilities. Then, when he entered high school and found the work difficult, she continued aiding him. This help has gotten to the point now where he not only expects it but demands it. She has became a crutch. Differences in opinion on this subject between my mother and myself have caused many heated arguments between us, especially when she continues helping him.

One female narrator describes the plight of a younger brother as follows:

Because of my participation in high school, my brother was also expected to be active. Being small for his grade in school, he did not play in athletic events. This seemed to bother my parents because my boyfriend acquired nine letters in three different sports. But my brother could not take defeat and wouldn't participate in school sports. His favorite sport is golf, and when he entered high school, they formed a golf team. He lettered the first year and was pleased with himself because he met with success, something that he enjoyed. I do think that I did influence him to be more outgoing and to have more confidence in himself.

My brother does follow the youngest-brother-of-sister pattern. He expects women to care for him and love him without giving anything in return. When it comes to competition, he shies away from it and is not a very good leader. He procrastinates on almost everything he does, and when he starts something, he wants little interference from others or else his job is not well done.

Being the oldest sister of a brother, I've always been around a lot of boys. Besides my brother's friends, the neighborhood I grew up in had mostly boys. According to Toman's family constellation, men like me and confide in me. Looking back, I see where this is true. From little boys to guys in college, I've answered many questions and helped them make decisions. This has always given me a good feeling because I felt as though I've done some good for someone. I've never felt that I have had the capacity to compete with a man—I imagine because I've always known them to be the stronger sex.

Our experience with the four sets of dyads illustrate Toman's fundamental notions regarding sibling relationships and the nature of parent-child identification and relationships. We will now see how these concepts apply to larger groups such as male and female triads. This involves a new dimension; namely, sibling triangles.

Notes

1. W. Toman, *Family Constellation: Its Effect on Personality and Social Behavior,* 3rd ed. (New York: Springer, 1976).

2. J. Richard Udry, *The Social Context of Marriage,* 3rd ed. (New York: J.B. Lippincott Co., 1966), pp. 262–264.

3. Discussions on treatment of male and female dyads is also found in L.K. Forer, *Birth Order and Life Roles* (Springfield, Ill.: Charles C Thomas, 1969); and Margaret B. McFarland, *Relationships between Young Sisters as Revealed in Their Overt Responses* (New York: Columbia University Press, 1938).

7 Male Triads

We now consider sibling constellations of three brothers. This system has more potential for leadership, as well as more rebellion and physical combat, than male dyads. Rebellion may be instigated when the oldest brother torments a younger brother, or when an older one assigns to himself goods and privileges at the expense of a younger one. In this system there are no sisters to mediate. A mediator may be a middle brother, the oldest brother, or a parent. In dealing with three-child families, the importance of position of both parents and children becomes even more revealing.

In one such family the oldest brother vis-à-vis his next in line would say, when something nice was to be had, "I'll take it, I'm older." When a dirty job was to be done, "You do it, you're younger." The notion that privileges accrue to one because he was the first to crawl out of the womb is attractive to firstborns but anathema to secondborns. If the spacing between brothers is three to five years, the younger one is not in a position to retaliate physically, but when aroused to do so, it will be with the fury of desperation. Such an experience may produce a rebellious attitude toward authority figures throughout life. This rebellious spirit may lie dormant if the authority figure is competent, reasonable, and respectful; but if the authority figure is pushy, dictatorial, or incompetent, the rebellious person may erupt violently and often effectively to the discomfort of his superior. Some observers have believed that secondborns are more often leaders of rebellions and revolutions and that firstborns are more often despots and reactionaries.

If a tormented younger brother acknowledges the source of his latent rebelliousness, he may, long after he has made amends with his older brother, harness it constructively to suggest new and better ways to accomplish things, to criticize institutions, to write satire, or to be an activist.

The rebellious spirit finds expression in the youngest of three brothers. Notice that the middle brother is one year younger than the oldest and two years older than the youngest.

$$- - - - \triangle \triangle \; \blacktriangle - - - - - - - - - - - - - - - \quad (7.1)$$

My second brother proved to be another major influence on my personality, especially in the area of accepting authority. In our early childhood he continually teased and provoked me to a point of frustration and rebellion. When I fought back I got the worst of it because he was so much larger. My oldest brother and my parents were mediators, but my rebellion against demonstrative authority remains.

The narrator adds that the oldest brother became a leader with the characteristics of a firstborn. The second brother was also successful:

My two older brothers were both exceptionally good athletes, did exceedingly well scholastically in both high school and college, and were active leaders in all their extracurricular activities (both made *Who's Who in American Small Colleges*). For me there was only one direction—to follow in their golden footsteps! This proved exceedingly difficult because throughout my childhood and adolescence I matured very slowly compared to my classmates. There was and still is a constant pressure to excel in everything I attempt. My parents understood my predicament and never pushed me, but I still cannot help the feeling that I must uphold the family name by attempting to follow those golden footsteps. I feel this predicament is unique in my family constellation because Toman's concepts regarding the youngest brother of brothers do not apply. In may case, I was forced to assume responsibility and leadership in order to achieve the kind of visibility dictated to me by those golden footsteps.

The impulse to live up to family traditions was motivated, in part, by this lad's father for whom he had great respect and with whom he had a fine relationship.

In the next case there was an eight-year span between the oldest and youngest, with the secondborn in midpoint. The narrator, the youngest, explains how he came to outshine his older brothers and get a taste of leadership.

My father's father was killed in World War I. My parents were married just before Dad went into the service, and my mother had her first child while my father was overseas. My mother lived a lonely life in New York and survived on food stamps until the war was over and my dad came back. My father was released as a major. He was wounded and received a Purple Heart and the silver star. He was a small-town hero and had all sorts of write-ups in the paper. This is the point where my mother thinks my father underwent a big change in his life because he seemed to become somewhat hard and cold toward my mother. He made her feel that she was there as another member of the family and that was it. In fact, at times I think his three sons took priority over my mother. [The mother worked for wages to help finance the college education of her sons and, at the same time, did the domestic chores. She spent many weekends alone while the men went hunting or fishing.]

Since I was the youngest, I spent more time with my mother than my brothers did and got to appreciate her more. I would bring her little gifts for no special reason, and this pleased her. I began to bring my problems to her and we became close.

When I was about eleven, I was with my father just about every weekend and Mother was alone. This makes my father sound mean or something, but I think he didn't realize what he was doing. About this time I was getting interested in sports; of course, my father had something to do with that. My mother enjoyed watching sports also. My two brothers weren't very big, so they had a hard time, but I made first string on the football team and was champion city pole vaulter. I think both my parents were proud of me.

As the youngest brother of brothers, I agree with Toman by admitting that I am somewhat willful and capricious, somewhat of an irregular worker, soft with women, against strong leadership, and can accept competent leadership, but contrary to Toman, I consider myself a good leader. I do preserve property, and I accept and like children.

Because there were no girls in our family, all the men in our family have a lack of understanding of women.

In the next family, the secondborn of three brothers describes both his brothers as having most of Toman's traits for their respective positions, while he has a mixture of the two:

My oldest brother Bill, in a number of ways, resembles Toman's analysis. He is definitely a leader and a good worker. Bill accepts authority of the male superior, his boss. He enjoys building up property and has recently taken a test, which he passed, for a real estate broker's license. Bill is often tough with women. I don't know if this is a general trait of his or not, but he is a strict disciplinarian. His children are the best disciplined ones that I know. Bill's house is always in order as are his bills.

My younger brother Jack, youngest brother of brothers, also has many of the traits in the Toman constellation. Jack is without doubt a capricious person; he is not an irregular worker. Jack is neither a good leader nor a follower.

Jack does not like authority because it is too demonstrative. I know this to be a fact. With respect to children, the character fits Jack even better. He doesn't like to be around children. He just can't accept them. I do not know if it is because they threaten his status, as Toman states. Is Jack soft with women? Yes, he is too soft. Jack's outlook politically and religiously is liberal in context. He never liked dictators or strict clergymen.

Toman's family constellation does not have an exact classification for a middle brother, which is what I am. My unique characteristics, due to my family position, are mixed. I have traits of both my older and younger brother. All my life I have been a leader, a trait of the oldest brother. I run parties, picnics, and other activities. I also lead a workout gym in Chicago. I am neither a good worker nor an irregular worker. I do not like authority over me, and I don't take orders as well as some people do. With respect to children, I accept them, and I love them. I plan to have a large family some day.

In summation, I would say that I have characteristics of both the oldest brother of brothers and the youngest brother of brothers.

Next is a family with dystrophic overtones. The father was upwardly mobile, but the mother did not grow and the couple grew apart. There were no manifestations of affection in the family. The last paragraph reflects a longing occasionally expressed by students from unhappy homes. One of the narrator's brothers was four years older; the other, four years younger.

I am the middle son of three boys. My oldest brother always got new clothes; I got hand-me-downs; my youngest brother, being the baby of the family, got new clothes. I was the target of my older brother's physical strength. He had great dominance over me. Whenever my brother disliked something I had done, he beat me up. When I beat up my younger brother, my folks would reprimand me.

Since my parents showed their love for us by gifts and so forth, my brothers and I would compete to get the most. In our home, there was never a real closeness between parents and children. This made it impossible for us to go to our parents with problems.

My positions in the family and in the peer group seemed to be identical. In the peer group, I was never a leader but a subordinate. My parents would not let me play football, which forced me to strive harder to maintain my position in the peer group. I had to be tougher and try to achieve more to maintain my place.

My father spends very little time at home with his family. My mother henpecked me quite a bit, causing me to rebel against people of like nature. In almost all areas of my family life, the lack of closeness persisted. The family rituals were sparse; we had no family participation in anything. There was a lack of communication between my parents and no communication between me and my parents. Our companionship and cohesiveness centered outside the home.

In my family of procreation I want it different—I want a wife who will help me to obtain vertical mobility, while also gaining it herself. I would like to be the ideal family man. I place importance on family participation in all sorts of activities.

Families with three boys introduce the status of the middle child as one who blends the traits of oldest and youngest. They also reveal the handicap of not learning early in life how to relate to the opposite sex. We now examine girl triads who provide additional material on these themes.

8 Female Triads

The traits of leadership and the free assumption of responsibility in a competent manner seem to be increased for the firstborn when there is a succession of children of the same sex instead of just one younger sibling, because the management of several younger children instead of one provides more opportunity for the development of leadership skills. If the secondborn is of a different sex, then he or she might not accept the authority of the older because their task roles may be different.

The following was written by a girl who was the oldest of three sisters:

Toman's description of oldest sister of sisters really hit home. Each characteristic listed was not just vaguely applicable to me but was a strong trait. I examined my personality somewhat objectively for the very first time. I'm sure that had I not had to study myself for family analysis, it would have been a long time before I really attempted to change these aspects of my character that needed such drastic improvement. The quality that especially struck me was the fourth listed in Toman's constellation: May cut people short who know more about the subject. I think that I had subconsciously sensed this fault in myself, but I never consciously admitted it. It does stand to reason that in learning so much about myself, I would not be pleased with everything I saw.

Constellation 8.1 includes a statement of the oldest of three sisters who lived in a family with no cohesion and whose mother "never really seemed interested in any of the children. There was also a lack of communication in our home."

●○ _ _ _ _ _ _ _ ○ _ _ _ _ _ _ _ _
Joyce Connie   Mary   (8.1)

I am the oldest of a family of three girls. This has affected my personality in countless ways. Because I was always the first to receive privileges and responsibilities, I had to pave the way. Now I feel more at home in a new situation and am not afraid to try something different and to go off on my own. I also had the responsibility of watching over my younger sisters, one a year younger (Connie) and the other (Mary) ten years younger. I think this helped to develop my leadership and interest in actively participating in everything to which I belong. At about the age of ten, however, I resented having to take Connie wherever I went and having to dress alike as though we were twins. I felt she should make her own friends and do things on her own. This resulted in a strained relationship between us that has only recently been cleared up. So during the years of puberty and adolescence I turned to my friends for my closest relationships. These girls and their families influenced me as much as my own family did, and I'm afraid this contributed to drawing me away from my family emotionally.

The members of my family are not really close to each other. We have no confiding relationships because my mother never really seemed interested in the things we did and never actively participated in any of them.

In the second family in this series, we have an appraisal by the middle sister who mentions her role as arbiter:

There are three girls in my family. I have a sister two and a half years older than I and one three years younger. In our case, this closeness in age has made us closer to one another. Also, I think a lot of this is the way we were brought up. My parents have taught us that family is first.

My older sister is more of the dominant type. Being the oldest, she was given a lot of responsibility of setting an example. My parents never really treated her like a baby—consequently, she matured quite early. When she was little, she patterned herself after my mother. When I was born, she felt it was her job to take care of me. To prevent jealousy, our parents let her know that I was her baby sister and that she should watch over me. I can remember a few times when she might have resented the fact that I had to play with her and her friends, but I also remember she would never let anyone harm me. Now we're on an equal basis, she comes to me for advice, and I go to her. We usually see things on the same level.

My place in the family constellation has made me more aware of others and the need to consider their feelings. Being in the middle had made me more easygoing than the other two. I have learned that it's better to give in sometimes to keep peace. I'm sort of the mediator between my sisters. My parents seem to depend on me to help both my sisters with their problems.

Another thing I've found out is that I want to get close to the people I come in contact with. I need to know that people think enough of me to come to me with their problems.

My younger sister and I have attained one of the best relationships, I think, ever possible. It's more than just sister to sister, better than best friends; it's really hard to describe how we feel about each other. She looks up to me, and I look up to her as I do to my older sister. People have said we're the image of each other. I think this has more to do with our personalities than with our places in the constellation.

I think I have learned to get along with people better than my sisters do. In sibling fights, I have always been between the two. I can usually see both sides.

The following appraisal by the youngest of three sisters involves the social dynamics of a child's withdrawal from competition with two older and successful sisters. The number of parents and teachers who make the mistake described by this girl is appalling. Why teachers make this mistake is a great mystery to me.

There is one big disadvantage I have had to face in the past and will have to face in the future to a lesser degree. Both Ethel and Marian were and still are A students. Coming from a small community, most of the teachers knew all three of us, which caused them to make comparisons. I am not an A student, but I feel I can learn. By the time I reached high school, this problem of comparison became the center of my attention. It was a constant struggle to prove to the teachers that I was an individual with my own capabilities. I remember one incident very clearly. My biology teacher looked up both Ethel's and Marian's records to see how their grades compared with mine, since at the time I was doing average work. He thought I should be doing better and reported his research and conclusions to my mother during parent-teacher conference. In turn, my mother told me about the conversation. Before that time, the comparison between my sisters and me had remained beneath the surface, but now it was known that at least one teacher was comparing us. I then had pressure from the teachers to reach my fullest capacity—to be an A student like my sisters. My mother also put pressure on me to equal their academic records. Receiving this pressure from both sides, I started to rebel by doing the minimum amount of work to get through school. I realize now that both the teachers and my mother were trying to make me do the best I possibly could. If it weren't for parental insistence, I probably would have quit high school.

After high school, my parents' ambition was to see me go to college. From the start of planning for college, I told my parents I didn't want to go to Madison where both Ethel and Marian had received their Bachelor degrees. It was not only that they had gone to school there but also that I felt that I wasn't capable of doing the work there. My parents agreed to my choice of another state university, glad that I would at least try college. My motivation for being in school my freshman year was that my parents wanted me here, not because I was motivated to get a college education. Not until this year did I start to motivate myself to study and to see how well I could do in my classes. Being self-motivated made all the difference in my grades. I see the value I can receive from a college education and intend to gain it.

The oldest of three sisters in constellation 8.2 points out the difference between favoritism and a special relationship between parent and child that is understandable to others and that does not result in jealousy. This narrator does not use the term *favorite* but *closeness* and *bond* to refer to the special relationship her middle sister had with her mother. Reading between the lines, one finds the suggestion that one special relationship balances out the other and that both girls are happy. She did not say much about the youngest daughter, but she did refer to the handicap for all three in not having brothers.

Emma   Ruth   (8.2)

My father has always favored me over my two sisters, probably because I am the first child and physically resemble him. My father and I have always gone places together such as football games, downtown shopping, and to his office, and I've always felt a lot closer to him than to my mother.

Now that I have gone away to college, my sister Ruth has taken my place doing things with my father. But there is still a bond between my father and me—we can communicate on any topic from sex and morals to politics, and even when we disagree, my father respects my opinion and realizes that I am almost twenty-one and should have a mind of my own.

My sister Janice and my mother have always been close like my father and I are. Janice is more of the homemaker type like my mother, and she and my mother seem to get along great on the household scene. This is particularly true lately since Janice got married and has started a home of her own. Janice and my mother relate well; this is fine since neither Ruth nor I have any interest in homemaking, yet.

Because no child in my family is left out of being cared for by one parent, there are really no signs of jealousy, competition, hostility, or rejection. Because of my home life, I feel that I am quite tolerant of other people. The lack of static in my own family has helped me to appreciate how well I do have it, and I can sympathize with friends who are not as happy with their family as I am.

As I am writing this family analysis, I am quite surprised to notice that my family and the roles they play fit very well into the outline set down in Toman's family constellation. Because I was raised with all girls and no brothers, I have found out through experience that all three of us are handicapped in our relationships with the opposite sex. Not having a brother, I looked to my father as the outstanding male figure in my life, and I think he has had a great influence on the type of boys I dated.

A middle sister from another family wrote:

I always felt somewhat hampered in dealing with boys because I never had any brothers. This, along with my inability to take my problems to my mother, made me wary of boys.

Constellation 8.3 illustrates how the trait of leadership in the eldest daughter was dampened by circumstances in the peer setting as well as by having sisters so much younger since they were more dependent and less challenging. She also provides another slant on the term *favoritism*. This is a pantrophic family.

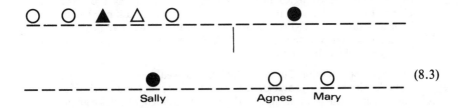

(8.3)

Since I was an only child for seven years before Agnes was born, I think there is a parallel between Mother and me. She often told me things she did as a child, and I would do these things myself.

When Agnes and Mary were growing up, I felt more like a mother since I helped take care of them. Because I was so much older, I could have more privileges, and I was at the age when I wanted to have responsibilities. Being left in charge of my sisters made me a more-responsible person.

I was happy when I got two little sisters, and because of my helping to take care of them, I now have a great interest in children. My sisters have often come to me for advice and guidance on their problems, and I think I have been more of a mother figure to them than just a sister.

I feel my parents have showed equal affection to us and treated us pretty much the same. What may look like favoritism is the different way they treated us because of our different personalities and also because of changes in cultural expectations while we were growing up. I don't think there is any real jealousy between any of us girls.

The following example, written by the middle daughter, explains why a child in a certain position does not fit the Toman categories, given the setting of the extended family:

My older sister, Arlene, could never be used as Toman's example of oldest sister of sisters. I believe the main reason she lacks traits for this position is that she was treated as the youngest of the family by my parents, grandparents, and uncles. The uncles were only a few years older than Arlene, and they bossed her around quite a bit and used her as a scapegoat. The difficulty Arlene had in trying to identify with a legitimate authoritarian figure among so many adults produced extreme stuttering. Within one month after we moved away from that place, her stuttering stopped.

In the next passage, the oldest sister implies that she did not acquire leadership traits because the parents usurped both leadership and decision-making functions themselves and because she was the youngest among her peers.

The three of us are quite different in both appearance and personality. Being the oldest, it is easy to assume that I am a leader type and rather dominant. This, however, is not true. I think my parents were overprotective when I was young, and consequently, I came to rely too much on others. I have had a hard time making decisions and find it much easier to let leadership fall elsewhere. Since I've been in college, I've made a conscious effort to overcome this. As a child I played mostly with girls two and three years older than myself.

My youngest sister Sue is unbelievable. At fourteen she is popular and comfortable with both boys and girls. She is a good student and excels in band. She is also president of the junior high student council. She has a great deal of self-confidence and is a little self-centered, which her age could explain. Part of the way Sue is could be due to the fact that she was a cute, bright little girl and is becoming a very pretty young lady. Also, being the lastborn child may have prompted her to strive hard to be recognized as an individual.

As a teenager I was shy around boys. I had no brothers, and none of my close friends had brothers. When I was a senior in high school I gained a little more confidence. Since I've been in college I feel more at ease.

9

Mixed Triads

Among the sibs in mixed triads, the mixture of both sexes eliminates extreme psychosexual imbalance since every child grows up knowing something about the opposite sex. In times of crises involving parental death, divorce, or gross inadequacy, the mutual comfort, cooperation, and solidarity of three children seems more marked than when there are only two. A common theme in mixed triads is that a person may have a combination of traits including those of oldest brother of brothers and oldest brother of sisters.

Boy and Two Girls

Our first subgroup in mixed triads is that of brother with two younger sisters.

$$ \_\_\_\triangle\_\_\_\bullet\_\_\_\bigcirc_____\cdot \qquad (9.1) $$

My brother and sister and I have always had a very close, intimate relationship. In fact, I have always felt closer to them and have had more confidence in them than either of my parents. Yet at the same time, I feel as though my middle position has somewhat given me an advantage because I feel as though I am more in favor with my parents than either my sister or brother.

My parents are in constant conflict with the youngest, my sister; in a little conflict with the oldest, my brother; but in no conflict with me. I established a good relationship with my parents because I did well scholastically and found employment to provide me with spending money. My parents had a high regard for scholastic achievement and hard work, and by excellence in these areas, I fulfilled their wishes.

Does the middle child have a better time perspective in the growing-up process? The narrator continues:

I can look back to when I was my sister's age and analyze her problems from her viewpoint, and I can also look ahead into the future to my brother's situation and visualize his ideas. By doing so, I am often able to iron out diagreements between family members.

A child pressured by the domination of two siblings or by a parent and a sibling reacts with rebellion or timidity. In one such case, the middle child, a girl, was dominated by her one-year-older brother and her three-years-younger sister. She wrote:

> For some reason my sister has become more dominating than I am, and quite often I find myself taking orders from her. I think I am so used to my brother dominating me that it seems only natural for others to dominate me also. I think that being the middle child and being dominated by an older brother and a younger sister has made me a timid person.

Note that, in constellation 9.2, the mother was the oldest of three children. From the record, she appeared determined to raise her firstborn to be successful, with frequent admonition. The youngest child reports:

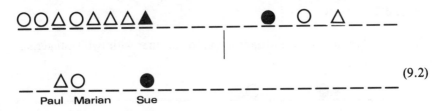

(9.2)

Paul Marian   Sue

> My brother is by far the most rebellious. He is not a leader. He was never active in school organizations and never held an office in any club. Unlike our brother, my sister and I were very active in school activities; we graduated with honors, and our brother did not. Being the oldest and the only boy posed problems for him. He was always henpecked by my mother, as was my father, which my brother will not tolerate. My parents were both very conscious of my brother's grades, how he studied, how he handled his money, and what hours he kept.

Sue explains that she was spoiled because in infancy she had had rheumatic fever and had received all manner of careful nursing and attention: "There was never any material thing that I really wanted that I didn't eventually get." She does not suggest how this might have affected Paul, but she does point out that parental rules established for Paul were greatly relaxed for her despite the difference in ages. She continues:

> We are all, except my father, very strong-willed persons. We have developed this way in reaction to Mother. Marian gets along best with Mother, but when Mother started to run Marian's marriage before it had even begun, Marian reacted violently. She warned Mother to stay out of her affairs.

Sue indicates that the mother is always ready to help any of her children in material ways.

> My brother and I do not get along with Mother as well as Marian does. My brother feels he must maintain his manly integrity, and I, being much influenced by him, want to maintain my individuality.

Although Sue did not mention it, we can imagine that the mother, because of her position, was in the habit of dominating her younger sister and brother, and Sue points out how she carried over this habit to her husband and son. The son likely felt that, because of his own position, he was entitled to exercise some domination, but he could not achieve it because he was so preoccupied with his rebellion. The father was lastborn in his large family, and there is no mention of his role in child rearing. When the only son is surrounded by achieving sisters and a mother (no matter whether she is rejecting, loving, solicitous, demanding, or protective), the role of the father is crucial to the son's development. In another family with the same sib configuration, the father, a firstborn, was overly dominant with the firstborn son, leading to similar rebellion.

Constellation 9.3 shows age spacing of siblings similar to the previous case, but the positions of father and mother are reversed, and the impact on the children is quite different. The mother is youngest; the father and son have identical sib positions.

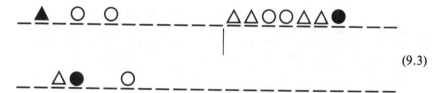

(9.3)

> My brother was the oldest brother of sisters in our family. He is the dominant figure in the family. Love is the most important concern of his, and he is always aware of how I feel or behave. Father is a thorough worker both on the job and at home. He doesn't go out for clubs and leagues in a big way; instead, he is at home most of the time, helping out.

> My mother is the youngest sister of brothers and sisters. Mother is very feminine, friendly, kind, sensitive, tactful, submissive but not subservient, devoted, and a good companion for my father. She is an excellent nurse both on the job and at home. Mother works easily under somebody's guidance. She married the oldest brother of sisters—her best match.

> My brother, like my father, is the oldest brother of sisters. He is sixteen months older than I. He is much concerned with love and tries to prove he is worthy of the love of other family members. He is a very independent person and very much against gangs.

I am the older sister of a sister. I can boss people effectively, but I feel my brother can boss me effectively because he is older. I do pretend I am surer of myself than I really am. I tend to cut people short who know more about a subject. At times when I cannot dominate (as with my brother), I am unhappy and angry. I am capable of leadership and have shown this in past years in clubs and organizations. I despise official female figures above me like a few of my female teachers in the past. I do obey my father more than my mother for fear of punishment.

My sister, two and a half years younger than I, is the younger sister of sisters. She is highly competitive in school and does above-average work. She likes adventure and travel, of which she has done an extensive amount. She's quite independent and makes her own entertainment. She is the type of person who constantly needs changes and challenges to keep from being bored.

In constellation 9.4, the father, a middle child, is a mediator and identifies with his daughter, also a middle child with whom he has a good empathy, but he has a poor relationship with the oldest boy who is adopted.

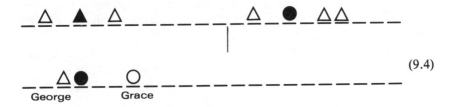

(9.4)

George   Grace

My father understood what it was like being in the middle of the family. George, my brother, is only a year and a half older than I, and Grace, my sister, is four years younger. The few children in our neighborhood were boys, so I had little choice but to play with them if I wanted to play at all. I was bound and determined not to be a sissy, so I learned how to play baseball and football with the best of them. I remember crying and asking my mother why I wasn't a boy. Through all this, I remained somewhat of a little lady. When I dressed up I acted like a prima donna, as my mother put it.

My mother always seemed somewhat to dominate the household. She would become angry, and my father would listen patiently to the day's upsets. To me it seemed my mother made it worse that it really was, and I would become angry in retaliation. My father would sympathize with my mother, which made me even angrier. Later he would come to my room to talk things over with me. Now that I can understand things better, I see what a wise man he is. When he talked to me, he always made me feel mature by explaining he couldn't argue with my mother because she was his wife and a family doesn't run smoothly if people are arguing. He would tell me to try and be more patient and understanding with my mother. I always felt much better and a little bit older after our talks. I guess I always wanted more of my mother's affections, but she seemed to favor my sister.

My father has had the biggest effect on my personality development. I've always looked up to him, and through our talks he helped me to grow up with patience and understanding of people. I can sit down and talk to him about anything, and he respects my ideas and judgment. I've told him many of my thoughts and plans for the future, and he listens and talks them over with me, adding ideas of his own. I've tried this many times with my mother, but she either dismisses the whole thing by telling me to wait until I've graduated before deciding anything or tells me I'm too young to know. I know I want to be a different kind of mother than she is, but already I do some of the things I've sworn I would never do. I just hope I've gained some of the good things my father has done for me.

Girl and Two Boys

We now consider cases in which a girl is the oldest sister of two brothers. She will have practice in caring for boys and learning something about men from her brothers and also from the friends of her brothers. In high school and college, she will often become the confidante of other boys who seek her advice. If her father is nurturant, she will identify with him, especially if he is the oldest of his family. She may identify ultimately with her mother if her mother is also the oldest, but in this case she may be in conflict with her mother.

From my samples, I would guess that the middle child in this combination is the one likely to have problems. In our society, the area of prevailing competition is in academic achievement, and here the girl has two advantages over the secondborn. She receives that special attention in parental training that makes it possible for her parents to brag that she knows her colors before the average child of her age; and she, as a girl, will likely outshine her brother in verbal and memory skills. Furthermore, he will be tempted to withdraw from competition if he has any doubts about living up to her reputation. He is more likely to be pressured by parents and teachers, with negative results.

Some observers have said that parents are more uncomfortable in rearing the firstborn for lack of experience but that they relax with later borns. However, could parents be tense about the firstborn boy because they might feel that he requires different treatment from girls?

Whenever the firstborn excels and the secondborn performs with mediocrity, a parent, in order to encourage the secondborn, tries to encourage him with compliments and neglects to compliment the firstborn, whose achievement may be greater. The firstborn is quick to notice this inconsistency. In one case, the mother approached the problem by complimenting the firstborn in private and soliciting her help in motivating the secondborn.

Constellation 9.5 illustrates, among other things, the impact of three women of different generations upon a boy who had a prolonged illness. It also illustrates how a girl can exercise skill in family analysis. When Joan, the oldest, was between the ages of eight and fifteen, her family lived with her maternal grandparents. They had little contact with her father's relatives.

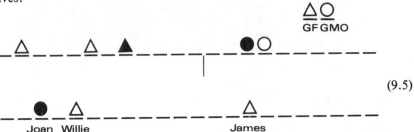

(9.5)

Mother relied on her parents for advice and conveniences such as babysitting and chauffering. In our childhood home, my two brothers and I had four parents telling us what to do. There was no clearcut delegation of authority; perhaps Mother and Grandma had the most to say about household matters and discipline. My grandparents were just like parents, and we were very close to them. Because I was the first child and grandchild, I occupied a favored position. When Willie was born, he was received with as much gladness and gratitude as I had eighteen months before.

To this day I am Daddy's favorite, but Mother and I are not very close. Dad's odd working hours made it impossible for him to spend much time with Willie, and he never took much interest in Willie's activities.

My brother Willie was a sickly infant and had several operations. He was coddled at all times. My mother became exceedingly attached to him and spent many hours nursing him because of his delicate physical condition. She took an interest in Willie's boyhood organizations and watched him perform. Although Willie is a personable, pleasant person, he has not one close friendship.

As a child, I was more of a leader than a follower. I led my brother as well as my playmates and initiated most of our activities.

James, my younger brother, and I are very close, but he is a lone wolf and doesn't like school; he has an unhappy look on his face. When James came along, Daddy devoted more time to him than to either of the other two children. Daddy became a father all over again. The sun rises and sets on James in Dad's estimation.

Notice that the father's position in his sib constellation is similar to that of James. It would be natural for the father to identify with James and to give him more attention than he gave to Willie.

Let us consider Willie's situation during his impressionable years. From the stance of psychosexual balance as it might impinge on Willie (before the arrival of James), there are three men in this family: grandfather, father, and Willie; and three women: grandmother, mother, and sister Joan. All three of the women are firstborn, but none of the men is. James, the younger brother, did not arrive on the scene until very much later, and when he did, the father, who had neglected Willie, gave all his attention to James.

The sister outshone Willie by a wide margin in academic and social achievement. Because Willie required special nursing attention during his infancy, the mother's strong emotional investment in her son crystallized into something of a symbiotic relationship.

> During high school Willie seldom dated. Then, in the second semester of his senior year, he met a girl on his intellectual and social level, and after a month they were going steady. Willie is quite short, and Mary, his girl-friend, is short also. This boosted Willie's male ego. During his freshman year in college, Willie came home almost every weekend to see Mary. He became extremely emotionally dependent on her. My mother did not like Mary and broke it up.

> Once again, Willie is, to a great extent, emotionally and psychologically wrapped up in his second girlfriend. This girl has dated as little as Willie has; she has recently lost weight and Willie is her first real boyfriend. The parents of Susan (the second girlfriend), are encouraging the relationship. My parents, especially Mother, are not.

> Mother and Daddy, especially Mother, do not understand Willie at all. I did make a suggestion to Mother one day as to why I thought Willie behaves as he does. She seemed to agree with me. I gave her the following analysis: Willie, all his life, has been in an inferior position with regard to the female members of his family. Mother is dominant and often uncom-promising; she has a strong personality, and one is aware of her presence and her opinions at all times. Willie has had an older sister (me) who has been in the spotlight because of her social and scholastic superiority over him. He has known his father to be a quiet, unusually submissive husband with a not-too-glittering personality. Willie was not very successful in social relationships and scholastic matters. Hence, when he met Mary and Susan, who were socially and intellectually his equals, Willie sought to develop these contacts in which he, for a change, was the outstanding, dominating, and leading member. Both Mary and Susan idolized Willie and praised him to the skies. Both their families made much ado over him. Willie, in short, was kingpin for a change.

We now turn to a family in which neither parent appreciated the smol-dering sense of injustice suffered by the narrator (boy in middle position) who appeared to have been discriminated against in terms of attention and material things. Both parents were eldest in the sib positions, but the mother had four sisters and no brothers. This would make it easy for her to identify with the oldest daughter and to fail to understand her son.

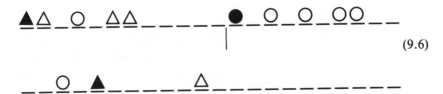

$$(9.6)$$

My older sister was very dominant and nearly always got her way when we were young. I remember that we used to play cowboys and Indians a lot when we were young. My sister always was the cowboy and I had to be the Indian. It wasn't until my junior year in high school that I started to rebel against my sister, and then all hell broke loose. I used to get disgusted over always taking the second part, but I seldom tattled because I felt that only sissies ran to their folks when they needed help.

What really disgusted me was that my sister always received the most money for clothes and that she always seemed to get more of everything than I did. I remember that my sister received not only a brand-new room when our family remodeled our home but also a whole net set of bedroom furniture. I never felt, though, that I was being left out of the picture because Dad always took me fishing a lot, and we later did a lot of hunting together. My parents explained to me that my sister got what she did because she was a girl and that I could get along with less. This satisfied me to a certain degree, but I guess I was still a bit jealous of the extra attention she received, especially considering that she usually did less work than I did.

One incident of rebellion against my sister in about my eighth grade in school stands out clearly in my mind right now. There was a TV special that I really wanted to see, but it was at the same time that my sister always watched one of her favorite programs. My sister used to watch TV for hours, and I seldom watched, so I felt it was my turn to have the program on that I wanted. My sister was in the other room, and during the commercial between shows, I turned to the channel I wanted. The program began, and I watched it for about five minutes before my sister came back and declared that it was time for her program. She headed for the TV set, and I countered by jumping between her and the set. My sister began to kick, scratch, and do everything possible to get me away from the set, but I was not going to budge and held my ground by pushing her away. It ended with Dad coming into the room and turning off the TV set for the night. This I felt to be unfair, but I still considered that I had won a major battle against my sister because, until this time, I had usually come out on the short string.

I remember that I used to get tremendously frustrated when my sister always got her way and when my parents went along with it. Violent fights began to break out between my sister and me, and by high school I was about fed up to the rim with anything to do with her (but she still was a part of our family, and if she had ever gotten into trouble in school, I'm sure that I would have tried to help her out). After my sister got married, I finally softened up and began to try to make conversation with her again.

The roots of resentment are deep, and I still would just as soon not talk with her because I feel uneasy, although I have tried to forget our past fights.

I remember that I was always fairly self-disciplined, and when I got frustrated and had no place to turn, I used to withdraw and not be seen for long periods of time. At times, no matter how hungry I was, I didn't come to meals, and I used to go sit in my room or go outside. My dad was pretty strong, and I never attempted to cross him up, so when he demanded that I come to supper, I usually did; but then I would come down feeling humiliated and would mope at meals. I just didn't know how else to react because I felt repressed at times, and I was frustrated as to what to do. To this day, I feel that I still get frustrated as to what to do; I seldom take a leadership role because I am unable to deal effectively with more than one person. I would sooner do my share of the work in a group and leave the leading to others. I am quite subordinate, even to people I know quite well, even if I consider that my ideas are better than theirs. I am petrified to speak to any group, and I am almost always excited when I get into any tight situation.

My mother had complete rule of the household, and I used to get frustrated over her lack of tact in dealing with me. I used to feel as though I was being taken advantage of, and my mother never seemed to iron out these feelings; she would brush over my problems as though they were not important. I always had the feeling that both my parents would do just about anything for me, however, and I respected them for this.

Although we do not have a statement of either parent or of the sister, this case suggests that when both parents are eldest, they should check their system of justice. A characteristic feature of pantrophic families is a sense of justice that pervades the family *hestia*.

A parent who is tired and frustrated over fighting among siblings may not have the energy to hold court, solicit testimony, and render judgment. In pantrophic families, however, the friction between siblings is less frequent and less intense.

In one family, the three children were wide apart in age. There was much conflict between the parents because of considerable drinking. The eldest child, a girl, began to take over responsibilities as the mother's drinking made her more inadequate. The two younger brothers placed more confidence and trust in their older sister, and the middle boy began to take over fatherly attitudes toward the younger brother. The secondborn wrote:

The indifference and rejection between my parents and their lack of love, respect, and warmth for all of us made us become more considerate and closer to each other. Many times we were awakened in the middle of the night by loud fighting and yelling between our parents. We couldn't sleep but wouldn't dare interfere in their arguments. Instead, I would huddle under my blankets trying to escape from the reality of a cruel family life.

Constellation 9.7 is interesting because it shows the sib groupings for three generations. Grandfather, father, and the narrator, Bess, were all firstborn, and each had at least one younger brother. When we have a succession of firstborn in three generations, the process of identification is strong, and the qualities of leadership and self-sufficiency become part of the family tradition. The leadership qualities of the firstborn arise from two factors: the first is scripting for leadership by verbal tradition plus modeling of the firstborn parent; the other is actual experience in leading and caring for younger siblings.

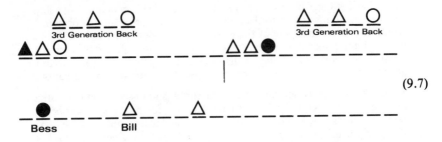

(9.7)

> In my family, my father identifies with me. He has always taught me to be a leader, to think for myself, and to be independent and self-sufficient. Although I am unlikely to admit it publicly, I feel that my personality is more like Toman's sister of sisters. My mother tends to identify with the youngest boy since she was the youngest child. As for the middle child, I guess it's no fun to be in the middle because he gets a little from both sides.

The mother and grandmother were youngest, having older brothers. Bess dwells on their skills in dealing with men. It is not hard to guess that the parents would have a good relationship.

> The communication between my mother and father is excellent. In the beginning of an occasional argument, my father is more dominant, and toward the end, my mother is more dominant and my father more submissive. [She quotes her father's occasional remarks,] "Behind every successful man is a more-successful woman."

The father's deference to his wife's ideas is understandable since both he and the grandfather had younger sisters.

Certain traits such as quick decision making, leadership skills, responsibility, dependability, and task competency are traits acquired by the firstborn, irrespective of sex. Of course, how the oldest boy or girl relates to the other sex depends on the spacing and sex of the younger siblings.

When three children are close in age like in constellation 9.8, we expect considerable interaction. We can understand why Libby became a tomboy. This is a pantrophic family with no favoritism and no jealousy. Note that no withdrawal from competition exists and that love is expressed freely.

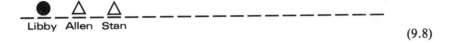

Libby Allen Stan

(9.8)

Because I had no sisters, I played with my brothers a lot and developed into quite a tomboy, playing cowboys and Indians and other rough games. I never liked dolls, although I got one every Christmas. I outgrew my tomboyishness when I started school and had other girls to play with. I never had any problems getting along with my brothers. I held the role of a typical big sister.

Between Allen and Stan, the situation was different. They were always doing little things to antagonize each other. This applies more to Allen. He just loved to tease Stan; this in turn made Stan angry, and then the fighting started. Mom and Dad would discipline the boys by talking with them, spanking, and taking away special privileges for a while. By putting an end to much of the teasing and fighting when they were younger, Mom and Dad helped the boys to grow up and get along with each other. They still have their differences, but if they didn't, I don't think they would be normal.

There has never been any favoritism shown in our family. I have gotten my share of discipline as I was growing up. Just because I was the only girl in the family didn't mean I got away with anything. When I was younger I had quite a temper, and I would become very sassy with my mother. I received more than one slap across the mouth for being disrespectful to Mom. Both Dad and Mom gave out punishments; however, Dad was the more authoritative of the two. The word *love* was used quite a lot around our house when we were young and it still is. Although my brothers and I love both our parents, we are still seemingly closer to one than the other. Both my brothers go to Mom first with a problem; I have always been a little closer to Dad.

None of us was ever made to feel that we had to compete with each other. Mom and Dad treated us as three individuals with three individual personalities, and they never expected one of us to be as smart in school as the other two. Competition didn't exist between us. We were always encouraged to do our best, and they were always there to help us when we needed them. My parents were firm, yet flexible in difference situations. Despite the firmness, Dad and Mom never failed to show us that they loved us and each other.

In constellation 9.9, we see how the transition to college marks a change from the dystrophic impact of jealousy and competition to pantrophic empathy and encouragement. Anne, the oldest, narrates:

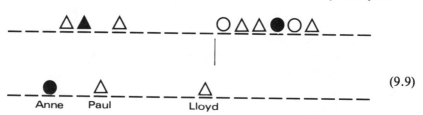

(9.9)

From the beginning, there was jealousy between Paul and me. He was able to get attention from me, but I was always right in there ready to get ahead whenever I could. We were never close—he was receiving the attention I could have had.

When Lloyd was born, Paul and I were in the background, and the baby was the pride and joy of the family. Since I was nine and at the helping age, I became the little mother. Thus, Lloyd and I received much attention and Paul was neglected.

I feel that Paul's lack of responsibility and immaturity are much my fault. I was always competitive in school and at home. Many times I would brag about my accomplishments and make Paul feel he had none. I was never close to him since my duties made me so involved that I forgot all about him.

Being the oldest, I had to break the ice for everything. This was not difficult because being a girl and being important in the family made it easy for me to get my wishes quite frequently.

I received still more attention upon entering high school where I became a cheerleader and had more to brag about. I had constant arguments with Paul over household chores. When I entered college, the chores devolved to Paul because Lloyd was too young to help, and Paul became withdrawn.

Since my freshman year at college, I have changed greatly. Each time I go home, I force myself to help Paul, realizing his need for attention. I find myself telling my parents to be more patient with him and to let him do more things on his own. When I am able, I will give him money or help him do things.

Girl, Boy, Girl

One might speculate, whenever we have three siblings of the same sex in a series with moderate spacing, that we should have more withdrawal from competition or conflict than in a system in which a middle child has an older and a younger sibling of a different sex. In the latter case the middle child should have different role expectations from the others, and the oldest and youngest would be separated in age. My small, unstructured samples support this speculation.

In nine of the eleven cases of a brother between two sisters, the oldest girl was described as a bossy leader, even though the brother might be only two years younger. In several cases the sibling arrangement of the parents was unavailable. Where available, the reader should notice how parallel positions in the two generations reinforce favoritism or identification. He will also notice parental patterns that promote sibling jealousy. A common feature to some cases is that students who perceived their parents as playing favorites during their childhood later decided that the parents had been fair.

The main contribution of the next excerpt, constellation 9.10, is a poignant phrase—"enough love to go around."

─●─ ─ ─ ─ ─ △ ○ ─ ─ ─ ─ ─ ─ ─ ─ ─ ─ ─
        John   (9.10)

> When I was six, I got a baby brother. At this age I welcomed John because, aside from all the positive stroking that made me confident that my brother wouldn't be taking affection away from me, my parents reassured me that they had enough love to go around. I remember that this reassurance really made me feel good. Furthermore, they played up my future role as a baby-sitter, pointing out how grown up I would be and that I would be given some responsibilities. This position of responsibility was furthered when I was nine and my siser Virginia came along. At that time I started changing diapers and feeding the children. The general effect of being the oldest was to put me in the leadership position.
>
> Also, I remember that it made me feel good and prevented any superiority feelings among the siblings when my parents told us that they had planned each of us; none was an accident. While we didn't experience superiority feelings, and while my parents tried to treat all of us equally, I was definitely my father's favorite. In fact, when Mom drove me back to school last year, she finally told me outright that I was Dad's favorite and that it was hard for him to see me go off to college.

After describing how her younger sister and brother were developing fine personalities, she added, "However, since we're so far apart in age, we can keep this competition lighthearted."

When this student says the children were treated equally and at the same time admits she was her father's favorite, is there a contradiction? By equal treatment, most students mean treated fairly in terms of attention, privileges, resources, and rewards. To be treated equally does not mean to be treated similarly because all parents know they must adapt their treatment of each child according to his age, position, temperament, and special needs. Special relationships do develop between a parent and a given child because of similarity of position, physical likeness, or temperamental compatibility. When there is enough love to go around, and when this special relationship is taken lightly, the other children understand it and accept it; but when favoritism involves a concentration of affection, resources, privileges, and rewards at the expense of others, they dystrophic consequences emerge. Appraisals of favoritism change over time.

The next excerpt describes the situation of a lastborn who is very much younger than her siblings. It could have been written by hundreds of students who were lastborn with a similar age discrepancy.

> My sister May is thirteen years older than I, and my brother is almost ten years my senior. In fact, I can't even remember their being at home except on weekends when they came home from college. I feel at times as if I were an only child and that my brother and sister were more like parents than siblings.
>
> My parents tell me that they had a harder time bringing me up because they were getting rather old. Things like school functions didn't interest them nearly as much as they did when Tony and May were growing up. Many times I felt the tensions that all these activities caused them, and many times I wished they had been younger so that we could have had more in common. The generation gap was very apparent.
>
> I had many more advantages than Tony and May, and they never let me forget it. They were off to school and I was home to grow up alone. The relationship between my older siblings and myself has been pretty fair, but we never lived together long enough for me really to get to know them in the family pattern.

Previously, I alluded to the difficulties of a child who is the recipient of pressures or abuse from any two members of his family. We may have similar difficulties when we have domination at home combined with a hurt in the schooling setting. The oldest in one family said the following about her next oldest brother:

> My brother is a very quiet person, and I often feel I am to blame for that. When we were younger, I always dominated him and told him what to do and he seemed to go along with it. Because he is so quiet, people have a tendency to walk over him. In the sixth grade he had a bad experience. His teacher favored him so much that the boys excluded him. He keeps things to himself. Mom complains, "He never tells me anything." He is an intelligent person and can do well in school if he feels like it. He seems to lack any kind of motivation. In his last year in high school, my brother opened up more, and he plays cards now with a few good friends. He won't give girls a second look. He's probably scared they'll be like his older sister. He gets along well with my younger sister, although he teases her quite a bit.
>
> It is hard for me to have a good relationship with a man, probably because I have not been able to understand my father's or my brother's feelings.

In our culture, so much stress is given to dominance and leadership that other traits such as empathy and judgment are neglected. Just having brothers when growing up is not sufficient for a girl to understand men in later life. She must experience a rapport with her brothers, their friends, or her father—preferably, with all three. The same goes for a boy in having satisfactory relationships with sisters, their girlfriends, and his mother.

The following excerpt reveals the attitude of a firstborn girl whose siblings were five and seven years younger. She alleged that she was spoiled because she was an only child for five years, that her brother was spoiled because he was the only boy, and that her sister was spoiled because she was lastborn. We may assume that, by spoiled, she means overindulged.

My parents looked to me for leadership—to set the right examples for my brother and sister. In many areas I am continually asked for my opinion. Because of my role as leader, I have become dominant in family matters. My parents give great weight to my opinions, and I influence their decisions greatly. All three of us children are close to our parents and to each other, although evidence of love and affection are more covert than overt.

Scholastically, competition exists among the three of us. If someone comes home from school with a bad grade, he or she is always questioned as to why by both our parents, and there are always remarks by the other children as well. One can almost predict, next time grades come out, that the deficient grade will have improved.

This kind of healthy competition is in contrast to the following, from constellation 9.11, that was ruined by a teacher:

(9.11)

In spite of the fact that my siblings were very much older, my teachers reminded me that I had an older brother and sister. My sister excelled in English, history, and German; my brother excelled in math. My sister and I had the same German teacher. She called me by my sister's name for two years. I tried correcting her, but she said she would never get it straight and that I should just answer to her name. I started out with an A in the course. The teacher would often comment on how much I was like my sister, but she was the last person I wanted to be like. She was a bookworm and sat home all the time, while I wanted to do things and go places. Competition started to get harder for me because more studying was required. I started to do B work, and the teacher kept telling me, "I know you can do better. Why, your sister . . . ." I then withdrew from competition, stopped studying, and was satisfied with Cs.

However, my brother and I had different math teachers so I felt some competition to do just as well as he. I would sit and study math for several hours compared to fifteen minutes with my German. I succeeded and got A grades. I looked up to my brother more than to my sister partly because my temperament and interests were more like his.

Boy, Girl, Boy

In the combination of daughter between two sons, the desire of the parents for sons has been satisfied, and their desire for daughters has been satisfied by the one daughter. There are advantages to the girl in this position. She gets to know men who are both older and younger, including the friends of her brothers. She learns to be a good listener, a good sport, and a confidante, especially to men. If there is some space between herself and her younger brother, she has an opportunity to accept responsibility for him and, thus, develops some competency in caring for children. These girls are apt to become tomboys before taking on feminine characteristics, and they often express preference for men over women.

Unfortunately, all my cases of this triad were written by girls. They described sibling relationships as being rather good. We would expect that the aggressive leadership of the older brother would be muted since he would not be so aggressive to a younger sister, whose roles would be different, or to a still younger brother. We would also expect that the youngest in this series would be different from the youngest brother of sisters because he has only one older sister to wait on him instead of two. He also has the advantage of an older brother. The few cases we have do not contradict these inferences.

In constellation 9.12, the sister is narrator; she has one brother two years older, another four years younger. Neither brother acquired Toman's traits for his position, but the narration provides the answers.

$$\underline{\quad\triangle\ \bullet\ \ \ \triangle\qquad\qquad\qquad\qquad}\qquad(9.12)$$

I am the only girl in our family and have both an older and a younger brother. Because my older brother and I were so close in age, we were together much of the time while young. My older brother was (and still is) a quieter and more-reserved type of person that I was or ever will be. He was always content to be a follower so I naturally took the role of leader. This role of leadership extended to our playmates in the neighborhood who were primarily boys. I was a tomboy but never really wished that I could have been a boy.

My older brother, until his recent marriage, always relied on my parents almost entirely. He was the center of the family before I was born. He has always withdrawn from competition. He was young for his grade in school and matured slowly. Of all the children, he stayed home the most. Throughout school he got below average grades, while mine were high. My parents were disappointed in him; yet they sent him to a private college where he did not do well at all.

As a child I was very willful and determined. Being a tomboy, I never played with dolls and spent most of my time outside. I never really cared a great deal for my mother, even as a child. I had a feeling of indifference for her. I like her, but we clash on so many ideals, objectives, and ideas that there is not much compatibility. My father, I think, is wonderful and he and I get along very well.

Because my mother started working when my younger brother was still quite young, he became very independent. He enjoys very much the few family activities we do have. He is a mature and responsible boy for thirteen years of age. He grew up fast due to the fact that he was living in a family of persons much older. He has always done well in school and has very many friends. He is active in school, church, and scouting affairs and enjoys activities with my father.

The older brother matured slowly among classmates older than himself. The younger brother grew up fast during the time his mother had an outside job and his sister was a tomboy. His father was his companion.

Note what the female narrators say in constellations 9.13 and 9.14 about how their contacts with the male friends of their older brothers increased their skill in dealing with men.

Jerry   Irma   Matt   (9.13)

To most boys I have been a confidante rather than a romantic interest. When Jerry's friends came to our house, they considered me his little sister, so none of them took me out. Since I'd rather listen to other people's troubles than talk about my own, I suppose I provided a sympathetic ear. This is true even with my girlfriends. They know me as someone to talk to and that whatever they tell me will go no further.

I developed a close relationship with my older brother and looked up to him. I was both a big sister and a second mother to my younger brother. He confided in me and sought my guidance and assistance. I was responsible for changing him and feeding him, which I loved to do most of the time. I assumed the authority of a big sister. I was my father's little girl, and I had a special closeness to my mother. We had sessions of girl talk between the two of us. Jerry and Father have a special closeness. Matt, the baby of the family, is spoiled.

                                                                             (9.14)

My father was the fourth of fifteen children, but since he was the oldest of a string of five boys, he was delegated the responsibility over them.

For a time we lived where there were no other children, and my brother and I became good companions. Later, when he brought friends to our house, I was always included in their activities. He was my protector and friend. I, in turn, did the housework without asking for his help. I'm also close to my younger brother, but in a different way. When my younger brother was in first grade, my mother went to work. My little brother depended on me for almost everything. I became a mother figure to him and a close friend. My brother assumed quite a bit of responsibility around the house even though he was the youngest. There was so much to do because both my parents were working. Since he was a much more-willing worker than my older brother, I found myself giving him many of the easier tasks.

All the relationships in our family are remarkably successful. I participated in all sorts of activities such as sports, hunting, and fishing with my father and brothers and their friends. From talking with my brother and his friends, I learned what traits boys like and dislike in girls. My parents, however, made it clear that I was a girl and not a boy. I developed very feminine characteristics. I feel I was very fortunate to have an older brother. It has helped me both in meeting and getting to know guys and in feeling at ease and having fun on dates.

In constellations 9.13 and 9.14, the sister in the middle of two brothers had satisfying contacts with her older brother and his friends and developed skills in relating to men. In both cases the younger brother avoided the unfortunate traits of the youngest brother of brothers (irregular worker, capricious, and willful) and of the youngest brother of sisters (expectation of being cared for by women, procrastinator, little ambition) because the mothers worked outside the home, thus thrusting task roles onto the boys under the direction of their older sisters who knew how to handle boys. Both brothers were independent and responsible.

Constellation 9.15 deals with high paternal expectations, withdrawal from competition, and blundering teachers. Note Monica's exuberant growth in the school setting. In this constellation, the reader may guess the extent the father identified with the success of his first two children as an extension of himself. The school difficulties of the third child are evident.

George   Monica Jim

(9.15)

George, or number-one son as my father calls him, was always given the greatest responsibility and leadership. At first he was Mama's little helper. He took us to school, changed diapers, and so forth. He was the first to get a job, the first to go to college, and the first to marry. He didn't need to be very domineering toward us because he was a lot older and we didn't challenge his authority.

Since I was the only girl, I became pretty much of a tomboy. My brothers treated me like one of the guys. I had a temper like a spitfire and could wrestle my younger brother and win, until he started high school.

I saw how proud Dad was that his number-one son was going to be a cadet, and I promised myself that I'd make him proud of me, too, by the time I graduated. I joined nearly every organization available and studied fiercely. After I had sung in a concert with the glee club, my Dad asked me why I wasn't in the a cappella choir. Undaunted, I auditioned for and was accepted by the choir. His remark was, "Of course, you're my daughter, aren't you?" I became valedictorian and president of my class. My Dad told his friends that his daughter could be nothing but number one.

I'm grateful that I had a chance to be active in high school organizations. Through them I developed an outgoing personality that I could never have developed at home. These groups helped me develop the leadership and individuality that my home life had stifled. Having two brothers taught me to be a good sport and buddy, but it didn't do much to fashion a young lady. Through my school activities, I met a wealth of people from whom I learned the give and take of cooperation and who, by inviting me to join their parties, instilled in me a poise and confidence of which I thought I could never be capable. I didn't shy away from social gatherings—I thrived on them.

Jim was always Mom's favorite perhaps because, like her, he was the underdog, the latecomer who got all the hand-me-downs. I took over George's job of taking Jim to school and watching over him, and he became my favorite too. He worshiped George and was lost when George left. I became Jim's second big brother. If he needed someone to help with his homework, there I was; or if he was lonely, I was good company. When he became a teenager, I taught him to dance and to drive.

According to the IQ tests given at school, Jim had the highest score of any of us. We all went to the same schools. Having to follow George and me, Jim just gave up. All he heard was, "Aren't you George's brother?," or "Isn't your sister Monica?" He flunked out of high school his senior year. He already had his cap and gown, new suit, and pictures when the news came. He finished high school at a vocational school and got good grades. He then joined the air force, and with family competition removed, got grades in the nineties in the technical training program.

Two Girls and a Boy

In groupings of two girls and a boy, the eldest was consistently bossy and domineering and had leadership ability. She often combined the traits of oldest sister of sisters with those of oldest sister of brothers. Toman described the youngest brother of sisters as one who expects women to wait on him, a procrastinator, less competitive and reactive, one who resents being pushed in work by men, and not a good leader. The sister narrators in five cases did not check their brothers on the Toman list because their brothers were too young to evaluate. However, three of them mentioned two or more of Toman's traits for this position; in one case the narrator said that Toman was all wrong about her brother but correct about herself.

Parental pressure often backfires, as in the following excerpt. The narrator had a sister four years older and a brother seven years younger. This girl was downgraded by her mother and was used somewhat as a scapegoat. She had a fairly good relationship with her father. She wrote:

My sister was the friendly, gregarious child, while I was the snob. My mother constantly nagged me to say hello to everyone. My sister could walk into a room full of people and start talking, whereas I would huddle in a corner. This nagging of my mother seemed to produce the opposite effect in me. Instead of being friendlier, I became rebelliously less so because I knew she was watching my interaction very closely. I developed an I'll-show-her attitude. My father was usually sympathetic to me.

I had no brothers near my age, so I looked upon boys as strange and rather frightening. I had no idea that boys were actually human and that they had feelings similar to mine until I started dating in college.

In constellation 9.16, the narrator alleges she has most of Toman's traits for the oldest sister of sisters and a few traits of the oldest sister of brothers. Her disdain for women in authoritative positions is marked.

(9.16)

If no one seems to be leading a group to get something done, I invariably find myself taking over. I have no trouble getting people to do things. I speak with much assurance, but down deep inside I'm praying that I am right.

I tend to identify with my superior as a father figure and am submissive and almost adoring if this male superior is older, dignified, and respected in his field. Conversely, I dislike taking orders from most women, feeling they are not as intelligent or as responsible as a man would be—or maybe as I would be.

Oldest sister of brothers pertains to me. My best friends are men. It seems that I can talk with them, joke with them, and generally enjoy their company much more than with women. Men do tend to confide in me, and I like to listen and give advice.

My brother fits none of the characteristics in the youngest-brother-of-sisters class. He prefers not to have women fussing over him. Another point of contradiction (Toman) is Andy's ability to compete. Whether in the classroom or on the football field, he does his best. The only tasks he really enjoys are those that present a challenge. My brother has often been called a born leader, and with his high intelligence and leadership qualities and love for competition, I am sure he will succeed in the adult world.

We may conjecture that the young brother became the opposite of the type Toman describes for his position because of his innate intelligence and dexterity in interacting with a peer group in which his talents were recognized. I feel, however, that part of his sister's analysis is significant:

> My mother tended to be more domineering than my father, who was more easygoing. My mother babied my younger brother, whereas my father treated my sister and me with great love and concern. My mother tended to dominate the whole family, especially me. I resented the way she dominated my father and the way my sister dominated her boyfriend, so I tried to be the opposite around boys. I hated to be a nag like my mother and sister, so I went to the other extreme and agreed with whatever my boyfriends said, thinking I'd lose them if I became a nag. I feel a lot of my mother's domination was due to her voice patterns that were irritating to all of us.

> Being in the middle, I am at a disadvantage. I always got everything secondhand from my sister, my brother was spoiled, and I just felt left out. My mother stated openly that she favored my brother. I am my father's favorite, but he would never admit it. My mother and sister would never give me a compliment to my face. I got the feeling that my sister was competing with me and that my mother was jealous of me.

> Reflecting on my childhood, I would say I was very happy because of my relationships in peer groups.

> When I began dating a certain boy, I let him dominate our relationship. This was natural for him because he was the oldest of four children. [He exploited her financially. She paid for the dates, gasoline, and so on.]

Two Boys and a Girl

If the parents of two brothers and a sister do reasonably well in child rearing, the oldest may take on the characteristics of both the oldest brother of brothers and the oldest brother of sisters. The second boy's problems may center around competition or withdrawal vis-à-vis the older brother. The sister learns to deal with men, and if the family functions well, she will have all the advantages of the youngest sister of brothers. In this position she may experience teasing from her brothers, ranging from banter to torment.

Of the six triad cases of boy, boy, girl, three were narrated by the daughter, one by the oldest brother, and two by the middle brother. In all six cases the sister came to understand and to like men—even the one who was plagued by a brother. The older brothers tended to describe themselves as the oldest brother of brothers and the oldest brother of sisters. The sisters alleged they had the traits of the youngest sister of brothers.

This combination of siblings seems to be a favorable one. The father and the brothers are happy to have a little girl in the family, and the mother has at least one female child. With one exception, family relationships eventually were satisfactory.

The loss of a parent when children are small seems to bring them closer together and gives them a sense of responsibility to make up for the loss. This is demonstrated in the following case. The father was divorced when the youngest, a girl, was two years old. The daughter, in her narration, gave her mother credit for supporting the family and making it successful; she displayed no favoritism. The daughter wrote:

Since I never knew my father, I've always thought I was lucky because I had two older brothers who in many ways represented a male figure in my life. There has never been any jealousy between either of my brothers and me. In fact, they play the father role to the extent that they both want to meet my boyfriends and give me their opinions of them. This means a lot to me. There has been very little competition between any two of us children, and even when we were small, we hardly ever fought among ourselves.

As a child, I grew up in a neighborhood with few girls so I played a lot with my brothers and their friends. This closeness to boys as just friends has had an adverse effect on my dating relationships. Because my brothers dominated me in a way, I can be dominated easily by most men, but I am beginning to overcome this.

In the next case, the mother and daughter had an especially strong relationship, but by the time the daughter was in college, the mother-daughter roles were reversed.

Now that I've been in college for two years, she still calls me and writes me often about her problems. In many ways I resent her doing that to me, especially because I feel that I have enough problems of my own without coping with hers. Once in a while I would like to feel that I have someone to lean on instead of being leaned on. Because of this, my mother and I haven't been getting along as well lately as we used to, and I don't go home as often as I did before. My brothers have a lot of influence in my choice of boyfriends. In the absence of a father, I have developed a strong ideal-mate image from my oldest brother. Probably I look for men like my older brother because he is much more dominant than the other brother and because I am attracted to people who are dominant.

Common usage has distorted the meaning of the word *dominance*. This girl had a loving relationship with an older brother who helped her make decisions. We can imagine how this kind of dependence made her feel uncomfortable when her mother reversed the mother-daughter roles and asked for advice. This daughter does not want to be dominated; rather, she wants an older man to protect her from all sorts of things, especially arduous decision making. We should learn something from the plight of the mother. She invested most of her relationships within the family so that when the daughter left the household, the mother had no close friend or relative of her own generation to whom to turn. The nuclear unit cannot be healthy by itself; it must have ties with a larger circle of friends and relatives.

The male narrator from another family had a brother five years older and a sister two years younger. The brother excelled in athletics, music, and scholarship. The narrator was self-conscious because of overweight and because he felt the pressure to keep up with his older brother. Although proud of his brother, he felt he could not catch up because of the five-year head start. "I gave up trying and withdrew as much as possible from competition. My father expected big things from me."

This boy entered high school just after his brother had graduated. He went out for sports, lost weight, and became a better football player than his brother. He transferred to a larger school where he experienced his so-called period of triumph. He was gratified that he had finally beaten his brother at something. Each was proud of the other, and they were on excellent terms. The writer was a leader among his peers, especially after his brother left home. Both brothers had a fine relationship with the very talented sister, although the narrator opinioned, "She lives in my shadow and doesn't like it."

The next report reveals how maternal overprotection, lack of supervision of children, and family friction produce a problem child. The narrator was a girl with two older brothers, one three years older and the other six years older. She wrote, "Since my mother worked from the time I entered second grade, the kids were left to fend for themselves." She was "pushed around by her brothers," especially the next older one whom she called a brat and a stinker. She alleged he teased and hit her for no reason. Even when the mother was home, the daughter maintained that her mother failed to reprimand the brother partly "because he was her favorite," She summed up the brother's situation as follows:

He is spoiled, rebellious, and cannot take orders from anyone. I believe he is this way because he has always done what he pleased and never suffered the consequences because he was protected by my mother. She has made allowances for him all his life, and today she says, "Let him have his way, it's too late to change him."

Among our mixed triads, this is the only case in which a mother's working was disadvantageous to the children. It might not have been disadvantageous in this family had the mother been able to discipline her sons adequately. It is risky business to leave a young girl with two older brothers unsupervised when the family has dystrophic features.

10 Fours and Fives

Constellation 10.1 represents a rural four-child family of both sexes with pantrophic overtones.

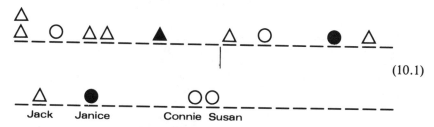

$$(10.1)$$

The attention Jack received while he was an only child is reflected to a considerable extent in his personality today. He still demands a great deal of attention and thoroughly enjoys being in the limelight.

A second influence on Jack's personality was the fact that he was the oldest brother of three sisters. Much responsibility was placed on him to take care of his younger sisters, and he was often given the role of babysitter. This, combined with his role as Dad's right-hand man with the farm chores, developed in him a strong sense of responsibility very early in life. This responsible attitude has continued to the present. He is a good worker—but, as Toman suggests is characteristic of an oldest brother of sisters, he works best alongside members of the opposite sex. Work experience with women came early for Jack as our farm work was always done as a family project. Now, he often depends on the services of his wife as a workmate in his own farm wok. This close cooperation with members of the opposite sex presumably has been a factor in his phenomenal ability to understand women. This understanding, together with a very strong interest in the opposite sex, led to a rich, varied, and very successful dating experience during his teenage years. His major concern was love, in the most romantic style, as Toman predicts for these outnumbered male siblings. Although presently performing the role of husband and father of two children, he still never lacks the time to notice and compliment a pretty girl or a beautiful woman.

Being a middle child in our family constellation, my status was never as well defined as that of my brother. Having both an older brother and younger sisters, I may be expected to develop some of the personality characteristics both of a youngest sister of brothers and an oldest sister of sisters. Because of the six-year age difference between myself and my next younger sister, I spent the most formative years of my life as the baby of the family, sharing my parents' attention only with my brother.

I was almost a complete opposite of Jack, a very quiet and reserved little girl who seemingly posed no threat to him. Thus, there was little jealousy between us and we became very close. The attachment I felt toward this brother undoubtedly formed the basis of my ability to develop very strong affinities with members of the opposite sex. This ability is so prominent in my personality that it becomes a weakness. It corresponds closely to a trait of the youngest sister of brothers noted by Toman: "If a man gets her, she will not let him go, even if he has serious faults and abuses her." Some effects of this personality trait will be shown in the discussion of my dating and courtship behavior later.

Other characteristics ascribed to a youngest sister of brothers seem to correspond to my personality. I have usually considered myself a feminine, friendly, kind, and sensitive person. I have proved myself on several occasions to be a submissive and devoted companion of men. My past two summers were spent as a secretary to men, a position I thoroughly enjoyed. Contrary to Toman's ideas, however, I have seen no indication that my ability to attract men is better than average, and I am too independent to work well under the direct guidance of someone else. The fact that I had only one older brother may account for the weakness of some of these characteristics in my personality.

Since the age differential between my sisters and me was so great, one would expect the characteristics of an oldest sister of sisters to be relatively weak in my personality, and I believe this is true. Possible exceptions may be my independent nature and tendencies to cut people short who are more knowledgeable in a certain area than I am and to despise official female figures above me. Through sharing the care of my younger sisters with Jack, I gained an ability to accept considerable responsibility and developed some of the leadership traits characteristic of an oldest sister.

My next oldest sister, Connie, acquired many of the characteristics of an oldest sister of sisters because of the large age differential between us. She has always taken a strong role as leader, with her sister Susan as follower. Establishing dominance has been relatively easy for her (some additional reasons will be discussed later), but if forced to submit, she is quick to anger. Her eyes flash and she stamps her foot.

Connie is truly a "self-righteous, conscientious queen." She is very close to her father, works well with him, and accepts responsibility extremely well. At the age of sixteen, she owns and accepts full responsibility for 100 chickens. One of Connie's most outstanding traits is her conservatism, politically and otherwise. She is an extremely independent person, however, and by her own admission, seldom confides in anyone. She gives every impression of being very sure of herself, yet her manner is often rather aloof and mechanical, making it extremely difficult to determine her true feelings.

My youngest sister Susan displays a personality directly opposite to that of Connie. Many of her traits correspond strongly with those Toman suggested as a characteristic of a youngest sister of sisters. One of her most noticeable traits is love of adventure and change. She is as liberal as Connie is conservative. She will work well at a novel task or one that she can carry out in a novel manner. She is very creative and will accept nothing at face value. To the dismay of her rather traditional parents, she cannot even mow the lawn or wash the dishes in a traditional manner. She is constantly asking why we do things the way we do and wondering if another way wouldn't do as well.

Susan's love for adventure is manifested in a love for mystery novels and television programs high in adventure and mystery. She has a great appreciation for social activities, sports, and most other forms of entertainment. She can be very competitive but, unfortunately, has developed quite a serious inferiority complex and often withdraws from competition, especially in the academic area, where all of her siblings were exceptional. She is a willful person, and the combination of this trait and her adventuresome spirit has led to considerable friction between herself and her parents.

From early childhood, Susan got along well with all her peers, especially with the boys, and was quite a tomboy. She is often willing to compromise or surrender her wishes and submit to those of her peers to maintain friendships that are tremendously important to her. She is a very sensitive person who finds another person's displeasure with her very hard to bear. This sensitivity and her submissive nature would probably prevent her from being a very effective boss or leader over others.

Parallel positions in their respective family constellations have probably been significant in establishing the close bond that exists between Mom and Connie. Both are in the third oldest position of their family constellations, and both have one older brother and sister, with a large age difference between themselves and their older sisters. In recent years this bond has resulted in considerable preferential treatment of Connie over Susan. Susan is often reprimanded for bothering Connie, and many privileges are given exclusively to Connie with the explanation, "Your time is coming. Connie is older." Much of this favoritism can be understood if we take a look at my mother's family of orientation.

Mom's younger brother Jim was always a distinct favorite of my grandmother's, a fact still evident today. He took full advantage of this, forever complaining of Mom's picking on him, convincing Grandma to give Mom most of the dirty jobs, and winning privileges for himself. Quite understandably, Mom has endeavored to avoid this overindulgence of the youngest member in her own family of procreation. Thus, she has a tendency to favor the older child.

Other factors increase the tendency for Mom to identify with Connie and strengthen her tendency to show favoritism. Mom was always a very petite, slender person and Connie is also small. By contrast, Susan is a large girl with a slight weight problem. Also, Connie's conservative personality harmonizes much better with Mom's traditional views than Susan's more liberal personality.

It would seem that the tendency toward favoring Connie would be somewhat eased by the fact that Dad is the youngest in his family and might identify more closely with Susan. This identification, for some reason, does not seem to have materialized. Perhaps the difference in sex is significant.

As we examine sibling constellations of four or more children, the number of middle children in which the traits ascribed to oldest and youngest are muted or mixed is increased. Also, a geometric increase in the number of relationships occurs so that the situations become so complex that generalizations in terms of position only are less useful. It becomes increasingly clear that many dimensions for analyzing one's family must be considered. I list some of the variations.

1. The parenting capacity of fathers and mothers can vary from excellent to poor. One facet of this is family leadership exercised with fairness, justice, and flexibility. Each parent may have both good and strong points in this role, and each may vary in his capacity to socialize children according to sex and age. In order to account for these variations, one must examine the childhood circumstances and constellations of both parents. It is also helpful to study the social and vocational settings of each parent. One function of each parent is to neutralize the mistakes of the other or to compensate for the inadequacies of the other.

2. Parents can vary from singling out a child for special treatment such as favoritism, affection, attention, or scapegoating to treating all children equally and fairly.

3. Skills of parents for motivating children to develop their talents and to achieve in appropriate fields vary. This is one of the highest of family skills, and our society is deficient in recognizing it, in formulating methods for developing it, and in providing training for it. Our case-history material suggests that parents low in such skills are those who make invidiuous comparisons, fail in the allocation of responsibilities for each child, neglect some children in favor of others, operate with rigidity, and permit destructive triangles to fester. Parents high in such skills tend to emphasize the idiosyncratic nature of persons; to distribute their love, attention, and concern equally among the children; and to give each freedom and encouragement to develop his talents and creativity.

4. Variation occurs in the achievement of high visibility of children's settings beyond the home. This visibility is improved by closer parent-teacher cooperation, by parental attendance at public events where the children perform, by making a home a favorite place for peers of children, and by parental participation in recreational activities of children beyond the home. Visibility is hampered by parental teasing of young love, distrust of child, and indifference toward their children's desires and activities. Although visibility of their parents' settings may be limited for the children by circumstances, some visibility in this dimension is helpful.

5. Variation exists in the extent to which the settings of each family meet the developmental and creative needs of each child. Some parents take it for granted that they have no control over the school and playground settings of their children. This is not necessarily the case because, when there

are options on where one might live, parents may choose a locale where good schools or a neighborhood with parks or playgrounds are available. If one is isolated from such advantages, the parent may take pains to transport the children to desired settings such as playgrounds, swimming pools, gymnasiums, and camps. The occupational settings of parents also vary. How happy parents are in their work settings is crucial to family functioning.

6. A final variation is the amount of time one parent is absent from the home. In case of permanent absence of one parent, the timing of the departure will affect children differently according to age. A variation in the number and quality of substitute parental figures will also affect the psychosexual balance of the family.

When parents examine these dimensions and act to implement them in the pantrophic mode, then they may improve the best traits that tend to accrue to a given position and lessen the weak traits. If they are able to influence the family, peer, and work settings, they may even assist a later-born to acquire the best traits of the firstborn. I therefore affirm that nothing is inevitable about position in the family constellation.

Contrasting Character Development between Older and Younger Sibs

A contrast emerges between the psychological milieu of the older and the younger children in the study of large family systems. The older ones are usually stronger, wiser, more capable, dependable, skillful, and knowledgeable. They have more opportunities for leadership within the family, are more often held up as models, have a better start in acceptance of household responsibilities, and more often act as teachers of their younger siblings.

The younger ones are disadvantaged as to power. They are more vulnerable to being teased, bullied, indulged, pressured, waited on, and sometimes exploited. The older ones grow up in a setting in which they received special attention from younger parents who were much in love and in good health. They also have a better chance of knowing their grandparents. The younger ones have less contact with both parents and grandparents but more contact with siblings. If one or two of the older children did well, the parents may relax on the supposition that the younger will do likewise. They may find it reassuring and comforting to see that the older ones are taking over the role of parenting. At the time the younger ones need shared activities with their parents, the latter are older, less vigorous, and less enthusiastic about the activities they had shared with the older children.

From the beginning, the younger sibs grow up in a family setting in which there are more relationships, more triads, and more potential for friction and conflict. While the younger ones are seeking to defend themselves against older siblings, at the same time they want protection and privileges. Since they cannot risk confrontations with more-powerful older siblings, they may develop great skill in covert strategies for getting even, such as tattling, dawdling, procrastinating, and surreptitiously instigating retaliation of an older sibling that is punished promptly by the parent. Sometimes they develop skills as mediators, and sometimes they learn to avoid family pressures by silently pursuing their own interests beyond the family setting. Older children have a right to complain that they had fewer material goods and less freedom than the younger ones.

We have observed in previous chapters the frequency with which the oldest brother and oldest sister have developed the qualities of leadership, responsibility, dependability, and capability and how often the youngest fail to acquire these qualities. There are exceptions, however, in both groups. A study of these exceptions leads to the identification of syndromes of circumstances that sometimes can be manipulated by parents so that, regardless of position in the family constellation, a child in any position can acquire desired traits.

Position does not automatically develop fine traits in the firstborn. These traits develop when the oldest takes on a useful function within the home that cultivates the skills for which he receives recognition. He receives additional recognition when his parents infer that he has the capacity to be a model for the younger children.

Early opportunity to perform useful functions revolves around housekeeping tasks and child care. A young child feels good about his first task accomplishment, and he feels even better when praised for it. He also places value on his achievement. A child who has just scrubbed the floor is the first to admonish against muddy feet.

In urban settings, opportunities for children to exercise their capacity for making decisions and judgments and carrying them out in a responsible manner deal more with outside jobs like delivering newspapers or with participation in group sports and school activities that require organizational, creative, or intellectual skills. Whether leader or follower, the essence of character has to do with the free assumption of responsibility for whatever needs to be done. The ability to identify quickly what needs to be done is a capacity greatly valued by employers. The free assumption of responsibility should not lead to exploitation. Parents sometimes exploit the oldest daughter who is overwhelmed with child care and household chores to the detriment of her social life. Single women are often exploited by married siblings who expect their unmarried sister to support and care for their aged parents.

Advantages in the development of leadership and responsibility are likely to accrue to the oldest child when we have circumstances including a parent (usually of the same sex) who serves as a reasonably good model for the oldest child and is thus in a position to suggest that the oldest serve as a model for the other children and a parent (also of the same sex) who is nurturant and supportive, orients the oldest to appropriate task roles, and has a reasonably good relationship with him. It is possible, however, for a first-born to acquire admirable qualities even though he has friction with the same-sex parent.

The essence of leadership is the ability to organize a group and to secure its cooperation without stirring up rebellion. A parent who induces rebellion in a child may be a poor model for training in leadership. In several of our cases in which the oldest son failed to acquire the desirable traits of his position, the father was absent from the home much of the time and was not involved in task roles or shared interests with his son.

Opportunities for training in leadership within the home are meager for the youngest child. He may, however, have an opportunity for such training in his peer group. This is why it is important for parents to have good knowledge of the peer setting of the youngest. This can be achieved by making the home a popular place for the peer group to gather. In the peer group, the only child exercises his ability as a leader. One reason why an only child is more likely to be a leader than the youngest of a large family is that the parents of the former are more alert for providing favorable group contacts.

To discourage the subtle, covert negative qualities of the youngest child, parents might refuse to accept tattling, protect the youngest from bossy siblings or from victimizing triangles, withhold nagging and pressures, and take special pains to introduce the youngest to appropriate task roles as early as possible. In the hustle and bustle of everyday life in a large family, these special pains are likely to go by default for a variety of reasons. Our data on the youngest is skimpier than for the oldest because, at the time a student from a large family is writing his family analysis, his youngest sibling often is still quite young.

Perhaps we should not leave our consideration of lastborn children without mentioning that they often make a great contribution to the family as a whole. I have in mind a family constellation in which the first three or four children are fairly close together and the youngest was born several years later. In one case the narrator said the birth of this baby was the best thing that ever happened to the family. She went on to explain how their quarrels abated as the whole family became interested in the growth and development of the baby brother. Another student wrote:

With the surprise coming of Jake three years ago, our family patterns changed considerably. First of all, he has united our family even more since we all are concerned with his actions. The beginning drift of the sisters away from the home influence has changed radically, and we are drawn to this center again. Naturally Jake gets much attention, not only in terms of love but also authority, since we all donate our ideas on how he should be raised. His arrival has given the whole family a sense of freshness as we watch him grow and learn, whereas otherwise things would be very dull and ordinary.

This paragraph does not tell us the whole story, but it does suggest that we should never neglect to recognize the contributions of young children to the growth of older family members.

All-Boy Families

In two families with four sons, there were boys without sisters in two generations. In both cases the mothers came from large families with both sexes. The secondborn son in constellation 10.2 wrote:

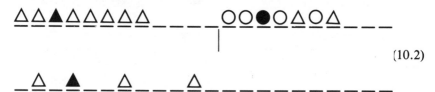

(10.2)

Unlike my mother, my father has more difficulty in relating to the opposite sex. I had no model to show me how a boy conveys his feelings to girls. I know that not having a sister, and thus not being exposed to the female point of view, has hurt me in my relationship with girls and my understanding of them. I never dated until my senior year in high school and then only sparingly. It wasn't until my experience with girls in college that I could understand them as persons.

My position as the second oldest has had a noticeable effect on my personality. First, my older brother used his superior strength to force me to submit to his will. This created rebellion on my part. In one traumatic episode, he broke his hand with a blow to my head.

Second, my parents often compared us by saying, "If it was good enough for him, it's good enough for you," and "If he did it, why can't you?" I rebelled at this kind of thinking until I developed a tendency to question traditional policies and became hostile to authoritarian figures that threatened my independence.

Third, there is something of a parallel between my position as the secondborn in a group of four boys and my father's position as thirdborn in a group of eight boys. My mother was also a thirdborn, but in a group of seven that included both sexes. My parents and I had to contend with older siblings and with younger ones. I think may father, especially, had a bit of hostility toward my older brother and found it easy to blame him for things. Possibly he displaced his resentment toward his older brothers onto his firstborn son.

However, one pattern of my parents did much to satisfy my ego and to increase my self-confidence. They praised my academic achievements and my superior athletic ability and made it plain that in these areas I was better than my older brother.

My youngest brother was spoiled. His desire for material goods has always been satisfied. He escapes from blame easily. He has been involved in delinquencies, yet he receives little or no punishment. This tendency to be so lenient with him on the part of my parents may reflect their experience in a previous generation in mothering and caring for their younger siblings.

We may assume from what was said and left unsaid that the youngest brother was indulged and not disciplined in task roles.

In constellation 10.3 we have another family of four sons. This family is hemitrophic—one parent is adequate and the other is not.

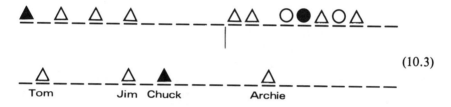

(10.3)

The father was oldest of four sons and possessed five of Toman's predicted traits for his position: leader, good worker, accepts the authority of those in a superior position, builds up property, and plans for his children's future. He was respected by his four sons. The other two traits (tends to treat girls like younger brothers and is politically conservative) were not ruled out.

The background of the mother seemed unfavorable. When she was six years old, her father died and she was raised by older, overprotective brothers. The narrator son wrote, "She seems to be a little girl always searching for a father." She married after a short courtship, and within a few years exercised domination over her husband through vociferous nagging and blaming. Her vindictive nature was illustrated by an incident in which she tore out the pages of her husband's high school yearbook that contained remembrances and honors he had received. It was alleged that the oldest son hated his mother for the way she treated his father. The narrator reported the second brother saying, "Because of the way my mother treats my father I learned to hate my mother as my father's wife, but as a mother to me I have great love for her." The father, described as a usually calm man, reacted to the verbal attacks of his wife with explosive wrath, producing constant turmoil and threats of divorce.

The oldest and youngest sons were especially sensitive to this conflict and were described by the narrator as nervous. The oldest son has none of the traits associated with his position in the family constellation. He entered a forced marriage with an immature woman who he feels tricked him into an unhappy marriage. He has, however, two beautiful children to whom he is attached.

Why did this oldest brother of brothers not acquire the better traits associated with this position? The answer is to be found in the character of the mother whose vicious, unwarranted verbal attacks on the father were deeply resented by all the sons. The narrator described his oldest brother as a sensitive person with many fine qualities who could have responded nicely to a mature and understanding wife. The father, also, was the oldest brother of brothers. Is it possible that men without sisters are disadvantaged in choosing a wife? The third son wrote, "Being in a family of all boys, I became quite shy around girls, and I still am in many aspects."

The youngest son was said to be overprotected by his mother, and Toman's characteristics for that position fit him well. "At an early age he constantly annoyed us, he is definitely an irregular worker, he can accept authority if it is not too demonstrative. Yell at him and he won't do it."

In another case, the oldest of five sons said he was more dominant and responsible than his brothers. However, he suffered from severe feelings of social inadequacy, not only because he had no sisters but also because of a bad family situation. His father was ignorant, domineering, and brutal. Internally the family was dystrophic, and externally it was isolated from the community. The father of these five sons had been cheated out of his childhood because, after the death of his mother when he was thirteen, he quit school to care for his younger siblings. The oldest son suffered from sexual ignorance and confusion until he reached college. He ended his paper with: "I doubt if I will ever establish my own family of procreation, but if I do, I will discard most of my present family's living patterns."

All-Girl Families

With respect to large families in our culture, it seems that it is easier for women in all-girl families to adjust socially to men than for men in all-boy families to adjust socially to women.

The spacing of the children in constellation 10.4 resulted in two dyads and one detached child. The emotional overtones were pantrophic, and the student referred to the excellent feeling among family members when they analyzed their family together. This was written as an alternate assignment after a family council discussion.

(10.4)

We have five girls born over a nine-year period. By the time the youngest was in the eighth grade, the oldest had moved away from home. The two oldest as well as the two youngest were close, while the middle one (myself) was distant from the other four. However, I always had my friends with whom I associated.

Although my parents made an effort not to show favoritism, each child at some time was considered by the rest to be the favored one. If one of us wanted something (like a new bike) and my parents could not afford a bike for each of us, no one got a new one. I respected my parents for this.

One feature that helps to distinguish pantrophic from dystrophic families is the presence or absence of parental favoritism. However, even in pantrophic families, children sometimes feel that a sibling is favored, but they get over such feelings later when they sense that the parents made efforts to treat them all fairly. Special circumstances make it difficult for parents to be convincing about impartiality—for example, the special attention a child with special needs requires or upward mobility so that younger children grow up at a time when extravagances are available.

In constellation 10.5, the three oldest girls constituted a dystrophic triangle in which the secondborn became the victim:

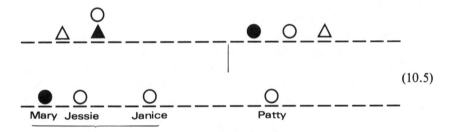

(10.5)

I (Mary) am the oldest of four sisters, and I've always had a great deal of responsibility. I've been able to exert a great deal of influence over my sisters as well as my parents. I've always been shy around boys. I often find it difficult to talk to them. This is probably due to the fact that I grew up without any brothers.

My father has a twin sister and an older brother, while my mother is oldest with one younger brother and a sister. This may account for my mother being somewhat more dominant than my father.

When my sister Janice, who is now thirteen, was a very small child, my seventeen-year-old sister Jessie and I used to compete for her attention. I always won probably because I was older and had more influence. For many years until the time my youngest sister Patty was born, Janice and I would team up against Jessie. Since it was two against one, Jessie often received much of the blame and punishment that Janice and I should have received. This is probably one of the explanations for the hostility we developed for each other. We often engaged in physical and verbal combat.

Although my parents have a happy relationship, our family has become somewhat unstable during the past five or six years. I feel that this has arisen from the emotional problems of my sister Jessie. She didn't create her own problems—she was forced into it by the treatment she received within our family unit. She was verbally and physically picked on more than the rest of us children and was made to feel inferior. This treatment caused her to run away from home a few times and even caused her to attempt suicide (although I don't think she ever meant to go through with it). I feel that I'm the only member of our family who even tried to help her. She has always looked up to me; she feels that whatever I say is right. I don't really know what I could do or say to help her except perhaps advise her to seek professional help.

Recently I had an exchange of correspondence with Mary who wrote that Jessie had been involved in a series of treatments by various professionals and that her prognosis for a recovery that would enable her to function as an independent member of society was not favorable.

Only Boy Oldest among Sisters

There were nine cases in which the only son was the oldest of three or four sisters. In one case the boy was mentally retarded. Of the remaining eight, three had problem sons who embarrassed their families. In these three cases, the fathers were deficient in the parental role, and the families were more or less dystrophic. This left five cases of the oldest brother of three or four sisters in which most of the boys had one or all of the traits as Toman described them, such as "Love is the most important of all concerns. Not a gang man. A good worker as long as there are female colleagues or co workers." In these five cases the younger sisters admired their brothers, and four of these families were reasonably pantrophic.

In constellation 10.6, the parents played a balancing-act game so that when the mother used a pet name for one child the father would counter with a pet name for the next older one, and this continued in a revolving pattern to include all four children.

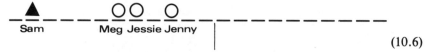

Sam   Meg Jessie Jenny

(10.6)

As Mom paid more attention to the youngest, my Dad seemed to give attention to the next one. When Meg was Mom's baby, I was Dad's boy; when Jessie was Mom's baby, Meg was his girl; when Jenny was Mom's baby, Jessie was his girl. Now that I'm Mom's baby, again Jenny is his girl. I guess it keeps all attention from one person. That's about all the favoritism you'll see in our family.

When we were all younger we fought a lot. I'd bait the girls and they'd bait me. We fought as couples and in teams of every variation. The baiting worked for a while, but then our parents must have figured us out, because later whenever we fought they punished all of us by not letting us play together. As we grew older, we fought less and less and now we seldom fight. There hasn't been any major jealousy between any of us.

This boy's report reaffirms the idea that no matter what the quality of the family, the success of parents in avoiding partiality among the children moves the family in the pantrophic direction.

In families in which the oldest is a boy followed by three or four girls, we may expect the oldest girl (secondborn) to take the lead in household tasks and become a proficient worker like the oldest sister of sisters.

Constellations 10.7 and 10.8 contrast the presence or absence of assigned task roles. Whether oldest, youngest, or middle child, the boy in this combination is surrounded by girls including the mother. It is important in such a combination for the father to present himself as a good model for the son, to allocate task roles for him, and to have one or more shared interests with him. Some fathers suggest to the son in subtle ways that, psychosexually, they are in the same boat.

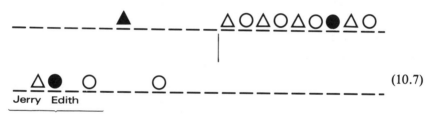

(10.7)

In constellation 10.7, the paternal grandfather was divorced soon after the birth of his son, who was then raised as an only child by mother and aunts. This child became, in the next generation, a father who was authoritarian, rigid, and unable to show affection. He failed to allocate chores or other responsibilities to his son Jerry, who was the oldest with three sisters. Household chores and care of younger sisters fell on Edith, who acquired the characteristics expected of her position. For a time the first three, who were close in age, formed an unstable triangle.

The mother came from a large family in which she was "picked on by older siblings," but she was said to be responsible, outgoing, fun loving and devoted to her children. This family may be described as hemitrophic.

In this orthodox family, the parents warned Edith, the narrator, against sexual aggression by boys and lectured her at length about the disgrace of a cousin who became pregnant premaritally.

Since there were no boys for Jerry to assume leadership over, the leadership position went to me. I had to watch the house and the girls if my parents were gone. Jerry could go off on his own merry way. When we were interacting, Jerry exercised the power of age; otherwise, I was in charge. Jerry didn't start dating until almost at the end of high school, and then because he was of the elite male sex, he could just about come and go as he pleased.

About this time, my eyes began to open as to how the double standard for the sexes operated. I could write volumes on Jerry's adventures and exploits. Maybe because he wasn't given leadership and responsibility, he has become reckless and irresponsible. He has quit school, taken off for months at a time, doesn't have any concept of how to handle money, feels the need to have sex with every girl he takes out, and seems to have more feeling for his friends than for the members of his family.

The family in constellation 10.8 is quite the opposite of that in 10.7.

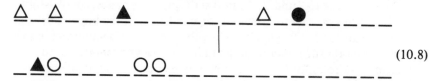

(10.8)

The mother suffered a period of poor health after the birth of her last child so that the brother assumed the responsibility for household chores and the care of his younger siblings. In this role he became unusually proficient. He said he became more fatherly than brotherly. He denied he had the traits of oldest brother of sisters, but his denial was a bit equivocal.

Love is important but not foremost. I am empathetic, not sympathetic. I work well with women, but most of my life I worked with men and I work well. Last, I was a member of a neighborhood gang, and competition seemed to be a spontaneous matter of self-pride.

Only Boy in the Midst of Sisters

The only son in the midst of sisters is worse off than if he were the oldest or youngest of sisters. His disadvantages can be overcome if the father establishes a good rapport with him. Sometimes a father will suggest in jest that he and the son form a defensive alliance. It is important for the father to participate in masculine activities with his son and be alert to neutralize overindulgence by women in the household.

The father in constellation 10.9 was alcoholic when the children were small, but later he became active in AA and was out of the home much of the time. When this father was a teenager, his own father died and his mother deserted the family. The oldest sister is narrator.

● △ ⃝ ⃝
Nancy Earl   June   Vi   (10.9)

I feel that my brother, being the only male sibling, was at the greatest disadvantage. Since my father was seldom home, it was up to my mother to discipline him. Having three daughters, she simply did not understand that a boy is by nature more aggressive and less sensitive than a girl. As a result, I think that my brother was sometimes unfairly picked on by all of the girls in the family, especially my mother. Sometimes, merely as a show of affection, he would throw one of us against the davenport or pull a ponytail. My mother would become quite angry at this and often forced him to spend the day in his room. My youngest sister liked to tattle on him, thus getting him in trouble. My brother so greatly resented the ensuing punishment that he claims he actually hates my littlest sister. After being sent to his room, he would usually displace his aggression violently by kicking holes in the walls or breaking the bed.

In constellation 10.10 the only son chafes because he was not given the same privileges as his older sisters. His resentment was increased by not being given the same liberties as his peers, who were alleged to be running wild. The situation was aggravated by conflict with the father over long hair.

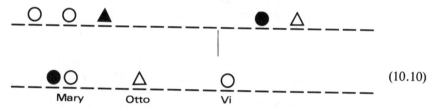

(10.10)

Mary   Otto   Vi

My brother seems to be the big problem. He's the only boy, and he feels "overgirled" and resents it. Otto rebels and does little or nothing. He says he's picked on—and to a certain extent he is—and his usual trick to get out of doing things is to go to his room or go outside.

In constellation 10.11 the only son is third with three sisters.

(10.11)

I was an above-average student, so naturally the teachers expected my brother to be exactly the same. As could be expected, he did exactly the opposite, withdrawing from competition and receiving very poor grades. When he got a D in English, my favorite class, the teacher said, tactlessly, "You're not much like your sister, are you?" My parents, however, reassured my brother that he was, indeed, a unique individual with talents of his own. After I went away to college, my brother proceeded to earn straight A's in math, physics, and chemistry—subjects I detested.

I think my brother has taken advantage of things given to him more than anyone else in the family. Consequently, he's the laziest, least thrifty, and is always looking for the easiest way out. While a child he was given the best opportunity to excell in anything, particularly sports, and as a result, he developed an aversion to them. Although he participated in sports briefly in high school, he never excelled, only playing to please society's concept of a man (or to sustain his self-concept as a man). During one season he sustained an injury that ended his sports career.

He later flunked out of college, worked in another city, and then came back to the open arms of Mom and Dad who financed him for a car and two more years of college. Finding he still wasn't a student, he joined the army.

This family had several strengths reported by the narrator, but the limited narrative does not explain enough. There is an implication of indulgence that may be significant, especially in the absence of any mention of task roles in the boy's life. It appears that the only brother of sisters has less opportunity to assume task roles within the home when older sisters have taken them over successfully.

The competent oldest daughter in the next case appraises the situation of her only brother. He had the advantages of sports ability and a stable family. The brother had two older sisters and two younger sisters. The oldest sister said:

Fred's position in the family has greatly affected his personality development. Being the only boy in the middle of four girls probably would have given any boy grief. All of us tend both to encourage and criticize him, mostly the latter. Fortunately Fred is very athletic, which pleases all of us, especially my father. We encourage his participation in sports because of his ability. Although he gets a lot of attention from us for being the only boy, he also receives a lot of static from us.

Our final case in this series is a boy with three older sisters and two younger sisters who did very well. The second daughter who narrates tells why.

Since my father and brother are outnumbered by girls, they tend to stick together. There is a definite favoritism here, but it's more or less of a joke in the family. My brother will be going around hitting all us girls, and Dad will come into the room and tell us to leave his boy alone.

We can sense from this excerpt that the father had a sense of humor and that he wanted to convey to his son that he understood how he felt in his sex isolation. In this family, roles were flexible and not especially sex typed. From the record I add this sentence: "When my father is working during the day, my brother can take over his role by making minor repairs, cutting the grass, taking out the garbage, opening pickle jars, and so forth." In this family the *hestia* obviously was fine.

A boy in the middle of many sistes is well aware of his status as such and so are the sisters. The latter want their brother to reveal his masculinity by being successful in manly pursuits. If he is successful, they are proud of him and often will "wait on him hand and foot." His status as an only boy among girls tends to make him overcompensate to prove masculinity. If he has a genuine interest in sports, he will have no problem, but if he gets off to a poor start, his interest in sports will be superficial and his participation will be only for ego gains on a temporary basis. As with all other cases, the background of a pantrophic family is most helpful.

Only Boy with Older Sisters

I have fewer cases of large families in which the lastborn is a boy with three or four sisters because, when any of the older sisters is in college, the youngest sib usually is too young to be assessed with respect to the influence of position in the family constellation. Five such boys were under seven years of age. Of these, two were said to be the center of attention, and one had the following of Toman's characteristics: expects and is willing to let women love and care for him without much regard for recompense; less competitive and reactive, procrastinates, works better with women than with men, and is not a leader. One twelve-year old boy was described as follows:

> When Tom was born there was real excitement among us girls. Tom was somewhat spoiled. He has had plenty of sisters to do things for him, and until he was six years old we really served him hand and foot. He is some-what of a procrastinator—and gets away with it. He is popular in his peer group and tends to be a leader.

One fourteen-year-old was said to be creative. He hitched his dog to a buggy with a long pole from which a carrot dangled in front of the dog's nose. The dog did not cooperate.

If a boy with older sisters is much younger than his sisters, he might grow up having three little mothers attending to his needs, and as an adult he might expect women to wait on him. The early departure of his sisters from home would leave him as an only child, as in several of the following cases.

In constellation 10.12 notice that the youngest is close in age to his sisters. The third sister narrates:

OOO● △ _ _ _ _ _ _ _ _ _ _ _ _ _ _ _ _ _ _ (10.12)
Tim

Tim, the youngest member of the family, contradicts Toman's ideas. Whereas he is expected to be some kind of spineless individual, he has become quite independent. Having three older sisters did not seem to bother him in the least. When people suggest to Tim that it must be hard to live with three older sisters, he reacts with complacency. To some extent Tim was spoiled, being the only son and youngest child, but this has never gone to his head. He has been kind and good-natured and has always been willing to go out of his way to help us. He has a tremendous amount of initiative and is finding new things to do with his time. My husband has called Tim the most well-adjusted member of the family, and I believe this to be true. He is now an activist in various causes.

In two cases, the youngest brother of three much older sisters described his own situation. Both families were stable and the parent-son relationships were good. Both boys felt they were handicapped by their position in the family constellation, but other factors hindered one boy and helped the other. The critical factor in the first case (constellation 10.13) was lack of physical coordination in a school setting where personal worth was rated only in terms of physical skills. Notice also that the age spacing is great compared to constellation 10.12. The boy Joe writes:

 (10.13)

My four older sisters and myself each were spaced exactly four years apart. They were so much older they were unbeatable in battle—verbal or physical—particularly with no brother to help me. Needless to say, I had little power in decision making and found myself enjoying playing games with the girls like dolls.

Such a position does not aid in the development of leadership or dominance traits, and it certainly didn't in my case. What it did produce was a feeling of insecurity within my own sex group and pretty much an overall shyness when confronting any persons outside my own family.

The oldest sister, twelve years older than Joe, left for college when he was seven. She seemed more like an aunt to him, and he had pleasant memories of her. The second sister was so dominant over him that he referred to her as one who "wanted to be a mother or prison guard or something. She was bossy and I used to have a few hot fights with her." He had a close relationship with the third sister and played with her and her girlfriends. He described his relationship with his father and his peers as follows:

I don't believe there was any favoritism on the part of my mother or father, maybe because I was the youngest and only son. I would consider myself as having been closer to Dad than to Mom, which I suppose is natural for a son. Both parents tended to stick up for me a little, being rather defenseless against my sisters. My role in peer groups was an unhappy one. Having all older sisters and no brothers, I was naturally uneasy with members of my own sex. Besides this, my father never taught me anything about baseball, football, or basketball.

When I entered school, my shyness, coupled with my inability to do things other little boys did, led to few acquaintances and to even fewer friends. It didn't take long to become known as an outcast. It always seemed wrong to me that our society put such emphasis on sports. I relied on my home life and would get home as fast as possible after school.

In about the fourth grade the teachers spent part of each day teaching the kids competitive sports and forcing them to play. My problem, however, was too complex to be resolved simply by learning the rules. For one thing, I have very little interest in such sports. Second, I had not developed the average degree of coordination that most other kids had. Third, having few friends, I had even less self-confidence—and for good reason, since I played "like a little girl."

From here the vicious cycle was set. The more I was forced to play these games, the more I made a fool of myself and the more I became an outcast. The more I became an outcast, the less self-confidence I had and thus, the less chance to learn. By the sixth grade I was used to being laughed at and pushed around and was well aware of being a coward—mainly because I didn't know how to fight and no one would back me up. When I got to junior high, with its formal physical education classes, things were much worse. I began to hate school with great intensity and would just dream about the weekend and getting home. My grades fell from straight As to Cs and Ds. I became afraid of people.

In high school people tend to grow up a lot. They start judging others more by who they are, rather than what they can do. So at this point, I made more friends and things were easier. Unfortunately, the damage had been done. I could not be an outgoing person and found myself terribly uncomfortable and out of place at social affairs or among any group of people. I preferred being alone. In short, I was, and to some extent still am and always will be, highly self-conscious and nervous around people.

As one might infer from what I have said thus far, any dating or courtship on my part was negligible until after high school. Actually, I never did go out with a girl until after I graduated.

Although the home setting in this case was quite favorable, the school setting was destructive. The unfortunate combination of poor physical coordination and a series of teachers, each of whom had a compulsion for promoting competitive sports, produced a synergistic effect that was devastating to the young boy's personality.

In the second case (constellation 10.14), the boy had good coordination that found expression in a favorable peer setting.

I must admit that I was a little shocked to learn of the unique characteristics due to position; I must also admit in all honesty that some of the characteristics of the youngest brother of sisters are applicable to me. Since my sisters were much older and since there was an absence of children my age, I had to entertain myself and make my own decisions. I think that I was sufficiently involved with my sisters so that I avoided some of the characteristics of an only child, which I was in a sense after my sisters left the household. (They all married at nineteen or twenty.)

I have always thought I am a capable leader and organizer and I recall that I considered myself the leader in my peer group. I organized baseball and football teams and made up schedules and rosters. I belonged to 4H, held offices, and worked on committees. Because I went to a small rural school for eight years, there was not much competition and I naturally became accustomed to taking the lead inside and outside the classroom.

In one case, the only boy in his struggle against three older and stronger sisters expressed a need for a brother who could be his ally. An adequate father figure who could convey to his son how he feels might be a boon to such a lad. In such unbalanced families, one may hear the facetious expression, "We men have to stick together."

It is apparent that, while generalizations about the relationship between sibling position and character traits are satisfying for scholars, they are of little value to a person who wants to improve his family unless he also analyzes his family constellation in several generations, taking note of age and sex differences, the operation of subgroups, the connection between favoritism and sibling conflict, and the settings of family members. Many of my students have expressed to me their gratifications for so doing. (A chapter with student excerpts that testified to the value of making a family analysis was omitted for lack of space.)

Two Boys and Two Girls

I now consider several cases in which we have two boys and two girls in various positions in families of four or five children. Notice how well the narrator in constellation 10.15 expresses the yen for self-identity and the preservation of her individuality.

This case alerts parents neither to reward children for passivity nor to suppress rebellious individuality just because the former is restful and the latter is annoying. The first three children in this case constituted a triangle in which the oldest sided with the youngest against the secondborn who wrote:

Bill   Lilly   Bobby

(10.15)

This led to much resentment and competitive feelings on my part. I felt that no matter what I did I could never be as good as Lilly in the eyes of my family. She seemed to go along with what anyone said. She never had opinions of her own. This agreeableness was pleasing to my parents. I, in contrast, had ideas of my own and too often did not go along with what the others said or did. Consequently, I was rebellious and resentful because they failed to give me credit for having a mind of my own. Often I thought it would be better if I only did and said what they wanted. I decided not to submit to someone else's opinions for fear of losing my individuality.

Then my first real break came. My mother gave birth to a baby boy. Lilly was no longer the baby of the family, and I was given responsibility for caring for Bobby. I now received more recognition than ever before. I was in charge. I became Mother's helper and received praise from morning to night. I was in the spotlight now and could show everyone that I was just as good as Lilly. Bill, Lilly, and I grew closer together. We joined clubs and showed similar interests. Since Bill and I were the oldest, we fought to get to do things (known as breaking the ice) while Lilly could step right in and do immediately what we had had to fight for.

Lilly seemed, through these years, much closer to our father than to Bill or myself. I feel that, since my father was an only child, he could relate better to Lilly who was the youngest for a period of eight years. I was closer to Mother because I was willing to care for my younger brother. I feel that perhaps Mother identified with me because in her youth she cared for younger brothers as I was now caring for Bobby. This seemed to draw us together. She trusted me and let me accept responsibilities at an early age. To my mother, Bill was a protector for his younger sisters and a masculine representative for the family.

The following relationships seem strongest: I to my mother and younger brother, Bill to both parents. Lilly to my father, Bobby to my mother and me. Through the years I developed a sense of responsibility and a watchfulness for younger people. Through these experiences, my personality has developed.

Assertive individuality is a precious thing to be fostered. In this case it found a legitimate outlet in the assumption of responsibility that led to growth.

We have been considering families that were somewhat out of balance psychosexually. Constellation 10.16 is different; it is in perfect balance.

(10.16)

Perhaps one of the main contributing factors to the happiness and success of my family is our evenly distributed family configuration. My family constellation is well balanced. I have an older brother and a younger brother eight years apart, an older sister and a younger sister six years apart, with myself acting as a fulcrum four years from either brother and three years from either sister. My parents knew how to keep the constellation in balance, showing no favoritism to any one member. They also kept it in balance by reprimanding one who was threatening to knock it out of balance and by praising one who did something good, thus strengthening it and keeping it in line.

Communication has played a very important role in the success and happiness of my family. My parents have never held themselves aloof from us. As a matter of fact, just to point out how they tried to keep communication with us, my mother would make a point of trying to stay in touch with the latest fashions and jargon of our generation. She wanted to be in the in crowd. I was proud to show her off to my friends. My father was a dedicated family man. He took on the role of a father with as much seriousness as his job. Pretty unusual, I learned, for a businessman. He even turned down a better job just so he could spend more time with his family.

Because my mother tried to stay with her kids' generation, the communication between us was tremendous. My father bridged the gap with his terrific sense of humor, often sharing jokes with us that his business associates had told him. Hostility, rejection, indifference, favoritism, overprotection, and other noncohesive family characteristics were virtually nonexistent. We never felt a need for love because we knew it was always there.

The narrator opined that, because of his position in the middle of the constellation, he had an advantage in relating to both sexes and to older and younger persons.

While each member in my family is an individual in his own right, our family hasn't set any goal so that one might accomplish it and one might not. Our family is flexible in order to take into account differences in each member. Values that one holds may differ from those of another, but each is respected and taken into consideration. Thus, each member gets a feeling that he is worth something. Because we all get a feeling of worthiness from our family, it has given us confidence and independence.

The chance of having such a family in perfect balance is remote, and perfect balance by itself is not sufficient to develop a pantrophic family.

Reverse Leadership

Our cases have indicated that, ordinarily, the firstborn takes the lead over the secondborn. Occasionally, however, this pattern is reversed and the secondborn takes the lead. I call this reverse leadership, and it comes about as a result of the convergence of several circumstances.

In the following case, Doris, the narrator and second daughter, developed a bond with her mother, also the secondborn, Doris developed a bond with her mother because of similar academic and domestic interests in contrast to Mary, the eldest, who had other interests. The father, next to the last child in a large family, also seemed to favor Doris in her disputes with

Mary. According to Doris, this partiality was increased because of her childhood illness.

> Toman's ideas on the older child dominating the younger do not apply at all to my family. Mary and I were born three years apart, and four years and seven years later two boys were born, also three years apart. As might be expected, my older sister Mary seemed to dominate in the beginning and to take the lead when we played, but only until I was about five. At this time many factors came into play that caused my parents to take my side more often during arguments. Now, instead of her winning because she was older and stronger, I was winning more often. I think the most important factor for my parents' attitude was my illness.
>
> It was not long before Mary realized that I was going to start taking the lead. Unconsciously, she withdrew from competition. The tables were switched. I was the leader, she the follower. By the time I was six or so we began playing my games and did things my way. When I'd have Daddy settle any disputes that arose, incongruously enough, the settlement went my way. As we became older, I made more decisions between us. I was always able to pull my dad's leg to get the car more often than she was, and whenever we got ourselves into trouble at home, it was always her fault because she was older and should know better, even when what we had been up to was my idea. This was never a conscious pattern. I am sure my folks never meant to be unfair; nevertheless, this pattern persisted for many years.
>
> About a year ago, Mary talked to her psychology professor, and as they were discussing family patterns, this subject came up. The professor made her realize that it was important not to let her younger sister win all the arguments—especially when Mary was right. I noticed a marked change in Mary's resistance to my ideas almost immediately and realized that I had been dethroned.
>
> The surprising part of it was that neither of us had consciously realized the pattern. It had begun when we were both so young, and it just continued to be more significant. I am sure that it has had more adverse effects on her than on me. It has been a big part, I am sure, of her relatively difficult adjustment.
>
> I can see this happening to the boys, too, although in their case it has not been brought on by our parents. Eric is fifteen, Mac is twelve, but already Mac is nearly as big as Eric. Eric has become less apt to start a fight with Mac now than he was even a year ago. It is not going to be long before Mac will be able to beat him. Mac is already able to beat him in their one-man sides of football. They don't play football as often any more. This is a more-normal pattern than Mary's and mine, and it is not apt to bring on any difficulties in adjusting. Eric prefers to study anyway, whereas Mac is more the energetic, nervous type. Mac and I have always had an easier time making friends, whereas Eric and Mary are the studious one and the serious type, like my dad. Mac and I have Mom's witty sense of humor.

Constellation 10.17 illustrates the importance of function. In families having both boys and girls, the girls are often expected to do the household chores and care for the infants. The girl in this case, although thirdborn, acquired leadership over her older brothers within the home because she took over the chores. Later, her youngest brother helped her with the chores, and he became a responsible person with none of the negative traits attributed to the youngest son.

△   △●   ○   △   (10.17)
Dan Joshua   Silas

Although I am in the middle of five children, my position as the older of two daughters has had a significant effect upon my personality and attitudes toward the other members of the family. I have assumed a position of leadership in some matters over my brothers and sister. For example, when my parents went out of town on business trips, I was left in charge of the household because my older brothers could not cook or clean the house. Many times I got my way by threats—either they listened to me and did what I wanted or else they could cook their own dinner and wash their own dishes. This position has given me a feeling of dominance and leadership and a high degree of responsibility in my work, especially when I am in charge of others. All this has given me the idea that age, sex, and position are less important than the free assumption of responsibility. Although my brothers were older, I dominated them like a mother in certain situations. Since I continually demanded equality with my brothers when I was younger, I instantly rebel against anyone who advocates inequality of the sexes. In return for my concern over my brothers' health and welfare, my parents assumed a protective role over me and defended me in any discord with persons outside the family. Thus, I hold the protective image of the man in high regard.

My youngest brother Silas has become a source of delight to the family. He loves to help with the chores because it makes him feel grown-up and he likes to have others depend on him. Silas is the opposite of Toman's characteristics of the youngest brother of brothers. He is responsible and affectionate.

Violation of Generational Role Boundaries

In most societies, reciprocal roles are divided according the generation—that is, some role relationships should be confined only to adults and others only to children. For example, a husband should play the role of lover only to his wife and not to his daughter. The incest taboo is almost universal. If the mother should act like a sister to her daughter, or a brother act like a father to his sister, we may expect confusion and disharmony. All such relationships that cross generational boundaries are unhealthy and dystrophic.

We have seen, nevertheless, that in large families older brothers and sisters play quasi-parental roles to much younger children. In these cases, however, the final arbiter is still the parent. The oldest sister in such cases is assuming authority over younger children temporarily, not as the mother but as the oldest sister who is accountable to the mother. If the older sister should try to exercise authority over her younger siblings as the latter approach adulthood, there will be trouble.

One of the strains in one-parent families arises from the confusion of roles when the oldest son, after the departure of the father, is required to play the paternal role for the family. Some students have said that after the death of the father, the mother took over the roles of both father and mother. As such, she might allocate responsibilities to the oldest son, not as the obligation of a father but only as that of the oldest son, with the understanding that the other siblings must share his burden as soon as they are able. The obligation of the state in providing support for fatherless children may be based partly on an unconscious desire to avoid violation of generational boundaries. The next two quotations illustrate, among other things, how the slightest tendency to play extragenerational roles leads to confusion and resentment.

> After my brother was married, he didn't seem like a brother to me at all but a father. I hated that. Although I was sure of his love for me, I felt like he was disciplining me and that I could never do anything right. Finally, one time when he was visiting, I became particularly upset and went to my room and cried. My mother came in and I told her the problem, demanding that she not mention it to Vernon. Well, she did out of concern for me. Later Vernon came to my room, never mentioning the matter in conflict, and just chatted for a while. Ever since that day he has returned to being my brother.

In the second illustration, a mother attempts two roles.

> My father's business kept him away from home much of the time. Victor was the lastborn, and we three older children exploited him cruelly for our enjoyment. He was the perfect scapegoat and stool pigeon, and we used him for both roles. Mother prodded and punished Victor for not attaining a satisfactory academic record. Her nagging, reprovals, and admonitions provoked strong resentment and disrespect toward his mother. As for myself, I have gone through greater conflict with my mother than with any other person I have known. Since early childhood, I have been a good student and usually assumed the role of leader. Perhaps because she never went to college herself, my mother has been somewhat jealous of my achievements in both scholastic and extracurricular activities. Trying to gain our confidence by being chummy and sisterly yet clinging to the authority of a mother, our mother has established a pattern of conflicting roles that has only further alienated her from the rest of the children.

Toman's statement that the oldest brother of brothers tend to treat women as younger brothers is summarized in his phrase, "tough with women." Very few students used this expression. One who did was the oldest of three brothers and two sisters with the sexes alternating at three-year intervals. He said:

> I think that the characteristics Toman lists as those of the oldest brother of brothers, even though I do have sisters, fit me perfectly. The one that hits home the hardest is the characteristic of being a tough guy with women. Because of this toughness and often cruel behavior, it has already cost me a couple of girls who would have been wonderful mates.

The oldest of three brothers and a sister in the next family deals with the same problem but from the opposite perspective.

> In my junior high school years, I had many friends of my own sex, but girls shied away from me. I remember reading an article in a magazine that said that girls don't like to be treated like fragile, precious things. The article went on to say that girls didn't like guys who were gentle, courteous, and kind. I realized then that I had been trying too hard, all I needed was to be myself. So I tried being Mr. Hard Guy and, to my amazement, it worked.

What Do Women Really Want?

I have been impressed over the years with the number of women who said they liked dominant men. Is this because they feel more comfortable in a follower role, that the presence of the dominant man absolves them from decision making, that dominance symbolizes material success, a mantle of protection and masculinity? Or are such women looking for a man who resembles their own dominant fathers? I come back to this question when discussing parent image in chapter 17.

In our consideration of families with dyads to families with four and five children, we have seen varying degrees of competition and varying methods that parents have used in dealing with competition among children.

Pantrophic families stress the uniqueness of each person and encourage each child to develop whatever capacites he has. They may also be alert to send certain children to different classes, different teachers, and different schools. They will find it helpful to chart the family constellation and examine relationships as my students have done.

11 Large Family Systems

As one considers families of six or more children, one sees complexities of structure and interaction that are baffling. The two are inextricably intertwined. I limit this chapter only to structure and touch upon questions related to size.

The very large family has a greater number of middle children who, at one time, may receive treatment as the youngest in a subgroup and who later command the position of oldest in a younger subgroup. Experience in both such positions may lead to more-flexible personalities compared to those who remain in either the oldest or the youngest position. A large family provides an expanded audience within the family for each developing ego, but this audience becomes more sib and less parental. Often when the oldest child leaves home, the next in line takes over leadership and quasi-parenting functions. Our excerpts contain increasing reference to the influence of brothers and sisters on personality development.

In spite of many children in a family, the number who influences any one in a meaningful way is limited. This is because the older ones leave home before the younger ones are old enough to interact with them. Some students wrote that such older siblings were more like aunts or uncles than brothers or sisters. In one family with twelve children, the last two were born while the narrator was in college. When she got home, "it was like they belonged to somebody else. It took me a long time to get adjusted to the fact that these kids were a part of our family."

In constellation 11.1, the middle child, a girl, is the only one among the children who has interacted significantly with all the others.

$$\underline{\quad OO \quad \triangle \quad \bullet \quad\quad\quad OOO \quad\quad\quad \triangle} \quad \text{(11.1)}$$

There is an age range of twenty-one years between the oldest and youngest in our family, with me falling about in the middle. In a sense, I'm the youngest of the four older children and the oldest of the five younger children. Being the youngest of the first troop, I have been compared scholastically with them at home as well as at school. I have been expected to earn similar grades and exhibit similar behavior. This wasn't difficult. Being the youngest also had its advantages. I was the baby of the family for six years and the center of attention. My older sisters helped me with feminine activities. I had to play rough games with my older brother or he wouldn't play with me, and there were no kids in the neighborhood.

As the oldest of the second group, I had many new responsibilities as soon as the older ones left home. I learned to take care of little kids, and I showed them the interest and concern that my mother was unable to give them. I also think I set a good example, not only for the little ones but also for my parents, because they could see that I got the results without using undue punishment. My sisters came to see me with their problems because my parents have never communicated well with their children. As the oldest at home, I took the majority of my mother's criticism when things went wrong. After so much nagging, one becomes indifferent to it and lets it go in one ear and out the other. My attitude of indifference isn't good because sometimes when my mother does give me good advice I refuse to follow it just because it comes from her. Another effect of her criticism is that I'm very unsure of myself at times, especially in stating my opinions and making decisions.

Large families have greater potential for the formation of subgroups of dyads, triads, or divisions such as the four big kids and the four little kids. Sometimes a laterborn group is referred to as the second family. Constellations 11.2, 11.3, 11.4, and 11.5 have subgroups as indicated by brackets.

(11.2)

If our family relationships were diagrammatically represented, permeable boundaries could be set up around certain dominant groups as indicated.

(11.3)

We often divided into pair groups: my sister and I, the two older boys, and the two younger boys. My mother encouraged this in many ways.

(11.4)

It is almost like there were two children from three completely different and separate families.

(11.5)

1st Family   2nd Family

The oldest daughter in both of these groups had similar bossy traits.

In constellation 11.6, there were three groups of sibs with three in each group.

△_O△_____△△△_____●_△__   (11.6)
                                                     △
                   Beverly

After commenting about the age discrepancy between herself and the oldest group, Beverly wrote: "I can cut the three oldest siblings off the list of family members who have influenced my life through family interaction."

As a young girl Beverly played the big-sister role to her younger twin brothers and to her male peers. She developed early the capacity to be a confidante to men. As such, the boys did not date her "because she made such a darn good sister." When she matured in her teens, she became more involved with the middle group of brothers who were six to nine years older and were now married. She describes her role as a sisterly confidante to them:

It is a feeling that I will never be able to express because it is so moving, so significant, and so beautiful for me to be so highly regarded by my brothers. To have these relatively unemotional men pour out their hearts to their little sister is touching. I treasure these moments as I know they do. This alone has done me more good than anything else I could ever think of. As far as my little brothers go, I can see them moving toward me as my older brothers have done. I don't regret not having more sisters because my brothers are and always will be some of the most precious people in my life.

As a member of a large family, Beverly makes some observations about competition and the expression of affection:

Competition—well, there was no detrimental competition. We are all so individual that no one tried to prove himself better than the other. The only possible bad competition occurred between the twins, and that only came about by other people comparing them. I'm happy with the amount and degree of competition in my family. As for dominance, submissiveness, hostility, jealousy, and cooperation, I feel my family fares excellently.

After commenting about the age discrepancy between herself and the oldest group, Beverly wrote:

The one area in which our family scores low is in the matter of expressing affection. Little affection is openly expressed, although I know it's there. To me, this is very sad. I well know that every one of us children has a little hurt in our heart from the absence of open affection. I have that hurt because, although I know my parents love me very much, I was never really sure because I'm the type of person who needs to be told that love is there, and I know that's true of my siblings.

Ordinarily, a middle child who plays the role of a younger sibling gradually changes his role to that of an older child. The reversal of such roles took place suddenly with the tragic death of the oldest brother in constellation 11.7.

△___○___▲_○___△○_____ (11.7)
Earl   Ellie Kevin Connie Wayne Meg

> I was a little brother to Earl and Ellie and a second big brother to Connie, Wayne, and Meg. I never saw myself as a big brother until Earl died, and then I found myself in a role with which I was unfamiliar. For quite a while I would compare myself with Earl and what I thought of him. There was no way I could measure up. Being a different type of person, I couldn't perform the role exactly as he had and thus ran into some problems. Once the role was altered to suit my personality, I felt more comfortable. Things were all right, at least in my relationship with Connie and Meg. I could never get together with Wayne, and this has been a source of guilt for me. I had difficulty in adjusting to the change from little brother to big brother.

When a dozen children are milling around in the living room, the parents may have more important things to do than to examine report cards and compare grades. The greater variety of personalities in a large family may increase appreciation for individual uniqueness. Out of seventy papers describing large families, only two mentioned that withdrawal from competition had been a problem. Many indicated that competition was fierce. However, it is not the kind of competition found in small families that is usually focused on a single sibling, but more like the scramble for food in a litter of puppies. We sensed this sort of competition in the next family, constellation 11.8, in which fourteen children were born within a space of eighteen years. The female narrator in the middle of the sib constellation writes:

_○_△○_○△△●▲__○△△△△__ (11.8)

> Relationships among the youngest children are characterized by quite a bit of dominance. Any child feels he can tell a younger one what to do. I have often heard the phrase, "Well, I'm older than you, so you do what I tell you to." The reply often is, "Oh no, Dad is the boss." In this group, rebellion and competition are high. There is competition over things such as who can eat the most, get their work done first, run the fastest, or hit the ball hardest. Of course, there has always been competition between all my siblings, each trying to be the best in something—grades, athletics, or sports.

It seems that in small families a child competes against a single rival but that in large families he competes against all. A number of cases give this impression. In a family of six children, the oldest daughter writes:

After a few years there was a lot of competition. My mother pushed this. We took lessons in swimming, tennis, piano, and guitar. We competed against each other in many kinds of events. This helped us develop in all sorts of ways.

In a family of seven children, the narrator writes:

There was no withdrawal from competition, but there was a sense of competition in our family. Although no one pushed me, I felt that I had something to live up to, and I actually did try just a bit harder to do better than my older brothers had done.

The oldest son in a family of nine children says:

There is almost always some degree of hostility within a large family. There's never enough to go around, so there's always fighting for the bike or the trucks, or who will wash and who will dry the dishes. In a large family it's hard to satisfy everyone at the same time.

As far as withdrawal from competition is concerned, there's never been any in our family. All the little kids are raring to get into whatever the next one is into. The smaller ones learn to accept things as they are and not be dejected if they cannot be as good as the older ones. In fact, it gives them an incentive to do better.

As far as jealousy goes, I don't think there is any. When one gets a good break or if he is lucky, the others are glad for him and are, in fact, proud of him.

When there is an ever-present economic squeeze, the family theme often centers around work and wages. Everybody is supposed either to work hard in the family enterprise or to earn money on the outside. Another hardship arises from overcrowding. There is more noise, confusion, disorder, and the ever-present lag in things to be done. One student in a family of nine children wrote, "I honestly feel that, if we had a larger house, the conflicts would be cut down by one-half."

Many references show how the hardships arising from a combination of limited income and a large family have spurred a child to develop skills relating not only to child care and housekeeping but also to budgeting, organization, and leadership. A secondborn and first daughter wrote:

I knew how to take care of babies, cook, sew, and clean by age ten. When I was nine I babysat for a neighbor who had five children. Everything I possess I acquired on my own. I learned how to handle money efficiently and became quite independent. My parents have a lot of respect for me, and I have the same for them. They admire me because I am very responsible. I show my individuality in my family in a dominant manner. I have a very good relationship with the other children in my family.

Another oldest daughter told me how the confusion and disorder of her large family in a house too small had driven her father out to find surcease in a tavern. He didn't drink much but he got a rest. The mother followed suit and joined her husband in the tavern, and the daughter proceeded to reorganize the household and became most proficient.

We tend to associate large families with greater economic and psychological strain, but among my sample of seventy families having six or more children, sixteen appeared to be in the high pantrophic range. The occupations of the fathers in this group were: two M.D.s whose wives were R.N.s, one successful attorney, one successful farmer, one airplane pilot, three businessmen, two managers, two truck drivers, one barber, one rural mail carrier, one school principal, and one semiskilled repairman. None of the student narrators in these families complained about economic hardship. The presence of wealth, however, does not prevent the development of dystrophic patterns. Among the dystrophic families were more laborers and very few college-educated fathers.

The oldest daughter in large families is often exploited in house-keeping and child-care responsibilities. One such girl, who had one older brother in a family of eleven children, wrote:

From the age of seven, I was introduced to housework and the care of younger children. I resented this responsibility. I did not explain how I felt since my father always told me that this was my duty as the oldest girl. I wanted to please him, but I resented him more because of it. My mother is obscure in my memory of those years. I never wanted to be like her; she was never free to talk or listen, always busy having more children and bringing in more work. I often thought of running away, even attempted it several times, with bitter results. The memories of home during those years are very unhappy. I never talked to my family except when it was necessary. This was probably another factor in my nervousness. Today I realize how these experiences have helped me. Being with my brothers and other boys taught me to be outspoken and to stand up for my beliefs. I have satisfying friendships with members of both sexes and feel confident in relationships with other people.

Some mothers, from their own childhood experience, are aware of the risk of overburdening the oldest. A daughter of such a mother wrote:

I think being the eldest of seven children has been advantageous to me. It made me capable of handling children. I understand them much better than do most girls my age, and I love them. My mother was careful not to tie me down with the children more than necessary. She often hired a babysitter so we could enjoy our own social lives. One reason my mother was so conscientious about this was that she often had been forced to babysit for her nieces and nephews, and she resented it.

In constellation 11.9, Daisy, the narrator, has three older sisters to take the lead in housework, pave the way, and make decisions.

_OO_ _O●_△_ _ _ _O_ _O_ _ _△_ (11.9)
                Carrie

The reader may speculate, since Daisy has three older sisters to take over feminine task roles, that there would be little for her to do. The older brother would take over male task roles. By the time the older sisters were out of the household, care responsibilities and leadership would devolve upon Carrie. This is what Daisy had to say:

> I was not a strong leader or dominant character at home. By being in the middle, I didn't have any responsibilities but to take care of myself. Many times I got out of tasks because someone else could do them. I tended to follow and go along with my older sisters, It made it easy for me to try things without everyone watching to see what would happen. Also, my sisters broke my parents into new ways and ideas so that, by the time I was ready to ask for a favor, it was readily granted to me. It is hard for me to make decisions on my own. I always wanted the advice of someone before I made a final decision.

In this family, the three youngest children constituted a satisfying subgroup in which the oldest (Carrie) was described as "definitely the leader and a very hard worker."

Constellation 11.10 has two groups: the big kids and the little kids. They are all fairly close in age, with the female narrator in the midst of five brothers. If a child is the oldest of siblings or of a subgroup, he or she will be cast (if functional opportunities are favorable) into the role of model, decision maker, and leader and, through the exercise of such roles, will become responsible, dependable, and capable. It makes no difference whether the oldest is boy or girl. Toman's traits for the oldest brother of brothers and the oldest sister of sisters should be recast to stress traits of independence, dominance, responsibility, dependability, and capability.

_△_ △_ ●_ △_ △△_ _O_ _ _ _ _ _ _ (11.10)

> I'm glad I come from a large family. It teaches you to live and get along with all types of people. According to Toman's family constellation, I fit into two categories: oldest sister of brothers and younger sister of brothers, although I have one sister eight years younger. I've had to stand on my own feet and take care of others since I started grade school. With my mother working all the time, I had to take on a lot of the responsibilities at home.

Presently I'm president of a sorority, and that certainly requires standing on your own feet and helping others. I know I cut people short in a discussion. I have a mind of my own when it comes to certain things. I stop and weigh both sides of a question, but once my mind is made up, forget trying to change it. I would like very much to marry an older man who is established in the world. Men tend to confide in me. This is especially true of my brothers. They tell me many things they would never tell Mom or Dad. They respect my opinion and ask my advice. This makes me very happy that I'm their sister.

What is the explanation for large families in the United States? Some writers explain it in terms of lower-class culture, ignorance, carelessness, nonavailability of contraception and religious taboos. These account for only part of the phenomenon; we also have large families among the sophisticated affluent.

The reader has noticed variations in the way parents react emotionally to offspring in different stages of growth from conception to maturity. Women may be either elated or depressed during pregnancy, elated or discomforted during childbirth, elated or frustrated during the early childhood of offspring, or feel a sense of fulfillment or disappointment during the adolescence of their offspring. These various feelings may be due to a variety of factors including the varying capacity of parents to nurture children at different stages of growth.

Husbands, likewise, experience different psychological states during these periods. One of the advantages of the two-parent family is the better chance that at least one parent will be adequate during each stage of growth for all the children.

Some readers, no doubt, can recall cases similar to the one we are about to discuss in which the mother experienced psychological elation during pregnancy and childbirth but who was quite willing to let others take over the nurturing after weaning. When this occurs the oldest daughter may be exploited, and unless the father is concerned and nurturant, the children may have problems.

The ideal situation would be two parents, both of whom have healthy emotional attitudes toward offspring of both sexes throughout every stage of child development but neither of whom would have any compulsion for multiple pregnancies that would entail exploitation of the oldest children or that would impair health or child-rearing processes. This, of course, does not take into consideration the ethics of overpopulation.

The yen to have many children is not to be explained entirely by commonsense logic. Some persons are fascinated by the growth of children as others are by the growth of flowers and pets. The desire for children and more children, or the determination not to have any at all, may be due to a learning process that has had its origin in childhood. With career women, the satisfactions of parenthood seem to be satisfied quite well with only one or two children.

In constellation 11.11, the female narrator, the oldest of eleven children, tells about her experience and tries to find out why her mother had so many children. After four children, her parents divorced, and after her mother remarried, there were seven more. They all remained with the mother.

(11.11)

Divorce

I have developed leadership qualities in the home because I was the oldest and had to assume adult responsibilities at an early age. I was also hot tempered and let my feelings and ideas be known among my siblings. In school situations I was not a leader and not very outgoing. I was oldest in the family but youngest in the peer group. I have the first seven characteristics Toman listed for the oldest sister of sisters and the first two he listed for the oldest sister of brothers. In addition, I tried to be feminine, friendly, kind, and sensitive. I still feel the need to compete with my siblings for my mother's love, possibly because there are so many among which to divide it.

I began to see myself as a mother image in fourth grade. I loved my brothers and sisters, not like a sister but like a mother. This created problems as my two sisters got older because they didn't want two mothers, they wanted me to be their older sister. I still haven't overcome this feeling, but I'm trying.

After a few more of my mother's babies arrived, I got sick and tired of dirty diapers, crying babies, playing mother, and a disordered household. I began to hound my mother, "Why, why, why, so many babies? Finally, after her tenth, I nearly had a nervous breakdown. I was almost sixteen years old and, as usual, had to take care of the household while she was in the hospital. I cleaned the house every day, the meals were well prepared and on time, and the kids behaved. I put my whole self into getting the place in order. When Mother came home that July day, I fell apart and needed a good day's sleep. I was always hurt by more babies in the house. I felt each additional one created a burden. The strange thing was, I was glad when my mother wasn't around, and I felt important accomplishing something. But I never received praise for caring for things well; I was deflated and hated each new intrusion. This formed my attitudes on the number of children I would ever have. Not many if any! I had dreams of adopting children or running an orphanage. I wanted to make the children feel wanted. I still feel strongly about adopting children.

I never had a room to myself because the houses we lived in were too small, and I never had the privacy I needed in my most crucial years. I have cold feelings toward anyone who delights in having a large family unless the children are adopted.

Because my mom has so many kids around, she tends to become overtired and irritated, and her voice patterns do change. She used to do a lot of yelling to get the kids to do something, but it never really worked. I always found it difficult to approach my mother with questions or problems. She was always too busy to have much empathy for me so I felt neglected. When I was in high school, I often brought up questions why the divorce and why so many kids. She would never tell me, and I would get very upset and hurt. I felt that this was not right and that I should know the answers. She would avoid my questions and tell me I didn't understand and it was none of my business.

The narrator in her following analysis loved her father dearly prior to the divorce, which occurred when she was nine years old. She describes eloquently the anguish she suffered because of the divorce and mentions guilt feelings that she had not tried to prevent it. After the divorce, she acquired from her mother a hatred toward her father and tolerated her stepfather with negative feelings. When she got a bit older, she renewed her love for her father and visited him in his new home with his second wife. The narrator describes her mother's background as follows:

Both of my parents were raised on farms. My mother's parents were quite strict religiously. She wasn't allowed to participate widely in school activities where she could socialize with her peers. Her father needed her to help with barn work more than her mother needed her in the house. I remember her telling me that she could keep a barn in A-1 condition, but not a house. Her standards of housekeeping were low, but she could do a man's job in a day.

My mother was very lonely as a child because her older brothers didn't have time for her. The youngest brother was seven years older than herself, and she was never close to any of them. This loneliness influenced her feelings toward having children and caused her not to take any precautions against having children. She had eleven children in her forty years of life, four with my father and seven with her second husband. I confronted her once with the question, "Why so many?" and she replied, "Some things happen without planning, but *each one was loved even before it was born.*" *My mother demonstrates affection to the babies of the family but seldom shows any as they get older* [emphasis added].

In summary, I conclude that in large families there is more of an overall scramble in competition with few instances of withdrawal, more sibling influence with less parental influence on the children, and more subgroups. In large families with a great age span, only the middle children have significant contacts with the oldest and youngest, and more of the children will have experience as the oldest or youngest of a subgroup. The motive to have many children is often obscure and not easily expressed by parents. Parental interest and affection for children may differ widely from one stage of development to the next. The increase in the size of the family does not seem to diminish the chances of family success if there is economic security.

It is apparent that the previous tendency of investigators to predict traits only on the bases of status as the oldest or youngest should be abandoned. If this approach is to be used with large family systems, it should apply to the oldest and youngest of subgroups, and it should be combined with an appraisal of opportunities for the free assumption of responsibility. Such opportunity within the home is determined by economic factors, sex roles, age space, and the parenting ability of father and mother.

**Part III
Family Patterns**

12 Family Rituals

The dividing line between family rituals and other types of ritualistic behavior is not a sharp one, but essentially, family rituals involve voluntary, repetitive family behavior that is gratifying to all family members. Rituals of baptism, confirmation, marriage, and funerals are prescribed by the state or the religious community and are usually experienced but once in the lifetime of the individual. Some crises of life may be associated with ritualistic behavior, such as birth, puberty, and death.

Family rituals, however, may occur repeatedly for decades. One student was required to attend family reunions, which he disliked because the relatives engaged in vicious gossip. If we were to include such behavior in the category of family rituals, then we should have to subclassify rituals that are negative and those that are positive. I find it more useful to define family rituals as positive experiences, hence this student's case would be ruled out because of its coercive and distasteful character. His family tried, unsuccessfully, to imitate a family ritual.

As I sorted out my papers, looking for those that had rituals worthy of mention, I suddenly realized that I had unknowingly sorted out the papers describing pantrophic families from those describing dystrophic families. Rituals that are colorful, meaningful, or creative are characteristic of pantrophic families. If the reader should take exception to this by thinking that he has a nice family with very few rituals, I hasten to suggest that his family possessed patterns of gratifying behavior that he may not recognize as rituals.

For clarification, following is a classification of family rituals:

Periodic rituals:
  Holidays,
  Religious,
  Sunday dinners,
  Birthdays,
  Anniversaries;

Seasonal and recreational rituals:
  Hunting and fishing,
  Camping and vacations,
  Sports events;

Strategic rituals:
    Family councils and rap sessions,
    Comforting rituals,
    Affectionate rituals,
    Work rituals,
    Mealtime and TV rituals,
    Kinship rituals;

Spontaneous idiomatic rituals.

Family rituals are important because they promote subtle emotional overtones by which family members sense their unity, identity, and uniqueness and because they provide opportunities for the growth of family members. These subtle emotional overtones that prevail with regularity constitute the family *hestia*. Although the students did not use this term or the concept, the reader will be impressed with how highly the students rated benefits to their families from rituals.

Periodic Rituals

Holidays

No two families celebrate a holiday in exactly the same fashion. When students describe their family holiday rituals, they dwell on detailed features that are repetitive and idiosyncratic, such as the same menu, timing, and sequence. The idiosyncratic process generates a feeling of cohesiveness and uniqueness. It seems to satisfy the yen for both individual and family identity. It is significant that, when students generalize about their family rituals, they invariably mention their relevance to family cohesiveness.

Many families incorporate ethnic traditions into their holidays:

> For as long as I can remember, we always celebrated Christmas eve by having a meatless dinner. We also serve a waferlike cracker. This involves an old Polish custom that my father experienced when he was a boy. The object is for everybody to have a large piece and then give some of his piece to each member of the family. This is to symbolize unity and friendship among us. I remember getting kind of sad at this time of the year. After that we would open our presents. As for other members of the family, I feel they enjoyed it a lot. It seemed the only time we are really close is at Christmas.

For children whose parents have divorced, the family *hestia* during the holiday season may be tinged with pathos. The following account was written by the girl, the oldest of three children, who described the family situation prior to the separation as:

Yelling, screaming, and hollering on the part of my mom. To these out-breaks my dad seldom, if ever, raised his voice. When he just couldn't take any more he would leave—sometimes slamming the door.

Her description of Christmas after the divorce follows:

There is only one ritual in our family, but this doesn't lessen its signif-icance. It is probably better termed a game than a ritual. This is our cele-bration of Christmas.

On Christmas eve, Dad comes over to the house in time for church. Al-though we split up for the two services, we meet back at the house after church. At this time Mom fixes dinner—all Dad's favorites. As we are all five sitting there, I get the feeling that everyone is trying to pretend as hard as I am that this is the way life usually is at the house—that we eat every meal around the same table. Although it is abstract and I can't prove it scientifically, I am almost positive of this mutual feeling. It is the one day of the year when my mom doesn't raise her voice. After the meal we all take turns opening the gifts. After this, a family that is very close to both of my parents comes over. Some time after midnight the friends leave, and shortly thereafter, Dad goes. Thus ends another annual ritual. Maybe it is not a ritual in that few specific concrete actions or traditions are involved, yet this abstract atmosphere is something that happens every year, and I have a very strong feeling that we are all aware of it.

Divorced mothers with children may retain and improve family rituals in spite of complications. One girl whose mother divorced her father be-cause of his alcoholism wrote, after her description of the Christmas ritual:

Our family is disorganized and solid at the same time. It's disorganized in the sense that one parent is not present. But the disorganization we had with his presence was far worse than with his absence. For the first few years, I missed not having a father in the home. However, now I no longer feel like anything's missing in our family life.

She then describes a series of gratifying rituals in which an older brother took over some of his father's roles.

Religious

Religious rituals, involving various modes of self-expression, play an important function in many families. Four excerpts follow:

Another example of our family coheseiveness was worshiping every Sun-day. Both my parents were Lutherans at the time of marriage, and we were devout churchgoers. Every Sunday, all four of us would go to church and usually visit our grandparents afterward. We would sit around the table and discuss matters pertaining to religion in which everone could express his own opinion and have a free voice on various matters.

Our worshiping together as a family I feel is a reason for our cooperation and happiness. It seems that the pervading philosophy at home is, "the family that prays together stays together." My brother and I sang in the church choir, attended youth fellowship, and went to two years of catechism. Mother babysits in the nursery and teaches summer-vacation bible school. Father is currently counting the Sunday morning offering and ushers for Communion services. I feel that performing services and worshiping together has improved the communication among members of our family.

There is one thing I will remember all my life, and that is going to my grandfather's house for dinner every Friday night when I was a little girl. When I walked into the house I could smell the Sabbath dinner, and there was a certain warmth I felt that seemed so very special. As I would walk down the hall toward the dining room, I could see the Sabbath candles twinkling on the table. I will never forget the feeling I'd have as I stared at those candles. They had a glow that seemed so warm, so special, so festive. Since the age of thirteen, I have lighted the Sabbath candles in my own candlesticks on Friday nights, yet they just aren't the same as the ones I remember on Grandpa's diningroom table. I truly feel that I have been given a heritage that I will some day be able to hand down to my own family.

My family practices many old Jewish rituals such as lighting the Sabbath candles on Friday night to give thanks for everything we have; Yom Kippur, a holiday on which one refrains from eating for twenty-four hours; Passover, when one eats unleavened bread called matzos; and Hannuka, which is the Jewish equivalent of Christmas. Sometimes we get together with relatives on my father's side and celebrate these holidays.

Sunday Dinners

The old-fashioned Sunday dinner has lost some of its style due to secularization, television, the dual-career family, and the trend toward eating out. Eating out on certain occasions like holidays has become a ritual, though. Also, snacks have been ritualized for specific events such as rap sessions or the practice of family members eating from trays while watching a favorite TV program. Some families still have a special Sunday dinner.

Birthdays

The following account of a birthday ritual is typical of many families. It was written by a girl whose full description of her pantrophic family was delightful.

For birthdays my mother makes a traditional favorite cake for the birthday boy (or girl). The special child doesn't have to do any work. This makes it a very special day for the birthday person because there is always a lot of work and to get a day off is really something. After our evening meal the cake is brought out, and we all sing the birthday song. When the birthday person tries to blow out the candles, we all make him laugh so it's hard for him to blow out all the candles in one breath. It's quite a ritual and a very enjoyable time. My mother gives the person a big kiss. We all laugh and the cake is cut. I really enjoy our family birthday parties because it's so happy and exciting in our house.

A girl from another pantrophic family added this to her birthday account:

When my sister and I turned eighteen, wine was served and my father proposed a toast. This treatment of birthdays gives each of us a feeling of being loved and appreciated.

Anniversaries

A description of an anniversary ritual follows:

My father never forgot to bring home a gift for Mother on their wedding anniversary. Mother was usually surprised because she was the kind not to remember important events. One time, Father took us kids into his confidence in order to organize a surprise party for Mother on their anniversary. On the eventful evening, the neighbors casually came in to visit until the living room was full of people. Suddenly Mother jumped up exclaiming, "Good land! This is our wedding anniversary and Pa's forgotten all about it!

Seasonal and Recreational Rituals

Seasonal and recreational rituals provide an emotional climate conducive to growth and opportunities for developing physical skills and cognitive learning.

Hunting and Fishing

The following account was written by an only child who suffered during his boyhood from loneliness and poor self-image. Later, his parents dealt more adequately with him and he improved.

The first ritual of the year is that of the Wolf River walleye run—an activity that my father loves. It is a very cohesive outing and brings us all together. My mother is a good sport and goes with my dad regularly each spring, and of course, I tag along to watch my mother catch a fish. Part of the ritual is to visit my mother's relatives just before the fishing season opens. The emotional feeling during these times is one of warmth and affection. This feeling is there in good times and bad. It is a feeling of deep acceptance and understanding from within, of affection and a deep care for all family members.

The following was written by a girl from a pantrophic family who had two older brothers and two younger sisters:

One very special ritual I remember revolved around Thanksgiving and deer season. This was the time each year my dad would head north for a week. On that trip my brothers marked their coming of manhood, the time when they also would be old enough to be trusted in the woods with a rifle. Deer season at home was also special. It was time for the women in the family to be alone together. We would make a special trip during this time to the downtown area to do our Christmas shopping.

Camping and Vacationing

When I was about twelve, my father thought it would be a good idea to have a weekend off. We would leave on a Friday in February and drive to a beautiful resort about seventy miles away. Our whole family would go skiing, skating, swimming, and bowling together. We would relax and have fun together for the weekend. It was fun to do things with my family for the weekend, and I always had a wonderful time at this resort.

Some of my happiest memories are from our family summer vacations. Every summer for the past thirteen years, the whole family goes on vacation. Besides having fun, we learn a great deal about the people and places we visit. I think my parents are absolutely wonderful to take us all on such wonderful trips. I really enjoy being with my family. We all come to know each other better and are drawn closer together.

Sports Events

Sports events are tied to seasonal change. Some families, or parts of them, may regularly go the ballpark in the summer and to the football stadium in the fall.

Strategic Rituals

Some rituals are not strictly periodic or seasonal but take place with the same pattern whenever occasion demands. I call these strategic rituals because they seem to have a purpose or goal of dealing with decision making and self-expression.

Family Council and Rap Sessions

The following two families with four children discussed family affairs as a group:

> We had what we called a family council. It was just our family of four. My father was the president, Mom was the vice-president, Mary was the secretary, and I was the treasurer. Even though no notes were taken and no money was handled, it made me feel important because I had a title. Once a week at the supper table we would conduct a meeting. We were allowed to bring up anything we felt important and it would be discussed. They always listened to us. I feel that it helped to keep the family a cohesive unit.

> Everyone had equal opportunity to state his opinions, and from these discussions, family decisions were reached. We also handled individual problems this way. Rather than have a one-to-one discussion, basic problems were always worked out as a group. This reduced tension and made it easier for the individual. Often these discussions took place at the supper table after our meal was completed. As I see it, these family discussions were our most important ritual. This practice tied our family together closely. It really worked great.

A characteristic feature of family rap sessions in pantrophic families is the complete freedom of the children to express themselves in spite of distortions due to immaturity. The parents seem to utilize the ritual to stimulate self-expression and judgment.

> The weekly rap session is my favorite family get-together. At these raps, all of the family will talk about whatever is important to them at that time. We may plan a vacation or weekend; discuss friends, school, and football; or decide on whether we'd like a pool table or craft for family entertainment. More fun yet, we often reminisce about comical family adventures. Most of all, though, at these rap sessions I enjoy our debates on politics; usually it is the left versus the right. We debate for the fun of debating, with one thing made perfectly clear by Father—no one is allowed to state his objection to someone's opinion until it has been stated. This is a far cry from the children-should-be-seen-and-not-heard philosophy of my grandparents. Mom and Dad will listen no matter what the idea or opinion we express, and only after we have finished will they reply, even if that may be, "Now young lady, don't you think that's a little out of reason?"

Comforting Rituals

A ritual may be developed for the purpose of comforting or diverting a family member who has had a bad day.

Talks concerning intimate matters were most revealing of personality in my parents. Usually it is my mother who is upset, and the minute Dad starts his low, melodic tone of voice, things settle down and Mom starts to brighten up. At times like this Dad is great for suggesting that they go someplace to get away from it all, whether it be out to eat or for a weekend camping. When Dad is down in the dumps, Mom performs a regular ritual that Dad has grown to depend on. Usually Dad becomes most upset on a long day that involves suppertime appointments, so on these days Mom feeds us and then whips up something special for Dad's supper. After dinner, they sit in the livingroom relaxing while us three kids do the dishes. During those discussions in the livingroom, my Mom is especially tuned to the thing (whatever it is) that is bothering my Dad and is always sure to add a few of her morale boosters to the discussion. By bedtime everything is pretty much at ease again, and in the final step of her ritual, Mom makes her entrance in a frilly nightgown and lots of perfume.

Affectionate Rituals

Affectionate rituals are characteristic of pantrophic families. Affectionate bedtime rituals are well known for their effectiveness in calming down children and getting them to bed at the proper hour. Kissing a spouse when he leaves or returns from work is ritualistic in character and seems to have as much effect on the children as on the spouse. One father related the following incident. One morning after a few unpleasant words, his wife turned her head to indicate her resentment when he was about to kiss her goodbye. The four-year-old son spoke up and said, "Go ahead, Mommie, it's good for you."

Our home always had an air of affection, cooperation, and mutual understanding. My father and mother rarely fought and were open in their display of affection. Dad never left in the morning without kissing Mother goodbye, and Mother was always waiting with a hug for him in the evening. I couldn't possibly count the times she has said to him "I love you" or he has said to her, "You look beautiful, Mary, and the dinner was delicious."

Students from dystrophic homes may note sadly that they have never seen their parents kiss or embrace. Such lack has consequences.

One thing I have missed extremely since I was quite small is expressions of affection. There is virtually no verbal or physical display of affection between members of our family. This lack of display includes special occasions such as Christmas, birthday, departure, and so on. I recall when I was small I wanted to climb on my Dad's lap and kiss him when he was reading the paper, and I was rather harshly rejected in my attempt. It seems to me that a number of such incidents with both my father and mother led to a squelching of any desire to express affection openly. That feeling of having love rejected by your parents is one feeling I never want my children to experience. It created in me a fear of love or affectionate situations that grew in me until I was a senior in high school when I finally learned through experience. I felt and feared that I would never know how to show a person that I loved him—that I'd again be rejected in any attempt, clumsy or otherwise, to express affection.

The lack of affectionate patterns may also inhibit communication.

I would have liked to talk to my mother more than I did and do now. I'd like to tell her about adventures and experiences, and I know she'd like to hear them too, but I just never had that relationship before and it's hard to start now. Of course, I never talk to my dad about anything. Mom always told him for me. I never knew what it meant to be Daddy's girl because none of us was. I envy girls who have this relationship with their fathers.

Work Rituals

When parents are both pantrophic and creative, they are able to transform drudgery into a family lark. The next excerpt is from a farm family with nine children:

Both parents are very creative. They enjoy dreaming up new things to build and new places to go. They are willing to try anything within reason that sounds like fun.

Every spring and every fall we had a cattle drive to a woods we own eight miles from our farm. This is something our whole family and neighbors enjoy. We drive the cattle with horses and on foot down the road to the woods. When we go by neighboring farms, they always come out and help us for about a mile past their home. Sometimes we pick up about six extra people on the way. It takes about four hours altogether, and we always go to the community store and have a treat for doing such a good job. It is really work, but we all enjoy doing it so much because it is such a united effort and it reminds us of the Old West.

Last spring our whole family went picking rock. One person drives the tractor, and we divide up equally on both sides of the wagon. We all sang while we worked and then had a picnic right in the woods near the field. This is something I will always remember doing because we were accomplishing so much and still having so much fun doing it.

A chain-store manager was about to be cheated from enjoying his children in the evening. His daughters describes how the problem was solved with a work ritual:

When we were small, my father almost always had to work at the store after supper. We all went along and, as small as we were, carried boxes filled with men's shirts, socks, and underwear from the basement. We learned to fill in the stock, take inventory, straighten merchandise, and break boxes.

Even now, as we build our house, we all work together. All of us can be seen digging the basement, putting the sealer on, back filling, putting on the insulation, and putting on the siding.

My family always did a lot of things together as a group. We do all of the big work projects at home together. We clean up the yard in the spring or clean out the cars as a family, each of us doing our part but all working together. We enjoy each other's company, and the constant joking makes the work almost fun. We also have a great deal of pride and a feeling of accomplishment for what we've done.

Mealtime and TV Rituals

Many families convert the mealtime into a discussion ritual:

One very important ritual in our family is that dinner is the time when you discuss what has happened during the day and anything else that happens to be on your mind. This was usually a very relaxing and enjoyable time.

One special occasion I'll never forget is when my father took my brother and me to lunch once a week when he worked nights. This became a sort of ritual among us and was always enjoyed because of the limited contact we had with our father.

The most important family ritual is eating supper together. Our suppers were always the time when we discussed matters of the day and matters of importance to family members. Some meals were disrupted by disagreements, but that was still communication. Sometimes the talks were about trivia and were good humored. I have a sense of peace in the family.

Another part of the routine at our house has been eating the evening meal together. We use our meal as a kind of round table. Here we have our discussions while the family is together for perhaps the only time all day. When I hear parents say kids should be seen and not heard, I really have to laugh because I visualize our dinner conversation. Dinner was our time to discuss politics, religion, school, and so forth. We were always free to discuss our problems or beliefs on topics concerning us, and on other subjects we became avid listeners. It is really surprising the amount a child can learn when things are discussed freely in front of him. It also made me aware of many subjects and gave me an active interest in them, and this helped me a great deal in school.

My father was a dentist and he liked onion on his hamburger, so an important ritual in our family was the Saturday night hamburger supper. It became the subject of many jokes and has carried over to my brother's family. I'm sure Saturday night won't seem the same to me without hamburgers. We also had popcorn and soda and watched Lawrence Welk on

TV after we took our baths. I remember these times as being very relaxing and happy.

In pantrophic families the habit of family members watching favorite TV programs with a snack becomes a happy ritual, but in dystrophic families the television may be used to prevent discord and to provide a way to avoid closeness. Dr. Rosenblatt and his colleagues at the University of Minnesota have found evidence to suggest that family members use television "to avoid tense interaction and the expression of anger and aggression."[1]

When I was small I thought we were really missing something because we didn't have TV—then we got it. After about three years I wished we never heard of it. If anything can ruin conversational ties that exist in a family, it is TV. It is really amazing what strangers the members of a family become when they see each other only in an entertainment room. It is a problem that is beyond solving in our family, but I certainly hope to put TV in its proper place when I have my own home.

Kinship Rituals

An important kinship ritual is the family reunion. Extended kin often participate in anniversaries, weddings, and funerals—indeed, some of these seem to be the only occasions when widely separated kinfolk see each other. When extended family members live close by, they may regularly participate in a family ritual like a Christmas trip to grandma's house. Some extended families get together camping, at resorts, at the seashore.

Spontaneous Idiomatic Rituals

One of our most important rituals, I feel, was our ritual of private jokes. Some of the best times I can remember were when the whole family was together at one time and we started going over humorous things that have happened to us. Usually a single line or a phrase recalled an incident to which we responded with fits of laughter. The jokes would be senseless to an outsider, but the story behind them reminded us of the happy times we have shared together and the closeness we have enjoyed over the years.

The biggest ritual in our house is May Day. Since our last name is May, we always figured it was our day. We make May baskets for each other, and my mother always fixes a huge meal with all the trimmings. It's a day that's long awaited at our house.

Since I come from a Polish family, we have customs that no one considers a family ritual. A change of pace plays a big part here. For example, when eating our first watermelon of the season, one family member will pull the ear of another and call, *Nowe,* which in Polish means "something new." This ritual is repeated every time something new or different occurs. These rituals produce a lot of fun as well as bring back fond memories.

Writing notes became a ritual. If we needed to ask Dad something, we'd write him a note. We never asked just a simple question but added all sorts of flowery phrases. Usually Dad would answer with a poem. He had a knack for making up poems. They wouldn't win a literary prize, but they were a lot of fun.

My grandmother's name was Em, and she had a habit of clearing the table as soon as she finished eating. Whenever anyone is going some place and is in a hurry to do the dishes, we call her Em because it reminds us of Grandmother. This always seem to put more fun in the rushing.

Rituals in the Family Life Cycle

Rituals seem to be the most numerous, exciting, and enjoyable when the children are young. This is the time they go to Grandma's house for the holidays and when family camping is at its height. As the children grow up and grandparents die and as the activities of job, courtship, and college conflict with family time, the rituals taper off. However, as the children marry, their families of procreation produce a new generation of children and a new surge of family rituals.

In many pantrophic families, the tapering-off process is slight. Boyfriends and girlfriends may be taken on camping trips. Newlyweds may join with their parents at Christmas and hang up their stockings. Touch football at family gatherings may become more important, as will beer drinking while watching sports events on television.

The following account explains how one family bridged the gap on a family ritual dealing with birthdays:

This year was the first year that I wasn't home for my birthday. I thought my family forgot me, but was I ever wrong. When I got back to the dorm after classes, I opened my room to find it full of my friends along with my family. Mom had arranged a surprise party for me with enough food to feed all the people on the wing. Was I surprised!

When Rituals Are Absent

There is little or no communication in our family. We celebrate all the major calendar events, but they are just customs with little enjoyment.

With everything considered, I feel and have always felt that I have lived in a house and not a home. I am looking forward with much expectation to a happy marriage and a home of my own.

Our family rituals are few in number and poor in quality. My family's social isolation has been a negative factor in the socialization process. For years my family has lived in almost complete isolation. Relatives rarely exchange visits and we have no neighborhood friends.

There is no unity in our family. No holiday seems to bring us any closer. Christmas is a time to buy presents, and Thanksgiving a time to overeat. No friends or relatives are ever invited over.

We have no family rituals. When Thanksgiving comes around, I make sure that I am on a trip of some sort.

My family has never really experienced any type of rituals. We never do anything as a family. As a result, I see us standing alone very much. We are independent and competent as individuals. We've learned to survive as loners. We are socially active but on an individual basis—with our peers. We find happiness in our individual lives outside of the family. We are successful with people at work and with our peers. As a family, we experience conflict and argument when we are together. Home is a sad place to go to after a day. I used to stay away as long as possible. When I get married I want to establish family rituals.

When Rituals Are Present

Family rituals were many and colorful while I lived at home. Every holiday had its own traditional family activities and patterns. Whenever one of these occasions is in the near future, it seems to have a big impact on the cohesiveness of the family. Everyone in the nuclear family realized the importance of this special event, and this seems to draw everyone together like a magnet. No matter what problem is facing the family at this time, it either seems to be solved or put aside in order to enjoy the special ritual.

The whole emotional tone of the family seems to take an abrupt turn for the better, and everyone in my nuclear family seems to take more of an interest in one another. Along with this, everyone, including myself, shows more consideration for the other family members.

The emotional outcome of these family rituals lasts for a time after the event is over. This acts as a cohesive type of bridge to keep the family somewhat tied together between the times of these occasions. Without the cohesiveness from these family rituals, I sincerely believe that my nuclear family would fall further and further apart until it would finally break up.

In my case, I can actually feel the tensions build up at times and be released by occasions such as Thanksgiving and the family traditions and rituals connected with it. It is at times like this that my nuclear family seems to function at its very best.

If parents take the philosophical stance suggested by the idea of the pantrophic family, then they will not accept traditional rituals casually but will take pains to utilize them effectively and creatively to promote the potential of their children in all facets of their growth.

We ordinarily assume that emotional security is basic to growth and that it is provided within the nuclear unit. However, rituals involving the extended family provide a larger base for security. A woman whose childhood involved many happy times with relatives said this experience was accompanied by the childhood fantasy that if anything dire should happen to her parents, "there would always be someone to take care of me."

Student accounts of family rituals tend to emphasize the enjoyment they provide not only for children but also for parents. Rituals also provide a means whereby adults can safely relive their childhood momentarily, and some can experience the lost childhood from which they had been cheated by circumstances.

The presence or absence of family rituals is more a symptom than a determinant of family happiness or unhappiness. A dystrophic family with its poor communication and depressed *hestia* might be unable to initiate satisfying rituals. They would do better to ask for treatment with a family counselor and, as they improved, to consider the initiation of such rituals. Families that do not require a family counselor have much to gain by improving the rituals they have and by creatively initiating new ones.

Another dimension that needs to be understood is that, compared to other cultures, ours is characterized by extreme age grading. When a young person spends nine months in a college dormitory, associating only with persons his own age, he finds it relaxing and gratifying to come home to associate with persons both older and younger than himself.

As families become smaller, more attention is given to providing one's children with contact with age-mates, but they also need contact with other age groups. The oscillation of children in their contacts with different age-mates and adults is therefore normal and healthy, and this condition is augmented by cultivating rituals beyond the nuclear unit in order to include all manner of kinfolk. To isolate retirees in retirement communities away from children is to diminish the contributions that each could give to the other.

The potential of a family for developing rituals is increased when there is no down-grading of in-laws, cousins, and other relatives. It is unfair to bias children against cousins who may not have the foibles of their parents.

Summary

Rituals promote a sense of family identity, pride, cohesiveness, solidarity, and continuity. They generate pleasurable anticipation, excitement, laughter, and joy. They improve the family *hestia*. They reduce tension and conflict and promote family cooperation and integration. They advance emotional growth and the capacity to express feelings. The effectiveness of rituals in cultivating these positive conditions is related to the degree that parents actively promote rituals and make a conscious effort to have the family function as an ongoing unit.

All this reaffirms some of the things Professor Bossard said about rituals in 1950.[2] While Bossard and Boll generalized that rituals increase in number, variety, and richness as one moves upward in the social scale, I postulate that when social status is held constant, this increase is related to the degree to which the family is pantrophic. While Bossard emphasized the advantages of rituals in terms of integration and harmony, I emphasize the use of rituals as growth-inducing processes because they provide opportunities to stimulate growth in self-expression, communication, rational thought, empathy, judgment, autonomy, creativity, and all other qualities in the pantrophic dimension.

Notes

1. Paul C. Rosenblatt and Michael R. Cunningham, "Television Watching and Family Tensions," *Journal of Marriage and the Family* 38 (February 1976):105–111.

2. James H.S. Bossard and Eleanor Stokes Boll, *The Large Family System* (Philadelphia: University of Pennsylvania Press, 1956).

13 Parent-Child Relations

Overprotection versus Rejection

That adequate nurturance of infants is basic to their growth and development is widely accepted. However, nurturance must end, and preparation for independence must follow. With birds and wild animals, the period before separation is fairly short, but for humans, it is long and often difficult. Training for ultimate separation takes place when the children are socialized within the home and venture into various settings beyond the home with increasing frequency and for longer periods.

We may have defects in nurturance and preparation for separation, or perhaps we should say defects in facilitating growth toward independence. Inadequate nurturance may involve parental abuse, rejection, and failure to protect against physical and psychological hazards. Defects in the independence dimension may involve clinging mothers and overprotective fathers in the home setting and trauma in the outside settings. Concerned parents may neutralize the effects of their mistakes if they have a deep and healthy love for the child.

A doting mother may claim to love her son overmuch, but it may be a fake love that leads to a morbid condition for both. It is not a difference in degree but a difference in kind. Maternal behavior that promotes the growth of offspring and that is carried out for the benefit of the child, not the mother, is healthy. If it stymies the growth of the child and is done for the gratification of the mother, it is likely to be unhealthy. More specifically, maternal behavior that restricts the child's capacity to make decisions and to accept responsibility for them and that prevents the normal separation of youth from the parental hearth is unhealthy. Conversely, maternal behavior that sets limits for protection, stimulates growth by the free exercise of responsible judgments, fosters self-discipline, and encourages the separation process at the appropriate time promotes healthy personality growth.

Parenting behavior designed to prepare children for adulthood must be done properly in the dimensions of time and degree. To overwhelm a child prematurely with freedom he cannot handle, or with responsibilities he cannot manage, will damage him. This is why parental roles call for artistry of the highest order.

Convergence and Separation

Two outstanding family therapists, Whitaker and Napier, have developed a concept that is useful in connection with convergence and separation.[1] They suggest that, all through life, family members tend alternately to separate and unite. The perspective is to focus on the two processes (togetherness and separateness) simultaneously. This idea fits in with the material on settings. The child ventures forth into the setting of his first grade (perhaps his first significant separation) and returns home at noon, where he is eager to express his enthusiasm or disdain. If family members provide a supportive audience, the child may return to his school setting in normal fashion. If both parents have stimulating settings and they exchange experiences, then every alternation of convergence and separation of family members may lead them all to a higher level of functioning and to healthier relationships. In such cases, the family circle becomes an audience for the converging members so that each is stimulated by the others.

I would like to use an elliptical metaphor for the path of a family member as he goes to and from his home setting to his school or work setting. This scheme fits the pantrophic family since it implies that travel in such orbits, like the movement of planets, is smooth and predictable, not stressful or unhealthy. It is exciting to venture forth to new school or job settings, and it can be interesting for family members to exchange their experiences with the others in the home setting. Convergence in the home setting with a delightful *hestia* can act as a recharge for family members so they go forth from the family setting to the other settings with renewed enthusiasm. In the growing-up process, the orbit for each child becomes elongated because the time spent in the school and work settings increases as the time spent in the home setting diminishes.

The outside settings have dangers as well as opportunities for growth. How do parents prepare the children to avoid the dangers while taking advantage of opportunities for growth? Throughout part III, the case histories show how pantrophic families have grappled with this problem successfully and how dystrophic families have failed.

As children grow older, nurturing gives way to succoring, and mutual succoring is characteristic of healthy families throughout the life cycle. I use the term in the broadest sense to include emotional support.

Mutual succoring among adult relatives is a sustaining force in family life. It has been facilitated by the inventions of the postal system, the telephone, airplane, and automobile. These have been a counterforce to the demoralizing effects of high geographic mobility. The two dimensions to the separating process are psychological and physical. Family members living in the same household may be divergent with respect to their emotional and intellectual lives. In one family the spouses did not say a word to each other for months on end; they communicated only through the children. College students whose parents are ignorant, authoritative, and rigid either will rebel openly concerning the parental values or will refuse to talk about divergent values. Sometimes physical separation is necessary to break up an unhealthy convergence. Unhealthy family relations may be broken up by factors such as marriage, going out of town to work, going to college, or going to jail. In pantrophic families, the convergence becomes rhythmical for mealtimes, pastimes, and family rituals. The dynamics of orbiting for various members are complicated and ever changing, depending on differences in age and in roles.

The orbiting of husband and wife in their respective settings in the upper-middle-class United States may pose a dilemma. One facet of growth is technological expertise. When each spouse pursues a narrow specialty, his or her capacity for being an audience for each other diminishes. If one or both become workaholics, there is very little time or energy for activities together. Both their social life and family life become increasingly diminished in time and richness. Their relationship becomes shallow, artificial, and fragile. A high degree of specialization has led to a good deal of alienation between spouses, and yet we think of the pursuit of a specialty as growth. Thus, we come back to the idea of quality in family living as a proper balance of time, money, and energy in various settings of life experiences.[2]

The tendency toward maternal oversolicitude of sons when the latter are in close proximity to maternal figures is worldwide. In societies where male infants sleep with their mothers, where postpartum-sex taboos are extended, and where young boys associate closely with maternal figures, then pubertal rites are severe. Conversely, societies without such practices have benign puberty rites.[3] In our society, puberty rites are haphazard and nebulous. In chapter 19, we see how some U.S. families have been creative in this regard.

In our society several factors counteract the constrictive process and permit healthier separation patterns to develop. One is the healthy orbiting of both parents in their respective occupational settings while reserving adequate time and energy for family affairs. Another is deliberate planning by the parents for task responsibilities for the children within or without the home, as I emphasized in chapter 10. A third factor is the size of the family, although in large families the handicapped son, the favorite son, or the youngest son may be vulnerable. A fourth factor is the skill of the parents in developing a *hestia* that radiates a sense of trust, self-direction, and self-discipline. Before discssing such a *hestia*, I deal with the two opposing and destructive parental patterns.

Scapegoats

The family situation that triggers scapegoating is one in which the parents have deep-seated hostilities toward each other, but in which neither parent can afford the risk of open conflict that would break the marital relationship and disrupt the family. There may be emotional and practical reasons why neither party can afford an open and irreparable break. In this situation they displace their antagonisms onto one of the children, which eases tension between themselves. Some believe this maneuver is functional because the family can continue as an ongoing system—the child scapegoat suffers and becomes dysfunctional, which does less damage to the family than to have both parents dysfunctional. Thus, the lamb is sacrificed for the solidarity of the group. This a summary of the classic and brilliant explanation of family scapegoating as given by Bell and Vogel.[4]

The recent interest in child abuse has led to use of the term *scapegoat* for other situations. For example, a perfectly healthy child may be victimized, not by parents in conflict but by parents who project their own unhealthy internal problems onto a child until he becomes psychopathic.[5] Sometimes the term is used to designate parental abuse of a child, regardless of the spousal relationship, until the child develops strong aggressive feelings against the abusing parent that are then turned inward against himself, causing aggressive and masochistic behavior that invites punishment from all comers.[6]

The broadening of the term *scapegoating* suggests that there are several kinds and various degrees of scapegoating in families in the United States. For example, we have a series of scapegoats beginning with the oldest child. When he leaves home, the parents then scapegoat the secondborn, and so on down the line as each of the children departs. Again, we may have two scapegoats, as in one case wherein the father scapegoated the daughter who looked like her mother, while the mother scapegoated a son who looked like his father. We may have a situation in which only one parent scapegoats a child. The extent to which the siblings of the scapegoat either cooperate with the scapegoating parent or resist such behavior is another variable. In some cases it seems that the children, by imitation of parental behavior, scapegoat each other until there is a babble of blaming in the family system, as described by Virginia Satir.[7]

If one suspects that scapegoating takes place in his own family, he should give some thought to how the scapegoat is selected. Our cases reveal that the scapegoat is often selected by the parents because the victim resembles one of them in looks, build, personality, or defective trait. In the last case, the wife's rage toward her husband is deflected onto the scapegoat, and the husband may displace his own weakness onto the scapegoat. At the same time, he is relieved to have criticism of himself deflected onto the victim.

Two other factors should be considered as influences in the selection of the scapegoat. One is position in the family constellation. One mother, who had deeply resented her oldest sister, selected her oldest daughter for scapegoating. The second factor is bitter resentment toward a pregnancy that takes place under a stressful situation. In one case the rigid and authoritarian father suffered business reverses because of conflict with an associate. He took out his frustration on his pregnant wife and later on his daughter, who resembled the mother. The mother became depressed and said that, if she had another baby, she would die and hoped the baby would not be born alive. The baby was born and looked like his father. The selection for scapegoating due to this resemblance seemed to be reinforced by her extreme aversion to his birth, as well as to the abuse she had received from her husband during pregnancy.

The influence of a resented pregnancy in scapegoating is made plausible by those cases in which children of later pregnancies not associated with conflict and tension were neither resented nor scapegoated. The following case illustrates how several factors influence the selection process and how the scapegoating by the parents permeates the family system.

> Archie, the fourthborn, is the spitting image of my father, and he became the family scapegoat. When he was born, both my parents made more complaints about having another child than they did about Laura, the fifth, and, oddly enough, about Lena who was born eight years later. I recall my mother commenting on what an ugly baby Archie was and how he was the least attractive of all of us. She compares him unfavorably to the rest of us, and she harps on him constantly about his low grades, bad temper, and laziness. Dad has no time for him. If anything is broken or lost, Archie is the first to be blamed by both parents. And now, my brothers and sisters and I find ourselves doing the same. As a result of this treatment, Archie is always on the defensive; he lies, screams, hits, and refuses to help at home. The more he becomes a nuisance, the more the family jumps on him, establishing a vicious circle. Neither of my parents realizes, nor would either of them admit, that Archie is their scapegoat.

The early literature on scapegoating implied that it was functional to the family because it permitted the family to continue as a system at the cost only of the harm to the scapegoat. My materials pose the dilemma of the parent who does not participate in the scapegoating and the dilemma of the siblings about whether to resist the scapegoating or to cooperate and connive with the scapegoating parent. The following case of Martin raises the question as to whether extreme scapegoating can ever be functional to the family and/or whether the damage it does is greater than the damage from a complete family breakup.

The Case of Martin

Martin was the third of seven children. He had two older sisters, one younger sister, and three younger brothers. There was much arguing and conflict between the parents. Both were described as stubborn, authoritarian, and rigid, and many arguments were over Martin. The parents were indifferent or hostile to the opinions of the children. The mother complained about her struggles to maintain the family on a meager income and expressed the wish that she had had only two children. The oldest daughter, Betsy, narrates as follows:

> In my eyes, my Mother hates Martin since there is absolutely nothing he can do to please her. She calls him Calf and requires that he eat with only one specific plate and fork; he cannot be in the livingroom but must stay in the basement or in the yard like an animal. Because of this, he doesn't always know when the meals are ready, and my mother won't call him or keep anything warm for him to eat. She favors one of the younger boys and will keep food warm for any of them. Martin must be in bed at nine o'clock, no matter whether his homework is done. My mother goes out of her way to find things to punish him for. If he tries to say anything, he is told to shut up and to do as she says. Martin refuses to discuss any of this with anyone because he is afraid of his mother's punishment if she found out he had complained. My Dad can't help the situation, mainly because she beats Martin while my Dad is at work. If Martin should tell my father, there would be double trouble; so he tends to keep to himself. When my Dad tells Martin to do something my mother had specifically told him not to do, he is in a desperate situation, facing punishment from both. He usually ends up doing what my father says and then getting punished for it when Dad leaves for work. Martin is not very bright, so if he doesn't understand her directives, she hauls out a stick to slam him.

Betsy goes on the describe how the mother enlisted the cooperation of the four youngest children in the persecution of Martin. To this end they were favored and babied, much to the disgust of Betsy and her younger sister. The younger children were described as spoiled and arrogant, and in one case, toilet training was several years late. The two oldest sisters tried to remonstrate with the mother over the treatment of Martin, but they were told to shut up or she would throw them out of the house. When the two oldest sisters tried to remonstrate with the younger children and to encourage them to treat Martin better, the young one would tell the mother what had been said. Betsy put it this way, "My mother developed favoritism toward the kids to help her execute her plan against Martin."

While Betsy was in college she was greatly distressed about her family situation and talked to me at length about the possibility of getting a social agency to intervene on Martin's behalf. Since Martin had no broken bones or deep scars, there was insufficient evidence to impress public authorities so her efforts in her home county came to naught.

Some eight years after Betsy was in my class, I had an exchange of correspondence with her. Martin had left home and had his own apartment. The mother still raged when family members tried to help Martin and even raged when his name was mentioned. When the mother met Martin at her father's funeral, "there was a huge blow-up and she told him never to be in her sight again." This continued to the bitter end when the mother was fatally injured in an accident. Betsy described briefly how the mother's scapegoating had had deleterious effects on her father and on all the children. Unfortunately, we have no information on the mother's life history prior to her marriage.

In the case of Martin, all efforts by family members to make the mother realize the nature of her behavior were to no avail. This denial of scapegoating is one of its features, although several students wrote that, in milder cases of scapegoating, they were able to make the parents see the nature of their behavior and to succeed in ameliorating it. Another feature is for the parent scapegoater to play the martyr role and tell the children (especially the victim) how much better they have it than the parent had.

The Case of Jeannie

Jeannie's mother teased her daughter about her body build and forced her to wear old clothing in school. A brother spread malicious lies about her. The father approached her sexually and frightened her. The teacher loudly called her stupid in front of the class, and her peers rejected her.

When Jeannie went to college, she fell in love with a boy and briefly lived with him. After the boyfriend rejected her, she became depressed and attempted suicide. When she went home for comfort, her mother told her what a lucky girl she was, that her life was so much better than the mother's. After Jeannie left home, a younger sister became the recipient of scapegoating. When this sister approached her mother with personal problems, the mother would start yelling and telling her what a rough childhood the mother had had. There were several mothers like Jeannie's, and they all had, indeed, had rough childhoods, as had many of the fathers.

How do scapegoats react to their punishment? Some regress, others are arrested in development, but some stubbornly resist their destruction. In one case the parents had scapegoated the oldest daughter; when she left home the mother turned her venom onto the second daughter who wrote, "However, I had learned by example, and I simply remained indifferent when I was insulted, cross-examined, and so on." Because of her father's abusive behavior, this girl had developed a fear of men and her dating was nil. When her mother called her a whore, she laughed:

The only way I could stand living with my parents was to show absolutely no emotion toward their attacks. This has had the detrimental effect that I am often unable to express emotion with other people sufficiently.

Other scapegoats avoid the scapegoating parent, bide their time, and escape via college.

White Knights

The opposite number of the scapegoat is the so-called white knight, who represents an extension of the parental ego. Instead of being downgraded and blamed, he is vested with potential for great things and pressured to achieve them—all for the glory of the parents. The following case illustrates how maternal overdomination restricts a child's orbit, obstructs the separation process, and combines with covert white-knight induction.

> As an only child I became the apple of my parents' eye. I also caused difficulties between them. I have been especially close to my father who rarely disciplined me.
>
> My parents never pushed me for grades, yet I know I am the only one to make them proud. I have become extremely achievement motivated, and to this day I often become so nervous about grades that I break out in a cold sweat or cry before tests. In high school I gave up many social activities for schoolwork, and I graduated with a 4-point average—a total wreck. I am always afraid to hurt my parents' feelings, and it is very difficult for me to express beliefs or to act contrary to their wishes. I even have difficulty choosing my own friends. My mother dislikes many girls whom I consider wonderful people because they are not punctual or their mothers are not good housekeepers, and so on.
>
> Often I come into conflict with my steady boyfriend because of my relationship to my mother. If I want to go home with him to visit his family, I have to ask my parents first. We cannot plan anything without first getting their permission. I cannot even go out with my girlfriends without first getting permission. My mother is fond of reminding me of all they have done for me like putting me through school. I become angry with my boyfriend when he insists that I stand up for my rights. Between him and my parents I am being torn apart, and yet I know that he is right—that I must break with my parents somehow if I am ever to live a full life of my own.

When parents pressure a child to become a white knight, he may backfire as did the boy in the following account:

> I think at times my parents were disappointed because none of their children excelled in anything. They would tell us of the achievements of the children of friends and relatives and ask why we couldn't do likewise. I often got the feeling that the only reason they wanted us to excel was so they could have something to brag about. Our achievements were for their pleasure and not for ours. As a result, I never did try to achieve anything and usually just did enough work in school and in other activities to keep from getting scolded.

I now present a case in which there was no scapegoating, no induction to white knighting, no overprotection, but resistance by the father to separation. How this resistance was overcome is a bit dramatic.

Fern was the fourth child in a rural family of fourteen children. She had three older sisters who helped their father with the farm work while she helped her mother with the housework and caring for younger siblings. She wrote:

> This training has helped me to be the hard and enthusiastic worker I am today. Accepting reponsibility at an early age helped me to mature faster. From a very young age, I exerted my individuality and was not afraid to exert it. I received many a punishment for this, but I wasn't afraid of punishment and, in a way, it was my means of getting attention from Dad.

When Fern was sixteen her father was hospitalized for a month, during which time she helped with the barn chores. Her dislike for these chores, combined with the ever-pressing emphasis on work, made her decide to leave the farm and go to college. This ambition had been stimulated by a high school teacher who became her mentor and did much to stimulate her leadership ability and creativity.

Fern knew that her father would object to her leaving for college, so she bided her time until graduation from high school. Then she planned to take a summer job in another state and go to college in the fall. On the day of her leaving, she announced her plans, anticipating that her father would be angry enough to tell her never to come back home. He did exactly that, and then she retorted with a long-thought-out speech. She told him she really didn't care to come back and why. "I left home with the idea that I would never have a home to come back to." A month later her mother wrote to say that everything was all right and that she could come home any time she wanted to. Her father later showed interest in her work and was proud that she was working her way through college.

Trust, Distrust, and Privacy

In pantrophic families a prevailing sense of trust is part of the family *hestia*. This sense of trust, I think, arises from the personal integrity of the parents. Early in life the children in such families sense this integrity and the unwritten standards and values associated with it. A trusting *hestia,* the integrity of the parents, and the value system constitute a precondition that makes it possible for parents to risk giving their children freedom to make decisions as they orbit in their respective settings.

When my students wrote about trust, they dealt largely with the trust (or mistrust) the parents had in them to handle the dating situation wisely. Some parents would restrict their children by proscribing dating partners because of religion, social class, or appearance; they would also be restrictive as to where the child might go and when he should return. Other parents would give their teenager freedom to select his partner and to determine the nature of the dating activity and would rely on his judgment to come home at a reasonable hour.

In dystrophic families wherein the *hestia* was marred by distrust, the parents were prone to control dating behavior by threats and restrictions. In pantrophic families with a benign *hestia,* the parents gave their children freedom to make judgments about most things relating to dating behavior—in short, they trusted them to make decisions and relied on inner controls to measure up to parental expectations.

Since we are dealing with parent-child relations, in any discussion we must determine the direction or flow of trust: Is is trust of the parent in the child or trust of the child in the parent? Corazzini has given the concept of trust several dimensions[8]:

> As an expectation by one person that another will tell the truth or carry out his duties,
>
> As reliance on others to be responsible in carrying out their respective roles,
>
> As faith of one person in another to be exemplary in his behavior,
>
> As the surrendering of control over another person to give him freedom to act in certain areas,
>
> As the confidence one person has in the other to be consistent in his reactions to similar situations,
>
> To include the element of mutality so that two people trust each other.

These ideas contain considerable similarity and overlap. Let us, however, combine the first and the fourth and apply them to the trust of parent and child in dating situations.

Expectations

The parent expects the teenager to, within the dating situation, exercise good judgment in fostering relationships with commendable partners and to terminate those with undesirable partners, that he will exercise inner controls for maintaining behavior compatible with family values, and that he will come back to the parent for help in times of accident or crisis and be truthful about such episodes.

The teenager expects the parent to trust him with freedom to exercise his judgment without undue restriction in the dating situation and to give this freedom with a feeling of reliance that the teenager will measure up to parental expectations. Teenagers further expect that, in time of accident or crisis, the parent stands ready to facilitate self-disclosure and render assistance. Finally, if the teenager does succeed in measuring up to parental expectations, he expects to receive the approval of his parents.

If the expectations of both parent and teenager are fulfilled, both will have a sense of well-being; each will take pride in the other, each will respect the other, and the result will be mutual trust.

The following excerpts illustrate a trusting relationship between parents and their sons and daughters with regard to dating:

> I was fortunate to have parents who trusted in my judgment in different circumstances. For instance, my parents never set a specific hour for my return home from a date. Due to this trust I've always made sure that I was home at a time they would feel to be reasonable. I have felt that I must live up to their expectations since they put so much trust in me.

> In regard to dating and sex, my parents gave me no actual advice, but I feel they gave me something more important—trust. They never told me what was right or wrong but that they felt I had good judgment as to the type of boy I wanted to date and how I would act on a date.

> One of the things I respected my parents for was their trust in my judgment. They never forced their ideas or beliefs on me. I was allowed to make my own decisions concerning dating, clothes, and friends. I have also had a voice in family affairs. The emotional tone of my family is excellent. Our family is stable. Everyone is relaxed, happy, and satisfied with life. The environment I grew up in was wonderful. I respect my parents very much and I hope that I will never do anything to make them ashamed or embarrassed.

When parents have no confidence in the inner controls of their children, they become anxious about the risks of dating. When a daughter gets pregnant, they resort to threats and sermonizing to safeguard the other daughters. For example, when an older sister got pregnant as a senior in high school and quit to get married, the father then turned on his younger daughter with a pointed finger and said:

> "Now let that be a lesson to you." From then on, I've been required to make up for her mistake. For a year after her marriage (I was a freshman at the time), morning, noon, and night they laid into me about my sister having to get married. But I do resent the fact that from that point on my parents never trusted me. I received numerous sermons day in and day out, and my life at that time was genuinely unhappy. My graduation from high school came as a blessing.

After two years in college this daughter planned to marry. She added to her story:

My dad did say, though, only a couple of months ago, that if I ever had to get married I wouldn't be allowed to come home again. It wounded me deeply.

When parents try to control the sexual behavior of their daughters by threats, the results are often counterproductive. For instance, the father makes his affection for his daughter conditional on her behavior. He is autocratic and refuses to permit his children any self-expression on family matters. The parents are more concerned about how the misbehavior of the children affects their own public image than how such behavior affects the children. One girl said, "I have often felt that my parents consider me an appendage of themselves rather than a person by myself." The father told his daughter that if she ever got pregnant, as her older sister had, she would be thrown out of the house. Eventually the daughter went to college, fell in love with a boy, and got pregnant. The boyfriend was willing to leave school and marry, but the girl was terrified at the thought of explaining a hasty marriage to her father. The threat of being an outcast from her family and the uncertainty of the future of her boyfriend if he sacrificed his education for marriage increased the stress arising from her dilemma. One young woman wrote:

> My father's threatening words echoed in my head all those weeks. I never felt so alone in my life. I kept shutting out my boyfriend and hurting him because I wanted him to feel as bad as I did.

Finally the couple made a decision; they went to a distant city where the boyfriend paid for an abortion.

There is a good deal of speculation as to the conscious or subconscious motives that lead a girl to have intercourse without protection. A common reaction is expressed as follows:

> We had often talked about contraception, and I had agreed to go on the pill. I kept putting it off. Only other girls get pregnant. My only excuse is that I did not want to admit to my actions (repercussion from my father? I think so). By going on birth control I would be admitting my behavior.

She might have added that by not going on birth control she also had a chance to get even with her father.

Distrust

Occasionally, the parent does not trust the denial of a child who is falsely accused of a misdeed and, without further ado, administers punishment. Children never forget such an outrage.

Honesty was one point both my parents stressed throughout their lives, and I've always had a very bad conscience as a result of this. But it also developed a great deal of pride in me as far as trust goes. My deepest hurt comes from a feeling of not being trusted, and to this day, I can remember an incident where my sister said I lied (to save her skin) and I got my mouth washed out with soap for telling the truth. That was the epitome of insult as far as I was concerned. When people doubt me, I am deeply offended.

Sensitive teenagers are especially hurt when a mother questions her daughter like a suspicious district attorney when she comes home from a date. Such mothers may have suppressed guilt feelings of their own. One girl said the implications of immoral conduct from her mother's habitual questioning after each date made her so angry that she said, "I might as well have the game as the name." The greatest resentment on the part of daughters is when the mother says, without justification, "Are you pregnant?"

A trusting relationship involves the flow of trust in both directions, but the two go together. In addition, it improves self-respect and self-confidence.

As I grew up, my parents trusted me to make more and more decisions for myself. Now that I am away from home and away from any direct parental control, I feel that they have a deep feeling of trust for my behavior. For me to feel that I have betrayed their trust would hurt me more than any punishment. Small incidents in my life have led them to trust me and me to trust myself, and this sense of trust is important to me.

Privacy

Trust seems to be closely associated with respect for privacy, and many students talked about privacy in their discussion of trust. We do not ordinarily associate respect for privacy with trust, but the quickest way a parent can lose the respect and trust of a child is to snoop in the child's room for love letters and to eavesdrop on telephone conversations. A few excerpts illustrate this behavior:

The most maddening thing that my mother ever did was to disregard my privacy and read my diary. She even had the nerve to write comments in it and argue with me about the passages in the diary when I complained about her. She was also very nosy about my personal life and would ask questions about my relationships with my friends that I thought were none of her business. My belongings and my room underwent inspection by her quite frequently, and my drawers were often spilled out on my bed when I got home from school. She excused herself by saying she decided they were messy. When she did disregard my privacy I would become very angry and we would fight.

I've always felt a special tenderness for my father that I can't arouse for my mother even though I don't communicate with either of them very often. Perhaps the reason for this is that when I do tell my father something I feel as though he is sympathetic and know he doesn't relate my confidences to anyone. Conversely, I have always regretted the few confidences that I put in my mother. If I should tell her about some mistake I made that was troubling me, she would listen, but invariably she would twist it a little and throw it back at me the next time I did something to displease her.

Pantrophic families with a trusting *hestia* may have rules to safeguard privacy. In one family, all family members were required to knock on any bedroom door before entering.

Each of the children had his own room. Everything in our rooms was our own and we had to take care of it. After we were big enough to clean our rooms and make the beds, Mom never came upstairs at all unless it was to get something out of the attic. We were also told that we never go into other people's purses or billfolds. Opening someone else's mail was an offense that was punishable by giving your allowance to the person whose mail you read.

I was able to have my own room when I was ten and was given complete privacy. If my little brothers went into my room to snoop, they were disciplined. When I needed to be alone, I could go to my room and would not be disturbed. They didn't eavesdrop when I was on the phone or had friends over. They didn't read my mail or anything. Privacy is one thing I am really grateful for.

Pantrophic families have genuine concern for the well-being of family members by other family members as well as respect for each other's privacy. Are these two attitudes incompatible? The following excerpt suggests that the parental approach should be different for different children and perhaps for the same child at different times:

My mother respects my privacy at all times and will never demand knowledge of my personal affairs unless I choose to tell her or unless it is something of grave importance. She has always let me make my own decisions, yet she is there to help me if I need it. She will not let me make a serious mistake but influences me in such a way that I want to do the right thing because I do not want to hurt my family. As I said, Mother will not pry into our personal affairs because she is afraid of invading our privacy. My sister took this to mean that my parents are not concerned about her. This sister needs to be asked about her affairs so that she knows that our parents are interested in her welfare. The family got together for a long talk in which this problem was openly discussed, and then things improved.

Middle-class Americans with smaller families are now often in a position to give the older children rooms of their own. To what extent is a bit of living space that one can call his own important to the human psyche? In many cultures it is considered important for every infant to have a crib of his own. Even in large families, living in crowded conditions, children desire a bit of space for their possessions, even though it is only a cupboard, a shelf, a cubbyhole, or a box. Many years ago I was called one evening to the home of one of my probationers because of a family uproar. There were about a dozen children in this family. One of the little girls had her dolls and other possessions in some kind of small cupboard. The uproar occurred when a brother broke into her cupboard. To what extent does the principle of territoriality apply to the private space of a little girl? Is there any similarity between the resentment of a teenager to one who violates the privacy of his bedroom and the fierceness with which a people resist an army that invades the homeland? However that may be, it appears that trust and respect for one's privacy are closely related.

Positive and Negative Stroking

It seems as though parental behaviors that increase growth for children come in clusters that reveal the nature of the *hestia*. We have noticed that genuine love, parental recharge of children that facilitates separation and convergence, trust, and respect for privacy are often found together in the same family (usually pantrophic). Likewise, the clusters of opposite patterns tend to promote dystrophic families. Such clusters have either a positive-feeling tone that makes the children relax and enjoy a high level of self-esteem or a negative-feeling tone that makes the children tense and that undermines their self-esteem. From transactional analysis I have borrowed the terms *positive* and *negative stroking* for the behaviors that produce these opposite feelings in the children. The following excerpts illustrate pantrophic and dystrophic differences respectively in this dimension of the family *hestia:*

I feel a major factor in our family's success was my parents' attitude toward our individualism. They've always praised everything we've done well, but have never expected too much, so there was a relaxed atmosphere and no feeling of failure for not fulfilling all expectations. They made us feel successful. My mother is a good listener and very understanding.

For putting down my individualism, my father is a master at dogmatic derogation. My mother tended more to sarcasm. Their method of socialization was heavily laden with guilt-inducing admonitions. My self-esteem was crushed. My parents' only real interest in me was in preserving their image as perfect people. Had it not been for preserving some such reputation they would have thrown me out. I definitely felt hated and unwanted.

Attitudes toward the Outside World

Another feature of family life has to do with the attitudes of children toward the world outside the family. Adults who were rejected as children tend to have negative world view and consider people to be unfriendly and untrustworthy and the universe to be an insecure and hostile place. Such adults may convey to their children a similar world view.

Anthropologist Ronald Rohner had made a worldwide study of the effects of parental acceptance and rejection upon children.[9] Among other ideas, he associated a positive world view with accepting attitudes of adults toward children and explained how the nature of the world view in each society is reflected in its magic, religion, and art. His findings also substantiate what I have implied regarding the effects of many pantrophic and dystrophic parental patterns. He implies that all or most families in a given society have similar family patterns and feelings. This may be true of small, nonliterate societies, but my material indicates that it is certainly not true of our society.

The following two excerpts illustrate how positive and negative stroking affect the world view of children:

> One thing I really love about my parents is that they made us children feel important and needed. I have always felt that we provide a sense of pleasure to them. My parents have given me the impression that life is a beautiful experience and that, on the whole, people can be really great. They did this through their reactions to other people. There are very few times that I ever heard them cut anyone down.

> My father never openly praised me for things I achieved. I feel they have little respect for me. My parents gave me the idea that the world was a tough place to live in.

The case-history material indicates that praise from peers, teachers, and the general public is not enough. The ultimate in praise comes from parents and not just one but both. For example:

> After some experience, I got a job as master of ceremonies for an accordian concert at the auditorium. After much work on the program, the big day arrived. The 4,000 seats were almost filled. The show went very well, and afterwards, my friends came up to congratulate me. I could not wait to see my parents as I knew they would be proud of me. My dad told me I was very good and he was proud of me. I waited for my mother's comment with great anticipation. All she said was, "How come it lasted so long?"

Attendance of parents at public functions in which their children perform provides an opportunity for positive thinking. Such attendance is very important to children as indicated by the following:

My parents have stressed that each one of us is an individual and that we all have our strong points. My parents have been interested in every one of us and have never missed a piano recital, a football game, a play, or any other event that one of us has been in. This has been so appreciated by us when other parents do not attend such functions. We kids all have pride in ourselves for what we are, and we are all proud of each other.

When parents fail to attend public functions in which their children perform, an emotional letdown occurs, as indicated in the next example. (See also the case in chapter 2 of the undersized boy whose father did not see him make the winning touchdown because he had gone home at halftime. Halftime fathers miss a great opportunity to contribute to the socialization of their sons.)

When I was in the little league, I pitched a game and drove in the winning run with a home run. Happiest little fellow in town, but no parents around to share with.

Parental Influence on Self-Image of Children

In some families the body image of the teenager is built up by appropriate remarks. For example:

My father has a very high regard for women and has treated his family accordingly. Ever since I can remember, my father has told me I was an attractive and interesting girl.

Conversely, we have families in which a mother will chide her daughter for being fat or ugly, and a drunken father will hurl epithets at his daughter such as tramp, whore, or slut, without the slightest justification. One girl stopped such epithets in the following manner:

Because Mother didn't show affection, I felt that something important was lacking in my life—love—and I looked forward to the day when I could start dating boys and find someone to love. It seemed as if I was constantly looking for signs of affection or recognition from both playmates and teachers. I became a very good student, eager to please my teachers.

During my high school years I had a good deal of conflict with my mother. When she was angry she called me all sorts of things, such as fat and ugly, giving me an inferiority complex that I haven't overcome to this day.

One day I made a list of all the names my mother had called me, and I put it where I knew she would see it. After she read it, she told me that it wasn't necessary to write down things like that. My method must have been effective, though, since she didn't call me any names after that.

The Importance of Timing

When children come home from school or a social setting, they are primed to tell parents the events of the day. It appears that it is important for parents to play the role of audience at this critical juncture.

> About the time I was twelve years old, I had a great deal to talk about. After school I would come into the house brimming over with what I thought was important information. In the telling of it my little brother would interrupt constantly, and then Mother would say, "Tell me about it later dear, when I can give you all my attention. You're older and you can wait." Because of my age and of my resentment toward my brother, I did not want to wait. When later did come, I did not feel like talking and gradually grew away from telling my family much about my feelings.

There is a time for praise and a time for correction. If a child has recently suffered rebuking by his teacher, teasing by a peer, or beating by a sibling, he is not in a mood to accept lecturing by a parent. A child should not be confronted at bedtime with any subject that will cause him embarrassment, anxiety, or fear. Some well-functioning families have a rule that unpleasant subjects are not to be aired at the table or at bedtime.

Courage to Face Dystrophic Realities

Some of my students and some of the readers of this book may have families that are thoroughly dystrophic. It is not easy to face such a reality for analysis. The following excerpt shows how one girl, Bridget, from such a family met the challenge of the analysis.

> For a considerable time I had difficulty writing this paper because my mind comes up blank. I think this is because I have so many negative feelings about my family. It is hard for me to talk, think, or write about it. My frustration makes me cry as I write. Your outline prompts positive reactions to most of the questions. When I look at them, I realize I've no positive things to say about my family. I feel there must be something wrong with me. I began to think I had a message telling me I got what I deserved. The outline was a sting and hard to bear because it didn't seem to apply to my family. It seems unbelievable that there is so little good in my family. Yet I know it is true. The only reason why my parents don't get a divorce is because they have too much pride and because they have no one else to turn to.

Bridget described the impact of her mother's behavior:

> It destroyed your individuality as a person; she had her own mold for you, and as a perfectionist she wanted you to fit into it perfectly. It was like

being a robot. If you rebelled, you were almost disowned, and my dad sat back and watched. I wanted to get out, so I went to college. Since then there are two teams at war: my mom and sister versus my dad and brother.

During her high school days, Bridget's social life was limited, partly because she had to help with work at home and partly because her parents restricted her social life. Nevertheless, she was elected to some class offices and won a number of school awards.

Never once was I complimented. I would run to tell them what honor I had received, and all I would get was a blank look. Just recently I won the presidency of my dormatory that houses 300 girls—what I thought was a real honor. I was so excited I phoned my parents, and when I told them, they simply said, "So what? Is that all you called for?" I guess I was starved for a little praise. Because of their treatment of all of us, I've lost respect for them. They hurt me so much. It took me until this year to realize that I was somebody and not a worthless nobody as so many parental messages told me.

The compulsion of parents to downgrade and the failure to upgrade their children usually arise from the dystrophic influences in their families of origin. Sometimes the narrator gives us a glimpse of these difficulties and sometimes not. The more Bridgets we have in our society, the more important it is for the rest of us to give them an uplifting word.

Some parents seem incapable of distinguishing between a trait and the person who at the moment displays the trait.

Father could not overlook minor faults in me and never ceased to harp on them till I came to believe that all he said was true about me. I felt a dissatisfaction in my person, my schoolwork, and my friends, all of which I wanted to shield from his scrutinizing eye. My shortcomings were failures to him that tarnished his armor of perfection. He personalized everything. His incantations on my person made me feel stupid, unwanted, and belittled. I had little confidence when associating with other people and tended to withdraw from any competition for fear of failing. Whenever I was home, his criticism and rules regarding my conduct made me feel suppressed, as if something heavy was always upon me. In social situations where I was having fun, I would feel guilty for fear that my father would find out about it and disapprove. I had dreams in which I rebelled against authority.

Parental failure to praise children leaves a vacuum that is easily filled with criticism. It is difficult to assess consequences from these patterns in the children because there are so many other factors in dystrophic families, but we may surmise that the absence of positive stroking and the persistance of negative stroking tend to:

Crush the ego and stultify growth,

Intensify feelings of inadequacy and worthlessness,

Lead to loss of respect for parents,

Induce hatred of parents when severe enough,

Arouse in children ideas of being unwanted and unloved,

Discourage self-disclosure vis-à-vis the parents.

Parental Attitudes toward Peers of Children

Another pattern that makes children either happy or unhappy is the attitude of parents toward friends of the children, especially when the friends come into the home. Children are quick to ascertain the degree to which they are welcome in the homes of their friends. In every neighborhood, children congregate in a few homes and avoid certain other homes. Some of the reasons why a child will not invite friends into his home are:

Constant quarreling or fighting between parents;

Hostile or critical attitude of the parents toward his peers;

Tendency of parents to judge friends on superficial characteristics;

The fussing of immaculate housekeepers;

Fear that a parent will be rude, discourteous, or vulgar to friends;

Fear that a parent may be intoxicated;

Ashamed of dirty or disorderly home;

Ashamed of parents or siblings.

In pantrophic middle-class families, the parents tend to encourage the association of their children with their peers in all sorts of organized activities, and they often chaperone such activities. They also assist their children in organizing house parties and are courteous, cordial, and helpful to the friends of their children. A number of students have mentioned the satisfaction of having parents who promote peer friendships in such ways. We have seen other students from unhappy homes describe the satisfactions they had from visiting the homes of their friends (see chapter 2 for the case of the girl who fell in love with her boyfriend's family). This attitude of parents toward the friends of their children is a prelude to how they will greet the dates of their children during the dating and courtship periods.

Parental Controls

Psychologists have distinguished between the long-term effectiveness of punishment with short-term effectiveness, and they usually concede that physical punishment is associated with the latter. Persons from pantrophic families do not use the term *discipline;* it is not necessary. Such parents, however, develop the inner controls of their children quite successfully. The following is a typical example:

> My parent are easygoing and very proud of their family. They never believed in physical punishment. Whenever we did anything wrong, they would sit down and discuss it with us, and sometimes this would hurt more than a spanking. They would point out what we had done wrong and why it was wrong or ask us why we had behaved in a certain manner. Because we had to answer for our own actions, we learned to question ourselves as well, thus developing a conscience. They never had any real discipline problems with us, I think basically because they have always trusted us completely and always believed that we were telling the truth. Because they did trust us and put their faith in us, we always tried to live up to their expectations and act accordingly. We didn't want to lose their trust. None of us children has ever rebelled against them because there was nothing to rebel against. My parents have never told us what to do; they have asked, suggested, and encouraged but never ordered. They have always assumed that we had a mind of our own and expected us to use it.

Several bizarre types of punishment came to my attention. One mother, when frustrated, would carry out her threat to leave the children. She would be gone for three or four hours, and the children would become hysterical. The eldest wrote:

> You can't imagine how alone you can feel when your father is almost a complete stranger and your mother walks out of the house. And there you are left alone. I used to wish I were dead on these occasions.

Another student wrote:

> My dad was never very affectionate, and I was afraid of him. He was very strict, and our punishment was that of being whipped with a belt on our bare rears. One particular instance is especially vivid in my mind. My youngest sister, who was about four years old, had lit several matches in our bedroom. I was five years old and my brother about eight. My dad felt she should be punished to teach her not to play with fire. My brother and I had to hold her hands and feet down while my dad beat her with a leather strap.

In the next case, the parents employed different methods of control, both of them harmful:

Neither of my parents has much tact concerning the punishment and correction of children. My father uses sheer physical strength to punish us. He lets his temper override his better judgment and proceeds with punishment before finding out what has happened and who is to blame. Thus, an innocent victim often received unjust punishment, leading to rebellion and resentment among the children. My mother is very inconsistent with punishments. When she is tired or angry, she will punish one of us for something, and later when we do the same thing, she'll overlook it.

It is not uncommon among families that tend toward the dystrophic end of the scale for the father to say to a child who protests an order or a restriction, "If you don't like it here, you can always pack up and leave." The children in such families typically react with resentment, rebellion, hatred, and a breaking of communication.

The following excerpt indicates the feeling of one student regarding various methods of parental control:

My parents trained me by striking, yelling, reasoning, and withdrawal of privileges. The two latter were OK, but the two former I'll never use myself. I hated it when they hit me; it made me feel infantile and ashamed, and I thought less of them too. Yelling is the worst though. I can't take it. It's like knives in the ears. Yelling drove me away from home sometimes. [Toward the end of his paper this young man wrote] The prospect of raising children scares the hell out of me.

From my papers I have roughly classified various kinds of parental controls from the least effective to the most effective. Evaluating such controls within the family is complicated because of varying degrees of harshness, the counterinfluences of the other parent and siblings, and the age and personality of the child. I list, according to effectiveness, a rough description of the kinds of parental controls I found:

Physical punishment by an arbitrary, authoritative, demanding, angry parent administered to an innocent child;

A mixture of yelling threats combined with physical punishment administered inconsistently;

Physical punishment administered by an authoritative parent who uses punishment consistently;

A combination of physical punishment with withdrawal of privileges;

A combination of reasoning with physical punishment and withdrawal of privileges;

Withdrawal of privileges and reasoning;

Reasoning in the context of a trusting *hestia* and development of inner controls.

Communication

Parental methods of control over a child affect the nature of communication between the two. A well-functioning family system requires a good communication system, with the parents as models for the establishment of communicative patterns. Quality in communication involves what to say, what not to say, how much to say, when to say it, and how to say it. Parents convey things to children not only with their vocal apparatus but also with their eyes, facial expression, bodily stance, touch, and gestures. There should be a congruence between the content of what is said and body movements. If the latter are inconsistent with the former, the parent is putting the child in a double bind, and the situation is unhealthy.

Previous cases have suggested what to say in terms of manifesting affection, praise, trust, encouragement, and so on, but what about things that should not be said? We might have bedlam if family membrs communicated all their irritations. Sometimes nothing is to be gained by hurting one you love by blurting out the brutal truth—that is, the truth as it is perceived. On closer inspection, the brutal truth may involve the person less and the circumstance more. It may turn out that the truth regarding the behavior of the other is partly the consequence of your own behavior or of someone else's behavior.

However, some circumstances warrant loud and clear communication to family members that undesirable behavior on the part of one member is damaging to the person and to the family and that it will not be covered up as, for example, when a family member is on the verge of alcoholism.

If parents observe that a child seems to be hiding resentments or is covertly suffering from anxiety, knowing what to say, what not to say, and how and when to say something to ventilate the child's feelings calls for empathy and skill.

How to talk to a child involves an examination of parental voice patterns. Verbal expression is the prime mode of family communication, yet very little attention has been given in marriage and family literature to the differential quality of voice patterns within the family and how such patterns affect the family system. Often the way something is said can have greater impact for good or ill than what is said. For example, a student confided to me, "When my mother asks me to pass the milk at the breakfast table, she says it in such a manner that I feel like throwing the milk bottle at her."

How can parents organize patterns of family behavior in order to pre-

vent emotional blockage and to improve communication? Chapter 12 provides a few illustrations of family councils. There is no standard practice for
such councils; they range from those that are regular and a bit formal to
those that are more spontaneous and informal. However, whatever type
prevails, they seem to be developing in middle-class families with beneficial
effects. In the following case, we have a pattern of a family council that
seemed to facilitate, along with other elements in the family, the one-to-one
communication between parent and child on a deeper level. This was a pantrophic family. The student reported that both parents had a high degree of
empathy, and the children were encouraged to voice opinions on all matters
affecting the family. Family discussions usually took place during the evening meal and sometimes continued for hours. Affection was openly
displayed.

> Though supper was the time when everyone got into the act, there were
> times when I could be alone with my parents to talk to them in private.
> After supper was a quiet time, and if I wanted to say anything to either of
> them, I would simply go up to one and say I wanted to speak to him, and
> then we would go for a walk or to an empty room and hash everything out.
> I never had difficulty communicating with my parents. I've enjoyed con-
> versing with them. I value their ideas and experience, although I don't
> always agree fully with them. Many of my friends envied the easy and in-
> formal relationship my sisters and I maintained with my parents.
>
> The main elements that make our family so stable, I think, are the genuine
> love expressed and well-established communication. Communication is the
> main element, I think, that gives our family its solidarity and stability. It is
> this communication from which all other elements seem to stem. Com-
> munication is something that every member is involved in. No one person
> does all the talking.

In contrast, I quote a paragraph from one student's experience in a
dystrophic family:

> Our opinions were never welcomed. Children should be seen, not heard. I
> think I've been told to shut up more often than being greeted with a hello. I
> can remember finding, when I was seven or eight and trying hard to make it
> through the day without a fight with my mother, that I couldn't do it. Even
> when I said nothing at all, she would get mad.''

Most textbooks on the family point up the cultural expectation that
men have task roles while women have expressive roles.[10] My experience
with students suggests that a considerable percentage of fathers are superior
to their wives in developing empathic relationships with their children. It
would be interesting to know what this percentage is and whether it is increasing. The following example is one of many of its kind:

It was always easier for me to talk to my father than to my mother, and I think my brothers and sisters felt this way also. When we had a problem my mother would be very pragmatic about it, and emotions were very seldom considered. She had no patience with someone who is emotionally torn about something or is depressed. Her solution was simple: "You just don't think about it."

Conversely, my father would listen to a problem, sympathize, and, although his solution would invariably be the same as that offered by my mother in a given situation, he would make us feel that he understood how we felt and that it wasn't necessarily a sign of weakness to be depressed about a problem. He always managed to give me confidence in my own feelings and decisions, and I would feel better just having talked things over with him.

In the following case the reader can sense how the negative *hestia* of the family was influenced by the nature of its communication. The two following excerpts imply that the absence of patterns expressing affection is a deterrent to effective communication. The oldest son left home ahead of the other children and established an enviable record in his profession. When he returned home for a visit, his siblings, although proud of him,

were bashful and polite. It would have been hard to tell whether he was our brother or a stranger. In evaluating the negative aspects of our family, I think the foremost disappointment is lack of communication and closeness my parents had with us. The extent of confiding in our parents was almost nil and can never improve. This I regret and resent.

Although we seem to be unusually considerate of each other, we were raised in an atmosphere where little or no affection was displayed between parents or between parents and children. We know they love each other and us, and yet I have never seen them kiss each other. This seems to be an important reason for our being reserved and polite in childhood. Even with close friends, I often feel unable to express myself for fear of being laughed at or ignored. Being sensitive and insecure prevents me from cultivating the people I like. I have resented this fact for a long time. My resentment is aimed at my parents' inability to teach me to reach out to people and not be afraid of them.

If parents are rigid, authoritarian, and have limited education compared to their children, they may stifle self-expression in their offspring; communication between parent and child thus is not only stymied but also the assertiveness of the child is damaged. In many cases the generation gap is apparent.

I hate to hurt my parents, but I really don't know what to talk about when I am around them. We have so little in common. If I said something or broached a subject they considered inappropriate for may age, they were quick to tell me that I "shouldn't know about that stuff." I actually became afraid to say anything in front of them, unless I was dead right. Even today I don't find it easy to converse with anyone unless I am sure of the person or unless I know I'm right. However, I did get to be a good listener.

My parents and I do not communicate very well because they think I am a brainwashed college student who is just trying to show them up and reject their ideas.

You couldn't reason with my father. I learned not to argue with him on anything, and because of his inability to reason, I could never confide in him.

A father who is preoccupied with his business or profession, shares no activities with his children, and sees them briefly on rare occasions will hardly get to know them. His communication with them will be artificial, and his indifferences toward them will be reciprocated by his children.

If children are encouraged to elaborate on their experiences in their school settings, to participate in family discussions on general news, and encouraged to express their opinions on family affairs, they will get some preliminary practice in articulation, thinking before an audience, and assertiveness that will be advantageous to them in the outside world.

Voice Patterns

It would be logical to treat voice patterns of the family in a single chapter, but I find it necessary to treat them in both subsystems: parent-child and husband-wife (see chapter 14). Parents have influence on the children's habits of communication that will later determine how well the children will be able to attract friends and lovers—that is, how well the parents as models instill in their offspring the habit of speaking in a pleasant tone.

Without regard to content, a voice can please and soothe a child or sting him into panic. The reactions of children (and adults) to the same unpleasant voice vary tremendously, and this leads to my theory that sensitivity to the tone of voice varies tremendously from person to person, and perhaps in lesser degree with the same person from time to time, depending on his fatigue and frustrations.

The speech habits acquired in childhood are likely carried over into adulthood without modification. These speech habits are of two varieties: relaxed tonal quality and angry tonal quality. As most people move from a state of relaxation to anger, the pitch, loudness, quality, and inflection of their voices change markedly. The tongue now becomes a stilleto. Some people seem immune from verbal stabbing, but others are wounded.

Some families are loud speaking, others are soft speaking. Differences in sensitivity to loudness could be explained partly by backgound factors. One girl said that her parents spoke softly and admonished her during childhood to speak in soft tones—so much so that she longed to run out in the open and scream to her heart's content. She might suffer, however, if she married a loud-speaking man.

I theorize that sensitivity to unusual voice patterns can be so extreme as to take on an allergic character. If this be so, it would explain in part why a father who was prosecuted for homicide after striking his child said to questioning authorities, "The kid was screaming and I lost my head." Other cases of extreme reaction to painful voice tone are given in an article I published in 1960.[11] In this article I set forth some findings from the use of a questionnaire that my students had filled out, giving data about the nature of the voice patterns of their parents and the reactions of the listening spouse.

Scolding, yelling, and screaming parents alienate their children and impede parent-child communication. The sad part of this situation is that the offending parents may never come to realize that the children may be reacting painfully to the voice far more than the adults in the family. Parents also do not always appreciate how they are setting the pattern for yelling so that the children also contribute to the bedlam. For example:

> Whenever some one person has something to say to someone else in our family, it seems that they can't say it decently but that they have to yell or holler at the person. I get the habit of yelling from my parents, and everyone in the family does the same.

Alienation of children and the withdrawal from communication because of unpleasant voice patterns are illustrated in the following:

> In your questionnaire, you asked us to estimate how much each parent suffers from the unpleasant voice tone of the other. I feel it was I who suffered from unpleasant voice tones. To this day I am very intolerant of people who speak in a harsh, strident tone. I do not feel it necessary for mature adults to resort to this childish mannerism. When a point must be made, a well-modulated voice will keep an audience much longer than a harsh, shrill one. It is often true that the tone of voice can be much more offending than what you are saying. The effect all this had on me is hard to measure. One result is that I am not very close with my father. It has caused me to be reluctant to discuss problems with him. The tendency of my father to raise his voice when he is mad or irritated has been a definite reason why we kids don't show any real emotion toward him.

When parents argue in loud tones, they may be oblivious of the effects on children who may not manifest outward signs of distress. In one such case the husband downgraded his wife with harsh tones. After suffering from his ranting, she would rebuff his affectionate overtures and a vicious circle was established by mutual feedback. In this case (a family of seven children), an eight-year-old boy was invited by a friend to go as a guest to a professional baseball game. The friend's father had the tickets and would provide the transportation. However, he declined the invitation. Later the mother questioned her son as to why he did not go to the ballgame. He finally blurted out, "What if they [the parents of his friend] should get into an argument?"

Loud arguments with nagging and yelling consume so much nervous energy that none is left for constructive pursuits, as the next case indicates.

> My father would yell at the top of his voice, and my mother would also raise her voice and her tone would change into a screech. They argued loudly like this about eight times a week until our relatives were talking about it. My father is impulsive and my mother is untactful. She nags and nags until a person could scream. Her voice can be very unpleasant. The fights, the tension, and the voice tone can actually make me sick. I get splitting headaches. Everyone in the family is very nervous. If something is bothering someone, he gets excited, tense, and irritable. All these things cause arguments to get out of hand.

> Since my home was always noisy with five children, it was difficult to concentrate on one's private affairs. This noise is the paradox of my family life, for while there was constant chatter among the members, the level of communication was very low. We all seemed to be talking at one another. It was difficult for me to confide in my mother, because she never really heard me. There was little communication of ideas or opinions between my parents. Their differing backgrounds made it difficult for them to see eye to eye. My mother's inability to convey her ideas produced a steady rise in the pitch of her voice. We all suffered, but this was almost unbearable for my father, and soon his voice would begin to get louder, but it never rose in pitch like Mother's. Daddy was always sensitive to the volume of conversation, and we children were taught to restrain it as much as possible.

This lack of communication was most evident in time of family crises, when both parents' first reaction was panic. This panic engulfed the children too.

> My family was characterized by tension, fear of inadequacy, and continual nervous chatter. Both parents had rigid personalities; they were products of insecurity and were confused in their roles. Consequently, their attitudes to each other and to their children were in a continual state of change. All this produced confusion in each of us that only found its resolution outside the home.

The student who wrote that excerpt indicated on his questionnaire that each parent suffered greatly from the voice tone of the other, that they had considerable conflict, but that they did show some affection for each other.

The following excerpts were taken from papers describing the nature of communication in pantrophic families.

> The quality of communication between my parents is excellent. My parents always seem to understand each other's views and motives. They respect each other's ideas and always reach an agreement on a problem that is satisfying to both of them. Both my parents have soft voices, and they rarely raise them. They have similar gestures. They never seem nervous but give the impression of being relaxed. When I hear my parents talking, I get a feeling of satisfaction. My mother never lost her southern accent, and her soft southern drawl is very pleasing to the ear.

> Problem solving in my family is done through democratic discussion. If a problem arises that affects the whole family, each of has a voice in its solution. I would say that my parents have equal power concerning family affairs.

> The general emotional tone of my family is excellent. Everyone in my family is stable, relaxed, happy, and satisfied with life. The social roles in my family are congruent.

> My sister Susie told my mother recently that she thought she had the best parents in the world. I agree with Susie. The environment they created when I grew up was wonderful. I respect them very much and hope never to do anything to make them ashamed or embarrassed for their son.

In my previous discussion on affection, trust, respect, and positive stroking, I suggested that these favorable traits that are found in pantrophic families seemed to cluster. To this cluster, or syndrome, we can add adequate communication between parents and child facilitated by pleasing voice patterns.

In selecting excerpts to illustrate problems in communication between parents and children, it is not possible to go into the details of family history to show the complexities that led to chronic and violent argument over trivia. If parents comprehend any such situation in their family, they should contact a family counselor forthwith.

Although there are some advantages in dealing with parent-child relations as a subsystem of the family and husband-wife relations as another subsystem (chapter 14), there is also a disadvantage because it is often impossible to disentangle problems of communication between parent and child from difficulties in all other relationships. I shall lead up to this dilemma in the next case. Occasionally, a parent will be so hurt by his spouse that he solicits help and comfort from one of the teenage sons or daughters. If the parent, in addition, recruits the teenager as an ally against the other spouse, the situation is unhealthy and calls for treatment by a family counselor.

In one situation, the older daughter (whom I shall call Phoebe) had a good rapport with her father. Phoebe conflicted with a sister, Jo, who was three years younger. Whenever the mother became upset by the behavior of the father, she would take her complaints to the three oldest children, Phoebe, Jo, and a brother. The brother tried to remain neutral, and Phoebe resented her mother's attempt to involve the children in the spousal quarrel. Jo readily sided with her mother against the father, and Phoebe found herself defending the father. This situation was most distressing for Phoebe, who was now in conflict with both her mother and Jo. According to Phoebe, "My mother became very resentful toward my father whenever he and I agreed or even attained any level of communication."

In the scapegoating phenomenon, the parents displace the venom they have for each other into the scapegoat child, but in this case the father, who covertly loved his daughter, was pressured by the mother to overtly express hostility toward her. This was the interpretation of Phoebe, who wrote:

When I was about seventeen, things reached a peak, and in order for my father to maintain a civil relationship with my mother, he was forced to express disgust and dissatisfaction toward me whenever my mother thought it was necessary, and she thought it was necessary often. This was another destructive force in my relationship with my mother because I felt as though I had lost my one important contact with my family. My father and I have grown quite distant, but I still have strong feelings toward him. Perhaps I am being unfair to my mother, but I blame any problems I have with my father on the interference of my mother when I was younger. I have always felt that my mother was unconsciously jealous of the love my dad had for me and that she tried to destroy it. As I begin to write about the kind of communication my family has, I realize that this is the basis of all our difficulties. The communication between my parents and us children is shallow. When I was younger, my mother would set my hair every Saturday night, and this process would take about twenty-five minutes. I think this was one of the most dreaded experiences because we would be alone and I just would have to listen and always be on the defensive. Even now when we are alone, a tense and uncomfortable atmosphere prevails. Because of this, we have grown further apart until it has reached a point where we barely know one another. It is really pathetic how I feel comfortable to be free and open with my friends' mothers but cannot be like this with my own mother.

It must be obvious that there is something lacking in the emotional tone of my family. Neither of my parents has been affectionate toward the other or toward us children. I've grown up longing for this affection and feeling that what love is present is little and shallow.

This plea for more genuine manifestations of parental love runs through hundreds of my papers. The number of children who suffer the handicaps to growth emphasizes how badly our society has need of family counselors.

Notes

1. Augustus Y. Napier and Carl A. Whitaker, *The Family Crucible* (New York: Harper and Row, 1978).

2. Elihu M. Gerson, "On Quality of Life," *American Sociological Review* (1976):793–805.

3. John W.M. Whiting, Richard Kluckholn, and Alber Anthony, "The Function of Male Initiation Ceremonies at Puberty," *Personality and Social Life,* ed. Robert Endleman (New York: Random House, 1966).

4. Norman W. Bell and Ezra Vogel, *A Modern Introduction to the Family,* Rev. ed. (New York: Free Press, 1968), pp.412–427.

5. K.M. Tooley, "Irreconcilable Differences between Parent and Child: A Case Report of Interactional Pathology," *American Journal of Orthopsychiatry* 48 (1980):703–716.

6. B. Bender, "Self-Chosen Victims: Scapegoating Behavior Sequential to Battery," *Child Welfare* 55 (1976):417–422.

7. Virginia Satir, *People Making* (Palo Alto, Calif.: Science and Behavior Books, 1972).

8. J.G. Corazzini, "Trust as a Complex Multi-dimensional Construct," *Psychological Report* 40 (February 1977):75–78.

9. Ronald P. Rohner, *They Love Me, They Love Me Not* (New Haven, Conn.: Human Relations Area Files Press, 1975).

10. J. Richard Udry, *The Social Context of Marriage,* 3rd ed. (New York: Lippincott, 1974).

11. Gordon Shipman, "Speech Thresholds and Voice Tolerance in Marital Interaction," *Marriage and Family Living* 22 (August 1960):203–209. Copyrighted 1960 by the National Council on Family Relations. Reprinted by permission.

14 Husband-Wife Communication

Noise Pollution in the Home

Recently, both psychiatrists and acoustical experts have emphasized the need for sound control in the home. Noise pollution from a dozen or more electrical appliances is the background upon which we must consider the effect of voice patterns in husband-wife interaction. Dr. Jack Westman has provided charts to indicate how the noise in decibels from sixteen different electrical appliances in the home is related to annoyance; activation of the automatic nervous system; increases in adrenalin, peristalsis, and gastric juice flow; and reduction in work efficiency.[1] This strain is superimposed upon the existing auditory stimulation from radio, television, stereos, and the crying of children. This accumulation of auditory stress, along with other stresses, increases the likelihood of scolding and shouting by parental figures with tones that are loud, shrill, and harsh. This kind of strain is intensified when large families are crowded into small living quarters; my students from such homes have reasoned that this situation had increased disorder, tension, and conflict. When family sociologists chart the rise and fall of marital satisfaction during the family life cycle, they should also chart the rise and fall of noise pollution in the home. It would be interesting to know whether the decrease in marital satisfaction during the middle years, when children are of school age, coincides with a period of increase in noise pollution.

When a couple marries, each brings to his or her system of communication the peculiar speech habits of their respective families. Such variations are numerous and complex, with nuances of inflection, emphasis, and quality.[2] Some families are loud-spoken; others are soft-spoken.

Speech Patterns and Communication

The speech patterns of parents greatly influence the nature of communication throughout the family system. Children acquire similarities in voice quality of their parents through inheritance and nuances of emphasis and inflection through learning in the context of their family cultures. Let us now identify some speech patterns that have a bearing on communication.

219

If we give our attention to speech patterns of husbands and wives, we should hear differences among couples in their tendency to use a given syntax or kind of sentence when they want a spouse to do something. Let us suppose a wife wants her husband to fix a dripping faucet. She could address him in one of three different kinds of sentences as:

1. Declaratory sentence: Honey, this faucet needs fixing.
2. Imperative sentence: Honey, please fix this faucet.
3. Interrogatory sentence: Honey, will you please fix this faucet?

Declaratory sentences are welcome when they convey compliments, frustrating when compliments are not forthcoming, and damaging when they are derogatory. Imperative sentences can be destructive, and too many interrogations can be irritating. Thus, in family life, one is damned if he says the wrong thing, in the wrong way, too often, and damned if he does not say the right thing, in the right way, often enough. One has to be alert to establish a pantrophic family.

Threshold of Verbalization

I now examine another feature of speech that seems to be an aspect of personality and fairly constant for most people. I call it the *threshold of verbalization,* which roughly measures the readiness of a person to speak in a social situation.[3] On the one hand is the compulsive talker; on the other hand is the person in a catatonic stupor. The former speaks as soon as he sees you and is not inclined to stop. The other will not say a word until he has been manhandled and shouted at. Most people are somewhere in between. The threshold of verbalization, therefore, is the amount or degree of social stimulation necessary to induce a speech response in a person. The low-threshold person tends to interrupt others and speaks more frequently and perhaps longer in ordinary conversation. The high-threshold person would be more deliberate with his speech responses to social stimulus. He might pause, swallow, clear his throat, and then slowly say something. The threshold by itself is not especially meaningful; a person with any reasonable threshold may be delightful and charming, or he may be a nuisance. In the study of couples, the threshold of verbalization is meaningful only when a wide discrepancy exists between spouses or when it is associated with certain other characteristics of speech.

Threshold Differences

In developing my study of voice patterns within the family, I gave a questionnaire to my students. On the first item the student rated the threshold for his or her father and mother on a seven-point scale. According to student perceptions (table 14–1), there was a significant trend for mothers to have lower thresholds of verbalization than fathers. Furthermore, anxiety lowered the threshold for 60 percent of the women but for only 35 percent of the men, while fatigue raised the threshold for 40 percent of the men and only 28 percent of the women. In other words, the mothers were prone to talk more when anxious, and a good number of men were prone to talk less when fatigued. One sample of ninety couples indicated that mothers were more nervous and anxious than fathers in fifty-two cases, while the reverse was true in sixteen cases.

One might speculate that couples with extreme differences in thresholds have wide differences in temperament or in activity levels. The only significant relationship we can find between happiness and threshold of verbalization is to be found in threshold differentials among couples, as shown in table 14–2. Slight differences in thresholds of verbalization are more common with happy couples, while greater differences characterize the unhappy couples. When we analyze the interaction patterns of unhappy couples, we seem to find certain syndromes or configurations, one of which I anticipated from my casework experience. In these syndromes (to be described presently), wide differences in thresholds were an important feature.

In my student questionnaire, the students rated their parents on a five-point scale on numerous items including: voice tones from the very well modulated to quite strident and harsh, each in normal conversation and when tired or angry; happiness of parents' marriage; the extent to which

Table 14–1
Relation of Threshold of Verbalization to Sex, 271 Couples

Threshold	Fathers	Mothers
Above midpoint	102	43
Midpoint	70	60
Below midpoint	99	168

Source: Modified from Gordon Shipman, "Speech Thresholds and Voice Tolerance in Marital Interaction," *Marriage and Family Living* 22 (1960):206–208. Copyrighted © 1960 by the National Council on Family Relations. Reprinted by permission.

$X^2 = 42.6$
$P \le .01$

Table 14-2
Differentials in Threshold and Happiness Scores of Husband and Wife, 270 Couples

Differential in Threshold	Unhappy and Very Unhappy		Average		Happy and Very Happy	
	Number	Percent	Number	Percent	Number	Percent
4 or more	7	22	21	23	13	9
3	7	22	9	10	14	9
2 or less	18	56	60	67	121	82
Total	32	100	90	100	148	100

Source: Modified from Gordon Shipman, "Speech Thresholds and Voice Tolerance in Marital Interaction," *Marriage and Family Living* 22 (1960): 206–208. Copyrighted © 1960 by the National Council on Family Relations. Reprinted by permission.

each suffered from the voice of the other; critical rate and annoyance thereto; degree of conflict; dominance-submissiveness; mode of argumentation; and conflict.

It happened by chance that 32 couples out of the 270 rated very high in happiness and 32 couples rated unhappy or very unhappy. A comparison of these two groups is made in figures 14–1 and 14–2. Figure 14–1 gives the voice scores for the happy and unhappy couples during normal conversation. Figure 14–2 gives the scores for couples when they were tired or angry.

Among the very happy couples, the wives had better voice tone than their husbands in normal conversation and less strident voices when angry. The percentage of wives in the well-modulated categories was 75; for husbands, 56. The percentage of happy wives in strident-voice categories when angry was 62; for husbands, 66. Among the unhappy couples it was just the reverse: the unhappy wives had smaller percentages fitting into the well-modulated voice categories for normal conversation, 31 for wives and 44 for husbands, and larger percentages than their husbands in the strident-voice categories when angry, 94 to 78.

This reversal on a sex basis from the happy to the unhappy couples in terms of voice modulation suggests a greater variance in the function of speech among women and that, in family interaction, the female voice has greater potential for good or ill. It also suggests that the emotional tensions of women find release by way of the speech apparatus more often than those of men. Sixty percent of the unhappy wives were rated as being nervous and anxious, while only 3 percent of the happy wives were so rated.

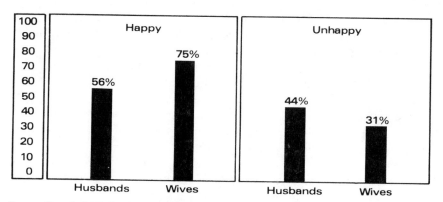

Source: Data is from Gordon Shipman, "Speech Thresholds and Voice Tolerance in Marital Interaction," *Marriage and Family Living,* 22 (1960). Copyrighted © 1960 by the National Council on Family Relations. Reprinted by permission.

Figure 14–1. Percentage of Good Voice Scores among Happy and Unhappy Couples

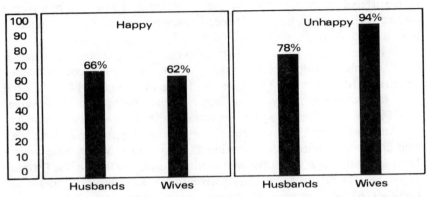

Source: Data is from Gordon Shipman, "Speech Thresholds and Voice Tolerance in Marital Interaction," *Marriage and Family Living,* 22 (1960). Copyrighted © 1960 by the National Council on Family Relations. Reprinted by permission.

Figure 14–2. Percentage of Strident Voices among Happy and
Unhappy Couples

We should keep in mind, however, that the quality of a wife's voice may be a reflection of how well or how poorly her husband treats her.

When under stress, women increase the pitch of their voices from a higher base than men—their normal pitch being one octave higher. Thus, the perception of this change in pitch by the listener will be greater compared to a similar change in men's voice. In normal conversation the voice of a man is ten decibels louder than that of a woman. This involves twice the loudness and three times the energy.[4] This supports my previous observation concerning the tendency of men to talk less when fatigued.

Much of these data fit in logically with lower verbalization thresholds of women when anxious. One possible explanation for this was suggested by a colleague: "Wives sometimes attempt to cope with anxiety by talking, partly in response to the husband becoming more quiet when she is anxious. She may be trying to goad him into discussing a subject while his defense of withdrawal protects him. His silence may be as hostile as her speech."[5]

It is not always the husband who withdraws, or the wife who nags, as we observe in the following case:

My father nags my mother until she finally gives in. If his nagging doesn't work, he resorts to shouting and swearing. My mother hates it when he swears and so she withdraws, leaving the room or sometimes the house. My father withdraws when my mother brings up something he doesn't want to discuss. My mother tries to avoid conflicts and often will not discuss a problem with him but takes care of it herself. My father has a very bad temper, and he often starts these conflicts. My mother's voice can be shrill and high and even sarcastic. My father is very loud, and this really bothers my mother. It also scares my younger brothers as it did me when I was young. My father can be very childish. He often pouts or refuses to go somewhere. He does this as a way of punishing my mother. My mother has learned to ignore him when he is like this as have the rest of us. Communication in my family is very poor.

The fact that my students have described many more illustrations of offending voice patterns of mother than of father requires some explanation. In this case, the mother had a shrill voice and the father had a loud and threatening voice. When partners are angry it seems typical for the woman's voice to rise more in pitch and the man's voice to rise more in intensity or loudness. For children, the reaction to the mother's shrill tones is annoyance, while the reaction to the father's loud and threatening voice is fear. Since women are usually more nurturant and make the greater adjustment in marriage than men do, we may have more cases of mothers whose nurturant qualities are appreciated by the children. If we have a mother who has many fine qualities, her scolding voice may stand out in such contrast to her other fine attributes that the son or daughter is given to describe it because of the contrast. There is perhaps another explanation for the syndrome of the scolding wife and the withdrawing husband. Our culture puts a damper on the expression of emotion by men; it permits them, however, to indulge in aggressive behavior, both active and passive. Although middle-class mores forbid them to strike women, the culture permits them to swear and to withdraw. Opportunities to exercise passive aggression by withdrawal seem to be greater for a man than a woman. Society permits him to withdraw, without giving reasons, to the basement, the workshop, the club, the fishpond, or the tavern. A wife who withdraws to like places is castigated for neglecting her home.

Three kinds of withdrawal patterns result from verbal clashes: (1) The first is more of a truce during which each partner can find surcease from his tensions, reassess the issue, and consider how to make amends. Many students devoted some attention to how their parents released tensions in some constructive way like heightened physical activity in kitchen, workshop, or garden. When the adrenalin has drained off, the couple is in a better mood to resolve their differences. (2) The withdrawal may be a justified move for self-protection as when one withdraws from a partner whose rage or intoxication presents a physical danger or when relief from nervous tension is imperative. (3) Withdrawal may be an act of passive aggression in which silence, secrecy, and refusal to resolve an issue or to take responsibility for a decision is paramount.

Since it is neither possible nor desirable to withdraw from the source of an irritating voice, except on rare occasions, it is appropriate to study the voice patterns of men and women as to quality and their reactions to the voice of the other. Table 14–3 shows the extent to which happy and unhappy couples suffered from the voice patterns of their spouses. Although happiness is definitely related to the absence of irritation to the voice tone of the partner, a few in the happy group still suffered considerably from voice tone of the partner. However, nearly 60 percent of both husbands and wives in the happy group suffered only slightly or not at all from voice tone. Note also that the unhappy husbands suffered more than the unhappy wives from the voice of their partners; in the happy groups it was just the reverse.

It is reasonable to assume that students from pantrophic families, compared to those from dystrophic families, are using a different subjective scale in judging both voice tone and reaction to it. We can speculate that a student from a soft-spoken pantrophic family would rate a slightly angry tone much worse than a student from a loud-spoken dystrophic family. If such differences in judgment could be corrected, the results probably would be more in the direction of my theory.

Rates of Irritating Expressions

I now examine three verbal patterns in which the meaning and frequency have significance in interaction irrespective of voice quality. I define the *critical rate* as the number of criticisms a spouse directs to the other per unit of time. The results in percentages are given in figure 14–3 for 32 happy couples and 32 unhappy couples out of 270 couples. Among the unhappy couples, the fathers were usually or always blaming or criticizing the mother in 53 percent of the cases, while the mothers did likewise to the fathers in 72 percent of the cases. Among the very happy couples, the corresponding high critical rates were 12 and 9 percent.

The second pattern deals with the extent to which a spouse puts the other on the defensive. Questions like "What did you do with all that money?" can put one on the defensive and elicit feelings of guilt or resentment. This pattern is labeled *interrogation pressure*. Figure 14–4 gives the percentages for the same numbers of happy and unhappy couples involving high rates of interrogation pressure. Among the thirty-two unhappy couples, the interrogation pressure of the fathers toward their spouses was strong in 34 percent of the cases, while similar pressure of mothers toward their spouses was present in 59 percent of the cases. Similar percentages of fathers and mothers, respectively, in the very happy group were 12 and 9 percent.

A third pattern that delineated the meaning of verbal expression is neutral in the elicitation of positive or negative feeling in the listener, but the repetition or rate of expressions is the annoying feature. Sometimes a

Table 14-3
Association between Sensitivity to Voice Tone of Spouse and Marital Happiness, 270 Couples

Level of Sensitivity	Unhappy to Very Unhappy		Average		Happy to Very Happy	
	Number	Percent	Number	Percent	Number	Percent
Husband						
Much and very much	14	44	18	20	18	12
Some	12	37	32	35	43	29
Slightly or none	6	19	40	45	87	59
Total	32	100	90	100	148	100
Wife						
Much and very much	11	34	28	31	35	24
Some	11	34	24	27	27	18
Slightly or none	10	31	38	42	86	58
Total	32	99	90	100	148	100

Source: Modified from Gordon Shipman, "Speech Thresholds and Voice Tolerance in Marital Interaction," *Marriage and Family Living* 22 (1960): 206–208. Copyrighted © 1960 by the National Council on Family Relations. Reprinted by permission.

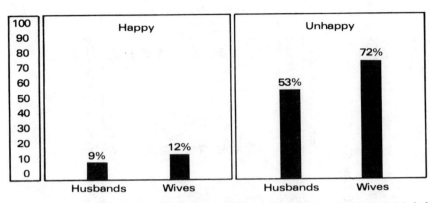

Source: Data is from Gordon Shipman, "Speech Thresholds and Voice Tolerance in Marital Interaction," *Marriage and Family Living,* 22 (1960). Copyrighted © 1960 by the National Council on Family Relations. Reprinted by permission.

Figure 14-3. Critical Rates among Happy and Unhappy Couples

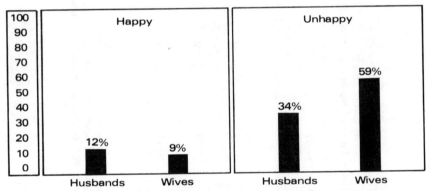

Source: Data is from Gordon Shipman, "Speech Thresholds and Voice Tolerance in Marital Interaction," *Marriage and Family Living,* 22 (1960). Copyrighted © 1960 by the National Council on Family Relations. Reprinted by permission.

Figure 14-4. Interrogation Pressure Rates among Happy and
Unhappy Couples

well-meaning spouse will request, direct, admonish, or correct certain behavior of the other. I call this the *admonition rate.* Each directive by itself may be sensible or even necessary, but the repetition of such directives leads to an accumulation of tension in the other spouse until an explosion occurs or the listener retreats with a slow burn. The annoyance may be due not only to the excessive rate of such expression but also to a sense of frustra-

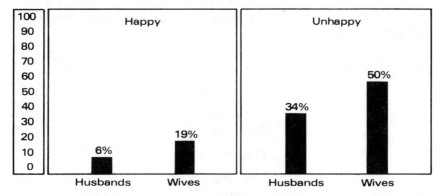

Source: Data is from Gordon Shipman, "Speech Thresholds and Voice Tolerance in Marital Interaction," *Marriage and Family Living,* 22 (1960). Copyrighted © 1960 by the National Council on Family Relations. Reprinted by permission.

Figure 14-5. Admonition Rates among Happy and Unhappy Couples

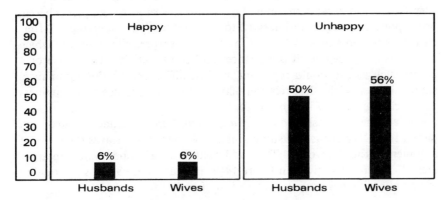

Source: Data is from Gordon Shipman, "Speech Thresholds and Voice Tolerance in Marital Interaction," *Marriage and Family Living,* 22 (1960). Copyrighted © 1960 by the National Council on Family Relations. Reprinted by permission.

Figure 14-6. Annoyance to Admonition

tion for lack of freedom and autonomy to perform a simple operation in one's own way. The percentages of high admonition rates for the thirty-two happy and thirty-two unhappy couples are given in figure 14–5. The percentages of annoyance to such rates are given in figure 14–6. The concept of the admonition rate is not as clear cut as the critical rate or the interrogation pressure, and I am not sure about its usefulness. However, observe that the unhappy couples had much higher rates and suffered much more annoyance than the happy couples.

A number of studies have indicated that equalitarian patterns are associated with marital happiness. Mine are no exception. My students checked their parents as in the following:

Father		Mother
_____ 5	Quite dominating	5 _____
_____ 4	Somewhat dominating	4 _____
_____ 3	Equalitarian	3 _____
_____ 2	Somewhat submissive	2 _____
_____ 1	Quite submissive	1 _____

We can imagine that a couple could be listed as reasonably equalitarian if a student checked any combination of 3-3, 4-3, or 3-2. Contrasting the very happy group with the unhappy group, the ratio of couples wherein both spouses are equalitarian is 12 to 1. Combinations involving a difference of two points such as 4-2, 5-3, or 1-3 would represent a couple in which there was some degree of dominance; and combinations involving 3 or 4 points such as 5-1 would represent marked difference on the dominance-submissiveness scale. The relation between such differences and happiness of the couple is given in table 14-4.

In another item called *mode of argumentation,* the students rated each parent from "vigorous and successful in argument" to "leaves the scene of argument without a word." The middle caption was "about equal in argument." The results, given in figure 14-7, indicate that patterns of equality in verbal exchanges are related to happy family life.

Analysis of Student Perceptions of Parental Voice Patterns

In the absence of standardized scales dealing with the quality of family life and quality of voice patterns, my students could only appraise the voice and interaction of patterns of their parents according to their impressions. How valid are such impressions? They may be better than those of an outside observer since the student has lived with his parents for twenty years or more. To get at these questions, I prevailed upon a few students to take home three questionnaires in order to get the evaluations of husband, wife, and student. I collected a dozen such triads.

I examined the ratings of husband, wife, and student on two items: (1)

Table 14-4
Differentials in Dominance-Submissiveness as Related to Happiness, 270 Couples

Differences	Unhappy and Very Unhappy		Average		Happy and Very Happy	
	Number	Percent	Number	Percent	Number	Percent
3 and 4	11	35	19	21	15	10
2	10	31	45	50	38	26
Less than 2	11	35	26	29	95	64
Totals	32	100	90	100	148	100

Source: Modified from Gordon Shipman, "Speech Thresholds and Voice Tolerance in Marital Interaction," *Marriage and Family Living* 22 (1960): 206–208. Copyrighted © 1960 by the National Council on Family Relations. Reprinted by permission.

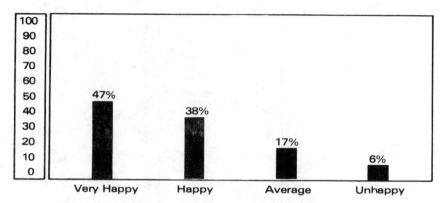

Source: Data is from Gordon Shipman, "Speech Thresholds and Voice Tolerance in Marital Interaction," *Marriage and Family Living,* 22 (1960). Copyrighted © 1960 by the National Council on Family Relations. Reprinted by permission.

Figure 14-7. Equality in Argument

the degree to which each spouse suffered from the voice patterns of the other, and (2) the degree to which each spouse was annoyed by the critical rate of the other. Each spouse rated his own discomfort from the voice patterns of the other as well as his estimate of the discomfort of the spouse from his voice patterns. The student rated the discomfort of both parents on both items. I tabulated the results, including underratings and overratings of all the raters, not only in the direction of the ratings but also in the number of deviating points.

Two significant trends emerge from this small sample. The ratings of the students are superior to those of their parents. This we would expect since the student was not involved directly with the marital exchange. There was also a marked tendency on the part of all raters to underrate rather than overrate the discomfort of the spouses to the voice patterns of the other. This reinforces the hypothesis that spouses suffer a great deal from the voice patterns of the other without anyone appreciating it. Communication within families is deficient on this problem.

A therapist might argue that the voice patterns of a spouse are the product of deep-seated animosities that, if ventilated by family therapy, would automatically be taken care of. Maybe so, maybe not. Do unfortunate voice patterns become such an integral part of the personality that their change is difficult even with therapy?

In my study of voice patterns within the family, I have identified two kinds of dystrophic syndromes. The one anticipated from casework practice was discovered as the most prominent among the thirty-two unhappy couples. This configuration has the following characteristics: considerable difference in thresholds of verbalization, with the lower-threshold partner being dominant, having poor voice score, and being vigorous and successful in argument; while the high-threshold partner is submissive, suffers markedly from the voice tone of the other, tends to leave the scene of the argument without a word. In addition, the low-threshold partner had high scores on critical rate, interrogation rate, and admonition rate, although there may be exceptions on any of these last mentioned patterns. This configuration characterized thirteen of the unhappy couples, plus three others in which the threshold differential was only one point. In three cases the low-threshold partner was the husband, and in ten it was the wife.

In this syndrome the withdrawal patterns of the high-threshold spouse vary. Some, with considerable stamina, turn a deaf ear to the constant talk of the other. Some will take verbal abuse in silence until a slow burn reaches a climactic explosion; others will retire to the basement, the workshop, the sociability of the tavern, alcoholism, the other woman, and even suicide. The effect of this and other syndromes on the children is devastating. It makes them most unhappy and insecure and gives them a profound distaste for marriage. However, when there is good communication between parents, the children will notice how their parents confide in each other and how they discuss their mutual concerns quietly at regular times. When this takes place, children experience feelings of extraordinary contentment and security. I now submit two illustrations of the first syndrome.

Father has excellent empathy, but my mother has very little. My father talks very little at home, but my mother doesn't do anything but talk. She is very dominant and has the upper hand in all communication. My father has gotten to the point where he says nothing. I don't think he even listens to her anymore. She constantly yells at him for things that happened in the past. Once in a while my father really blows up, and then my mother limps away like a wounded animal.

Interpersonal relationships within the family were extremely poor. Father existed only for bringing home the paycheck. Mother complained and nagged him incessantly. She was always talking; she never shut up. Her voice was loud and sharp. From morning to night she was hollering at somebody. She usually had a strap in her hand, and I got it most often. She didn't like anything about me. I was just an ungrateful brat who almost killed her when I was born. She didn't argue or discuss anything. She just threw a fit by threatening murder, suicide, or anything else that came into her head.

Father was a soft-spoken man. Even when he was angry he didn't yell. He was a courteous man and never spoke sharply to the children or anyone else. Arguments between him and mother were one sided. All the neighborhood could hear her, but nobody could hear Father. We kids often wished he would strap her once in a while. Sometimes my mother would end the argument by telling my father to leave. Usually he did, and then we children would worry about his coming back. Sometimes Mother would leave, and then we would have a few hours of peace and quiet.

Mother seemed to reject us. We were only burdens to her. She didn't show us any affection. Mother was always threatening. She talked about suicide and claimed that her difficulties were all our fault. The twenty years I spent at home were bedlam. We could not have any satisfactory rituals because there was continual bickering and mother's constant hollering. I remember only unhappiness, misery, and fear. Though it was hard for me to forgive my father for committing suicide, I can fully understand why he did it.

The second configuration is that of couples in which partners were equally dominant, had similar thresholds, and were vigorous in verbal combat. The following case that illustrates this syndrome involves parents who had six children and a marginal income. Both parents had been severely deprived in childhood. The narrator-daughter wrote:

Both my parents are dominant and neither takes a quiet side in an argument. Their voices become gruff and shrill, and Dad's is brusk and bellowing. Usually verbal battles occur at the supper table in front of all the children. Conflict and arguments are loud, long, and frequent and may last for days. It is an unusual day when tempers don't flare and arguments aren't heard. The usual subject of arguments is money. Yelling and screaming and frequent name calling make ours a loud-voiced family. There is seldom a quiet moment. Once an argument begins, it repeats itself in other minor incidents and may go on for days. Most of us are tense and nervous and easily upset. The slightest incident might trigger hours of screaming and crying. Daddy suffers from migraine headaches after these verbal battles, even if he initiated the argument.

When parents use up a great deal of energy in verbal conflict, they may have little time and energy to nurture the children. There is a suggestion of this neglect in the following:

I wanted someone to love me, love me, love me. Since my parents' marriage was unsuccessful, I was constantly observing the marriages of the parents of my friends and judging what I believed made them happy. I have had enough experience to prove that a marriage fails without communication. Mother persists in nagging my father about his inability to support her and his lack of masculinity in letting her work. They argue as often as they see each other, and much of it involves my father's drinking. I've prayed for, wept for, hoped for, and finally given up the idea that my parents could talk to each other without arguing. When they argue their voices reach a pitch that makes the wailing of alley cats sound like a choir of heavenly voices. My father is the more sensitive of the two, and when he can't stomach any more, he turns to alcohol to forget.

When a husband is narrow minded, opinionated, and dictatorial, he may terrorize his wife and children into submission so that no open communication is possible for family members. Thus was a father described by his son:

My father insisted on being the head of the household in the manner of a German dictator. His extremely domineering attitude polluted the whole family relationship in that there was little respect for him because of lack of love—he for us and we for him. My father had a violent temper, and when he was angry his voice was terror made manifest and reason completely left him. He was like a raging animal. My mother was always submissive to his wishes, opinion, and actions because she feared going against him. If there was any sign of compatibility, it was based on fear.

Between the pantrophic and the dystrophic families are the hemitrophic families. In a minority of cases the father is the nurturant one and the mother is deficient; in the majority of cases the mother plays the role of wife and mother in such a way that, in spite of an inadequate father, the children do well.

In the following report a son describes how his father destroyed his communication with the mother:

My mother represents to me a type of ideal woman. She has always been so kind, so naturally unselfish, that I can't believe it. She thinks of those she loves before herself, and this I see in everything she does. She is a real and full person and has probably been the single most positive influence on my life. She lives her life from day to day; that's just the way she is.

Next, I come to the most tragic episode in my family analysis. This is the communication between my parents; to put it more aptly, I would have to say the gross lack of it. Normal conversation about everyday things is a rarity between them. My father is extremely impatient and quite frequently yells harshly at my mother. Then the conversation is over. He gets very impatient over little things and has never learned the joy of sharing his life with his wife. No affection is ever displayed between them. Ninety-nine percent of the time my father's will is the law of the land.

Importance of Background Factors

Voice patterns operating in marriage cannot be separated from the deep-seated emotional disturbances the spouses bring to the marriage from their childhood. The patterns of shouting, yelling, screaming, and nagging between spouses are characteristic of dystrophic families. When students describe such behavior, they do so in the context of poor communication. When reading such descriptions in a student paper, I turn to the introductory pages to look for information about the childhood of the parents. Typically I find that both parents were brought up in orphanages, that one or both parents experienced a cold and demanding parent or stepparent, that one or both suffered the loss of a parent through death or divorce, or that one or both were emotionally deprived at a tender age. Superimposed on all these factors might be a family history of alcoholism, mental disease, and leaving school at an early age.

When the children in such families become adults and have children, they will be parents who have never learned how to exchange simple questions and answers to resolve ordinary problems. Their children never see a good model. Learning how to conduct such an exchange may be no more complicated than learning how to tie one's shoestrings, but it seems as though some adults have learned how to do the one but not the other.

Undue Emphasis

Another common irritating speech pattern is called *undue emphasis*. If, for example, the wife puts a question to her husband that requires an answer with a simple yes or no, he may give undue emphasis to his reply in one of several ways. Instead of replying pleasantly with a single word, for example, he may give her a lecture loudly with a twist of inflection to imply that she was quite a fool not do have known the answer. This sort of thing may happen when a child puts a question to a parent, and when the child reacts defensively to the undue emphasis, the parent most likely fails to understand his child's reaction. Persons who habitually use undue emphasis in replying to questions are quite unaware of their habit and fail to recognize it even when others attempt to point it out to them. My guess is that persons with this habit more often are the quick decision makers with a low threshold of verbalization, such as the oldest brother of brothers or the oldest sister of sisters. Undue emphasis conditions other family members to associate discomfort with questions; the resulting reluctance to ask questions impairs communication. One student wrote:

> My mom is extremely dominant, authoritarian, and intelligent and makes people feel she is always right. Even when she believes she is talking in a normal tone, it sounds to others like she is shouting.

Origin and Cure of Poor Speech Patterns

Irritating speech patterns probably originate from one of four influences: (1) habits of speech acquired unconsciously in the microculture of the family of origin, (2) underlying emotional problems that find expression in conscious or unconscious vocal aggression, (3) failure to socialize children in the process of family decision making, and (4) stressful marital situations. These are not mutually exclusive.

   Alcoholism may be a complication in situations referred to in numbers 2 and 4. The relationship of alcoholism to the tragedies of family life would require a volume; the relationship of inability to communicate in a loving way with family members to fostering alcoholism would require another volume. My papers are replete with the anguish and pathos of students as they wrote about drinking habits and the destruction of their families. When I was engaged in social work, I was amazed to see how often a spouse would attempt to reason with or admonish a spouse when he or she was drunk or half drunk. Unfortunately, we have too many sophisticated people in our society who try to do the same when the spouse is only one-quarter drunk. The widespread use of alcoholic beverages in our society has obscured the fact for all classes of people that it is quite futile to attempt the resolution of marital conflict, or any delicate marital problem, when one or both partners have just had a couple of drinks.

Whether irritating speech patterns are habits or symptoms, is it advantageous to treat a person with such patterns directly in order to improve communication? If so, how might it be done? For many years I have thought of a possibility. All sorts of electronic equipment such as myographs (to measure muscle tension) and multiphase polygraphs now exist to detect physiological reactions to stress. We even have sound spectrographs that portray the shape of sound waves of a voice. Suppose we had a couple in which we suspect that a low-threshold wife with irritating voice patterns is disturbing to her highly sensitive husband, and further suspected that some kind of covert or overt behavior is frustrating to the wife. We proceed to get the husband's tracings on the polygraph when he listens to a tape of his wife's voice as she passes from a pleasant mood to undue emphasis to an angry mood. We also get tracings on the polygraphs of both partners during an altercation. We show the tracings to each partner, then point out the behavior of each that produces an exaggerated reaction in the other. We may then proceed with a program of operant conditioning or other type of therapy.

One category of events to which people respond with a wide diversity of behavior is accidents. Some people faint at the sight of blood from a cut finger; others approach with a zest for bandaging. Family members discover from experience which one of them responds best to each category of accident. Most accidents elicit a variety of vocal outbursts. Family members suffer not only from the inconvenience of an accident but also from an excessive outburst over a minor incident.

We have seen how conflicting behavior of married couples with distressing voice patterns often has a background of family disorganization, poverty, stress, and personality distortions from emotional deprivation and heavy drinking. We have noticed how spousal relationships have been contaminated by extremes of dominance and submissiveness, authoritarian rigidity, aggressive verbal combat, one-sided verbal expression combined with withdrawal and passive aggression, and mutual or one-sided downgrading. Furthermore, much of this conflict has taken place in a *hestia* of dread and fear. From all of this, spouses and children have recoiled in pain.

Ritualization of Communication

Sometimes a couple ritualize their communication by talking things over at certain times of the day, which they come to enjoy and look forward to.

> Every morning at the breakfast table my parents would talk for an hour or so about the day coming up as well as events that have taken place. They talk a lot before they go to sleep at night. It seems when they lie abed and relax they can communicate very well. Occasionally I've seen my mother very upset, but after she has had a chance to talk to my dad, things are greatly changed for the better. It seems a simple talk can do miracles for my parents. When they talk their voices are pleasant. One thing I like about my mother's voice is its excellent expression. You can tell the way she feels by the tone of her voice. She can use it in a number of ways.

The next report also illustrates how the ritualization of communication by parents has a benign effect on their children. This is quite a contrast to descriptions of children weeping in their beds when they hear their parents in loud verbal combat.

> My parents do most of their communicating when they are alone. Often I hear them quietly discussing something domestic and important before falling asleep. It gave me a very warm and secure feeling to hear them talking together late at night.

Pantrophic Syndromes in Communication

The following excerpts illustrate pantrophic syndromes in communication. Notice the repetition of certain themes.

> Our family is basically equalitarian. Neither of my parents is a dominating person; they reach decisions after discussion together. The quality of communication between my parents is good, both through words and through gestures. They don't bottle things up inside themselves; if something is wrong, they discuss it and things are better after the air is cleared. Dad is fairly easygoing and seldom raises his voice to Mom; the same holds true for Mom except when she is tired. Then Dad goes out of his way to do little things for her.

> The quality of communication between my parents was excellent. In my twenty-one years of living at home, I never once heard them raise their voices to each other or in any way give any indication of serious discord. I did not feel that this was at all unusual and assumed that this was the way a marriage was supposed to be. My father seemed to put my mother on a pedestal for us and for everybody else. The surest way to elicit a slap in our

family was for one of us kids to raise our voice to my mother in any way that was the least bit disrespectful. He introduced my mother to others as "my bride." In return, my father seemed to be the most important thing in my mother's life. While she could influence him, she usually deferred to his wishes graciously.

The quality of communication between my parents is good. My parents possess a high degree of empathy, but at the same time they retain their independent thoughts and ideas. They are equalitarian and willing to compromise. The voice patterns of both parents are soft and melodious. Decision making in our family is the same as problem solving: by mutual agreement. The opinions of my brother and me are taken into account.

My parents are in love, they love me, and I love them. The quality of communication between them is good. Both have relatively low thresholds of verbalization. Nervousness, anxiety, and fatigue do not greatly alter their communication. Problems can always be talked out, maybe not immediately but eventually. Both parents have a good sense of humor. Both are extremely tactful and have a great deal of empathy. Their voices are normally well modulated and pleasant. When they are tired or angry their voices tend to get a little strident and harsh, but nothing severe. Neither suffers too much from the other's strident voice. One rarely criticizes the other. Appreciation is shown by words of thanks or by some action. Both my parents are always ready to express words of comfort, encouragement, and consolation to each other. Sometimes this is not verbalized, but a facial expression will convey the meaning. They respect each other's opinions and judgments too. One does not wholly rely on the other. They are able to function as unique individuals and still have a strong relationship and a happy marriage.

When problems or decisions arise, my parents are brought closer together. Each voices his own opinion, the opinions are then weighed, and the decision is made. My father is the final voice of authority, though. My mother sometimes can sway his decision. If an argument comes up, which is rare, it reaches a peak, then is dropped, and the issue is settled later when tempers have cooled and rational thinking has returned. Tensions are released by diversionary activity. Mom releases her hostility by cleaning the house, doing the ironing, or working in the kitchen. Dad will calm down by working in the garden or tinkering in the basement. Affection is expressed sometimes verbally, sometimes by a kiss, sometimes by facial expression, but mainly just by the way they are: kind, courteous, and gentle to each other all the time.

My sister and I were always included in family affairs. We were allowed to voice our ideas and opinions on all matters and they were respected. This taught us to think and reason logically. Our wishes were not always granted, and if we were denied, we were always told why.

I have dwelt on the factors that impair the development of good communication within the family, but if we are to conceive the family as a system whose function is to promote the growth of all family members, then it seems appropriate to summarize the positive contributions my students have made. In chapter 13 and 14, we have seen that in pantrophic families the adults listened respectfully to what their children and spouse had to say. A listening pause in a discussion is just as important as a rest in music. Playing the audience is stimulating to thought. When spouse A approaches spouse B with a problem of concern to A, B may listen intently, and while A is explaining the problem, he comes up with his own solution. B has made a contribution by playing the audience role, and A's creative thinking during a period without interruption is stimulated by his own words.

Good communication and a healthy relationship are two sides of the same coin; progress in one promotes the other. In this chapter I have treated some of the manifest, or overt, behaviors involved in communication. A family counselor works with the covert elements to improve the relationship while reading all the signs in overt behavior. I believe, in families in the middle range where there are no deep-seated emotional problems, that improvement in communication can be made by consciously improving the overt processes of communication.

In the light of the foregoing materials, I list some factors that promote effective communication within the family:

Character of parents:

> One or both parents have reasonably pleasing voice patterns.

> Parents are mutually affectionate.

> One or both parents have a reasonable degree of empathy, tact, and good judgment.

> One or both parents are flexible and adaptable.

> One or both parents are patient, concerned, and loving.

Family patterns:

> Family is equalitarian.

> No extremes of dominance and submissiveness exist.

> Appropriate communication is ritualized.

> The family has a relaxed *hestia* wherein laughter and good humor prevail.

> Members show their feelings without hesitation.

> The audience role is played by parents and sometimes by the whole family.

Parents play a firm and united front in family leadership. This leadership must be such that each child feels free to be assertive about his feelings of injustice or other problems, that he is free to participate in appropriate family discussions and decisions, and that his contribution will be respected.

Notes

1. Jack E. Westman, "The Need for Sound Control in the Home," A statement prepared for the U.S. Commerce Committee, 28 June 1971.

2. For treatment on what a professional can learn about a patient from the nature of his voice, see Paul J. Moses, *The Voice of Neurosis* (New York: Grune and Stratton, 1954).

3. Gordon Shipman, "Speech Thresholds and Voice Tolerance in Marital Interaction," *Marriage and Family Living* 22 (August 1960): 203–209.

4. H.K. Dunn and S.D. White, "Statistical Measurements on Conversational Speech," *Journal of Acoustical Society of America* 2 (1980): 228–288.

5. Dr. Pamela Kemp, assistant professor, Department of Home Economics, University of Wisconsin at Stevens Point, 1980.

15 Family Patterns in Sex Education

If the reader is a youth who finds it difficult to approach his parents for sex information, or a parent too embarrassed to impart sex information to his or her children, I hasten to reassure both that plenty of people the world over feel the same. Why is this resistance to communication on sexual subjects so prevalent and widespread? David Mace, who noticed this phenomenon in all the countries he has visited, speculated that it is in some way related to the incest taboo.

A superficial examination of ethnographic literature suggests the hypothesis that hardly any society has an institutionalized pattern of verbal sex training between parent and child within the nuclear family unit. Sex training seems to be relegated either to kinfolk in the extended family or to adults with specialized training functions. The taboo on parent-child sexual behavior may be strong enough to make any verbalization about sex in this relationship symbolic incest.

If the incest taboo puts a damper on sex discussion between parent and child, such reluctance becomes one of several defenses against incest. If we were to plot a curve representing the likelihood for parent-child incest in the life cycle, it would begin at zero point for infancy, rise to a peak at the bloom of adolescence, then decline as sons and daughters become oriented toward courtship, marriage, and departure from home. In my study of this problem in 1968, I discovered that the exchange of questions and answers between mother and children is greatest in early childhood and declines in late adolescence.[1] The significance of this drop is increased by the finding that, as children grow older and become of dating age, their questions and anxieties escalate. The older they are, the more questions they have and the more they turn from parents to seek answers elsewhere.

What about other defenses against incest? There is a strong tendency in Western culture for parent and child to deny the sexuality of the other. This denial is implicit in parents who think that their child will be safe from sexual problems if he does not see the genitals of the opposite sex, does not fondle his own genitals, does not hear vulgar words or sexual terms, or does not learn anything at all about sex. Such parents may think that if their child learns nothing and experiences nothing, he will be safely neuter and that the longer he is neuter, the better. Sexologist Dr. John Gagnon stresses

243

this point when he describes the phenomenon of nonlabeling—that is, the refusal of parents to use the proper terms to assist the child in the learning process.[2]

As the child grows older, other defenses come into play. Although the spontaneous exhibitions of young children are treated indulgently by adults, there comes a time when the defenses of isolation of the sexes, training in modesty, secrecy on sexual matters, separate bedrooms, locked doors, prudish behavior, and embarrassment on sexual themes set in. In young adulthood, however, when children return from college with fiancé or spouse, they may relax and discuss sexuality with others including parents.

In chapter 13, I noted the need for privacy of children, but parents also have a special need for privacy in their bedroom. Mutual respect for these privacies is conducive to the maintenance of generational boundaries and lessons incestuous fantasies.[3] However confused a child may be about sexual knowledge, he may correctly associate sexual activity with nighttime sleeping arrangements. For an adult to approach a child in his bed at night and abruptly confront him with a sexual lecture doubly violates his self-identity, his need for privacy, and the sanctity of his territorial space. David Mace reports the case of a man who said that, when he was a boy, his father did approach his bed at night to discuss sexual subjects and that for the rest of his life he suffered nightmares. My material reveals few such cases, but it does emphasize the idea that sex education for a child should not be attempted at bedtime. One student said that when she was three years old her father said something to her when bathing her at night. She could not recall what he said but it frightened her terribly. This occurred a day or so before the father left home prior to divorce. From then on she:

> Was scared to death of men including my grandfather. I wouldn't stay in the same room alone with a man, and if one should touch me I would cry uncontrollably. When I had my first date at age 16, I had nightmares revolving around that last experience with my father.

Presently I shall deal with the trauma young boys experience at the first ejaculation. Such episodes usually take place in bed during the night, and the nocturnal context undoubtedly intensifies their fears.

Sex Education between Mother and Daughter

Sex education in the home may exist in four relationships: father-daughter, father-son, mother-daughter and mother-son. In U.S. families, the only relationship in which sex training is significant is between mother and daughter. From my 1968 study (involving data collected between 1965 and

1967), I found that some 70 percent of the mothers of 400 students did reasonably well in handling the questions of small children and that some 60 percent prepared their daughters for menarche. Only a fifth of the mothers mentioned reproduction. In 1980 I replicated part of my previous study on a smaller scale, using similar questionnaires.

Between 1966 and 1980, good quality of instruction in preparing girls for menarche went up by ten or twelve percentage points for mothers, peers, and school. The number of mothers who went beyond menstruation to give information on reproduction increased from about one-fifth to one-third. The percentage of cases in which no communication at all took place on sex matters between mother and daughter decreased from 34 percent to 23 percent. There still remain, however, about 25 percent of daughters whose sex inquiries were rebuffed or postponed and 34 percent whose questions about reproduction were evaded or answered only partially. It is quite possible that, as mothers become aware of the increase in family-life education in the schools with all their facilities in visual aids, literature, and teaching skills, they are willing to let the teachers take over some of the instruction on menstruation and most of the instruction on reproduction.

A slight majority of girls learn first about menstruation from within the family—that is, from mother or sister. This did not change much between 1966 and 1980. There are a number of reasons why mothers should always be the first to advise their daughters about it. In all my samples, the age range for menarche was nine to seventeen years, although greater extremes are on record. Mothers are in the best position to observe the physical signs that indicate that menarche is soon to occur. Instruction about it should not be an hour late lest the girl, in ignorance, suffer fright at the first sight of menstrual blood, as 10 percent did in 1966 and 1980. As we shall see presently, however, girls may suffer fright at menarche even though they have been advised previously about its nature. Instruction, therefore, should be not only timely but also of continuing high quality.

One reason many mothers can do well in explaining menstruation to their daughters is that neither mother nor daughter perceives menstruation as a sexual phenomenon. A mother can explain the beginning of the menses as a growing-up process that enables a woman to conceive and have children, that marks the transition from girlhood to womanhood, and that is a process independent of male behavior. The only damper on the discussion is the mother's fear that the girl will ask how the sperm reaches the egg, and that definitely is a sexual question. How do some parents do well in overall sexual training of their children? Is it possible, when some of the pantrophic patterns listed in chapter 16 prevail, that the generational boundaries become so well reinforced that parent and child can relax and orient sex learning in the direction of growth with positive connotations? We can imagine that parental sex education would be easier in a family wherein the *hestia* is happily relaxed, the children participate in family discussions, love in all relationships is freely expressed, casual nudity coincides with respect for privacy, the children can sense that all is well in the parental bedroom, and patterns of trust and respect prevail. In contrast is a family wherein marital discord persists, parents solicit support from children in spousal battles, mistrust and disrespect exist, privacy is violated and one parent takes his bed elsewhere, or when a seductive stepfather is present. It may be that when both parents and children feel secure within their respective generational boundaries, embarrassment on sexual discussion wanes enough to permit sex instruction.

While excellent parents are waiting for their child to mature enough for his next lesson in sex training, all sorts of things may happen to him or her in school and playground. It is therefore important that the child's settings in both school and playground have high visibility for the parents. For example:

> By the seventh grade, all the girls had heard The Big Lecture from our junior high gym teacher. This old maid set back sex education about two centuries. She made us think that the most ghastly thing in the world was to tell or have a boyfriend find out when you are having your period. Then, after telling us how animals mate when the female is in heat, she led us to believe that if a boy knew when you had your period he'd attack you or something and you'd get pregnant just like the mares, sows, and cats in her examples.

> By eighth grade I had been left behind in the shuffle. All my friends were now women, and I was still a little girl (and they reminded me of it constantly). In an attempt to be like them, I quit wearing an undershirt. My mother took the hint and bought me a bra so "I wouldn't catch a cold." My father said I needed that like he did, but it didn't make me one of the crowd.

Most of the following reports were written in the 1960s and, happily, are not representative of sex education in parochial schools today.

> I had never had any sex education because I went to a Catholic school. In the eighth grade I remember the boys being herded out of the room, and one of the nuns got in front of the class and warned us not to touch ourselves. This was evil. Well I had no idea what she was talking about, and I mistook it to mean we were not to touch our breasts. I was very careful not to touch myself when I took a bath. Well after a week or two I decided I'd rather be clean and evil than dirty and good. I thought this was a stupid idea of the church. It was not until I was a senior in high school that it dawned on me that she had been talking about masturbation.

> When I was about eight years old, my mother was pregnant and explained the birth process and menarche. My peers, however, had a more-intriguing

explanation that all you had to do was to be in love to get pregnant so I thought my mother must have been mistaken. From Catholic teaching, I knew that another way of getting pregnant was the Immaculate Conception, so I walked around trying not to fall in love or to be immaculately concepted.

My friends told me that if you didn't menstruate on the correct day you were pregnant. If I was three days late I'd lie in bed at night and worry to death. Even if I hadn't gone out with a boy all month, I'd worry until I was thinking up all sorts of ridiculous ways of becoming pregnant.

This priest gave us a talk in the eighth grade. He gave us a sex talk that all but made us girls condemned as tempters. He made boys sound like sex maniacs who were looking for the least bit of skin. He told us never to walk around the house with just a slip on because our brothers would get sexually aroused. Well, Mom used to walk around in her slip and I would think, Oh my God! I was positive that my brothers were just going wild. So ended my formal sex education.

As parents cooperate more closely with schools on family-life education programs, they appreciate better the resources of libraries in schools, audio-visual aids, and teaching skills. The task of preparing daughters for menarche cannot be delegated to the school, although some children with negligent mothers have been saved anxiety and fright by school programs. If a daughter is precocious in development, she must learn about menarche before she reaches the fifth or sixth grade when it is usually covered by the teachers. A daughter slow in glandular development will have special psychological concerns as well as need for medical attention.

If a mother should try to explain menarche in terms of transition from childhood to womanhood to a little girl who has had very little experience in childhood, we might have a situation as follows:

I saw this movie one week before I started menstruating, and I shudder to think of the consequences if I hadn't seen it. As it was, I was very much frightened when I started menstruating and didn't tell my mother until the third day. Some of my friends were excited when they began to menstruate. I was very unhappy, however, because I looked upon this as an end to my childhood, which I was reluctant to abandon.

On the one hand, a girl may be reluctant to end her childhood symbolically for another reason. In one case, the oldest girl in a large family was exploited in having to care for the younger siblings. When friends came to play she was so detained by her work that her friends got tired of waiting and left. She wrote:

My parents seemed removed from me in the joy they showered on this long-awaited child. I suddenly realized that if growing up meant this, I didn't want it. In contrast to most children, I wanted to remain a child. When I first began to develop a bust, I cried and cried, pounding on my chest unmercifully. I had my mother tightly sew in all my bras, and I nagged her constantly to reassure me that I was still her little girl and that she loved me.

Late developers, on the other hand, are reminded by peers that they are really late. Such girls are apt to worry that they are abnormal in some way. One such girl was so late that she was taken to the family doctor, who reassured the family that she only needed a bit more time. The girls continued to worry and, on her own initiative, consulted a specialist who diagnosed thyroid deficiency.

There is a real problem when a physician suddenly decides to give a young girl a pelvic examination. In one such case the mother was hesitant, but the physician proceeded without concern for psychological repercussions. The resulting trauma to the girl was devastating, and she suffered nightmares for years.

In another case the mother, a nurse, prepared her daughter for a pelvic examination by talking about the kindness and expertise of the gynecologist, and the result was no trauma.

Parents are confronted with a dilemma: If they barge ahead to give sex information in spite of their own embarrassment and that of the child, the results may be disappointing to both. If they say nothing, the child may be the victim of frightening misconceptions promulgated by peers and sometimes by teachers. This difficulty is understandable, especially for women who are the heads of one-parent families and who have sons. I was confronted by such a woman in a class where I was a visiting speaker. I suggested, in part, that she frankly admit to her son that she felt inadequate to give him the information he needed but that she would do her best to provide him with pertinent literature on sexual development. I mentioned the fact that, although most boys are grateful for such literature, a few of them disdainfully refuse to read what a parent offers. To forestall this possibility, I pointed out that she could truthfully observe that even the experts do not pretend to know all about sex and that they are continually researching the subject. I thought it was important to make the son feel that the mother was concerned about his sexual well-being and that she would always be available whenever he was concerned about something or had a question. In this connection, parent surrogates can be helpful.

A confiding relationship between parent and child facilitates communication on sexual subjects. When such a relationship cannot be established, it may be better for the parent to utilize outside resources for the sex training of the child. For example:

The lack of communication between my mother and me made the process of maturing very difficult. There were times when I needed a mother badly, just to cry on her shoulder or something, but I couldn't. Everybody in my family has a wall around him. Sometimes I think they feel as I do. I'm sure of it, but I just can't do anything about it. The facts of life were not discussed with my mother because of this lack of communication. I cannot bear any intimacies of any sort with my mother. When I began menstruating, the difficulty was not in my attitude toward menstruation but toward my mother's finding out and playing her motherly role in giving me the necessary equipment. There was no explanation or heart-to-heart talk, for which I was definitely grateful.

I do not think a mother should abdicate her role in giving her daughter psychological support at menarche just because the school is doing an excellent job in this area. For example:

In my preparation for puberty, I felt I knew more than my mother did. I had seen some films in the sixth grade, but when the time came for me to become a woman, I was quite frightened. I woke up from a sound sleep with a terrible pain in my stomach and saw a pool of blood. I knew what it was but never thought it would be like that. I was mad at my mom for not having prepared me. She should have realized that I was in eighth grade and could have it any day, but she didn't. That's the way my mother was, never prepared. Next day, my mother told me not to tell anyone what had happened to me. This gave me a feeling that it was something I should hide, something I should be ashamed of.

Fright at menarche, however, is not confined to girls who know nothing at all about it. A number of reporting girls had been given some information but were frightened anyway at the appearance of menstrual blood. The overall feeling tone of the family has a bearing on a child's reaction in these cases. A child whose mother radiates warmth, security, and concern for her daughter will produce quite a different effect from that of a mother who is reserved, careless, and indifferent. In each home are all kinds of parents, patterns, feelings, and relationships. The same is true of school and playground settings. In all of his settings, including the home, the child is subjected to a hodgepodge of facts, misconceptions, half-truths, and fears about sexuality. These are acquired on the one hand with connotations of evil, secrecy, embarrassment, and danger and on the other hand with connotations of parental support, enjoyment, love, and beauty. Such experiences will orient the girl positively toward her self-image, sex, marriage, and motherhood or negatively to all of these. The following excerpts seem to emphasize that a program of sex education for both parents and teachers is in order.

I started menstruating when I was twelve years old. I didn't know what was happening to me. For three days I walked around thinking I was dying of cancer. I finally told my dad, and he had my mother talk to me. Her first words were, "This is something you must not talk about to anybody. Do not even discuss it with your brother." She went on to say what a curse this was and that I would be sick for so many days. She told me that if I ever missed my period, it would mean that I had done something bad (I didn't even know what she meant—I thought it meant kissing a boy) and would become pregnant.

I was not prepared for menarche at age ten. I was completely shocked. I felt alone and afraid and unwilling to tell my mother. I thought I had cancer. For several years I hated menstruation and felt it was a complete inconvenience.

When mothers fail their daughters at menarche, a resentment often develops that destroys whatever confiding bond may have existed between them. For example:

Most of my sex education came from conversations with girlfriends whose mothers had given them information or books to read. In such discussions I would have to stop and ask what they meant and, on occasion was made to feel stupid. This made me very resentful of my mother for she in no way ever prepared me or even recommended a book for me to read. I felt that if my mother couldn't confide in me about sex, then I could never confide in her about anything, and so to this day I seldom tell Mom anything.

This theme of how failure to communicate with a child on sexual subjects (especially menarche) destroys communication in all other areas is very common.

Schools as an Alternative

Previously I gave a few illustrations of unfortunate happenings in schools wherein teachers were ill prepared for sex instruction. The number of homes in which parents are ill prepared is many times greater. The orientation of children toward sexual functioning in dystrophic homes is so deplorable that the schools can act as an alternative against ignorance, misconceptions, negative connotations, confusion, anxiety, and terror. The students from pantrophic homes wherein sex instruction has been adequate and wholesome can act as catalysts in school discussion groups. One can imagine how a good school program in family-life education could help the following cases:

When I was in the third grade, my father told me to expect to start bleeding some day within the next few years. I was terrified and burst into tears, whereupon my father became disgusted, threw up his hands, and hastily left the room. I worried a great deal about what he'd said because I wasn't sure the bleeding would stop after it started. It sounded terrible to me, and I was too ashamed to ask anybody questions about it.

Occasionally, a boyfriend or a father will overcome the negative connotations from mothers at the time of menarche. For example:

When I was nine years old, my mother said it was about time she told me about the problems of being a woman so I wouldn't be frightened. She called it getting sick. She explained it was a messy nuisance women had to put up with. She scared me half to death. She did give me hope, though. She said my aunt had not gotten sick until she was eighteen. I prayed and prayed that this would never happen to me. When I was ten, we had a movie in school concerning the details on menstruation, "Very Personally Yours." It was very cute, but I still prayed that I wouldn't get sick.

I got my first period when I was in the eighth grade, just when I thought I had escaped the malady. I could not believe it. I thought I had hemorrhoids. The next day in school I was so frightened that I fainted. The principal had to call my father to take me home. Mother never explained the process of reproduction to me. I never asked any questions because I was rather embarrassed with Mother. We don't have any rapport. I never confide in either of my parents. She did say, however, that men are all alike and marry only for one reason. She also said that a man wouldn't marry at all unless a girl refuses to let him touch her until they get married. She also said that boys only date girls to see how far they can go. I was scared to death of boys until I had dated my fiancé for three months. In fact, I never wanted to get married because sex, what little I knew about it, sounded so ugly and predatory.

This girl's boyfriend was sympathetic, patient, and hopeful, and she learned to confide in him. His influence completely reversed her attitude toward her periods. The mother came from a most dystrophic family and undoubtedly had severe sexual problems herself.

Negative Introduction to Menarche

Resentment against mothers for not instructing their daughters is not uncommon, as illustrated in the following case. When she was eleven years old, this girl learned about menstruation from a friend. It was crudely described as horrible, involving bad blood that makes you hurt every month: "The very day she told me I suddenly felt a surge of hostility toward my mother. I was furious at her for having kept that secret from me." That same year she had a date with a boyfriend, age 13, who explained intercourse in crude terms. She was shocked and wanted to have her mother deny it all but never had the courage to approach her.

> I again felt deceived by my mother and father because they were leaving me out of everything. I asked her many other things but never got any answers, and I just gave up. As a result of built-up apprehension, I developed an inward hatred for both parents and cried almost every night before I went to sleep.
>
> When I was thirteen, I had my first view of bad blood. I was so shocked that I forgot about my girlfriend's explanation of two years before. I thought I was going to die. I remember screaming and running through the rooms looking for my mother, hoping she could stop the bleeding. When she saw me, all she said was that it was a natural occurrence and that I shouldn't be afraid. She said that she had meant to tell me but had forgotten. I was too scared to ask questions, but the only other thing she told me was that it would happen every twenty-eight days. When she gave me the belt and the napkins, she answered my astonished gaze by saying, "My mother never helped me so why should I help you?" That ended all conversation between me and my mother on sex. She never asks whether I'm regular or if I have pain or anything. Somehow I felt ashamed of it, and I was brought up to be so prudish that I am ashamed of being a woman. She gave a connotation of bad to girls who enjoyed fun and a connotation of good to studious, serious girls. As a result, I neither feel at ease on a date nor can relax enough to enjoy any particular activity just for fun.

The key expression that helps to explain why this mother was so neglectful is to be found in her words, "My mother never helped me so why should I help you?" If we could probe the mother's life history, we could better appraise the extent to which she is displacing onto her daughter the hostility she had toward her own mother. Another rationalization when a mother is confronted by a daughter who wants to know why the mother failed her duty is, "No one told me anything and I was none the worse for it." Conversely, we have mothers who, because they had been frightened in their childhood because of ignorance, took special pains to educate their own children about sexual phenomena.

Many adults, when dealing with preparation for menarche, stress the notion that it marks the transition from childhood to womanhood. When this notion is ritualized within the family, it crystallizes the gender identity of the girl as feminine and one approaching adulthood. If there is no preparation and the transition is not ritualized with the moral support of the parents, the transition may not be smooth.

I was not told about menstruation before it started. I was so upset by this new functioning of the body that I almost wished I had been a boy. My mother gave me a book to read that gave me little consolation. It is hard to grow up overnight, to be a tomboy one minute and a young lady capable of childbearing the next.

The Yen for Maternal Support

Another theme is common to many of my papers. No matter how well the daughter has learned from school or peers about sexual matters prior to menarche, she still yearns for communication with her mother about it.

My preparation for puberty and my sex learning were from school and reading. My mother did not tell me one fact about sex, reproduction, or menarche. I informed myself in these areas mostly from reading and second from my peers. One incident I will never forget. I checked out a book from the library on teenage girls growing up and how their bodies develop into young women's. I had my mother read the chapter on menstruation and reproduction, hoping that she would tell me herself about these facts and maybe answer some questions that I wanted to ask. She said nothing to me and handed back the book. I experienced a feeling of resentment.

The big day came when I had my first period, and I was just frightened. I knew what it was and why I was having it, but the hardest task for me was to tell my mother about it. I should have been happy about this physical change, but all I could feel was hurt. It would have meant so much more if my mother had prepared me for menarche. I finally got up enough courage and told her that I had started my period. There was so much tension built up in me that I just stood there and cried hysterically. All she told me was that it happened to every girl and that I wasn't to be afraid. This caused my mother and me to become very distant in our mother-daughter relationship, and I knew that if I ever wanted any information on sex or reproduction I could never ask my mother about it.

From that experience I have learned that I will make it a special effort to tell my children about menarche, "spermarche," and reproduction. I can see that it might be a hard task to do, but if one develops an open mind and tells his children about sex in general, it would definitely strengthen the parent-child relationship.

Role of Nudity in Sex Education within the Family

It is hard to ascertain the amount of nudity and the degree of modesty in U.S. families. It ranges from families in which the children are not permitted to come to the breakfast table in their bathrobes to a family in which some members eat breakfast in the nude. Occasionally a student will confess to feelings of embarrassment when she sees her mother working while nude in the kitchen. My material contains frequent reference to family members bathing together, especially when the children are small. I do not recall any cases in which nudity was used by a family member in a seductive way, even in incestuous cases. Neither do I recall any case within the family in which nudity was exhibitionist in character. Nudity seems to nullify secrecy about things sexual, and secrecy is associated with shame, guilt, curiosity, evil, and even danger. When students mention nudity in connection with sex learning, they do so in positive terms.

When parents set the pattern of being relaxed in the presence of nudity or partial nudity, it has for the children a connotation of naturalness about sexuality, and this may be considered a part of the family *hestia*. The students did not always spell out the time element, but nudity in bathroom procedures usually occurred when the children were young, and partial nudity was tolerated in a relaxed manner when the children were older and the need for privacy more pronounced. The following excerpts are typical of those families in which the narrator dealt with the subject.

> Our family is very affectionate. When we were little, Dave and I went to sleep many times with each other and with both parents. We took baths together, I with Dad, and Dave with Mom. Very few nights have gone by without a kiss or hug from both parents. Thus, we have few inhibitions about the body of the opposite sex, and also I am a very touching person. Because of the physical contact I had as a child, I need to touch someone's arm or give a pat on the back, despite their sex.

> I associated menstruation as a totally physical change, not as affecting my sexual attitudes that consisted of a gross curiosity of the male anatomy. The women in our house were used to each other's nudity, but for some unknown reason, father was never seen in this state. We were told to close our eyes if we ever walked into their bedroom unexpectedly. When our curiosity got the better of us, we were scolded and shamed. This leads to an incident in which a neighbor boy four years younger than I offered to show me his penis, an invitation that I accepted.

> Another circumstance helping my sexual development was my parents' attitude toward nudity. Whenever I happened to walk into a room where one of them was dressing, they always acted natural.

> My psychosexual development was normal and probably better than most. From earliest childhood on, I was always well informed. Because my mother was a very talented artist, I learned to think of the human body, either nude or clothed, as a beautiful and graceful object of art.

> When my first menstrual period came, I was prepared and knew what was happening. My mother treated it as a natural and healthy bodily function.

About a third of my knowledge regarding sex was gained by reading or in biology classes. What I also believe put me at ease about sex was that my parents didn't try to conceal themselves when nude. We children were taught right and wrong and not to hide ourselves or be afraid; yet we were modest. This built a healthy, wholesome attitude toward sex. Religious training in our family was quite strict and stressed self-control.

My parents had a type of their own sex education in that throughout my life, in our home, nudity was something you didn't have to be ashamed of. A simple but casual exposure of my parents after a shower was not a rare happening. I feel this is very important to youngsters because otherwise a child could get a feeling of being ashamed of his or her body that could imprint a mark on him for the rest of his life. This was one of the ways my parents gave us our sex education, and even though it was without words, I felt it is important in a child's growing-up process.

Is nudity, as an element favorable to sex discussion, inconsistent with respect for privacy? I think not. Respect for privacy strengthens generational boundaries so that family members may better relax and then discuss taboo subjects. To respect the privacy of a person is to respect the person. One function of the incest taboo is to discourage a forbidden relationship that can only take place with secrecy and privacy. Casual nudity in a pantrophic family wherein the parents are compatible and loving with the children is one thing, but nudity in a dystrophic family in which parents are incompatible and the unloving father a weak character is another thing.

Role of Fathers at Menarche

When mothers are inadequate in sex instruction, fathers may play a positive role with daughters. In one case, a curious little girl asked her mother about the source of babies while the mothers was playing cards with relatives. The mother's angry reaction convinced the daughter that "babies came from something bad. After that I didn't ask her anything." At the time of her menarche "my sister was laughing, but I was ashamed, crying, and mad at her." The mother reacted with cool assistance but gave no explanation. The daughter wrote:

After that, I was depressed every month when my time arrived. I skulked around as if I were committing a crime for those few days. One month I got very sick with my period. My dad came into my room and told me he knew why I was sick and tried to comfort me. He didn't act like it was a bad thing, and he sympathized so strongly with me. I liked that attention so much I was almost glad I had my period. After that day, I felt I was more girlish and a lot more lovable whenever I had my period. I was much better adjusted after that.

The following excerpt indicates that the daughter's sex training was handled by both parents and her seven older brothers.

> When I got my first menstrual period, I think I had mixed emotions. Although I had been told about it both at home and in school, there is definitely some feeling of anxiety and fear. However, also there is a certain pride in being called a woman. I remember my mother was very kind and helpful and calm—I thought that this was important at the time. All I remember about my father's reaction is that he smiled and seemed to be extra nice to me, but he did not actually say anything to me about it.
>
> I think, naturally, that my brothers played a bigger part in sex education than anyone else. They were always interested in me and willing to talk about it. I was not afraid to ask questions and I feel they gave good, clear, and healthy answers. I never had any bad or dirty ideas about sex. I think my parents had such a good and healthy relationship that I got the view that sex was something beautiful and that marriage is something to work toward. Sex was usually talked about fairly openly in our family although I think the boys had an easier time talking about the girls they had taken out than I did of the boys. I feel this was because I was outnumbered. All of us talked more freely with my mother than with my father. I can honestly say I did not have any unhappy or traumatic experiences in my psychosexual development.

Although it is an advantage for both parents to participate in the sex education of their children, it can be done very well by either parent. The next excerpt shows how the sex education of a daughter was undertaken by the father when the mother (a nurse) seemed uncomfortable with the task.

> When I was in seventh grade I was informed by a classmate that her mother had told her that girls can get pregnant by flirting with boys. As usual, I went to check this information out with my father, whom I regarded as being extremely knowledgeable on all subjects. He assured me that it didn't work that way and invited me to go for a ride with him in the car.
>
> Taking a long ride alone with one of us was my father's way of encouraging conversation and confidences and a means of showing individual attention. It was the method he used when he wanted to discuss something with one of us, and we were all eager to take him up on such an invitation. On our ride he explained the process of procreation very effectively, emphasizing its role as part of marriage, and the responsibility and judgment one has to use in regard to sexual relationships.

If the incest taboo is an obstacle to sex training within the home, we would expect an unconscious resistance to sex learning. My case-history material suggests that some children do not grasp simple explanations the way adults expect them to. It is a great mistake for a parent to think that a single brief explanation on sexuality will suffice for a child the rest of his life. The mother in the following case considered sex learning as a continuing process that was not to be forced.

I was fortunate to receive my sex training at an early age from my mother who is a nurse. She talked to me first about menstruation and reproduction, encouraging me to ask questions as she went along. Then I was given some books to read, and again she encouraged me to come back with questions. This was done even before we were shown the traditional reproduction movies in the fifth grade. Her explanations were good, and she always referred to the act of intercourse as a way of expressing love and of creating children from that love. I think this helped me to gain a healthy attitude toward sex. As I grew older, she presented me with the books again and said perhaps I would want to look them over again to clarify anything that may have seemed hazy to me the first time. She said that if I didn't want to it was allright with her. I was glad to have the chance again, and the books seemed even clearer the second time through. Again she asked for questions, and now that I look back, I hope I can do such a good job in telling my daughters about reproduction. On the whole, I think my attitudes toward the opposite sex are healthy ones, and I can honestly say that, after my mother's training, I looked forward to the time when I would cease being a little girl and would become a woman capable of producing life.

Probably one of the happiest memories I hold in growing up is the way my mother explained menstruation and sex to me. I remember for years she would read a story to us from a magazine about a young mother and her little son. It concerned the relationship between them as time grew closer for her to give birth to a second child. On the day she told me about menstruation, she first read this story to me again. She also had been reading some little books with titles such as *Now Your Are Nine* and *Now You Are Ten*. On this particular day she read the latter and then, calmly and with no embarrassment, explained about menstruation and growing up as a woman. She made it seem like one of the most beautiful times in the life of a woman. When I finally had my menarche, the summer of my tenth year, I was not in the least frightened. It was a time of joy, and Mom and Dad made it a very special day. This, I am sure, has a great influence on how I feel about menstruation now. At this time each month I feel especially feminine and glad to be a woman.

My brother received much the same instruction from our father. Then later Mom used the magazine story in explaining about sex to me. She was clear and precise, bringing in the joys of love shared between a man and a woman in love. I do remember being a little amazed and thinking, "My Mom and Dad do that," but there was no revulsion about it. She again answered my questions and has continued to answer new ones as they have arisen over the years. My dad also shows no embarrassment in answering our questions in honest terms. It has always made me feel that I was very fortunate when I compare my sex learning within the family with those of my gildfriends who experienced terror at menarche and who thus regard sex as dirty, frightful, or something to tease boys with.

The positive or negative attributes of a mother's treatment of her daughter's puberty may have considerable repercussions. One little girl was nicely prepared for menarche by her older sisters, but her mother spoiled it all.

I had my first menstruation at the age of thirteen. When I realized I had started my period I was overjoyed. At last I was a woman. I ran quickly to tell my mother who had just returned from shopping. She soon squelched all my excitement when she responded indifferently to my news. We went to my parents' bedroom where she showed me how to use a sanitary belt and napkin. All the while we were there she seemed to talk only of how much trouble and work it is to have a monthly period. I didn't agree with her, but I remained silent and let her do the talking. She upset me to talk like that. That night I cried on my pillow before I went to sleep.

Another girl wrote, "One thing I distinctly remember my mother telling me was that it would not hurt, and to this day, I have not had cramps."

Some girls who were instructed in positive terms and elated at the onset of menarche said they felt more attractive to boys during their period. It would be interesting to determine the relationship between the extent of physical distress of women during their menstrual periods and the way their mothers had prepared them for menarche. Another question is whether there is any relationship between the nature of learning about intercourse and the attitudes arising therefrom and sex adjustment in marriage. Since I have a number of cases in which boys and girls who suffered severe trauma in sex learning were able to make a good sexual adjustment later, it would appear that intervening variables should be considered. One such intervening variable would be a change in attitude toward sexuality effected by a confiding and affectionate friend of the opposite sex. Another might be an opportunity to experience emotional catharsis by analyzing one's history of sex learning and experience in the presence of a good listener.

Ritualizing Menarche

We can see from the experience of girls in the happier families that a tendency to ritualize menarche had developed within the home. For example, after describing how well her mother had explained the approaching menarche, this girl went on to say:

When I discovered it, I called my mother and she showed me what to do. Then she did something I'll never forget. She told me to come with her, and we went to the livingroom to tell my father. She just looked at me and then at him and said, "Well, your little girl is a young lady now." My dad gave me a hug and congratulated me, and I felt grown-up and proud that I was a lady at last. That was one of the most exciting days of my life.

In one family it was traditional for the pubescent girl to wear her first lipstick, notifying everyone in the family about the event. The star in this family drama may be excused from washing the dishes, served her favorite dessert, presented with her first high-heeled slippers, and congratulated by her father.

The improvement of sex education in school and home, together with improvement in literature and visual aids, seems to have reduced the advent of menarche to the commonplace. If this observation is correct, then it would explain why the percentage of girls who looked forward to the occurrence of menarche decreased from 44 to 21 percent between 1966 and 1980 and why those who accepted the idea with indifference or resignation increased from 46 to 68 percent. Those who were elated or thrilled decreased from 23 to 11 percent. However, negative feelings increased from 10 to 13 percent, and those embarrassed increased from 13 to 19 percent. Mere information may not be enough. Maybe we should structure some puberty rites for all children of both sexes. The problem is to get the parents, the schools, and the churches to cooperate on developing puberty rites. As my materials indicate, some parents do not wait for the schools or the churches; they develop their own rituals. In ritualizing the event of puberty, parents crystallize the child's gender identity, giving him a tremendous boost in self-esteem, and so orienting the psychosomatic system toward health.

The Crisis of Puberty for Boys

I suggested before that most mothers and daughters are able to overcome the sex taboo in discussing menstruation because they do not consider it a sexual process, that it has to do with becoming a woman and the capacity to have children. This avoidance technique cannot be applied to sex training for boys because it is hard to deny that ejaculation is a sexual phenomenon. Because of this difference, our society (like a parent) is able to label the onset of puberty for girls but not for boys. Thus, we have the term *menarche* but no comparable term for the male phenomenon. This avoidance and nonlabeling within the family is similar to that in the larger society relative to the first ejaculation. This avoidance also represents a cultural void likely perpetrated by the incest taboo.

The term *menarche* is from the Greek. *Arche* means the "beginning of" and *mens* is the word for "month"; thus, the *beginning of the monthlies.*" In 1968 I proposed to label the onset of male puberty "spermarche," the beginning (or first appearance) of sperm.

The attention and concern of parents for the onset of puberty for girls and their neglect for the onset of puberty for boys is also found in nonfamily institutions. We have, on the one hand, a plethora of reading materials, slides, and films used in schools and churches to explain menstruation in nonsexual terms; on the other hand, in preparing boys for their first ejaculation of life, we do not usually show on film the erect penis discharging semen. In some nonliterary societies, the sacred importance of semen is ritualized, but in our society we do not know what to do about it. We have sanitary napkins and tampons for girls but no corresponding padding for semen. With the exception of the Jewish community, our society has made the onset of male puberty an experience surrounded by secrecy, mystery, embarrassment, and fright even after boys have been taught the rudiments of reproduction.

In 1966 and again in 1980, I asked on questionnaires how the first ejaculation was produced. The results are given in table 15-1.

The majority of boys experiences the first ejaculation via nocturnal emission, next is usually through masturbation, and third outlet is through intercourse.

In a sample of 146 college men in 1966, about 90 percent indicated that they had received no information about nocturnal emissions from either parent and that what little they had learned from peers was most inadequate. Their knowledge about masturbation was received from peers or from their own experience. If the first ejaculation was from a dream with emission, the incidence of fright was 15 percent; if masturbation, 20 percent. Typical negative reactions from spermarche, resulting from ignorance, by either outlet follow:

It scared the hell out of me.

I was shocked and horrified and thought I was physiologically out of order.

I was filled with horror; I woke up thinking I was on the way to meet my maker.

I thought I had hurt myself, a very fearful experience.

Confusion about spermarche may arise from sexual misinformation from peers or school. A boy can be frightened by spermarche even after he has learned about intercourse and reproduction. For example:

Most of my information concerning intercourse, masturbation, and nocturnal emissions came from peers. We had discussed many times that an emission occurred during intercourse but had no idea what made it occur then or when it occurred without intercourse. Also there had been some mention of wet dreams, but I did not know the meaning of this, and none of my friends associated their dreams with sexual activity. I was totally unprepared for the occurrence of my first seminal emission or wet dream. I was frightened at first, but I enjoyed the pleasurable sensations that accompanied the emission. Later I came to realize that the pleasurable feelings connected with seminal emissions were associated with intercourse in some way.

The confusion about male puberty is so great that a boy may be embarrassed by his first nocturnal emission and later frightened by his first masturbation. This combination may lead to negativism toward intercourse.

Table 15-1
Outlets for First Ejaculation in Life

	1966		1980	
Outlet	Number	Percent	Number	Percent
Nocturnal emission	82	56	54	78
Masturbation	63	43	12	17
Intercourse	1	1	3	4
Total	146	100	69	99

Source: Data for 1966 is from Gordon Shipman, "The Psychodynamics of Sex Education," *Family Coordinator* 17 (January 1968):3–11. Copyright © 1968 by the National Council of Family Relations. Reprinted by permission.

> I was not prepared for my first seminal emission, which occurred as a wet dream. I did not know what it was and tried to cover it up because I was afraid I had wounded myself and that this weird flow might never stop. Then I found out what the wet dream really was and was all the more embarrassed. I never tied these occurrences with the onset of manhood, merely thinking it was something I might have done all my life had I known about it. The only connotation this held for me was fear and something to be avoided. I experienced the same fear and disgust when I first learned how sexual intercourse took place.

When a boy is ignorant, the first ejaculation via masturbation may be more pleasurable and dramatic but also more fearful than when achieved by a nocturnal emission. The following case illustrates how a surge of erotic feeling can be combined with fright:

> By nonverbal means, our parents conveyed to all of us the message that we were not to talk about sex. When I was eight years old I watched wide-eyed as the farm animals were being bred. I also observed the birth of calves. It wasn't until the eighth grade that I had my first shocking experience with sex. One day a friend told me about the pleasures of masturbation. A few days later I started playing with my penis. Soon each stroke began to feel more delicious than the preceding one, and as the moment of ejaculation neared, I was aware that my heart was thumping so loud I feared someone would hear it. Suddenly my whole body was seized with an overwhelming physical ecstacy, and I watched in shock and wonder as the semen shot in spurts from my penis. It was so delicious I didn't want it to stop, yet even during this most exciting moment I became afraid. I feared that maybe it wouldn't stop; that my intestines and stomach would shoot out too. During that split second that lasted an eternity I panicked and was on the verge of shouting for help, when as quick as they had begun the spasms ceased. I was so relieved. Then I began to suffer from feelings of guilt and shame. I imagined that Grandma Jones and God must have witnessed the whole thing, which is strange because she had been dead for over ten years, and I did not have much religious background.

From Innocence to Intercourse

The next case illustrates the worst possible sex education for a boy who was immersed in prudishness, secrecy, nonlabeling, avoidance, and guilt. It also shows that the terribly negative sexual connotations arising therefrom can be overcome provided the victim establishes an affectionate and confiding relationship with an adequate partner:

> When I reached puberty, I was frightened that my father might explain the facts of life. Sex seemed too terrible a thing to discuss, especially with one's parents. As I later discovered, my fears were unjustified. My father had no intention of relieving my mind of misconceptions.
>
> One day when I was about four years old, I pondered the question about the origin of my birth while my mother prepared dinner. When I asked her how I had been born, she almost dropped the pan whe was holding. After making a few unintelligible utterances, she told me to ask my father. Although my curiosity was strong, I decided not to bring up the subject again. I now knew that sex and birth were things never to be mentioned, that they were terrible. I was afraid to ask my father.
>
> When I was about seven years old, I picked up the word *fuck* from the playground and asked my mother what it meant. My question figuratively blew the roof off our house. My mother's eyes widened, her jaw dropped, and she stuttered in a quivering stance, "Where did you learn that word?" Upon witnessing the convulsive excitement in my mother, I tried desperately to keep myself from crying while I asked her what it meant. She then lectured me on how disgusting and filthy this word was and warned me never to use it again. Once again I asked her what it meant, and she said indignantly, "Ask your father." I was petrified at this idea. I had learned my lesson well. Sex was not to be discussed, and I never asked my parents another question. Two years later an older friend verbally sketched the process of the sex act. My friend was confused about many things; I was confused about everything. The whole business was repulsive. I could not imagine how the partners could be seen without their clothes on because my mother told me we must not undress in front of people. Therefore, I was shocked when I had to undress before strangers when I went into the swimming pool. By the time I reached puberty, I was filled with misconceptions. I was ashamed of my physical signs of maturity and afraid of becoming an adult. When I took a bath or changed clothes I was careful to lock the door and close the bathroom window. I didn't want anyone to see me. Not only was I ashamed of my body, but also I was afraid that my father might note my maturity and tell me the facts of life.
>
> When I had my first nocturnal emission I was terrified. The bed was wet and so were my pajamas. I thought the dampness must be blood. I turned on the light—no blood at all. Then I remembered a joke about a wet dream that had made no sense at the time. Now it was plain to me—I had had a wet dream. My fright turned to embarrassment. I put my bed clothes in the bottom of the hamper and scrubbed the sheet with a wet cloth. I was so embarrassed I could not stand the thought of my mother asking what happened.

In my second year of catechism, the minister lectured on the unfortunate consequences of sex. He plunged into a discussion of venereal disease and truck drivers visiting call girls and getting funny little sores on their lips and other parts of the body. I'll never forget the look on the boy's face sitting next to me—he had a cold sore on his lip. The minister's diatribe filled me with fear. When I get my next cold sore, I was positive it was a chancre. I looked up the symptoms of syphilis. The more I pursued the subject, the surer I was that I had the disease: I had never had sexual relations. Even this fact did not put my mind at ease. My fear lingered for many years.

I needed the affection of a girl, and yet I did not trust myself with one. I became infatuated with a girl in one of my classes, and for the first time, I had the opportunity to show a girl some affection as well as to receive some in return. This girl decided, however, that she was looking for a friend with money and a car, and she rejected me. This episode crushed me.

In my sophomore year I came out of my shell and began dating again. A friend fixed me up with a blind date. That night we both drank too much liquor, and going home that night, we had sexual relations. Guilt gnawed at my insides like a cancerous growth. I never was so ashamed in all my life. What if someone should find out? What if she became pregnant? I never wanted to see her again.

When I met my future fiancée for the first time, I was determined not to make the same mistake. I still craved affection and companionship. The only way I could attain them was to show the girl that I liked her for herself. I can't say I really loved her until the night we sat and talked about a wide range of subjects. This was the first time that I had ever been able to speak to anyone. When I told her this, she revealed that it was the first time she also had been able to speak her mind. That night I knew I loved her. At last I had found someone I could confide in. My dreams became her dreams, her wishes my driving force. She measured up to my idea of the perfect girl. One night I took her to a restaurant and who should turn up as the waitress but my blind date. My fiancée couldn't understand why I lost my appetite.

My fiancée and I experimented in heavy petting, but we managed to stay away from sexual intercourse for the first eight months. When we shared in sexual relations it seem natural. I had no feelings of guilt as I had before. Sexual intercourse was a magnet that drew us closer together. I was now concerned for her welfare. Her problems became mine. We became one. My misconceptions and fears of sex diminished. Sex is no longer a problem, and I am looking forward to married life.

Ritualizing Spermarche

In some 1,200 papers studied, the number of fathers who prepared their sons for the spermarche and who ritualized it enough to make the boy proud of his entry to manhood was exceedingly rare. In the family in the next excerpt, both parents were Polish and had only eighth grade educations. The father was a millwright and held a supervisory position in a paper mill. There were several healthy, wholesome children in this family, which was described as happy and smooth running. Family relationships involved "cooperation, love, and affection. There was fun and joking." The narrator was a middle child with four sisters and two brothers. His account follows:

> My father prepared me quite well for puberty. He made it possible for me to accept my physical changes without much trouble. When my first emission occurred, I was thrilled, not only because of the physical pleasure but also because, according to my father, I was a man. This emission occurred in a dream, and when I woke up, I immediately ran and told my father. He congratulated me, and the next morning he did a very unique thing. He called the whole family into the living room and told them that he felt it was about time the family started treating me as a young man. Therefore, he said, I was no longer to be referred to as Willie but as William. Well, I must say that I did feel a little embarrassed but I also was the proudest boy in the world that day.

Three other reports follow in which the son was well prepared for his spermarche. The reader will notice two things: these boys were very grateful to their parents for training them so well, realizing that their peers had no such training, and the boys reacted as proudly to their manhood as the girls to their womanhood.

> I was prepared well in advance on the subject of puberty, and my first seminal emission wasn't a big surprise to me. Although my parents contributed more to this subject, I did receive some valuable extra information from church and school. Mostly my father used to sit down with me and talk over the subject of sex. He prepared me for manhood when I was eight years old, and I felt that I was ready to go out and conquer the world. I knew about sexual intercourse and where babies came from before any of the kids on our block. I was shocked when I found out that many members of my peer group did not yet know anything about the birds and the bees. I laugh to myself when I recall how I used to bring these ignorant little children together and preach to them about the fundamentals of sex. Many of their mothers came over to our house after this and told my father they would prefer to teach their children about sexual matters, although it could be inferred from what some of them said that I was quite qualified on the subject.

> Because I was informed about sex dreams at this early age, I was not really surprised, shocked, or embarrassed when my first seminal emission came in a nocturnal dream. For the first couple of seconds after the emission I was rather frightened, then I came to my senses and realized that this is what my father had been preaching to me all along. He told me that I would be entering manhood one of these days and that there should be no cause for alarm when it happens. The next morning I told my father that the previous night I had received my first evidence of puberty and that I wasn't embarrased or shocked but happy and thrilled that I was entering manhood. He said that he was very proud of me and was glad that it had happened this way.

My parents taught me to cherish sex, to hold it in high esteem and to look at it as something clean and pure, while my peers considered it something filthy, vulgar, and dirty. I received a fairly decent education on the sex issue from my parents, school, and church. I feel that a person's whole attitude toward sex revolves around his parents. I am so grateful to my parents for the well-rounded knowledge they gave me on the subject of sex.

When I was thirteen, my father presented me with a book on where babies came from. This was an admirable idea, but the book was keyed to the mind of a six-year old, not a freshman in high school. This actually turned out to be a good thing because it prodded me into badgering my father for information about sex. He patiently explained everything to me that he could, and he got some books on sexual reproduction from the library. He also made a very good explanation of nocturnal emissions that completely baffled me until about a week later when I had my first one.

I'll never forget how proud of myself I was, the morning after my first wet dream. Since my father had explained everything to me, I wasn't the least bit worried or upset by the situation. The only thing that bothered me was that I couldn't for the life of me remember what the dream was all about. I was thrilled with the whole idea of the thing and felt like Joe Stud for the entire day. It made me feel like such a man that I smoked my first cigarette.

Problems Concerning Male Puberty

From the case-history material, one can see that, for many boys, the first ejaculation of life, by whatever outlet, is a profound experience. For the vast majority of boys, the order of experiencing ejaculatory outlets is nocturnal emission, masturbation, intercourse. Since, according to my data, the average age at first masturbation for both 1966 and 1980 was 12.7 years, we may speculate that the age for the first nocturnal emission was slightly younger. This suggests that private and public rituals to prepare boys for puberty should begin at least by age twelve. How important is it to prepare young boys for the advent of puberty, and to what extent has sex education for boys improved since 1966?

The emotional reactions of boys to their first nocturnal emission for the years 1966 and 1980 are given in table 15–2.

The percentage who experienced shock and fright decreased considerably from 1966 to 1980; surprise and wonder doubled. The percentage of those who were embarrassed and of those who did not understand the phenomenon decreased. In 1980, only 24 percent indicated they well understood the phenomenon, and 8 percent developed feelings of pride because it marked the beginning of manhood.

There is still great need for improvement, and the potential for parents to crystallize the gender identity of sons at puberty and to improve their self-image as persons growing into manhood has scarcely been tapped. I alluded previously to the rewarding ritual of some families at the menarche

Table 15-2
Reactions of Boys to Nocturnal Emissions

	1966		1980	
Reaction	*Number*	*Percent*	*Number*	*Percent*
Shock and fright	22	16	2	3
Surprise and wonder	14	10	15	21
Embarrassment	45	32	7	10
Did not understand phenomenon	37	27	9	12
Vaguely understood phenomenon	21	15	16	22
Well understood phenomenon	—	—	17	24
Feeling of pride because it marked the beginning of manhood	—	—	6	8
Total	139	100	72	100

Source: Data for 1966 is from Gordon Shipman, "The Psychodynamics of Sex Education," *Family Coordinator* 17 (1968):3–11. Copyright © 1968 by the National Council on Family Relations. Reprinted by permission.

of their daughters. Imagine a thirteen-year-old son coming downstairs where his mother is preparing breakfast and exclaiming, "Mom, guess what? I had my first ejaculation in a dream last night and now I'm a man." If this quotation brings a laugh, it shows how lopsided our culture is. This failure in preparing boys for puberty is still with us, as revealed in table 15–3 that compares the adequacy of such preparation in 1966 with that in 1980. Unfortunately the samples are small.

The increase in the percentage of fathers in 1980 who were adequate in preparing sons for the spermarche (19 percent) over those who did likewise in 1966 (6 percent) is nullified by an increase in the percentage of fathers who did poorly. Although the percentage of fathers, mothers, and siblings who instructed not at all declined since 1966, the percentage is still much too high. Apparently, the programs in a majority of schools are pitifully inadequate.

Table 15–4 sheds some light on the sources of learning about intercourse. Peers as teachers in this area seem to have declined, while information about intercourse may be increasing slightly through reading materials.

Young boys in our society are being crushed psychologically by increasing sexual permissiveness and sexual activity on the one hand and by ignorance and irresponsible attitudes on the other. I recall my first case of a young simple-minded probationer who had impregnated a girl. He told me about the circumstances of his intercourse, and I inquired if he had used any precautions to prevent pregnancy. "No," he said. Then I asked, "Did you

Table 15-3
Adequacy of Preparing Boys for the Occurrence of Nocturnal Emissions
(percentage)

Preparer	Adequately 1966	Adequately 1980	Poorly 1966	Poorly 1980	Not at All 1966	Not at All 1980	Total 1966	Total 1980
Father	6	19	2	13	92	68	100	100
Mother	7	14	5	13	88	73	100	100
Sibling	3	8	5	17	92	75	100	100
Peers	9	34	45	37	45	29	99	100
Reading materials	39	38	61	21	0	41	100	100
School or church	0	22	0	27	0	56	100	100

Source: Data for 1966 is from Gordon Shipman, "The Psychodynamics of Sex Education," *Family Coordinator* 17 (January 1968):3–11. Copyright © 1968 by the National Council on Family Relations. Reprinted by permission.
Note: Total for 1966 sample is 146. Total for 1980 sample is 66.

think about it?" "No," Many years later a senior at the university was in my office to discuss how the lack of a credit might bar him from graduating. He said, "And this isn't the only trouble; I got a girl pregnant and I don't want to marry her." Then I asked exactly the same questions I had put to my probationer forty years before and received exactly the same answers. We have a vast literature on why girls get pregnant. Maybe we should give more attention to why young men do not think about it.

Table 15-5 shows two time dimensions involving increase in anxieties for sexual phenomena. First is the increase for individuals as they progress from puberty to adulthood as shown in the horizontal columns. Thus, anxieties over masturbation and petting are high during puberty and adolescence and decline in adulthood; anxieties over intercourse and venereal disease rise from puberty to a peak in adolescence and decline in adulthood. The second time dimension is the increase in anxieties from 1966 to 1980 as shown in the vertical columns. The percentage of anxieties over intercourse and venereal disease increased sharply during this period. In most cases it doubled and tripled, and the percentage of adolescent anxiety over venereal disease went up five times. Dramatic increases of like nature were associated with the possibility of impregnating the girlfriend and the anxiety from her actual impregnation. The trends they imply are reinforced by similar trends in my tabulation on mild anxieties and by the impressionistic experience of the counselors at the university. They were also consistent with a great many studies showing the increase in sexual activity of college men and women during the past two decades.

To what extent do such anxieties impair the health of students, their

Table 15-4
Source of First Knowledge about Intercourse for Boys

	1966		1980	
Source	Number	Percent	Number	Percent
Peers	77	72	48	57
Reading	13	12	16	19
Father	7	6	4	5
Mother	3	3	4	5
Teacher or clergyman	6	6	7	8
Pornography	1	1	5	6
Total	107	100	84	100

Source: Data for 1966 is from Gordon Shipman, "The Psychodynamics of Sex Education," *Family Coordinator* 17 (January 1968):3–11. Copyright © 1968 by the National Council on Family Relations. Reprinted by permission.
Note: Sample for 1966 is 107. Sample for 1980 is 75. Multiple choices increase total to 84.

academic efficiency, their work, their relationship to lovers, their readiness for commitment and the breaking of commitment, and their later adjustment in marriage? Case histories in chapter 16 have relevance to some of these questions. Anxiety and its aftermath are the price for adolescent sexual freedom.

Sexual Encounters of Women from Childhood to Adulthood

In 1966 I gathered material concerning the extent to which women had suffered from various kinds of sexual encounters from childhood to the time of the questionnaire, when most of them were university sophomores between twenty and twenty-one years of age. I replicated this study in 1980, using the same questionnaire, and compared the two findings. In 1966, 263 women indicated they had experienced 448 sexual encounters, averaging 1.70 per person; about 25 percent had had no encounters. In 1980, 180 women had had 334 encounters, averaging 1.85 per person.

These data indicate that the percentage of female students having encounters in the following categories did not change appreciably between 1966 and 1980: voyeurists, males who followed making obscene remarks, males who were obscene over the telephone, rapists, and child molesters. (To simplify table 15–6 I listed only percentages.) Encounters with exhibitionists went down by 11 percent. Encounters with males who were aggressive in suggesting intercourse went up slightly, while those whose aggressiveness

Table 15-5
Sexual Anxieties of College Men Associated with Various Types of Sexual Experience from Puberty to Adulthood

Focus of Anxiety	Year	Puberty		Adolescence		Adulthood	
		Number	Percent	Number	Percent	Number	Percent
Masturbation	1966	15	14	20	19	9	8
	1980	19	26	14	19	3	4
Petting	1966	5	5	8	7	8	7
	1980	9	12	8	11	4	5
Intercourse	1966	10	9	17	16	12	11
	1980	16	22	20	28	9	12
Venereal disease	1966	4	4	6	6	8	7
	1980	11	15	23	31	16	22
Possibility of impregnating girlfriend	1966	7	6	16	15	28	26
	1980	16	22	38	51	29	39
Actual impregnation of girlfriend	1966	1	1	3	3	5	5
	1980	5	7	19	26	9	12
Total	1966	42	39	70	66	70	69
	1980	76	104	122	166	70	94

Source: Data for 1966 is from Gordon Shipman, "The Psychodynamics of Sex Education," *Family Coordination* 17 (January 1968):3–11. Copyright © 1968 by the National Council on Family Relations. Reprinted by permission.
Note: Sample for 1966 is 108 college men. Sample for 1980 is 74 college men.

had to be resisted by force went down slightly. Fright from males who aggressively suggested intercourse remained at about 50 percent; fright from rape remained at 100 percent. Fright in all other categories went down in varying degrees; reaction of disgust increased in all categories.

These data should be considered in the light of two trends since 1966: increasing sexual permissiveness and increasing enlightment regarding nonconventional sexual behavior.

My 1980 questionnaire elicited information on the age at which females progressed from first experience in light petting to heavy petting, to petting in which the partner has an orgasm, to petting in which both achieve orgasm, and finally to intercourse. The data on these are given for 178 women in table 15-7.

When teenagers are permitted freedom to fondle each other in private, the progression we find in table 15-7 is inevitable. The disastrous effects of pregnancy on young girls and their offspring, in terms of health and marital hazards and in educational and economic deprivation, are well known. If

Table 15-6
Unpleasant Sexual Encounters of College Women
(percentage)

Encounter	Type of Encounter		Felt Fright or Terror		Felt Disgust	
	1966	*1980*	*1966*	*1980*	*1966*	*1980*
Exhibitionist	29	18	76	38	24	66
Voyeur	7	6	68	20	32	60
Man who followed, making obscene remarks	27	28	89	35	11	57
Man who said obscene things over the phone	23	26	59	51	41	68
Man overaggressive in suggesting intercourse	31	47	50	49	51	61
Man whose sexual aggressiveness you resisted by force	35	29	74	62	26	51
Man who forced you to intercourse	3	4	100	100	0	57
Older man who enticed you into sex when you were a child	4	7	100	75	0	50

Source: Data for 1966 is from Gordon Shipman, "The Psychodynamics of Sex Education," *Family Coordinator* 17 (January 1968):3–11. Copyright © 1968 by the National Council on Family Relations. Reprinted by permission.

Note: Sample for 1966 is 263 women. Sample for 1980 is 180 women.

Table 15-7
Selected Types of Sexual Experience of 178 Women according to Age at First Experience

Age	Light Petting	Heavy Petting	Heavy Petting— Partner to Orgasm	Both Achieve Orgasm	Intercourse
7-11	3	1	1	1	1
12	6	1	0	0	0
13	13	4	3	1	2
14	14	6	2	1	1
15	39[a]	17	10	4	6
16	34	31	21	15	11
17	15	35[a]	24[a]	24	18
18	11	22	26	25[a]	33[a]
19	0	2	7	13	12
20	1	4	3	6	7
21	0	0	1	3	4
22	0		0	0	2
Total	137	123	97	93	87

[a]Median mode.

society were to taboo opportunity for youngsters to fondle each other in private, we might delay the petting-to-intercourse syndrome for a few years. Such a program would outlaw youngsters as couples from engaging in certain types of recreation in private places like outdoor theaters and would call for an enlargement of professional and lay supervision of recreational activities.

By subtracting the percentages listed in table 15-7 from 100 percent, we have the percentage of teenagers of a given age who have not had the type of experience listed in each column. This gives a substantial percentage of youngsters who are not a risk for premarital pregnancy. These nonrisk percentages may be related to the substantial number of families in which dating in private is not permitted until after a certain age.

Another approach to consider is that most pregnant teenage girls are from dystrophic families wherein negative psychological pressures are conducive to all sorts of disastrous consequences. Pantrophic families rarely have delinquency, drug addiction, running away from home, truancy, and teenage pregnancy.

Learning about Contraception

In my 1960 questionnaire, I sought information about when students first learned about various types of contraception and from whom. The students were given a grid listing the sources of learning at the left of each row and the types of contraception at the top of the columns. They were instructed to list their age in the appropriate square to indicate the age at which they had learned about a given contraceptive from a given source.

In table 15-8 for women and table 15-9 for men, I tabulated the number of learnings by sources and then computed the weighted percentage of learning by sources. Note from the right-hand column that, for women, first learning about contraception from peers and public schools is way out front. Women also learn more from mothers and college courses than men. For men, learning from peers is way out front, 42 percent, with public schools next, 27 percent. More women take courses dealing with child development, marriage, and family, and they have more to lose by not understanding the use of contraceptives.

Apparently, both men and women first learn bits of information from a variety of sources about various types of contraceptives between the ages of ten and twenty. There was little difference in the age range according to source except that learning at college took place between age eighteen and twenty. The age range for schools was twelve to eighteen. The percentage of learnings about each type of contraception was very close for both sexes.

Just how well or how much children learn about contraception from

Table 15-8

Source of First Learning about Various Methods of Contraception for 156 Women

Source	Number Who Learned of Method, by Source							Total Number Who learned of Method, by Source	Weighted Percentage of Learning, by Sources
	Condom	Pill	Foam	Diaphragm	IUD	Rhythm	Withdrawal		
Father	0	1	0	0	0	0	0	1	0
Mother	5	25	9	8	6	11	5	69	8
Sibling	13	17	5	5	6	4	6	56	7
Peer	65	46	30	23	20	25	35	244	29
Public school	24	26	39	40	38	41	35	243	28
Parochial school	5	8	5	5	4	6	5	38	4
College	7	9	15	23	19	13	12	98	11
Other	3	12	18	22	23	12	17	107	13
Total Number of Learnings, by Method	122	144	121	126	116	112	115	856	100

Table 15-9
Source of First Learning about Various Methods of Contraception for 74 Men

Source	Number Who Learned of Method, by Source							Total Number Who learned of Method, by Source	Weighted Percentage of Learning, by Sources
	Condom	Pill	Foam	Diaphragm	IUD	Rhythm	Withdrawal		
Father	7	1	0	0	0	0	0	8	2
Mother	1	2	1	4	3	2	1	14	3
Sibling	5	6	3	2	2	2	0	20	5
Peer	36	22	23	18	16	32	29	171	42
Public school	12	21	17	21	19	13	11	114	27
Parochial school	3	4	3	4	4	6	3	27	6
College	0	0	1	2	2	2	0	7	2
Other	4	8	11	9	7	8	8	55	13
Total Number of Learnings, by Method	68	64	59	60	53	65	52	421	100

different sources is problematic. They may learn only the term for a given method without understanding much about it. In view of the increasing incidence of sexual activity as children approach late adolescence, some agency like the schools must take responsibility for a systematic educational program.

Conclusion

In concluding this chapter, I wish to reemphasize what I consider to be the main function of the family in the orientation of children to sexuality, a function that cannot be done by other agencies—that is, the orientation of children to their appropriate gender roles.

The origins of homosexuality and transsexuality have not yet been clearly and finally established; I suggest that those interested in these problems investigate what happens within the family at the onset of puberty. In the meantime, I suggest to parents who would like to maximize normative gender identity that they ritualize puberty along the lines that my case-history materials have suggested and that they do not openly express disappointment at the sex of the child.

An effective puberty rite within the home requires the cooperation of both parents. The mother's role is to advise the daughter something about the approaching menarche. If the daughter learns all about it in school, the mother must acknowledge its imminence and give the daughter positive moral support as a woman. The father's function is to congratulate his daughter. For the boy at puberty, these parental roles are reversed. The father instructs his son about nocturnal emissions and gives him moral support at spermarche, while the mother congratulates her son. The term *congratulations* is not to be taken literally but should include any expression that inculcates a sense of pride.

Another conclusion may be made from my data. Whether or not we give credence to the theory that the incest taboo places an obstacle to sex education within the home, there are cultural obstacles to free and easy communication on sexual subjects between parents and children. Sex education programs must be staffed by classroom teachers who have had special training in order to accomplish what most parents cannot and will not accomplish. These programs can be conceived in part as a second line of defense to succor the children from dystrophic homes and to prevent a great deal of anxiety and misery.

Notes

1. Gordon Shipman, "The Psychodynamics of Sex Education, *Family Coordinator* 17 (January 1968):3-12. Copyright © 1968 by the National Council on Family Relations. Reprinted by permission.

2. J.H. Gagnon, "Sexuality and Sexual Learning in the Child," *Psychiatry* (1965), pp. 212–228.

3. J. and B. Whiting, *Handbook of Research Methods in Child Development,* P.H. Mussen, ed., (New York: Wiley, 1960), p. 937.

16 The Vicissitudes of Courtship

Parents sometimes spoil the mate-selection process before it even gets started by teasing son or daughter about the first dating. The damage such teasing does to the social growth of children is substantial and blocks the visibility of their settings for the parents. In chapter 4, I mentioned several cases in which the teasing of the father about his son's first dating built up a barrier that completely cut off visibility of the son's social life. Such teasing affects daughters also:

> My brother could never bring any of his girlfriends home, and I never have and never will bring any of my boyfriends or my fiancé home. My father teased us about our dates, saying cutting remarks about them although he had never met them or knew them. I know he did it just in fun, but sometimes he really hurt us, so we avoided the possibility of great embarrassment.

I found a number of pantrophic families wherein light teasing about dates was acceptable and even enjoyable. A man with two brothers and two sisters wrote, "I've always received a normal amount of teasing within my family about girls. This I accept and enjoy and love to return heartily."

The variables that determine whether teasing about dates is damaging or enjoyable are (1) timing (age and experience of youngster at first date), (2) nature of the teasing, and (3) nature of the family *hestia*. A good rule is to avoid teasing about first dating unless all circumstances are favorable.

Parents with a shy child sometimes get pushy in thrusting the child into the dating pattern, with negative results. For example:

> I didn't start dating until I was about sixteen because I was afraid of boys. Another reason I wasn't interested in dating was that my mother tried to push me into it. It was very important to her that I go out with boys, and I think I kind of resented it and almost out of spite made no effort to date until I was good and ready.

At the other extreme are parents who hamper the social life of the daughter by discouraging all contact with boys during early adolescence. This may be due to unfortunate life experiences of the mother or older

277

daughter. In the following case a daughter explains what happened when the mother squelched her social life:

> My parents failed to realize that my interest in boys during early adolescence was quite normal. I suppose they thought that if they didn't squelch my interest immediately I would wind up a tramp. With that attitude, they proceeded to rip down any self-confidence I might have had in the presence of boys. They harped that I was too young, that nice girls aren't interested in boys. As a result, I withdrew from as much contact with boys as possible. On several occasions when I developed crushes, I attempted to tell my mother, but she became so highly critical and disapproving that now I tell her as little as possible about my social life.
>
> Such parental attitudes stymied my dating, cut down my self-confidence, and made me withdraw into myself. Ironically, as I got older, my parents began to worry because I didn't date.

Parental Influence

Fathers sometimes bluntly tell their sons what physical types are to be desired in wives. One father maintained that the ideal woman should be slender; another father said the ideal woman was chubby. Both sons accepted these judgments without reservation.

Very often, parents who have been indifferent to the dating of their children suddenly take action when the son or daughter gets serious about an objectionable dating partner. One woman said that, when her parents considered her dates suitable, they were lenient about her dating rules, but when she dated a man her parents did not like, they were restrictive on such rules.

Sometimes when parents are distraught because a son or daughter is committed to an objectionable partner, they will not only beg their child to reconsider but also will implore friends, relatives, and their pastor to do likewise.

Another method of exerting influence is for parents to criticize the objectionable partner and/or to extol the merits of the favored one. The case-history material suggests that overt criticism is counterproductive. It often produces rebellion and tremendous emotional conflict, as in the following report. A couple who were sophomores at the university became engaged. The parents of the girl became fearful that their daughter would get pregnant and not finish her education. The woman wrote:

> My mother turned on Jerry with everything she had to break us up. She was rude to him, called him a no-good, and made her objections known to friends and neighbors. I could have withstood my parents' objection to my engagement but not their failure to support me in front of others. I seri-

ously began to doubt their love for me. It seemed that as long as I was doing what they wanted and bringing honor to their names, I earned their love but that when I chose to do something contrary to their wishes, I was excluded from the family without understanding and gentle persuasion. My mother was so desperate she said that if I decided to love Jerry, it meant I didn't love my parents.

This was a terrible time for me. I was torn between my love for my parents and my love for Jerry. We argued constantly. Jerry was starting to hate my parents for what they were doing to us, and I was starting to hate him for being right about my parents. Finally, we broke the engagement until a later date, and I wrote home that we still planned to marry but that we'd wait to become engaged until just before the wedding. I also told them that was all the farther I would go in their direction and that I demanded respect for Jerry's acceptance of my love for him. Since we were doing things their way, they should now accept the fact that we were in love. I realized it was a time I really needed guidance and love from my family, but I didn't get it and I'm still quite hurt about it all.

Immediately after that, they treated us sweet as pie and Jerry was accepted. We were both slow to accept this seemingly false acceptance, but we both realized that my parents played a big role in my life as well as in our lives together.

During this stressful period, the mother had surgery for cancer and was going through menopause. The father had started a new business and was under terrific pressure. The daughter continues:

About that time, my mother started to drink heavily to steady her nerves. I confronted her about the drinking. We had a great talk; she knew that I cared very deeply, and I helped her face a problem that she had been unable to face.

My goal is to have my mother play a big role in planning my wedding and to reach a closeness that is rare between mothers and daughters. I am going to help her in the transition of a hopeless, lonely woman to someone who can accept the worries of life with a driving spirit.

The last paragraph in this quotation illustrates the fundamental desire of daughters to have their parents cooperate and give them moral support during the wedding festivities. A second fundamental desire is to have unfettered freedom to make their choice of a partner.

My parents never said anything to influence me either way about the people I dated. They feel that it's my life and that I should do as I please.

Children reared in a pantrophic family develop two expectations regarding their choice of a mate: (1) They expect to choose a mate who will be acceptable to their family and who will fit into the extended family system, and (2) they expect their parents to receive such a partner graciously.

My parents have never influenced me on whom I should or shouldn't go out with. They were always friendly to everyone I brought home. My parents left this decision completely up to me because they wanted me to make that choice on my own.

This is how they will be until I bring my life mate home, and then they will treat him very well and will give him the same love and attention they have given to all of us. This is what they have done so far, and it has worked out marvelously.

I have never let my parents' preferences decide whether or not I continued a relationship. I hated parental interference. I refused to tolerate any attempts at running my life. I want to be trusted to make the right decisions myself. If I make a mistake, I will have no one to blame but myself, and I am willing to accept this responsibility.

Another mode of parental objection is to threaten noncooperation and nonattendance at the proposed wedding. This is more likely to be a retaliatory gesture than a way to prevent the marriage. It is quite devastating in its effect, especially on brides who long for the emotional support of their parents at this time of their lives.

I have one sad case in which the old-world culture of the mother collided with the dating pattern in the United States in order to prevent dating by the daughter. This family was socially isolated from the community and the members emotionally isolated from each other. There were no manifestations of comfort or affection. Tragedy for any family member was met in silence. When the mother received word from a European country that her father had died, she burst into tears, but no one expressed sympathy or comfort. The daughter wrote:

If anyone suffers in our family, he suffers alone. When one of us breaks down and shows emotion, it is an embarrassment to the rest or else a big laugh. Whenever my brothers are feeling depressed over a girl, my mother will ridicule the poor boy.

When I was little, my mother lectured me on the evils of boys. Later when I was about to date, these lectures became fantastic ravings. When The Boy came along and asked me to go steady, I was very happy. My bliss was shortlived. I was forbidden to see him in any place outside of school or even in the library. Because my parents didn't trust me out of their sight, I had to turn down an active social life.

The situation hasn't changed now that I am in college. My battles are not as lengthy or tearful, but they are just as heated as before. My parents cannot and will not understand the U.S. dating system. Mother views it as corruptive and degenerate. My brothers, however, have an easy time compared to mine.

If I should meet a boy I could love, my mother would be the last to know. My mother not only criticizes every boy I date for the silliest of reasons but also she criticizes and ridicules my girlfriends, which is painful to me.

Subtle methods of parental influence are more effective than other methods as they seem to involve families that appear to be in the middle or upper ranges of the pantrophic-dystrophic scale. These families have a degree of mutual love, trust, and respect between parents and children. Each of the following cases contributes certain nuances that need no explanation.

> When I was finally permitted to date, in the summer of my junior year in high school, my parents established rules for my dating and trusted me to obey them. The rules concerned things such as time to be in after a date, number of dates per week, and going steady. My parents preferred that I date more than one boy so I would learn from differing personalities. These rules were reasonable, although I chafed somewhat because my friends were not so restricted. Now I am happy they restricted me.

Although this family was religious, the girl was not limited in her dating by this factor, although she implied that social class in a subtle way was something of a factor in her dating.

Many students have implied that their choice of dating partners was influenced by parents in a variety of subtle ways, although none would accept a partner who was specifically recommended by a parent. For instance:

> My mother attempted to influence my dating by telling me that she liked a certain fellow and implying I should too, but I was determined to date whomever I chose. As a college freshman, I made friends with every different group of people I could—the artists, the rebels, the math majors. She didn't approve; she thought I wanted to be one of them. She kept watching over me until one day she saw me come home with this fantastically ugly foreign student. He had a nose bigger than Cyrano de Bergerac's. After that I dated anyone I wanted to, and she accepted them for fear I bring Cyrano back.

For a parent to be hospitable to all dating partners of the children and give the children a sense of freedom to date whomever they please seems to provide an entree for the parent to make an effective generalization about types. This tactic avoids any implication of criticism. For example:

> My friends have always been welcome at my home. During a college recess, my brother and I bring home friends so that our house is like home for them. Mom never goes to a lot of work preparing for guests, but she makes them feel welcome and comfortable.

> Mom and Dad have always liked the boys I have dated. There were many boys whom my parents felt were not my type, but with a free hand in dating and in having them come to my house, I soon realized that fact and dropped them. The fellow I am now dating is the son of parents who are friends of my parents. If any of the parents had suggested we date, we probably would have declined. None of them pushed us but accepted our dating as they had done when I went with other partners. Jim and I get along very

well with each other's parents and family members. We have attended social functions with both sets of parents.

Both sets of parents believe in trying hard to like whomever their children date and marry. I would rate my family as one with internal and external cohesion and very happy.

Appraising Prospective Partners

One perspective for appraising a person as a marriage prospect is a work setting in which both partners participate. A better opportunity for such appraisal is visitation in each other's homes. What they observe there will lead to a greater understanding of the partner's personality and how he or she developed such a personality. Observing a partner in his or her home setting provides a perspective for analysis far superior to that of seeing the partner in the artificial situations of parties and outings. It also provides material for discussing the kind of family and the kinds of relationships they wish to establish after marriage. How a given partner functions in the dynamics of his family constellation will give a clue as to how that partner will function after marriage. Parents who wish to encourage or discourage the romance of their son or daughter should encourage such visitation without making prior judgments.

> My parents usually approved of my dates. They wanted to know whom I was going out with, but they didn't wait up for me or pry into my personal affairs. As a result I told them about my dates of my own accord. I respected them for giving me privacy and, in return, enjoyed talking to them about my dates.

The expectations mentioned here are expressed even more strongly in the next report. It amounts to the prior consent of the parents to accept and love whomever their son might choose.

> My parents were not concerned about the girls I dated because they trusted me. This trust made me look at possible dates for respectability because I did not want to embarrass or shame them.

> My parents have always accepted my dates whenever I have taken them home. Each one has received the approval of my relatives, and each has felt very much at home. My parents have told me that they will love any girl I might fall in love with and marry.

Both parents and their children may be disturbed by cultural restrictions on courtship, such as age, social class, religion, and race. Since most young people have only four or five years on the college campus, differences in age are not often important. In the state universities where I taught, social-class differences did not seem to pose grave difficulties, although a bit of snobbery became apparent between sorority girls and non-fraternity men.

Interfaith Differences

In the 1950s, my students who were getting serious about their boyfriends and girlfriends of different religious affiliations were much concerned about possible difficulties arising from interfaith marriages. In response to this concern, I organized student panels in my marriage class to discuss this problem. The panels consisted of students whose parents were originally from different religious denominations. Although some couples involved in interfaith marriages have suffered considerable anguish, I think the students were surprised to learn how many couples were able to resolve satisfactorily the interfaith problem. In the 1960s, the intense interest in interfaith marriage seemed to have subsided, and the panels were discontinued.

My impression is that, among college-educated people, differences in religion moved from conflict to confusion to tolerance between 1950 and 1970.

Some years ago, a certain bride and groom were members of different synods of the Lutheran church. There was no agreement about resolving this difference so that each attended his or her own church, and the religious conflict simmered for years. The children did not join any church, which was very disturbing to the parents and grandparents.

Conflict with Parents over Interfaith Marriages

Some parents make known that they prefer their child to marry someone of the same religion but, when confronted with the possibility of an interfaith marriage, are flexible enough to cooperate in resolving the issue. This is demonstrated in the following story, which also illustrates the advantages of trust and respect in the parent-daughter relationship.

> I guess my parents felt I should date more boys from my own faith. We had a few fights over religion, but there wasn't a big hassle, even when I started going steady with a boy who had a strong Catholic background. However, it did bother my parents a bit. It didn't become a big issue until we decided to get married. In the end we did work out the difficulty and were happily married.

Another dimension of interfaith difficulty within families is the objection of parents to the interfaith dating and marriage of their children. Following are listed summaries and quotations to illustrate how young people have handled this difficulty between 1958 and 1972.

A Jewish man was married to a Lutheran woman. They had a liberal attitude toward all religions until their daughter began to date a Jewish boy:

> Within the last year, my mother has fought my dating a Jewish boy, and this has damaged my relationship with my mother. She sees in my boyfriend (unconsciously, of course) all the heartbreak, faults, and problems with the family that she had to contend with. I have always considered my mother to be almost perfect because she has been such a wonderful mother to us all. Lately, however, she is distant to me and terribly rude to my boyfriend. My image of her is rapidly being destroyed, and I have tried everything possible to get her to accept this boy. We are planning to marry within a year and a half, and we are hoping she will accept him before then.

Tension due to interfaith marriages is severer when conflict over the issue between the partners is overlaid with conflict between the fiancé and the girl's mother, as in the following case:

> Roger was four years older than I and was graduating from college when I graduated from high school. He invited me to the university for his commencement with this parents. Enthusiastically, I went to seek my mother's permission and got slapped down for wanting to do something as vulgar as going out of town to chase a boy. Nevertheless, off to the university I went, and two weeks of silence followed at our house.
>
> In January I will be twenty-two, and in June I will graduate from college. I have long since paid my way, with the exception of room and board. I am still going out with Roger and am very much in love with him. We want to get married, but due to our religious convictions, we find it impossible to agree on training for our children. June will find us completely separated or married because self-control is fast losing ground. I need Roger and cling to him for the love and warmth I had never felt until we met. We have not made our relationship a steady thing, and both of us have gone out with others. For a period of six months after Roger had gotten his master's degree, we broke up, but then, as usual, we came back together.
>
> Mother walks out of the room when Roger comes in and raves at my frequent dates with him. I have little respect for my mother and feel that it is my life. I want to be the one to run it, not her. When June arrives, I want to leave home and teach somewhere far from home and Roger, provided we can't come to an agreement by that time.

A youth's negative attitude toward organized religion may result from a combination of factors: (1) chronic and severe conflict between parents over religion, (2) parental pressures concerning religion when the parents have severe character defects, (3) intellectual stimulation of the children, (4) religious education by persons whose interpretation of religious principles is narrow and unsophisticated.

The following case of a bright coed born of a Polish Catholic mother and a Greek Orthodox father illustrates severe and chronic conflict over religion. The father was a heavy drinker, and the distraught mother, with five children, made several attempts at suicide and was hospitalized for a nervous breakdown. The daughter writes:

> I was never a very religious person, so religion didn't make any difference as far as choice of dates. Although I was raised Catholic, I have grown to dislike Catholicism and all forms of religion, not so much because of the religious conflict between my parents but because most of the teachings seem ignorant and meaningless. Since I feel very strongly about this subject, I try to avoid dating devout boys.

In predicting how children will react to an interfaith marriage in terms of religious attitudes, I suggest that the following variables be considered:

The degree to which the parents are committed to their religion,

The nature of spousal conflict over religion,

The nature of the emotional health and the personal integrity of the parents,

The degree to which the children have been intellectually stimulated,

The nature of the religious training of the children,

The degree to which a person tends to compartmentalize his religious thinking from his other thinking.

Interfaith marriages between partners who are reasonably wholesome and harmonious tend to make their children more tolerant of religious differences and readier to accept an interfaith marriage for themselves.

Confusion

When parents of different religious backgrounds neglect the religious training of their children and only explain that they are to make their own choice on religion upon maturity, the children may react with confusion, as in the following family. The mother, a Christian Scientist, and the father, a Catholic argued over religion, but neither attended church services. The daughter writes:

> My sister and I were baptized in the Catholic church, but we were left to solve our own problems as adults. This resulted in insecurity and confusion throughout the adolescent years. My sister is now a practicing Catholic since this is her husband's faith. My fiancé and I are planning on joining

the Congregational church before our wedding this summer. My sister and I believe that religion is a very important part of family life and that the parents should be of the same faith.

I recall another student who said that her parents, of different religious faiths, likewise permitted the children to make their own judgments on joining a church upon maturity, but in this case it was handled so well that the children did not suffer from confusion but attended a number of churches and made their decisions without difficulty.

Tolerance

Tolerance of interfaith marriages is promoted increasingly by the trend toward the secularization of religious organizations, by improvement in the education of the clergy, and by the greater percentage of college-trained people in the population.

The following excerpts illustrate how religion has come to play a lesser role in marital choice. The trend toward a more-tolerant attitude toward interfaith marriages is not smooth because of differences in the orthodoxy of parents.

> Sam is Catholic and I am Lutheran, but we both feel that we are worshipping the same God so the particular religion is not important to us. However, I will change to Catholic because his family is very religious and would condemn him for leaving the Catholic church. My family is not particularly religious. My fiancé and I have the same degree of religiosity.

> It doesn't make any difference to me what religion a girl has. I never even think about it as a factor for influencing my dating.

Lonely and clinging parents are a real problem in the courtship of their children. The availability of premarital counseling would help young people to gain autonomy and to achieve separateness from such parents.[1]

Problems in Courtship during the Sex Revolution

A suitor's success in courtship involves not only getting the consent of a woman to marriage but also the successful wooing of the right woman. The counterpart of this is the acumen of the woman in selecting which of several potential suitors to encourage and her success in that encouragement. Success or failure in courtship often is determined by the fortuitous combinations of various initiatives in amorous behavior and the various responses to such behavior. If the sexual overtones are abrupt and extreme and the response equally so, the couple may enter a fragile marriage whose base is only temporary sexual compatibility. If the amorous initiative is considered premature in the relationship, the woman may reject a man who has good potential as a husband.

This leads us to consider how the vicissitudes in physical intimacies have affected courtship during the 1960s and early 1970s. This period was, for middle-class college students, a period of guilt, anxiety, frustration, and confusion involving decisions on sexual behavior. The time and degree of changes in sexual attitudes and behavior have been dealt with extensively by family sociologists, but the psychological milieu of such changes has received less attention. Young people neither embraced the changes uniformly nor accepted them nonchalantly.

Young women who enrolled as freshmen came from families idiosyncratic in family structure, religious orthodoxy, mode of imparting sex information, and the way sexuality is to be conceived, expressed, and controlled. In addition, each woman may have had an idiosyncratic history of sexual abuse, dating experience, and sexual encounters. She is at risk for negative sexual encounters throughout her college career and for the rest of her life.

Entering freshman men, likewise, come to the campus with diversities in family background and sexual experience, but they differ from the women in several respects. The women will have suffered more than the men from sexual abuses, incestuous contact, frightening sexual encounters, and rape. The women but not the men have been admonished, lectured, warned, and threatened by parents about dangers from aggressive men and about getting pregnant. Control of dating is more restrictive for girls than for boys.

At college entrance a larger percentage of men than women have progressed further in sexual expression and sexual maturity, although a small minority of women may have outstripped their male contemporaries. Women who have not masturbated and whose dating experience in high school was limited may arrive at college before their sexual awakening has occurred. These great differences in the readiness for sexual response of freshmen women are but dimly perceived by men on the campus.

Another difference affects all of us. In the past, men have been scripted by their culture via family experience, literature, the press, cinema, and television to assume they are destined to play primary roles in the workaday world and in the establishment of a family, while women were destined to play helpful but more-passive secondary roles. This unequal scripting operates at the subconscious level so that it was difficult for men to perceive how this lopsided scripting affected sexual discrimination in the workaday world, in the coding of family and criminal law, and in the administration of such law. Susan Brownmiller has attributed these lopsided scripts to the ancient conception of women as property and to the way this concept has fostered the rape of women through the centuries.[2]

Remnants of this scripting operates on the campus to make some men look upon women as sex objects to be pursued for their own pleasure without regard to the worth and dignity of the woman. Male students, as we shall see, vary extremely in their approach to women in dating and courtship; women also vary in attitudes toward men, including issues relating to the equality of the sexes. When men and women converge upon the campus with such great diversities within each sex and between the sexes, in a period of rapid social change in sex patterns, we have a dynamic mixture of attitude and behavior that is complex, sometimes painful, and difficult to organize.

It seems as though modern man has the ability to compartmentalize his view of people so that, in one perspective, they are objects and, in another, human beings. When a general estimates the number of civilian casualties in a nuclear first strike, people are objects; when he dances with beautiful women at a military ball, they are human beings. Slavers and prison guards usually regard people as objects. In the realm of sexuality, it is easy for some to view people as sex objects, like when the military high command facilitates the establishment of brothels near troop concentrations. Both the generals and the patrons view the inmates of the brothels in the perspective of sex objects as do the rapist and would-be rapist and college men looking for a woman to seduce.

A male student said that when he was young, he considered girls as sex objects, and later he wondered how he had arrived at such a conclusion. Some girls have said they looked upon boys as sex fiends; one girl wondered if, in intercourse, the man bit the woman on the neck like a tomcat to keep the woman under control.

In all human relationships it is important to maintain the perspective of persons as human beings, especially in a sexual context. What kind of family influences encourage children to acquire the human perspective in a sexual context? In this connection, one girl from a pantrophic family wrote that two factors had determined her attitude toward sex: one was the casual nudity of the parents, and the other was open demonstration of affection between the parents. She went on to suggest a third factor:

> I look at sex positively and as an experience that is gratifying. My parents exhibited great respect for each other, and from their teaching about respect for people, I got the idea that women are to be viewed as people and not as sex objects. I can appreciate a woman's sexuality and her personality at the same time.

In the early 1960s, a majority of women entering state universities in the Midwest had had no experience with intercourse, but many had necked or petted. Those who were popular in high school entered into dating with enthusiasm, and most of their high school sweethearts were forgotten. Most of those who had done little dating in high school now found themselves in demand as dating partners, and their self-esteem increased suddenly. Many of these freshman girls accepted the prevailing sex standards of their parents and religious teachers that required them to restrict their petting and to abstain from sexual intercourse until marriage.

As the young women engaged in dating, they were confronted with situations in which they had to choose between the pleasure of petting and guilt and sometimes between the boyfriend and guilt. Some of the young men were subjected to the same orthodox culture that made them uncertain about expectations regarding the initiation of physical intimacies.

It is well known that the strength of religious feeling is inversely related to sexual permissiveness, but how did freshman and sophomore students overcome their religious scruples concerning sexual behavior so quickly? What were the influences that brought about change?

A common theme in the student analyses is the self-perception that a satisfying love affair not only provides affection but also improves personal growth. If a woman has suffered from inner conflicts that are relieved by talking to an understanding man, then she may associate her relief, personal enhancement, affection, and erotic pleasure with her more-liberal permissive partner. A certain young woman had refused to have coitus with her high school boyfriend. She resolved not to go beyond light petting at college, but in a certain dating situation, she thought she "wasn't giving the guy enough" and that her boyfriend might drop her. She wrote:

> If a guy was gentle enough, I enjoyed it too. I was faced with a dilemma. Religion says no, but then I felt I was missing something. I got so mixed up I went to a counselor, and when I left I decided on no petting. This resolution lasted about a week, and I continued as before. I decided to follow my generation and not go to church so much because it eased my mind. In college I began to reexamine my values along with other students and threw out many of the traditional values and sins. In deciding what is right, I take into account the time I've been dating a man, how well I know him, and who will be hurt by a given action. I use these criteria because I think the Catholic church is too far behind the times.

In another part of her analysis, she mentioned how one boyfriend helped her to see the good points of her personality and to overcome her defeatist attitude. Of her relationship with a later boyfriend, she wrote:

> Our relationship has had good effects. I have learned to be more tactful, understanding, and to speak up with more assertion but with softer tones. I'm still hung up about sex, but through his understanding and gentle approach, I have lost much of my apprehension about it.

Another dimension to a student's decision to change his sex standards may be considered. As I indicated in chapter 15, young girls invariably react with shock when they first learn about the nature of the sex act as described in the crude terms of their playmates—not so for the boys. This difference may be due to the external position of the male genitalia and widespread masturbation by boys. In both sexes, however, the beginning of sexual knowledge may be associated with dirt, vulgarity, and sin. When such children get to college and experience love affairs, they may sooner or later come to associate sexual activity with ecstasy and affection. What was vulgar and dirty becomes rapturous and beautiful. How could an intimacy that increases self-understanding, self-improvement, and love be sinful? Of course, it might not be all these things because perception may err and love affairs break up. In the meantime, permissiveness has steadily increased through the years.

The growth of sexual permissiveness has brought confusion. Young people who are derided by parents may be more vulnerable to confusion. A case in point is that of Gertrude. Gertrude's mother was silent on the subject of sex, but she zeaously noted Gertrude's blemishes. The mother laughed at her gait and said her breasts were too large and her buttocks too big. About her experience in college, Gertrude wrote:

> I had no idea that boys were actually human and had feelings similar to mine until I started to date. Then the problem of sexual behavior came up, and I became very confused. None of my dating partners was a steady boyfriend so I was constantly trying to decide when and if I should kiss or neck with a boy and if I should permit petting. I would go from one extreme to the other. On some dates I would drink a little, become amorous, and then feel guilty. Then I would go to the other extreme on the next date and not even permit a goodnight kiss. I had no help from my mother because I could neither confide in her nor trust her. Finally I went to the library, took out five books on sex, and read them with great interest. It was a relief to learn that my dilemma was a common one. My guilt was relieved and I learned many things.

One young man became confused but from entirely different circumstances. He wrote:

> My preparation for sex was horrible. At spermarche I thought I had a malfunction of the urinal tract. As for intercourse, I hardly knew what goes where and whether I was to lie down. My curiosity was satisfied in the ninth grade. I was at the home of a girl I was dating. We were alone and necking, when her hand gave me the surprise of my life. I bubbled over and she remarked to the effect that "there goes our child." An hour later she led me into her bedroom, gave me a prophylactic from her brother's suitcase, and increased my knowledge. After we broke up I took out other girls and was shocked to find that they not only didn't make advances but also didn't care for me to. I was utterly confused.

The progression from necking, light petting, heavy petting, to premarital intercourse can terminate at any stage prior to marriage. The final stage is determined by factors such as religiosity, family background, dating history, sexual trauma, nature of the lover, and timing. One girl wrote of an encounter with an exhibitionist that gave her an abhorrence for sex that decreased gradually as she became more attached to her steady boyfriend. "This abhorrence, coupled with my church instruction and moral standards, kept me from heavy necking and petting." In the middle of her college career, she had a love affair with a man who had similar standards. After an engagement of one year, they planned to marry. Her marriage was imminent at the time of writing. She was happy that she would be married as a virgin.

One syndrome that limits the sexual progression to petting prior to marriage is a combination of later age at dating, strong religious views by both partners, a short engagement, or opportunities permitting a reasonably early marriage. To be able to set a date for the wedding is a help in sexual restraint.

If a girl has not dated in high school and has not masturbated, we may assume that her sexual awakening has been delayed. At this point she is repulsed by the sudden approach of an aggressive man. She will, however, respond to a lover whose approach is gradual, attentive, and respectful. The following was written in 1971 by a college girl who had not dated in high school and whose parents stressed that she was not to get pregnant and that sexual relations were to be reserved for marriage.

> I had several very aggressive dates that I had to push away. When they pressed their bodies against mine, I hated it; it made me sick. When I met Steve, sex was beautiful. I wanted him sexually, and after some months, we petted lightly. It was different with him. He never forced himself on me. Things came gradually for both of us. As our love grew, so did our desire for each other. From him I discovered much about sex and sex play. He would answer my questions and never make me feel foolish. With Steve, my attitude toward sex became maturer. Sex became beautiful but somewhat frightening as I learned in later sexual intimacies more about orgasm and ejaculation. Even though our sex life is more involved, we have never engaged in intercourse. I couldn't change that about me. My parents pounded that into me too firmly. I want to be a virgin on my wedding day. My religion has reinforced this resolve, as has my father. I think Steve feels as I do. He wants to attain the ideal of having intercourse with only one woman and then only when she becomes his wife.

In the following story, the girl had many erotic experiences short of intercourse in high school. This girl said her sex education at home and in parochial school had been very poor. Kissing was a mortal sin. One night she and her boyfriend became amorous and petted heavily:

> It was like a dam had burst. It was one of the most traumatic things that ever happened to me. I cried and ran into the house. The next day Eric

came over so we could talk. I parroted to him my good Catholic rules, how I wanted to be clean and a virgin, while he expressed his more-liberal, but not extreme, views about love and sex. His ideas stimulated me to question my beliefs. I began to question but didn't change. We each went away to college, but we visited each other's campuses. I still had much conflict over sex and came close to breaking our relationship. I read books on reproduction, sex, religion, and psychology. I talked to friends, priests, non-Catholics. I had to decide whether I could freely indulge in any sort of sex or not. After much thought I decided I could. Since then, Eric and I have had many talks about the subject, and now we have a real understanding and a beautiful relationship going for us.

When young people begin physical intimacies in high school, traditional restraints are overcome more quickly, as expressed in the following:

Sexually I developed with Eddie. In high school we engaged in necking at first and, after about a year, in petting. The degree of our activity increased as we got older. After becoming engaged this summer, we became more open in the expression of our love. We have begun to engage in intercourse. At first I felt ashamed and guilty, but it is so wonderful to express your love the way you were meant to that this feeling of guilt has been replaced by guilt for not feeling guilty.

During the 1960s, there seemed to be more references to sex as something natural and, therefore, permissible. More criticism of the double standard developed. There was also disapproval of exploitive sex and a widespread preference for sex with affection.

When high school students progress through the stages of intimacy to intercourse, they find it hard to conceive how they are going to restrain their sexual activity until marriage, which seems a long way off. In the following quotation the girl implies that she is in favor of what might be called open engagement—a pattern likely to be followed by open marriage.

Gradually, sex became less revolting and more intriguing. I met a boy of my age (14) who interested me very much. After two months of necking, he started to pet and I slapped him. He apologized and went back to necking. He gradually introduced me to sex, never forcing me or becoming angry when I refused. We learned from each other. After four years of petting and mutual masturbation, we had our first intercourse. The idea of saving myself for marriage seemed silly. I wanted to experience it then and not have to wait eight years.

When I got to college I realized that most guys were out for one thing—sex. I hated it and let them know it. In two cases, after dating a few weeks, our relationship went beyond petting. I felt I was old enough to know what I was doing. I had no guilt feelings and didn't regret it at all.

[She finally got back to her high school sweetheart:] We both know marriage is in sight but not until we can afford it. Until then we are both free to go where we please, do what we want, and with whom we want.

Lack of high school dating and sexual activity does not guarantee that traditional values will be maintained. In one case, the young woman who did not date until whe was nearly eighteen suddenly found she "couldn't hold her emotions back," but she did not engage in intercourse in high school. She had sexual dreams, fantasies, and anxieties but could not confide in her mother. While in college she engaged in intercourse with a variety of men without emotional involvement. Contrary to prevailing ideas, she was least permissive with men she liked best and opined that she would not have become so permissive if she had dated earlier.

By the mid 1970s, for some parents the sexual revolution seemed like a flood from which they could not influence their children to maintain traditional standards. Consequently, parents take the position expressed by a student in the following language:

> Because my younger sister became pregnant, my mother has talked to the rest of us sisters about the advantages of birth control in case we choose to engage in sex. I have a feeling that my parents trust us completely but that they would rather not know what we do in private.

In our society, the establishment of a pantrophic family requires that the mate-selection process bring together people who are both marriageable and compatible. By marriageable, I mean the potential for being a good spouse. Our society does not know what to do with men who are severely nonmarriageable. These men clog our divorce courts, drive creditors to distraction, and fill up our prisons.

Some psychopaths are great suitors who like to pet and seduce. One hazard in courtship is that amorous activities can develop so suddenly and become so absorbing that judgment in the appraisal of personality is poor. In my experience in parole work, as well as with students, the most distressing and tragic cases involved superior women who were trapped by outwardly charming men who were severely nonmarriageable. One young woman who missed marrying a man who seemed a risky prospect wrote that she was "swept off her feet by Rodney" on a blind date. They immediately proceeded to heavy petting that led him to orgasm. The affair was broken up when he took a position in another city:

> Rodney was unpredictable and at times stubborn, but he could always make up for this with his charm. He gave me the feeling of being loved although I had doubts about the sincerity of his love. Our relationship wasn't secure because it was based too much on sex. I don't ever want to be involved again in a relationship placing that much importance on sex. I know now that much more is involved in love.

It is unfortunate for a woman to succumb to the desires of a man who, without regard to her feelings, will browbeat her into a sexual activity she does not want. Such behavior may be symptomatic of instability and immaturity. This is especially true if the man wants to proceed without regard for protection against pregnancy. For example, Lorna was a good student from a fine family. Just before she was about to leave for the university, her high school boyfriend begged for intercourse "just this once." She became pregnant and married him. Her parents agreed to finance the young couple through college, but the young husband's father did not offer to help with financial support. Whenever the husband's father visited the couple, the husband became critical, depressed, and abusive to his wife. She became so fearful of physical injury that she went home to her parents and filed for divorce. In reminiscing about her case, she wished her parents had been stricter with her dating activities in high school. She was grateful to her parents and admitted she had let them down. At the time of writing at the university, the daughter was three years old. She expressed a desire to remarry and felt that her daughter needed a father.

In another typical case in which the boyfriend begged his girlfriend for intercourse, assuring her that he would not get her pregnant, the girl's period did not come on schedule. Her sister had dropped college to enter a forced marriage and the father, like fathers in this situation, had lectured all the other daughters about not getting pregnant so they could finish college. He also threatened severe consequences if any of them should do so.

The guilt and physical pain of this first experience led to a hysterical reaction, and she told her boyfriend she wanted never to see him again. During the ensuing weeks when her period was overdue, she was tortured with the thought of facing up to her father and the ridicule of her family none of whom liked the boyfriend. She decided that if she was pregnant she would jump out the window, hoping for a miscarriage or death. However, her period did finally arrive and she went to college.

Many college girls with traditonal views regarding sexuality have high but latent sexual potential. When such girls get lonesome they may innocently drift into a bar near the campus where there is usually one male who is stupid enough to think he can seduce them by abrupt methods.

Female students do not dwell on their motives for going to these bars, but they express themselves on two points: They feel that opportunities for socializing with men on the campus are inadequate and that their experiences with men at these bars are usually unsatisfactory. For example, one girl met a male friend at such a bar. After conversing for a short time, he invited her to his room for some popcorn.

> He almost had the sheets pulled back before I got in the door. I left immediately, really disgusted with the whole situation. I just find it so hard to understand how a person can have so little feeling toward someone.

By the time young women reach college, they have a pretty good idea of how sexually compatible their parents are. If they have positive feelings about this relationship and if the marital relationship is reasonable good, they may readily assume, along with other elements of their culture, that love and respect should come before sexual activity. This association is reinforced by traditional attitudes. When the college man abruptly initiates sexual activity with such a woman, he produces the following typical reaction:

> I can't stand a smart aleck or a sloppily dressed boy. Maybe my kind of a young man is a dud, but I'll take him any day over the pawing, roaming, Casanova type of fellow who is looking for only one thing. I'd rather not have a date at all than to spend an evening with a man you have to fight with all night.

Another reason why the abrupt approach may produce a negative reaction, even with a girl who does not have traditional standards, is the possibility that she may have suffered from rape or attempted rape. Her lingering fears and negative feelings toward men are then activated.

> I had one experience that greatly influenced my attitudes toward sex. In the summer after my senior year in high school, my girlfriend and I were invited to a party that many of my former classmates attended. When we got to the park and discovered it was a beer party, my friend went off to get someone to take us home. Meanwhile, I sat in one of the cars parked some distance from the partying group. Suddenly the car was surrounded by boys. Two got in front, one on each side of me, and several got in the back seat. Somehow I managed to get out of the car with all my clothes on. I didn't have any choice but to go home with one of the boys who had been at the party. All seemed well, and I felt relieved until I noticed that the boy was driving in the wrong direction. He started to slow down so I opened the car door and ran. I was really shaken up. He followed, grabbed me, and said he would take me home. Then he turned the car around and headed for town. He drove the car into a lot near a plant. By this time I was really upset. I got out of the car and ran as fast as I could through a wooded area toward my girlfriend's home. I screamed outside her bedroom window and woke up the entire family, but no one came outside to find out what was going on. I turned and told this boy that if he didn't take me home, I would call the police and report an attempted rape. He took me home. After this experience, I carried a knife in my purse.

> I don't see how the girls at this school, or any other school for that matter, can hitchhike to bars or walk around campus late at night. I think this experience really helped me mature. I have made it a practice not to go to bars. When I'm home, I don't accept a date unless I know in advance the boy has a good reputation. This experience has had a negative effect on sexual attitudes and emotional life.

The next case of sexual assault illustrates two principles that were stressed by Storaska in his book on how women should handle themselves when confronted by a would-be rapist. He advocates treating the rapist as a human being and keeping your cool.[3]

A girl visited her grandfather in another city. While she was waiting for a bus on a street corner, a boy drove up and asked if she were the one who lived in such and such a house on 25th Street. She said she was and he offered to drive her home. She accepted the invitation. The boy drove to a baseball diamond and parked behind the backstop fence so she could not get out of the car. He tried to neck with her but she refused. Then he reached into the back seat and came up with a baseball bat.

> I was really terrified by then, and I also felt very sorry for the fellow because he was to young and wanted so much what he could not have. I decided to talk to him and asked a few questions like his age. I told him I was not yet eighteen and that he might get into a good deal of trouble. After a while, he sat back and pondered what I had said. Then he started the car and drove at a reckless speed along city streets. I was lost but knew the general direction of my grandfather's home. I decided the only solution was to get out of the car. When he slowed down at the next corner, I rolled out of the car. He then sped off.

How do persons fare in later life when they have suffered sexual trauma in childhood and/or adolescence? Some recover amazingly well, and some are crippled emotionally and/or sexually for the rest of their lives. If a girl comes to the university with feelings of sexual inadequacy or fears of men and sex, how is she to overcome her difficulty? If she encounters aggressive men, her problems will be aggravated. If she meets up with a man who expresses interest in her as a person and draws her out with empathy, he can often effect a tremendous change. Many girls cannot confide in their parents on any significant subject, much less sex. In case after case, such women have said that certain boyfriends completely turned their negative attitudes toward sex to positive ones. Such men develop a confiding relationship first and then proceed slowly with physical intimacies.

A number of women have written or said to me that they were afraid of their own sexuality. I took these comments to mean that their yearning for sexual expression was so strong that they were afraid they would get themselves into difficulty with men whose desires were similar. This may be augmented by fear of the unknown, which is increased by guilt and ignorance. For example:

> Before going with my fiancé, I never had had the urge for coitus. This urge scared me, and I became uneasy with myself and my desires. I didn't understand myself or these desires, and I had many strange and confused conceptions about lovemaking and intercourse. One night when we were together, I became scared and began to cry. Floyd was very understanding when I told him that I didn't know the facts of life (not really) and also that my feelings and desires scared me. That night Floyd told me about life, and I grew to love him even more. He told me that my feelings weren't wrong but natural. I guess up to that time I had thought of sex as being dirty, but Floyd told me about life in the most beautiful way possible. We strength-

ened our confidence in each other and could discuss any question without embarrassment. I found confidence in Floyd that I never had in my mother.

Some girls, of course, are sexy go-getters. One man said of his high school experience:

Often the girl desired to be petted. I recall a girl I liked and respected who said there must be something wrong with me because I didn't go as far as other boys. I asked how far that was and she said just so we didn't do it. Girls were often as aggressive as the boys. I think my values changed when I went to college. I didn't care for cliques so I stayed away from fraternities and sororities. My social life was a success and I loved it. I dated a good-looking girl for three months. Then she joined a sorority and told me she didn't go out with anyone but frat men. I was checked, but I learned to put my values somewhere else.

From then on, I rated the girl's face and figure fifth instead of first. Once I was offered a choice on a blind date between a good-looker and one that was lots of fun. I chose the latter, who became my wife three years later. The good-looker has since been married and divorced.

The ups and downs of success in dating have an influence on the ups and downs of self-image. Jennie, from a dystrophic family, said her birth was a mistake and an unwanted one. She hated her father, mistrusted her mother, and had few friends. Her first fiance passed her up because he had a pregnant girlfriend back home. She finally developed a good relationship with a man whose ideas on love, sex, and marriage influenced her greatly. With respect to her ideal image, she wanted her future husband to be the exact opposite of her father, and she added:

I would like him to treat me with the respect and dignity due any woman. The one true love affair I have had and the infatuations I've experienced have proved to me that I am capable of enjoying life and, more important, capable of loving.

Sometimes a love affair that has progressed smoothly through the usual stages to a good marriage is sufficient to counteract unhappy experiences in the family of origin, and sometimes it is not.

Another woman wrote that she was shattered when her boyfriend deserted her and that she became moody. Her moodiness was then a handicap in trying to establish new relationships. She took cognizance of her problem and tried to overcome her difficulty. She finally met a man who understood her problem and took action to change her attitude.

The pursuit of erotic pleasure on the campus, even with a fiancé, may be hazardous to scholarship and peace of mind. Bertha came to the university with traditional sexual values. She fell in love with Pete, who had the same values. After dating for a year they became engaged, leading to a relaxation of previous standards. They were so involved sexually that her grades dropped and she was forced to leave school for a time. She was in such a state of confusion that she broke her engagement, which upset her fiancé. She attended a college in a different city, calmed down, and renewed her relationship with her former fiance. He was more careful in his amorous approach for fear of losing her again. However, she teased him into sexual activity again. She concluded her remarks:

> Recently, I've felt that we're beginning to enjoy sex for itself more than for each other. I've been doing much thinking about the effect this could have on our married relationship. We finally managed to get the subject out in the open, and we have been able to agree to make another attempt to discontinue such a trying relationship until it is legal and can be enjoyed in perfect trust and lack of fear of discovery by others.

This case brings to mind the ideas of Paul Cameron, who suggests that adults in our society should script adolescents to a progression of intimacies short of intercourse.[4] Such a script is said to be more in keeping with the concept of sexuality by adolescents, who tend to look upon physical intimacies as an end in themselves, as contrasted to the adult view that they are but a prelude to intercourse. The Cameron view would be midway between liberal permissiveness, with its promotion of birth control for youth, and the conservative view of stemming the tide of physical intimacies by means of suitable moral barriers. The middle position would emphasize the positive emotional components in the boy-girl relationship and hopefully would avoid the disadvantages of youthful intercourse by youngsters who are not emotionally mature enough to cope with it.

Those in favor of permissiveness scoff at Cameron's suggestion by minimizing the difference between a technical virgin and a person who has experienced intercourse. Physiologically, there is little difference between petting to climax and ejaculation with penis in vagina, but it appears that for many young people the symbolic difference is great, and symbolic thinking can be important. If Cameron's program could be implemented in a practical manner, it would reduce the disastrous consequences of premature pregnancies and would stress the moral and psychological nature of love.

Perhaps those who operate the media for motives other than the good of society have added enough pressure to the tide of sexual permissiveness so that it is now too late for Cameron's proposal. There is one drawback to this proposal that I do not wish to overemphasize but that I think is worthy of note. Young men and women who consider themselves in love will eventually progress through the various stages of intimacy to that of heavy petting. If petting stops at this point and continues for a time, it produces congestion in the pelvic areas of both sexes, which leads to a variety of aches and pains and to uneasiness and nervous tension. Each partner may come to associate the discomfort of these symptoms with the presence of the other partner so that this conditioning will trigger negative feelings when they are about to meet; at this point, they may argue over trifles. This difficulty in the relationship I call the petting-tension syndrome. The presence of the syndrome in partners who pet but do not climax was admitted by students on questionnaires and other written material. I have two reports for illustration.

Beginning in his senior year in high school, a man dated an outstanding woman for four and half years. They were devoted to each other and gradually progressed in intimacies to heavy petting that continued without climax or intercourse.

> For such a long time it was hard to stop. By the time I reached the age of twenty-one and was able to get married, we began to argue. She said she was unsure about me and decided we ought to break up. This led to many emotional problems for both of us. It is hard for me to forget her and hard for her to forget me.

A young woman describes a similar experience. Both partners were devout and petted heavily, and both had strong feelings against intercourse. After describing the rapture of their lovemaking, she wrote:

> We have been fighting occasionally lately. For a whole year we had only one fight, and now in the last two months we've had three. These fights were all my fault. I get moody and crabby and then I pick a fight or my feelings get hurt very easily. There are also times when I'm not sure just how I feel about him.

Both these reports were written in 1963. It is possible that this syndrome has not been common since then because petting couples more often proceed to climax or to intercourse. If Cameron's concept were to be adopted, the progression would have to be stopped prior to heavy petting or permitted to continue to petting with climax if the engagements were lengthy.

In the 1960s there was a good deal of concern on where to draw the line in the progression from light petting to intercourse. The following comment is typical of the conservative group:

> Ted and I found satisfaction in being with each other. We kissed quite a bit and started petting after we had been going together for a while. We discussed going further than this but decided we should wait until we were married. The way things turned out, I'm happy we didn't do anything. I feel that lovemaking is not something to fool around with. It is very important and should be left until marriage allows its full satisfaction.

Sometimes a girl will rhapsodize over the delights of her sexual fulfillment that is stimulated by an artful and patient lover. Later, she falls in love with another man with traditional values who is ignorant of her sexual desires and thinks she is still a virgin. Such women are frustrated until marriage, but they seem to manage. One of them wrote:

> Our sexual relationship is satisfying though we both desire more. During two years, we've stopped at heavy petting though we had many opportunities for sexual fulfillment. I have learned that such desire is better postponed and look forward to it as something to bind my marriage.

Effect of Trauma on Courtship

In chapter 15, I presented questionnaire data collected in 1970 that indicated that 75 percent of college women in the midst of their college careers had suffered from various kinds of sexual encounters and that this percentage increased to 80 percent in 1980. Other kinds of events in the lives of children and adolescents add to negative attitudes toward sexuality and members of the opposite sex. These unfortunate events may be divided into those experienced during childhood and those occurring during adolescence and young adulthood.

I list now a sampling of childhood traumatic events as they were described by the narrators:

> When in the sixth grade, a girl became confused and anxious when the boys kept asking her if she was going to have a baby.

> A loving father died when the daughter was ten years old. She became very quiet and shy. She lost all faith in men because her father had left her. The mother indicated that sex was a deep, dark secret.

> A boy was punished for masturbation at age three. When he was six, older boys forced him to attempt intercourse with a girl his age. Women became for him sex objects. He had no desire to date or to associate with women.

> A young boy was lured into a hotel room where an older man displayed pornography and masturbated him.

> A girl in sixth grade was shocked when told about intercourse by her peers. She then drew a picture of a nude man and woman that her parents found and confronted her with in such a fashion that she was overwhelmed with shame and embarrassment. She felt her parents hated her, were disappointed in her. She felt dirty, could not look her parents

in the face for a long time, and developed a fear of sex.

Between the ages of twelve and eighteen, a girl was raped by an uncle, fondled by a brother, and developed a phobia for dark rooms.

Just before a father left home at the time of his divorce, he said something (which she cannot remember) to his daughter, age five, that marred her sexual attitudes and caused her to suffer anxiety for years. She was unable to confide in her mother. She had a tendency to fear and distrust her father and all men.

A father went to prison for a long term when his son was five. The son and a brother were placed with grandparents where he felt unwanted, unloved, and a burden to others. He was threatened with insanity by a grandparent for masturbating. He had his first intercourse with an older girl at age thirteen. He joined the army at eighteen and became a "prolific woman chaser." He married at nineteen and divorced two years later.

Such children are disadvantaged in relating to the opposite sex, and this disadvantage may carry over to the period of courtship and even into marriage.

The sexual trauma suffered during adolescence and young adulthood may involve the kinds of reactions listed in table 15-6. During this period, girls suffer trauma largely from obscene phone calls, boys who are aggressive in suggesting intercourse, or boys who try to obtain consent to intercourse by trickery or a show of force. In one state university whose student body grew from a few thousand to nine thousand in a decade, the university authorities could not recall a single case of a female student being raped by a male student. Rather, they were raped within six or seven blocks of the campus by men who were not students. In some universities female students are warned not to loiter without an escort on certain streets near the campus where nonstudent rapists are known to lurk. When male students begin to tear off the clothes of their female partners, the latter are usually able to save themselves by breaking away or threatening to report the attack to the authorities. This threat is effective because the attacker knows he can be identified.

When a girl who combines strict religious standards with sexual naiveté arrives at the campus and encounters a sexually aggressive man, she may react with fright and anger. Such was the case of Ethel, who was beautiful and had an exceptionally feminine figure. During high school she had successfully slapped down boyfriends who wanted to pet, but she was soon to be disillusioned by her dates on campus. One night when she attended a fraternity dance party, a young man (whom we shall call Freddie) offered to take her home. As soon as they got into his car, he kissed her and reached under her coat. She immediately objected and Freddie said, "You are a college girl now, not a little kid. Come on." Ethel continued to fend him off, trying desparately to explain her feelings. Freddie was undaunted and begged her to have intercourse with him in the back seat. When she told him she was a virgin, he guffawed and said, "There are no virgin women in college." She continues:

> My fright turned to anger as I told him I'm neither an animal nor so cheap that I'd have intercourse in the back of a car. If I even considered it, it would be in bed or not at all. When he finally realized his attempts were in vain, he took me home.

Freddie is similar to the type of rapist described by Storaska.[5] Such a man interprets every glance, every gesture, every posture, every remark as a teasing invitation to intercourse. The rapist, of course, is intent on giving a woman what he thinks she wants. Thus, having failed in his first attempt, Freddie tried a bit of trickery. Four months later, he phoned Ethel and invited her to another fraternity dance, pretending to have reformed. Ethel agreed to go, but when she got to the fraternity house, Freddie took her upstairs on the pretext of having a gift for her. At the head of the stairs he opened the entrance to a darkened room and asked, "Which bed do you want?" Again there was panic and a scramble as Freddie tugged at her clothes, while she screamed and resisted. Ethel could hear couples fornicating in other rooms. She sought out a girlfriend and left. I am happy to report that, in the end, Ethel recovered enough to fall in love with a man who had the same standards as her own.

Fear of Commitment

A trite expression found in some textbooks says, "Men want sex and women want commitment." Early in their college careers, neither usually wants sex unless the partner, the relationship, and the timing are right; and neither wants commitment. There is good reason for reluctance to commitment. Many freshmen, upon entering the university, are confused about their careers. The pressure to decide on a major is great for sophomores because, if they dally in this decision, it may require more than four years to graduate. I have said to my students occasionally, "There are two kinds of students on campus: those who take the wrong major and know it and those who take the wrong major and don't known it."

In addition, there is a plethora of sports and extracurricular activities that requires choices and budgeting of time. In an age of specialization, confusion about how to shape up a college education in order to earn a living frightens students when there is a suggestion on commitment to marry. The love affairs of upper classmen have matured to a point at which commitment seems more urgent, but the longer period of training for a specialty and economic uncertainties may still hamper commitment. This trend and the trend toward sexual permissiveness make cohabitation almost inevitable. This is what some students have said about commitment:

I have been infatuated with a few boys but never in love with them. I do not want to become serious with anyone because I want to finish college and travel after I graduate. Therefore, I will not be able to marry for at least another four years. Some boys are looking for wives, and when they size me up as a good prospect, I become cold and withdrawn.

Throughout my college years I have never suffered from lack of dates or male attention. I have had five more-intimate relationships with discussion of marriage. I feel that these relationships increased my overall human understanding. They also gave me an opportunity to be very flexible. Furthermore, I felt that all these people had qualities I really loved and were people with whom I might have been happy, but I never considered myself ready for marriage because I wanted to travel.

I am now going with a graduate student in engineering who is five years older than I. He has all the qualities I like in a man and I love him very much. He wants me to marry him at the end of this school year. This would be wonderful if I wanted to get married but I don't, not yet anyhow. I am not quite twenty and definitely not ready to settle down with a husband, a home, and children.

I met a college junior who proposed marriage after graduation, but we broke off when we saw that we had to wait awhile and realized that, as time went by, we would get more involved with physical attraction. We decided it was best for both of us to stop seeing each other for awhile. I'm afraid I'm just not ready for marriage, and yet I long for my own home and family.

Rae was two years older than I when she left for college. We continued to go steady throughout that school year and a portion of the next, until we separated during my senior year in high school. The reason for our breakup was the prospect of marriage. Rae began to speak often of marriage at that time and the idea scared me to death. I was too immature to consider it at that time. I had many plans for the future: getting a college degree, playing college basketball, and the like. I wish to achieve these goals before even considering marriage. We finally disagreed so strongly on the issue that we broke off our relationship completely.

This man in the midst of his college career, fell in love with another girl. He wrote:

> She and I discuss our love freely and are planning to be married. If it were
> not for financial difficulties, we would be engaged, but are planning to do
> so as soon as possible.

A few students seemed to indicate that a sexual relationship adds another dimension to a responsibility they wish to avoid. A sophomore man dated a girl steadily and had regular intercourse with her. This relationship became a strain and he broke up with her, leaving a bitter feeling in both. He wrote: "Having intercourse seemed to change us by adding a responsibility that neither of us wanted."

A man who broke with his girlfriend had several motives: He was afraid of marital responsibilities and desired a wife who was willing to work, and he was afraid that what he disliked about his parents was also what he disliked about her.

> The one thing I learned from my parents' arguments is that someone must
> give in. My girlfriend has one trait I don't like: She will never admit she's
> wrong even when she knows she is. My greatest fear lies in being tied down.
> I recently broke up with my girlfriend after two and half years of steady
> dating. She was badly hurt. The only reason I could give her was that I
> couldn't be tied down just yet. I'm really confused now because I like her
> more than anything in the world and would do anything she asks, but I just
> can't face the responsibilities of an engagement and possible marriage. So
> there are two persons being hurt, she and I, and maybe me a little more
> because I'm the one who had to do it. I want a wife who is willing to work
> and help me get ahead in my vocation. I sure wish I could find the answer
> because I'm not happy the way I am. But I know one thing, when I marry I
> want it to last with a love that gets stronger through the years and not a
> relationship tied by obligations.

Fear of Being Hurt Again

Some partners are so hurt by rejecting lovers that they are wary of the approach of others lest they suffer again, as the following excerpts indicate:

> When she severed our relationship, I was deeply affected. This experience
> has led me to be defensive toward becoming emotionally involved with
> women. However, my feeling toward that particular girl subsided quite
> normally. Because of that experience, I am afraid that if I extend myself
> initiating a relationship with a girl I will be hurt again.

> In high school I dated a boy with whom I thought I was in love. When he
> wanted to pet, I said no. He said he would find a girl who would and
> dropped me for another girl. This really hurt me, and as a consequence, I
> have a fear of being hurt again. I also want to graduate, and when I get
> emotionally involved with a fellow it upsets my studying.

The girl in the following case had more than one reason to be wary of men. At age thirteen she was saved from being raped by a sixteen-year-old boy in the home of a girlfriend when the parents of her friend came home at the critical time. She was also frightened by a mentally deficient man who lived across the street and exposed himself in a revolting fashion. After graduation from high school, she became engaged to a boy who had quit school and joined the marines. After five years of courtship she broke up with him for very good reasons, but the emotional shock was severe for her. She could not date again for six months, and then it was not enjoyable because of fear of being hurt.

How children relate to the opposite-sex parent has an impact on how they relate to peers of the opposite sex. When a girl feels that she cannot trust her father to love her, or when she feels that instead of receiving love she receives hate from him, she may be afraid of a close relationship, as in this story:

> I think the reason that I am afraid to form close relationships stems from my fear of being hurt the way my father once hurt me. On that occasion I had every reason to believe he hated me. I think that the only trait I have for my image of the ideal mate is a deep understanding of me and undying love for me. I do not even picture the ideal mate as a person, but rather I just imagine myself in the presence of this approving love.

A successful suitor would have to break through this girl's wall of fearfulness and provide the undying love she craved.

In the next case, the hate for a former lover, the negative reactions related to intercourse, and the breakup made the girl fearful of another close relationship. She was deeply in love with a certain man. They petted heavily and planned to marry. He decided to quit college and join the army. They both agreed not to have intercourse until marriage. He changed his mind, and after much persuation over many weeks, she finally consented. This one experience led to remorse and guilt, and she refused his later sexual overtures. He thereupon broke the engagement. Her remorse and disappointment were so severe she began to hate all men:

> I never wanted another man to touch me again. Besides that, I felt I was no good for any man. I felt I was ruined forever. It was useless for any fellow to date me because I had built a wall around myself so I would never get hurt again.

> [Later she met another man who dated her regularly.] He is the sweetest fellow I have ever known, yet I think I hated him unconsciously because he was a man and could hurt me. I hid behind my wall so I wouldn't get hurt. Soon he began to know and understand me, but he never forced me to do anything. If he had, I would have hated him intensely and rejected him. After many months I changed my attitude and have grown to love him. I

know I may get hurt, and I may lose him, but I'm willing to take the chance. One thing is certain, I will not have intercourse with him until after marriage, and he agrees with this.

Fear of Marriage

Children in dystrophic families may develop an aversion for marriage because it signals distress. The following case illustrates this and shows how role confusion develops when the strongest child is called upon to help the others.

The father disliked his work and was alcoholic. The mother was hospitalized several times for nervous breakdowns. The daughter Ethel became the rock of the family and succored the others. She suffered sexual trauma at the age of twelve when boys on either side of her in a theater tried to fondle her. Ethel wrote:

> I suffered from role confusion because I was no longer the older daughter. I was a companion to my mother, a mother to my brother, and an alien to my father, although I knew he needed me. I had immense guilt feelings for shutting off my father. In my freshman year at college I was still dating my high school boyfriend. He wanted to become engaged at Christmas, and it scared me. I didn't want anything to do with marriage because I felt that I could not become involved in something that had destroyed our family—so I broke up with him.

In the following case, there was very poor communication within the family. Both parents were alcoholic, and they did not sleep in the same room. The student did not seem to perceive the connection between her dystrophic family and her fear of marriage.

> I would go out with a boy until a serious relationship seemed to be developing; then I would find fault with him and never go out with him again. I don't quite understand why I am like this, but because of this reaction, it is almost impossible for me to imagine myself ever getting married.

In the next case the father was irresponsible and alcoholic. The parents were divorced when this daughter was nine years old. Because of the pain of the divorce, she decided she would be extra careful about getting married.

> I have gone through one divorce in my life and never want to go through another. The divorce did affect me seriously in one way: It made me critical of people. I had little good to say about anyone. To get me over this, my mother introduced a game to me. Every time I said something nasty about anyone, I was to find something nice about the person. This game really worked, because I not only liked the people better but also I was happier with myself.

Women's Differences on Feminine Roles

When the women's movement was making headway in the 1970s, some
women seemed to object to its aims and philosophy. One of my students
was in this category.

> I take great stock in being a woman. It bothers me to see women taking
> over men's roles. Somehow they are losing their femininity when they cry
> out for equality for women. I don't want to be equal to my man—I want
> him to be the boss, the dominant one in the family. To me, that's what sex-
> uality is all about—being a woman and playing the role of a woman to
> satisfy a man. I think, by doing this, a woman can also satisfy herself.

How shall we account for antagonism to equality for women? From
this girl's description of her experience at dance halls, one gets the impression that she considered the maneuvering of social relationships as a game,
a game that improved her capacity to emphasize with and to maneuver men,
which she thought hastened her maturity. Another quote from this girl may
throw light on her conception of male and female roles:

> Since first grade, there has always been a boy in my life. I went through the
> usual stages of liking the opposite sex—from the earliest stage of liking a
> boy but pretending one doesn't care at all to chasing boys to being chased.
> I'm in the last stage right now. I'm enjoying my sexuality to the hilt.

The art of maneuvering a social situation so as to be chased is here considered to be a feminine role and the propensity to chase as a masculine role.
The greater these roles are exaggerated, the greater the enjoyment of the
game and the greater the perceived differences between the sexes. The propensity to chase is considered both masculine and aggressive, which may
support the notion of inequality. A puzzling feature of this case is that the
girl's parents were equalitarian in their relationship and had a good marriage. In her childhood, she played with a brother two and half years her
senior. She considered herself a tomboy and at one time refused to wear
dresses.

While antagonism to equality for women by women is sometimes baffling, the opposite kind of woman is easier to understand. In one case, the
parents offered to finance a college education for the son and bought him
an automobile, while they discouraged a daughter to earn her own way
through college and forbade her to buy a car, even with her own money. She
voiced disdain for the prerogatives of men and their superior position.

The next girl formulated the art of managing boys in terms of a "conquering instinct." She wrote from a broader perspective:

> I dated quite often but never with more than one fellow too often because I
> never really wanted to be tied down by the opposite sex. I think now, look-

ing back, that I actually like to lead boys on. I was probably developing a conquering instinct, built up from my perception that the male members of my family were superior. However, I always admired and liked dominant boys, maybe because they were more of a challenge to me. My ideas, however, have changed since I've realized I could never marry someone I'd feel inferior to. I'd rather enjoy equality. All of these infatuations were good for me, though, because they made me realize that real love is not a game of hide-and-seek, an effort to make the best deal, or to win the best trophy. People are not shells, but personalities, each with a shell, and the shell must be opened to get at the fruit.

The Yen for a Dominant Man

This elusive pining for a dominant husband occurs in several facets of courtship. I deal with this factor in chapter 17 in connection with women who admired their dominant fathers and who projected dominance into their image of the ideal mate. I shall illustrate cases in which the woman put into her ideal image the trait of dominance to counteract her own tendencies to be bossy. This hankering for a dominant husband also involves other themes. One is the acceptance of the cultural script that prescribes the husband as the head of the house with superior status, power, and authority. This script tends to equate dominance with masculinity and dependence with femininity. A girl who has feelings of insecurity may imagine her future husband as one with traits that lead to wealth in a competitive society. If she is the indecisive type, she might think of her future husband as a leader who freely assumes responsibility and makes decisions easily. The following excerpts indicate a mixture of motives for wanting a dominant husband.

> There were things I didn't appreciate in my father, such as his drinking and his inability to play the dominant role. I always wanted Dad to stand up to Mom. My boyfriend seldom drinks, and he dominates me like I want him to. He never overpowers me but is dominant in such a way that I associate it with security.

Some sociologists are so impressed with the pecking order in chickens that they carry over the concept to human beings in their discussion of dominance and power. It seems essential to make a distinction between dominance and strength of character. The latter is not easy to operationalize for research, since it takes us into the realm of morals, but morality and strength of character are embedded into the *hestia* of pantrophic families. The student in the next excerpt uses both the term *dominated* and the expression *strength of character*. The latter emphasis may be replacing the former.

I need someone I can look up to, but I also want to be able to contribute as
much as I can to the relationship. One thing I don't like at all in a guy is his
being dependent on me. I have to feel that I really need him, and he has to
be able to keep me in my place. I guess I want to be dominated. Maybe it's
an unconscious desire for punishment, but I'm happier if the guy I'm dating makes me feel unsure of his love. I'm happiest when he keeps me in sus-
pense. My father was always such a strong figure, and that is why I admire
strength of character in any guy. My mother seemed so weak and dependent, which explains my dislike for dependency.

There may be a tendency for young people to replay, in their own marriages, certain interactive patterns of their parents—sometimes to their
delight and sometimes to their sorrow. In thinking ahead about the replay, a
woman may opt in her imagination for a husband pattern that is the opposite of a paternal pattern from which she has suffered. A daughter explains
that her father, who had emigrated from the Near East, played his authoritarian role vigorously with his wife and children. However, his mother, who
lived in the house, was in charge. He consulted her on all family decisions
and always took her position against that of his wife, whose ethnic background was different. Wife and mother-in-law clashed bitterly, which
greatly distressed the daughter. On such occasions, the daughter watched
with dismay when her father invariably sided with his mother against his
wife. This injustice was aggravated by the clannish behavior of the father
with his own relatives while excluding, in an obnoxious manner, all the
wife's relatives from family gatherings. It would be logical to assume that
the daughter would hope for a husband who would protect her from all
comers, including a mother-in-law. The student groped in that direction but
did not quite make it.

I don't know how to explain the fact that I want a man with a dominant
personality when I have always resented my own father's domination over
me all my life. I may not know why I want what I want, but I do know that
I want it, and I won't settle for less.

In our culture, the term *dominance* has such an impact that it has been
used inappropriately as a cure-all, and it has obscured insight into an understanding of family relationships.

Premarital Pregnancies on Campus[6]

Premarital pregnance of a college woman throws both partners into a
dilemma. If they are devoted to each other, have the financial resources to
continue their educations, receive moral and material support from both

sets of parents, are both highly marriageable, and can find suitable housing near the campus, then they may enter into a successful marriage. However, if these factors are not present, then the prospect of successful marriage is dim.

University administrators have little or no data on how many college women become pregnant, requiring them to terminate their education, or what happens to them. No one knows the percentage who opt for various solutions, the success of those solutions, or how many return to college. The material I have indicates that an unwanted pregnancy of college women is frought with panic, guilt, shame, and anxiety and that the worst part of their immediate concern is the prospect of telling their parents about the situation.

Abortion was not well established during the 1960s so that, except for marriage, the remaining options for an unwed mother were either keeping her baby (usually within her own family) or adoption. The following pregnant girls expected their boyfriends to marry them.

Phoebe had been having an affair with a boyfriend and decided too late to go to Planned Parenthood. When she confronted her lover with her pregnancy, he outlined the options: abortion, adoption, or marriage. He preferred abortion and she, marriage. He acceded to her wish and she made plans for the wedding, only to be frustrated again and again as he failed to show up for appointments to discuss and ratify her plans. His vacillation was so pronounced that even his mother advised the girl not to marry him. She poignantly described her anguish during this period. Fortunately, her parents gave her moral support and offered to adopt the baby. However, she refused to burden them with additional responsibilities and placed the baby out for adoption. She related how her emotions welled up on each anniversary of her child's birth.

Jan had been having intimate relations with her boyfriend for several years; when she discovered she was pregnant, she expected him to marry her. He rejected the idea. Jan was too ashamed to tell her parents, so she went to a city a thousand miles away where she gave her baby up for adoption. She wrote:

> The moments of terror and anxiety I felt can never be expressed in words. I suffered severe emotional strain and became mentally maladjusted. I decided that the only place I could straighten myself out was home, so I returned. I told Mom and Dad the whole story. They were both very kind and understanding. For a long time after my return, I was very leery of men and felt quite unstable.

The next report illustrates a different reaction. Jenny was engaged to a man with the same background as hers in every way. He had been a attentive lover, and a date had been set for the wedding. When she discovered her pregnancy, she panicked, renounced her lover, and called off the wedding.

She made secret plans to visit a brother three thousand miles away where she gave up her baby for adoption. She wrote:

> I haven't been able to understand why I couldn't go through with the marriage. It seemed as if I were totally in love with him and then suddenly turned off. My feelings of going it alone may stem from my sister's experience with my parents before me. Upon telling them of her pregnancy, my sister found herself blocked out of the family. My mother wouldn't even come to her wedding.

The next history points up the ethical and legal rights of a man to be consulted about the disposition of his unborn child, especially when he and his girlfriend are devoted to each other. Derek was ten when his parents divorced. While in high school he was seduced by a girl and thereafter had considerable sexual experiences. He became devoted to a high school senior before going to college. During the summer after his first year in college, he became intimate with his girlfriend. He had been using withdrawal but was worried because he "hadn't been too careful." In October she confirmed her pregnancy.

> I broke apart emotionally and couldn't bring myself to do anything. I felt very alone and as though I could not tell my folks. I sought religion and it settled me some. The pastor was very understanding and made me feel more at ease. I decided to go home and discuss things with her folks. I told my real father, and he condemned me just when I really needed some family support. When I got home, she told me that her folks didn't want to talk to me. They had decided with her to take her to get an abortion. I was left out and didn't feel like I was worth much. They didn't want my opinions, my support, or anything. I told my mother and stepfather, and they told me that I really didn't have any right to question anything anyway. I returned to school very bewildered and mixed up. She wrote and informed me that she had had the abortion and that all was well. Things were still not well with me. I just couldn't see how I was going to act in future times when I saw her again. I was very hurt and wanted the best for her, but it seemed like I could do nothing anymore. Now her folks act as if nothing ever happened, and I am still going with her, but I think I am losing respect for her because of past memories.

Some very young couples who drifted into heavy petting, intercourse, and pregnancy during the 1960s were grossly ignorant about the physiology of sex. One girl became so alarmed about heavy petting that she approached her mother to get information on intercourse. The mother told her daughter that she should not know about it until marriage. Shortly thereafter, the girl became pregnant. Later she said, "If only my mother had told me more about sex." Another girl whose sex life began in high school wrote, "As I look back on the situation, I really must confess I didn't know what I was doing."

By the 1980s, college women were reasonably sophisticated about sex, reproduction, and contraception. However, an amazing phenomenon has transpired. In a state university of 9,000 students where the health center offers contraceptive services, some 300 to 400 women come in every year for pregnancy tests. Of these, 80 to 100 are found to be pregnant; their pregnancies are terminated by abortion in approximately 90 percent of the cases. These estimates do not include students who handle their pregnancies without going to the health center.

How can we account for such a large number of unwanted pregnancies in a sophisticated population? Many experts have stressed that young adolescents are too immature to manage the emotional and sexual complications of intercourse. Should we revise our thinking now and say that even the older adolescents cannot manage them? A professional in the counseling office put it this way, "There is a massive denial of the realities that lead to pregnancy."

Although the counselors much prefer to handle pregnancy cases as couples, there is no systematic breakdown on the number of couples who come in for counseling compared to the number of women whose boyfriends commit themselves only to pay for an abortion and the men who make no offer to help at all. Emotional turmoil from worry about whether the woman is pregnant, the shock of pregnancy, and the bitterness against men do not end with the abortion. Eventually counselors are confronted with these same women who arrive in a state of confusion—a confusion traced to the emotional aftermath of the abortion. How much emotional and financial support pregnant women on the campus receive from their boyfriends is unknown. Some men pay for the abortion; others do nothing.

Life histories of students reveal that many decide for practical reasons to forego their active sex life for a time. They may decide that a sexual affair is not worth a replay of the anxiety, shock, cost of an abortion, and loss of a girlfriend or boyfriend. Some men may reason that premature sexual activity is a handicap in sorting out women as prospects for future mates and a handicap to courting a girl they really want. They may also reason that working one's way through the university makes it more necessary to utilize every moment for study and that the demands of a sexual partner or the upsets of that partner may hinder the pursuit of a career. The histories of female students reveal that many of them have been hurt by sexual partners in a multitude of ways so that some have resolved to discontinue sexual activity until they are able to calm down, their education is no longer in jeopardy, they find a man they trust, they become engaged, or they marry. Many women resent the implication that they need contraception as soon as they matriculate or that they will need it throughout their college careers. If there is any advantage to freshmen in pursuing their studies without looking for sexual partners, the faculty and staff have kept it quite a secret.

Universities reject the idea that, with reference to students, they are to act in loco parentis, but university personnel are confronted every day with students whose careers are in jeopardy because of a sexual crisis. Those in charge of student health are divided on suggesting options for students regarding sexual activities. Some advocate the option of playing it safe with contraception; others think this option should be balanced with that of refraining from intercourse until the quality of the relationship, the nature of commitment, and timing are in keeping with one's values. The latter option requires judgment and sobriety. Risk of difficulty in all options is increased by the combination of drinking and heavy petting.

In chapter 15 I described cases of sexual aggression of college men against college women during the 1960s. In the university mentioned before, there were, officially, seven cases of sexual assault by college men against college women in 1980 and six such cases in 1981. All cases were classified as third- or fourth-degree sexual assault, none of them involving rape.

A brighter side to the students' approach to the nature of their interaction becomes evident in the recurring themes they discuss. They place great value on friendship and the moral support they give and receive in such relationships. Many have expressed a preference that friendship develops prior to the love relationship. Another theme is that sexual activity should never be hurtful to the other partner or exploitive in any way but that it be considered a manifestation of affection. A final theme is a desire to establish a happy family.

To conclude this chapter, I offer a few suggestions to those interested in the mate-selection process. Mate selection is more effective when:

Partners have an opportunity to know and appraise each other before their judgment is impaired by sexual arousal or frequent and steady intercourse;

Commitment is deferred until one has associated with a reasonable number of people among eligibles during adolescence and young adulthood;

The partner who is more in love does not pressure the other for commitment when the other does not feel ready for marriage;

The person with a history of sexual trauma has been relieved of emotional problems by the other partner via understanding and encouragement before they become sexually involved;

Before commitment, a person who hates a parent, analyzes his family of origin with the aid of another, preferably a professional person, until inner conflicts are resolved.

Partners who are definitely attracted to each other defer commitment until each has observed the other in the context of their respective families;

Each partner has diagrammed a family constellation, discussed its implications with the other, and pursued the discussion to other aspects of the family system as revealed in part II of this book.

Notes

1. In 1977 I suggested that premarital counseling be made available on a countywide basis at the point of marriage registration. See Gordon Shipman, "In My Opinion: The Role of Counseling in the Reform of Marriage and Divorce Procedures," *Family Coordinator* (October 1977), pp. 395–407.

2. Susan Brownmiller, *Against Our Will: Men, Women and Rape* (New York: Simon & Schuster, Bantam Books, 1975).

3. Frederic Storaska, *How to Say No to a Rapist and Survive* (New York: Warner Books, 1975).

4. Paul Cameron, "Sexual Graduation: A New Approach to Sex Education" (Paper delivered for the National Conference on Family Relations, Portland, Oregon, October 1980).

5. Storaska, *How to Say No.*

6. For material on teenage pregnancies, see Jane Burgess-Kohn, *Straight Talk About Love and Sex for Teenagers* (Boston: Beacon Press, 1979).

17 The Image of the Ideal Mate

Sociologists have devoted much attention to finding out why, among the field of eligibles, a person is attracted to some but not to others. The kind of spouse one eventually marries is determined in part by the continuing behavior of parents from the time the infant recognizes them as parents to the time he grows up and falls in love.

In 1953, Burgess and Wallen, two outstanding sociologists, defined the image of the ideal mate as that idealized picture one develops in his imagination of the kind of person he would like to marry.[1] The source of the image may be romantic literature, the cinema, or dating experience. The nature of the image may be physical attributes, common interests, personality traits, cultural traits, or the quality of the love relationship. Burgess believed that the image of the ideal mate functioned largely to eliminate partners who were different from the image. Anselm Strauss, another sociologist, did a study that indicated that two-thirds of the men and women he interviewed believed that the image of the ideal mate was important to them in choosing their fiancés.[2]

The concept of parent image assumes that a person tends to fall in love with someone who has the characteristics of the opposite-sex parent. The nature of the parent image is similar to the ideal image in its inclusion of physical resemblance and similarities in personal traits and in affectional and emotional relationships. Burgess and Wallen treated the ideal image and the parent image as separate concepts. I feel that it is much more logical and more useful to merge the two concepts into one in which the ideal image is more general but in which the parent image is the fundamental core. My reasons for this merger should become apparent in the following pages.

Burgess and Wallen list five patterns of parent image that I reproduce with illustrations from my own material.

1. Positive image: The loved one resembles the parent of the opposite sex. The positive image is the fundamental one and is more common by far than all the others. It develops, for example, when there is any reasonable attachment of a daughter to her father or of a son to his mother; it takes only a few similar traits of father (mother) and boyfriend (girlfriend) for the daughter (son) to take note of the latter.

My image of the ideal mate is someone similar to my dad. I have never known anyone who impressed me as much as my dad. If I ever marry anyone who has his qualities, I will be very lucky.

I think the source of my image of the ideal mate is rooted in my mom. I want my wife to have all her qualities—I'd want my wife to be as sexy and as sweet as possible.

2. Negative image: The loved one is a person with traits opposite to those of the opposite-sex parent. This takes place mostly in dystrophic families in which a daughter or son has suffered from the behavior of the opposite-sex parent. I am attracted to personalities almost opposite to my father because I have come to hate his attitudes."

A negative image may arise, not only from the personal characterization of the opposite-sex parent but also from the occupational status of that parent. A woman whose father worked in a factory that was soon to close wrote:

I have no physical image of the ideal mate, but I will not seriously consider dating a boy who works in a factory or cannot provide a good future. When I begin to like a boy with no college education, I force myself to break off the relationship. My steady boyfriend is now my ideal mate. He comes from a high-income family, is nice in appearance, and is majoring in medicine at the university.

The next case of negative image deals with emotional and psychological dimensions of personality.

Although I love my father, my image of the ideal mate became anything my father is not. My father is cold and refuses to express his feelings. I married a very warm and expressive man. My father never spent time with our family. My husband loves children and I know he will want time with his family. Included in my image of the ideal mate was the idea that he be a psychologist. I married a man who is majoring in psychology.

3. Reverse image: In reverse image, a person is attracted to someone with traits of the same-sex parent.

My mother has provided me with my reverse image of an ideal mate. From her I have learned the importance of being kind and patient and of overlooking small faults, even grave faults if necessary, to prove the true depth of one's love.

4. Combination of positive and reverse image: In this case the person pictures a future mate as one who has the best characteristics of both parents. This image is more common in pantrophic families in which both parents have many excellent qualities.

> As I look back at my family of origin, I can see that my wife embodies a combination of the traits I found most admirable in my parents.

Students commonly said that their image of the ideal mate was patterned after the good traits of both parents.

5. Surrogate image: The surrogate image of a future mate is patterned after an adult who is not a member of the immediate family such as a grandparent, aunt, uncle, or the parent of a girlfriend or boyfriend.

> The sources of my ideal mate are many. I sometimes admired the man of the house where I babysat. Sometimes I felt he was responsible for instilling in his children the love, respect, and consideration they had for me and for other members of the household. I think the behavior of the children reflects the kind of relationship that exists between the couple.

6. Composite image: I have added a sixth source to the five listed by Burgess and Wallen. The composite image involves any combination of multiple sources within and without the family and is fairly common.

> I established my image of the ideal mate as I gained experience in dating. With each boy, I found qualities I liked and disliked. Personality was the biggest influence on my mate selection.

> My ideal-mate image is a composite of characteristics I've seen in many different women rather than just my mother or some other woman close to me.

These six types of image of the ideal mate are not discrete entities, for most people construct their images from multiple sources such as romantic literature, the cinema, television, and positive and negative traits of father, mother, siblings, dating partners, and acquaintances. In a sense, all image building for the future partner is composite in character and arises from a person's life experience from the time one learns something about the nature of spousal roles.

Furthermore, some images fade in time while others become clearer and more influential. Also, personalities are not discrete. The perceived self is fluid and dynamic, and it interacts with different groups in different settings as the self communicates with a series of dating partners and the family members. This interaction between the perceived self and others in the dating and courtship process improves not only the ability to appraise others but also self-appraisal, as indicated by the woman who wrote:

> I have dated so many different types that I have had an opportunity to grow in understanding individual differences. My past romances have helped me to know myself better.

This theme is very common. Burgess and Wallen say that the parent image is not a superficial but an affective factor and that it seems to function more effectively in terms of personality traits and affectional relationships. The concept of the ideal image, in vogue for only a few years, has since been neglected by researchers.

In view of my experience with students, I believe that the image of the ideal mate should be rediscovered. In my outline for the students' papers I mentioned ideal image, and the students knew that this expression included parent image. My students were exposed to all the current theories regarding who is attracted to whom and why, but when they wrote about their courtship, they employed the concept of the ideal image, almost neglecting all other theories.

The Importance of Image Making

Man is said to be a symbolic animal. By the use of symbols, he has been able to create images, and by creative imagery he has accelerated his culture in art, science, and religion. Artistic expression involves the manipulation of images to create all manner of emotional states.

In view of the importance of image making in the modern world, it would seem appropriate to rediscover the contribution of Burgess and Wallen on the role of imagery in courtship. In this connection, we shall consider how the self-image is related to the ideal-mate image. In courtship we have the self-image of ego reacting to the self-image of alter ego, both rising and falling according to the vicissitudes of courtship. We have also the ideal image of ego and the ideal image of alter. Thus, in courtship, four interacting images are in a state of influx. If we understand the structure and direction of this constellation of images, then we can predict the outcome of courtship.

Both the self-image and the ideal-mate image tend to reinforce homogamy. The self may feel uncomfortable when dating a person either much higher or lower on the social scale; one may also feel uncomfortable dating a person much taller or shorter or much higher or lower in intelligence. One young woman wrote:

> The greatest source of my ideal image has been my father. I look for intelligence and good character in boys—qualities I have noticed and appreciated in my father. I would also say that boys who appear lacking in education are taken off my list of prospective mates. My father's emphasis on cultivating an intelligent mind has become an important criterion for mate selection. Another thing I appreciate in a boy is the ability to articulate his feelings and to express his ideas and opinions on a subject. It is possible that the qualities I have mentioned may have been formulated indepen-

dently of my father's positive image. I feel I have many personality characteristics of my father, and I may desire a mate who is similar to myself in
many ways.

Thus, homogamy is reinforced by the father or mother image interacting with self-image. Anther feature of the perceived self also encourages
homogamy. The self-image involves various degrees of self-respect. A loving person with self-respect tends to project respect onto the beloved, and it
is difficult to love a person one does not respect.

The higher the quality of personal attributes of a person, the greater his
or her advantage in courtship competition. The level of desirability in a
partner that one feels he deserves is called the comparison level.[3] The nature
of the self-image influences the comparison level. Whether conscious or
subconscious, the self will tend to bring the resources of the image of the
ideal mate into some correspondence with his own resources.

In my experience, students do not seem to think consciously of a suitable partner in terms of what they deserve. Rather, they build up an image
of the kind of partner who will help them to establish a good marriage and
family. Their ideas of what is good or bad in this connection come largely
from their life experience, the marriage of their parents, and their family of
origin. If they come from a pantrophic family, they are able to ascribe quite
clearly the image of a partner they desire so that, as a couple, they will be
accepted by the members of both families.

A person's comparison level is determined not only by one's personal
attributes but also by the nature of one's family. Suppose a young man is
attracted equally to two women. The first one invites him to her home
where he is received graciously and wherein he senses a fine *hestia,* but the
second girl feels she cannot invite him to her home because she is ashamed
of her parents and her home. We may surmise that the first woman has an
advantage.

If children are programmed by parents to notice differences in personalities in a series of dating partners, and if the quality of family life is pantrophic, then I think images of a desired spouse will develop and be helpful
to the young people in their mate selection.

Changes in the Image

My material indicates that the image of the ideal mate changes over time as
a person matures. For example:

When I was younger, the source of my ideal mate was the movies and
novels wherein the romantic, handsome, rich hero was my image. But now

my image of the ideal mate is a dynamic picture subject to frequent modi-
fications as I face the realities of life. Today I value intelligence, compatibility, common interests, shared attitudes, a promising future, and a sensible outlook on life. This seems like quite an impressive list for any man, but
I plan to marry only once and want to marry the right man as he is, without
imagining that he can be changed.

Notice that this woman's image moved from physical traits to personality traits to desired relationships.

The next cases have a different slant on changing images. One stresses
similar goals; the other stresses the importance of peer judgments.

As for an ideal mate, my expectations are constantly changing. I feel this is
due to a change in values as I mature. When I was younger I always imagined the man I would marry would be tall, good looking, and very strong.
After I realized that these were just superficial things, I changed my mind
completely. I now feel my mate would have to be someone who is sincere
and honest. He must have at least equal intelligence to me, and I hope we
will have the same goals.

The source of my image of the ideal mate has changed over the years. Early
in my dating, my image of the ideal mate was mostly influenced by my parents and my religion. I went for the nondrinker, nonsmoker, and the athletic type who was handsome and smooth. During the next stage, my qual-
ifications for the ideal mate were most influenced by my peer group. I no
longer cared whether a boy drank or smoked, but he had to be smooth and
handsome. In the last stage, my source was more or less a compilation of
what I'd learned about boys through experience. Personality became more
important than looks; sincerity replaced smoothness; consideration, gentle-
ness, and maturity became important to me.

It bothers me when I know that my roommate or other friends don't like
the boy I'm dating. I usually don't stay long with a guy that my friends
don't care for. As far as the neighbors or other families are concerned, I
don't care what they think. They have no influence on my choice.

The next case suggests that the image may be submerged at various subconscious levels:

I felt I was too young to know for sure what I really wanted and that only
through more dating would I be given the opportunity to grow and recognize what I desired and needed. Surprisingly enough, I never created within
me an ideal like Mr. Wonderful who was an all-American boy that I
searched for—tall, handsome, intelligent, suave, and debonair. Yet, within
me, I did know that I had not met him yet, and I did have a vague inner
knowledge of the qualities and type of relationship I hoped some day to
establish instead of a stereotype. Yet, when I met him, I was able to recognize that this was he.

We have examples of positive images of fathers and boyfriends, but here is a case of negative image of a boyfriend combined with negative-reverse image of her mother. This girl had a boyfriend who dominated her thinking and bullied her into sexual activity that she disliked. He made her tense and nervous and was unconcerned about her feelings. He also down-graded her. This daughter was distressed over her mother's inability to express her feelings and her low standards of order and cleanliness.

> The two main sources for an ideal mate came through experiences I had with John and my feelings toward my parents' marriage. I want someone to respect my feelings and let me do my own thinking. I am repelled by a person who wants to dominate me. I want a mate to love me for myself and not for sex. I also have negative images of my mother's marriage.

The following quotation suggests a continual comparison between the ideal image and the partner, which sharpens the image:

> To me, my fiancé represents the ideal mate, but if you had asked me what that image was a few years ago, I could not have told you. Each day I add new traits to my list of those contained in the ideal mate, and each new trait I add comes from knowing my fiancé just a little better as time goes by.

Her report fits in with the finding that longer engagements are associated with successful marriages.

Need Themes

Few students mentioned the theory of complementary needs.[4] In the following analysis, a woman expresses in the last sentence her need for a man who would compensate for her special weakness in order to improve their image as a couple:

> Like most girls, I had an image of the ideal mate. Perhaps this image was colored by TV and movie stars. I know that the boy I fell in love with would have to have certain characteristics, most of which are patterned after my father. I want him to be kind, gentle, loving, and industrious. Because I am not an outgoing person in unfamiliar groups, I want someone who is outgoing.

This type of need is one of compensation in a couple relationship, which is quite different from an individual personality need.

One woman was determined that she would not dominate her husband when she married as her mother had dominated her father. To reinforce this eventually, she imagined her future husband as the dominant spouse:

> My parents determined the type of person that attracted or repelled me. My mother's dominance helped me decide that I want a dominant husband or, even more specific, that I don't want to have to play the role of a dominant wife.

The real reason for wanting a dominant husband is not that she had a need for being dominated; she only wanted a husband whose initiative and strength would prevent her from becoming a bossy wife like her mother. Other women have expressed themselves in similar fashion. Another daughter is a similar situation wrote:

> I feel that since I think my Dad is just great in every way, he has affected me in the kind of man I look for. My mother's bossy attitude has made me turn toward a man who argues and does not keep things to himself.

We might label this case as a positive image with a reverse-negative feature. This woman was assertive, like her mother. She described her mother as a woman with a strident voice, high on dominance, and high on both critical rate and interrogation pressure. Her father was sensitive to quarrels between mother and daughter and presumably sensitive to his wife's verbal behavior. This daughter is thinking that the way to correct any tendencies she might have in repeating her mother's objectionable behavior in marriage is to marry a man who will counteract such tendencies instead of correcting them herself. If we knew nothing about this woman's parents and only heard her say that she "wanted a man who is masculine and bossy," we might explain her preference as a dependent person having a need for dominance and thus reinforcing the theory of complementary needs.

However, in light of what we know about her and her parents, the theory of complementary needs does not apply. What she really wants is a loving husband like her father but also one who is assertive enough to prevent her from becoming shrill and bossy like her mother.

In the first case, the ideal image was formulated to compensate for a weakness; in the other two cases it was formulated to counteract anticipated undesirable traits in the young women.

It would seem that we might predict, among acceptable social eligibles, the kind of person that one is attracted to by analyzing the dynamics of the family system and studying the sources and nature of the image of the ideal mate better than by resorting to need theories.

In another case a man described his mother as beautiful and brilliant. He said he wanted a girl "who would lend herself to being dominated because I disliked the way my parents had arguments over trivial things." Here, again, the student seems to be molding his image of the ideal mate and his relationship to that mate into the stereotype of dominance-submissiveness. In writing about his family he implied that the bickering between his parents occurred during a period of years when his mother's alcoholism was not treated, but he failed to suggest a relationship between the drinking and the bickering.

The students who distorted their images because of the stereotypical thinking along the dominance-submissiveness axis are not the only ones to do so. Such thinking pervades our culture and our social science. Stereotyped thinking along with dominant-submissive axis is an obstacle to finding the real difficulties in a poor relationship.

Choice and Exchange

Can we speculate that self-centered persons develop an image of the ideal mate for all their needs without thinking about what their perceived self has to give to a future spouse? It is hard to conceive that comparison level does not operate in courtship. Is a youth from a pantrophic family more able to articulate clearly the attributes of the ideal image, and is he more aware of the attributes each will contribute to the marriage? One student, after describing her positive image, went on to imply that she had an obligation to contribute an equal measure of fine qualities to the marriage when she wrote, "I would also try to manifest these qualities to my husband and to the children."

My students sensed that there must be some correspondence between what they had to offer in marriage and what they were to receive in return. In short, a choice among eligibles might be made according to an assessment of rewards and costs by each partner.[5] We might say that when a student deals with image building, he is formulating an ideal picture of the person who would give him the greatest rewards at the least cost. If so, then the concept of the image of the ideal mate, the processes involved in its formulation, and the reactions thereto blend with the theory of choice and exchange. This blend presents two difficulties. First, an underlying assumption of choice and exchange theory is that people are rational. When lovers idealize each other, rationality wanes. The second assumption implied in the theory is questionable—that people are highly motivated by the calculus of self-interest. To lovers, this sounds like crass commercialism. There seems to be an antithesis between unselfish devotion on the one hand and calculated self-interest on the other. It has been suggested that genuine love involves concern for the well-being of the beloved without thought of recompense. Persons most concerned with self-interest may become selfish and unhappy. I do not wish to press this contrast too far because a reasonable regard for one's self-interest is a mark of a healthy person.

When students who are fairly even in personal resources analyze each other, their thinking does not seem to resolve around the personal resources of ego and alter as bargaining chips. Rather they seek a partner with potential for becoming a good spouse and parent and, in addition, one whose needs, habits and tendencies will blend best with their own. Working with the image of the ideal mate clarifies this kind of thinking. When extremes in personal resources are involved, or when the self-image is low, choice based on exchange is pronounced. A lower-middle-class man will not attempt to court the beautiful daughter of a millionaire. In one case a girl wrote a pathetic narrative in which she portrayed herself as a tall, gaunt, ugly duckling. She quickly accepted a proposal of marriage from a man whose personality attributes were comparable to her physical attributes "before he had time to change his mind."

The students who applied the theory of the ideal mate to their own courtships turned out to be a select group. They were middle-class students at Midwest universities who were motivated to take a course in marriage and the family; a course, furthermore, in which the instructor outlined the theory and suggested they apply it to their own life experience. The readers of this book who are involved in the mate-selection process may wish to do likewise.

Influence of Position in the Family Constellation

In part II, I dealt with influences arising from position in the family constellation and suggest how such influences could effect harmony or discord in marriage. In the following quotation the young woman deals with complementarity of position in describing her ideal mate. She was the younger sister of a brother who dominated and teased her. In this conflict she received support from her father but not from her mother. She said that all family members agreed that she possessed the traits that Toman had allocated to her position—that is, "can attract men better than other girls; at work, an ideal employee who does best working under male guidance." She traces her description of the ideal mate from physical traits to personal traits and then writes:

> To please my parents, the boy would have to be white, Protestant, and have a college education. I think it important to look at a fellow rationally. However, if I fall in love with a man who doesn't have all those traits, I will marry him anyway. I have always followed orders from an older brother and respected his judgment. I have had lots of practice getting along with a man. When I am with a man, I look to him for decisions. Most men feel

they are in command, and this is why I think I get along with them well. I also fit the description "submissive but not subservient." I do not like to lead although I will not do anything someone wants when he or she tries to take advantage of me. The boys I have been attracted to the most have been fellows with younger sisters. According to Toman, they are my best match.

Failure of the Ideal Image to Develop

I have mentioned how some parents encourage the dating of many partners rather than going steady. Such encouragement seems to be effective in the absence of pressure and when parents are gracious to boyfriends and girl-friends. Conversely, we have the case of a girl, the older of two sisters, who was enmeshed in a steady relationship with a boyfriend she did not respect. This resulted from a combination of circumstances. She wrote:

> I was elected to carry out most of the ideas my father had for a son. In my efforts to please him in the attainment of high goals, I became a loner.

This tendency was increased by the neighborhood girls who considered her far too young to associate with them. In order to secure acceptability with her peer group at school, she went steady with a boy she described as "the youngest and most spoiled child in the family." She continued this relationship from the tenth grade until she went to college, much to the disgust of her parents who tried to break up the affair by restricting her dating. This produced rebellion and she wrote:

> Actually, I feel I was attracted to him because of the strife between my parents and me. I feel that going with this boy for so long under the pressure of my group of friends hindered my real personality development. Since I had no alternative except either to be with him or by myself, I was forced into being still more of a loner. My boyfriend was the complete opposite of my dad who is ambitious, while my boyfriend was weak and unambitious. They were complete opposites in physical appearance. Because I went with this boy for so long at an early age, I didn't acquire an image of an ideal mate.

Advantages of Freedom and Trust

The next report illustrates how a family *hestia* with implications of freedom and trust in the dating situation leads to strong positive image and the internalization of parental standards for a partner.

> My parents never instructed me on my dating behavior. I knew they expected me to follow the Catholic ideal, and my father especially simply

trusted me not to deviate. When my dates came to pick me up, I always invited them in to meet my parents. My mother made them feel welcome and would converse to make them feel at ease no matter who they were. My father would say hello and then go back to reading his paper. My parents rarely expressed an opinion on my dates. They may have thought they didn't know them well enough, that I wasn't serious about them anyway, plus the fact that they expected me to have internalized their standards. I knew the types of boys my parents would disapprove of, and I never went with such boys.

If I had to pick any one source from which I derived the image of my ideal mate, it would be my father. He has the qualities I admire greatly. He is quiet sometimes but he also knows how to have a good time. He is responsible and I always felt secure when he was near. He rarely criticizes, and when he does, he tries to be tactful. He displays affection for me, and when I do something well he displays his pride. He builds up my ego and is comforting when I feel bad. He always makes my troubles look smaller than they first appear, and he gives me emotional support when the going gets rough. I think the reason I chose my steady is because he is like my father in many ways.

I pointed out, as did Burgess, the tendency of young people who develop positive images to pass from physical traits to personality traits to relationships. In the last category, students are concerned about happiness in the marital relationship. Some of the students also directly or by implication carry their image to include all family relationships. If I had developed my concept of the pantrophic family years sooner, I am sure the students would have formulated their image of the ideal mate as one who could best cooperate with them to form a family high on the pantrophic scale.

The following case is unique in that it involves not only the idealistic traits of the father but also the ideal marriage of the parents. It suggests that lovers should know when to go slowly in pressing their suit. We may call this the *marriage image*.

During high school Phoebe had gone with a certain boy for three years with whom she was emotionally involved. Just before college, she broke up with him and was determined not to get emotionally involved with another until she was ready to marry. Meantime, another man became attached to her, but she refused to be tied down with a commitment.

He said he understood but that he loved me and would wait. He never pressured me, and we dated occasionally for nine months. Gradually, I began to see all of the wonderful qualities he possessed, the qualities that I had always thought of when I described my ideal mate. Tim is a very dependable person and extremely responsible in any job he undertakes. He is intelligent and graduated first in his class. He is a natural leader, and he possesses a wonderful quality of having a deep insight and understanding into the feelings of other people. He is well liked by others—adults as well as persons his own age. He has high ideals and the determination to achieve them. Some of the other qualities for which I have sought (and found) in my mate are kindness, thriftiness, and wisdom with money. He takes a genuine interest in my problems, gets along well with my family, is popular, and displays a genuine loyalty to me and our love. By observing my parents' marriage, I have formed an ideal of what I would like to see in my own marriage and family of procreation. My parents still appear to be very young and very much in love after twenty years, and I hope that after I'm married that long I can be as happy and content as they now seem to be. I am even happier in my choice of a mate because my parents like him so much and heartily approve of our forthcoming marriage.

Is it possible that in the friendly interaction between engaged couples and their prospective in-laws that either or both sets of parents provide a subtle influence that inducts the future son-in-law or daughter-in-law into the desired marital roles? If so, we might then think of images of the ideal son-in-law or daughter-in-law. Parents with such images could exert a positive influence only when one or both sets of parents have pantrophic families and when all involved have fine relationships.

On the other hand, suppose each partner has positive parental images and, when they visit in each other's homes, they realize that many fine traits in their own parents are also possessed by the prospective parents-in-law. In such case, the positive parental image of each is reinforced by the prospective in-laws. We can imagine that this would produce a fine *hestia*. The following couple seem to approach this happy situation.

I have gained several images of the ideal mate from my father. He has been a wonderful father and husband, and I would like to marry someone like him. I admire many of his qualities, and I include these in my image of an ideal mate. The guy I am going with has many of my father's qualities. My boyfriend's family also has had a big influence on me. I really enjoy visiting with them. His family is a close-knit one, and I always feel so welcome and at home. He has acquired several very admirable traits of his father. Like my father, his father is sincere, trustworthy, honest, congenial, and compatible.

Voice Patterns in the Ideal Image

Several students mentioned their desires for a mate with good-quality voice patterns. For example:

A voice of good quality is one element in the ideal mate that I require. I see a definite relationship between the high quality of the voices of my parents and their successful marriage.

Life Experience and the Image of the Ideal Mate

What a person says about his image of the ideal mate cannot be appreciated unless one knows how that image arose from life experience within the family. In the following excerpt, that experience is related to the student's image.

> Because of my unhappiness within the family, I expect my boyfriend to be a confidant, counselor, and a thousand other things. He must have the good qualities of the men in my family (attractiveness, intelligence) but none of their faults (loud voice, quarrelsomeness, prejudice, sloppiness, and a lacking of understanding and gentleness).

> I have noticed that I am more attached to men who can handle themselves well in situations where aggressiveness or defensive strength is needed. Since, throughout my life, I have been pushed about, physically and verbally, I am delighted to have someone stand up in my defense. And I cannot respect a man who cannot stand up in his own defense.

The next report reveals how strength of character is forged in childhood and adolescence by a series of traumas and hardships and how such life experience affects the ideal image. When the male narrator was six years old and his only brother eight, the parents were divorced. The father was a large man who disciplined his sons harshly and arbitrarily and who met their efforts at self-expression with a slap. His brash infidelity led to constant arguing with his wife. He tended to favor the older boy. After the divorce, the mother was forced to work outside the home, and the two boys were alone much of the time. The mother, however, was described in laudatory terms. In describing the situation shortly after the divorce, the student wrote:

> I can remember countless nights, after going to bed, when I would hear my brother softly crying in his pillow. Then I would feel a petrifying fear inside, one that I will never forget. At that moment I felt more alone than ever. I think I must have looked up to my brother, and when he broke down, it completely demoralized me. It was evident that my brother displayed a definite need for a father. The feeling of insecurity that developed during the next few years would be impossible to describe.

> As time went on, this fear slowly vanished, but in its place a feeling of uncertainty developed in me. There was a good deal of hesitation in decision making for I knew if I made a mistake there would be no one there to help me out or to stand behind me.

> Years passed, and the closeness with my mother remained, but my brother and I drifted apart because our interests became different. Throughout these years my relationships with my dad were limited. On occasion he would take my brother and me on trips up north where he passed off his lady friend as our mother.

The narrator goes on to describe how the father's errant behavior increased hostility between them. The favored older brother did not profit from the association with his father, but he did express a definite need for a father's attention.

When it was time for the sons to go to college, the father cashed in the insurance policy designed for their education and used the money to marry a woman the boys disliked. The father cut off both support money and alimony, and the boys had to earn their own way through college.

In the meantime, the mother and her two sons developed a strong, cohesive unit. The narrator's first love affair was broken up by the girl's mother because she considered him a lower-class man, much to the hurt of the young couple. The next girlfriend did not measure up to his standards, and he discarded her. The young man wrote:

> Through these two experiences and the kinds of events I have been subjected to throughout my life, I have developed an image of the ideal mate. The things I look for in a girl are an extremely neat, well-kept appearance, moderation in drinking, no smoking, and emotional stability with an endless amount of intestinal fortitude. She must be able to rise to most occasions with mental ability, and to take a get-tough attitude. Most of all, I look for a girl who can bring out the best in me. I have met all kinds of people with many excellent traits, but there is no one I would trade places with because I have developed an image not only for the ideal mate but also for the ideal life. I am sure that my attitude is such because of the absence of a father, but I am glad it is this way because I know that I could not possibly possess this attitude at my age if my father had been present. At this moment I can say I owe only one debt—to my mother—and someday I hope my brother and I can make up to her all she has been deprived of.

The Perfect Image, the Perfect Mate

We all take it for granted that there is a wide discrepancy between the image of the ideal mate and the reality one marries. I invite the reader to ponder the extravaganza in the following image and then read what developed at marriage when the man was twenty-two and his working wife, a college graduate, was twenty-four. The man's father was described as a heavy drinker, rigid, and inflexible. The mother was said to have a high degree of empathy and a pleasant voice and to be very adaptable. In high school and college this man played the role of leader and was very successful in many activities.

> My ideal mate should be a girl who is fairly good looking, is fairly tall, has good posture, is a good social mixer, is educated, is quick witted, and has a sense of humor and other traits that are necessary for a good individual. She should read good books, enjoy music and dancing, enjoy plays and ballets, be a good critic of the same, be a good housewife, and of course, be

a satisfactory sex mate. She does not necessarily have to be a virgin. She may even have several children. She should have a purpose in life and should be aiming toward some goal. I know that some of these characteristics are hard to find, but there are even more that I look for before I could even think of marriage. The most important characteristics I have found is the ability to sit down and talk things over sensibly and not argue. This will be a great aid in the success of our marriage.

I think I have found the girl who comes up to all the points I have looked for and even more. I do more than think so because I married her. When I first became engaged to my wife, I could not help but feel that what I had was too good to be true. In the past, all other girls I had gone out with could not meet these standards, and when I found her, I could hardly believe it.

My parents and brother also seem to agree with me on the qualities my wife possesses. I am not sure how my relationship to my parents affected this choice, but possibly I realized that in this role of favorite son, who could do no wrong, I had to produce the right woman who could live up to their standards.

In conclusion, we may say that the sources of the image of the ideal mate are legion and that they may be found in all sorts of combinations involving positive and negative traits from literature, art, family members, dating partners, and nonfamily surrogates. However, the central figure of the ideal mate is the opposite-sex parent. Excellent perception in image making is related to the quality of marriage. How the image emerges and how it functions can best be understood by analysis of the family system and the social settings of the person involved.

Notes

1. Ernest Burgess and Paul Wallen, *Engagement and Marriage* (Chicago: Lippincott, 1953).

2. Anselm Strauss, "The Ideal and Chosen Mate," *American Journal of Sociology* 52 (1946):204–208.

3. John W. Thibault and Harold H. Kelley, *The Social Psychology of Groups* (New York: Wiley, 1959), p. 21.

4. Robert F. Winch, *The Modern Family,* 3rd ed. (New York: Holt, Rinehart & Winston, 1971), p. 21.

5. Readers interested in choice and exchange theory should see Ivan Nye, "Is Choice and Exchange Theory the Key?" *Journal of Marriage and the Family* 40 (May 1978), pp. 219–233.

18 How Families Meet Crises

How well a family meets a crisis depends upon the quality of the family. With this in mind, let us review some cases dealing with crises such as the death of a family member, serious accident or illness, divorce, the complications arising from the sudden acquisition of stepparents and stepchildren, and alcoholism. It is difficult to organize materials according to any of these categories because they become intertwined in all sorts of combinations. I shall not treat family crises in a systematic fashion but will try to sift from student life experiences some reflections that may be helpful to readers who have suffered from similar hurts.

Bereavement and Divorce

A characteristic feature of dystrophic families is poor communication and the inability to express feelings openly or spontaneously. In one such family characterized by alcoholism, much conflict, unhappiness, and lack of expressions of affection, the mother died when the middle daughter was eighteen years old. This daughter was concerned about the grieving of the younger sister, and she wrote:

> I could not put my arms around my younger sister to comfort her. My feelings were inhibited because I had never experienced a releasing of such tensions. I found it very hard to reciprocate comforting expressions to anyone in our family.

There was no one else to comfort the middle daughter. About her own feelings she wrote:

> Mom's death and its emotional side effects had a traumatic effect on my disposition. I needed to share my feelings with people who cared and were genuine. I desperately sought an outlet for my screams of fear, loneliness, and overwhelming loss. I was so afraid—afraid of death, afraid of my friends, and afraid of tomorrow. When I reached out, no one helped. They did not seem to understand how I felt. Unexpectedly I was left alone to face the cold world. My independence became more and more dominant and I have learned finally to face things alone.

331

When a parent dies, adults must take pains to include younger children in the comforting process. One girl wrote:

> My father died when I was twelve, and since I was very close to him, his death was very hard for me to accept. It was my first experience with death and a very traumatic one. I felt betrayed by God and, for a short time, excluded him. The day of my father's death was a nightmare. I couldn't comprehend a sudden death. My older sister came and comforted mother—I couldn't. My brother, who was in the armed services, came and comforted her too. I felt like I wasn't a member of the family any longer and perhaps never have been. I felt a great deal of guilt for a long time.

Some dystrophic families are isolated from the community and the extended family. In such cases, the death of a child not only makes healthy mourning difficult but also leads to an aftermath of parental possessiveness of a surviving or later child. In one such family, the mother discouraged the children from bringing their friends into the home; she also discouraged them from making friends with the neighbors. She did not cooperate with her husband when he wished to socialize with his friends. Their first child was a boy, the second was a girl who died at the age of three. The narrator wrote:

> Mom was crushed and really went to pieces. It was almost three years before she began to face reality. To this day she cries over the loss of the little girl and freely admits that her loss was greater than when my father died.

The mother's grief was assuaged at the birth of a second daughter, the narrator. When the narrator was twelve years old the father died, and shortly thereafter, the older son married and left home, leaving only the mother and daughter in the household. She continued:

> Despite my mother's constant worry, I never felt loved or wanted. My mother became extremely possessive and wanted me home after school every night. I revolted and argued and the conflict has continued to this day.

The girl's determination to achieve independence and autonomy saved her. She secured a series of jobs throughout high school and was a leader in many school activities. She finally went to college, where she clung to her lover in spite of her mother's vicious opposition to him.

One might reason that the death of a hated father or mother would not leave the children or the spouse grieving. This could be true if the departed one had no redeeming features. However, few are the cases in which children have no memories of loving attention by a parent at some time in their lives. Even children of alcoholics have memories of their parent in moments of sobriety giving them loving attention when they were young. Love becomes more valuable the scarcer it is.

When a member in a pantrophic family dies, the survivors readjust their roles more easily, cooperate more effectively, and develop more cohesion. The following family had a daughter by a previous marriage; the second marriage produced nine children. The oldest of the second marriage was a girl who is the narrator. She was thirteen when her father died. She said the communication between her parents was excellent, and she described both parents in glowing terms. She made the following observations about how the family met the crisis of her father's death:

> My mother, being weak at the start and pregnant, found it difficult to withstand his death because she relied on him so much. She turned to me—the strong one, as she called me. I was much like my father, and even from the time of the funeral, I found myself being forced to take his place. Anyway, my position in this family has made me an easy listener and very compassionate. Being the strong one, I looked on this widow and her ten orphans and felt and saw all the grief. I got so that every job or grief of theirs was mine. When my father died things seemed to go poorly, but we stuck together and worked with each other to get back on our feet. My mother, with a new surge of strength, strove to become the aggressive and strong person—the head of the family. She succeeded to a great degree.

This girl went on to describe all the dilemmas involving her mother's working, her own responsibilities at home, and her college education. The mother thought the daughter's education should have highest priority.

The following excerpts was written after the death of the father by the youngest daughter in a family of eight children. This family had a fine *hestia* and excellent communication.

> My father died very suddenly due to a heart attack about two weeks after I started my senior year in high school. I feel that his death made our family more stable. It made the older children more protective of my mother and me. His death was a big shock to the entire family and drew us all closer together. Our family had always been quite close knit, and his death made it even more so. Each of us gave and received emotional support from the others.

One student, the youngest of four children, reported that her mother died when she was five years old. The older sisters and the father, who never remarried, divided up the household chores. All the children finished college and were successful.

The following was written by a girl from a farm family that was pantrophic in all dimensions:

All of us children were teenagers when I was a junior in high school. In the midst of the female subculture, I found myself in a world of beauty, clothes, and daydreams. I was caught up in this world of class rings and junior proms. I saw my mother growing thinner, but I laid aside the possibility of a serious illness. She thought it was a tumor and the doctors confirmed it. She was admitted to the hospital in early March and scheduled for surgery a few days later.

Meanwhile, I had been asked by the prom king to be his queen. Terribly excited, I rushed home to share the news with the family. My only regret was that Mama was not there to hear it. When I told Dad, he received the news in silence, asking only when it was. That night he paid a visit to my aunt and uncle.

The next morning, a cool spring Saturday, I was approached by Dad on the way to the barn and he said, "Your mother has cancer. There's nothing that can be done, it's only a matter of time." Then his voice broke. I kept walking in a daze. A week later she died. My mother had known about the cancer months before but had told no one except Dad about it. "Why make them all so sad?" she had said to my aunt toward the end. She had looked so thin the last time I saw her in the hospital; I think deep down I knew she was going to die, but I didn't want to admit it. I think of our last meeting and how cheerful she was. I'll never forget her smile.

My dad was with her when she died, we children were at home. Around eleven the telephone rang, and I knew. Susan came running upstairs and burst into my room—"Mama's dead!" She was crying in a hysterical sort of way. I put my arms around her and told her Mama would want her to be brave and that she should sleep with me. Stifling her sobs, she nodded and finally dozed off to sleep. Unable to sleep, I kept thinking, she's only fourteen—too young to lose a mother. I don't know how much of a comfort I was to her or the many others who tried to help. Somehow, by leaning on each other we made it through the ordeal.

Meanwhile, there still was the question of being prom queen. It was an honor, yes, but could I go through it all? The decision was mine. My family was behind me and I did it. The prom's theme was "This Magic Moment"— how many of them I had shared with my mother.

For the longest time we were unable to talk about her. My Dad would bring her up in conversation, especially around mealtimes. We would sit in silence, staring down on our plates. I remember those first telephone calls asking if my mother was home. I remember the lumps in the throat and the sick feeling in the stomach. For anyone who has never had such an experience, it is hard to explain. That is why some type of death education would be of such help. It is hard to get away from feeling awkward at such times, but even harder to fill an empty heart.

My family reached its depth in disorganization at this time, but we have managed to pull ourselves together. We are a happy family today; we can talk about her but we still all miss her. Because of this experience, I've tended to look out for my family. I know the hurt they all suffered and I don't want to be hurt again.

If a dying parent wishes to tell his child that he is about to die, how should he go about it? The following case tells how one father did so. This case also deals with the question of what to do with the offer of relatives to care for the children when the mother is impoverished.

On my tenth birthday, about a month and a half after my father had been admitted to the hospital, I had a big birthday party. Immediately after the party, I went to see my father to tell him all about it. I sat on the bed visiting with him for quite some time, and he was his usual cheerful self. Then he became very serious and told me that he had something important to tell me, that he wanted me always to remember. He started by telling me how very much he loved me and the rest of the family, but that some day he might not be able to be with us, even though he would like to be with us always. If that day came, he wanted me to take care of the family for him and to help my mother as much as I could. I asked him if he was going on another long trip, and he said no, not exactly, because when he left us he wouldn't be able to come back but he would always watch over us. I then realized what he meant and started to cry. He took me in his arms and comforted me and tried to ease my fears. To this day, I can't understand how he could be so calm and understanding while telling me of his approaching death. It was the last time I saw my father alive. He died a few days later while my mother and I had gone home to settle some business. The morning my mother received the call from the hospital, I went hysterical. I ran out the door screaming. My father's death was a difficult thing for me to accept because I had been so close to him. I went to his funeral, but even then I couldn't believe that my father was dead. My world seemed to have collapsed, and I withdrew into a dream world. I would pretend that my father was out of town on one of his trips and that he would be back again.

My father's death was a turning point in my relationship with my mother. Because I was the oldest child and the only one my mother could turn to, we became closer than we ever had been. The other children were very young; four years, two years, and nine months, so I was the only one she could discuss things with.

For a month following my father's death, we stayed with my maternal grandparents. One night the relatives had a family powwow; and although they thought I was upstairs, I was listening to them. My mother's family had decided that it would be too difficult for her to raise four children by herself. They told her that the best solution would be for each of them to take one of the children into their homes. My mother cried and kept saying that they couldn't take her children because they were all she had left. They warned her that she would never be able to manage and would eventually have to give us up. This experience had a great effect on me. Throughout my life I have had the feeling that I had to excel in everything I did in order to prove to my mother's relatives that my mother could do a good job of raising her children alone.

Due to my mother's determination to keep our family together, we returned to our hometown and Mother received Aid for Dependent Children from the county in order to provide a home for us. In our little community, there was no opportunity for my mother to get a job. She always said that it was much more important that she be at home with us anyway. Although we didn't have many material things, Mother provided a home with much happiness and togetherness.

Mother also seemed to have a determination within her to prove that is was possible for her to be both mother and father to her children. She took an active interest in us and would take up camping, hiking, and fishing and during the winter she would be skating and skiing with us. We became a very closely knit family and always did things together as a family. But each of us had to assume certain responsibilities, probably more than most children. Each child was responsible for duties that he was capable of doing. Being the oldest, I had the most responsibility, the main one being the care of my brothers and sister. Whenever I went anywhere, I always had at least one of them with me, but when I was younger I didn't seem to mind it. By the time I was a teenager, my mother no longer expected this of me.

Although I missed not having a father like the other girls, I was much closer to my mother than most of my girlfriends were with their mothers. Previously I had always discussed my problems with my father, and now I went to my mother. She never thought any problem was minor and showed a great interest in everything I had to say. In return, she discussed her numerous problems with me; the older I became, the more she grew to depend on me and to discuss family problems with me. Because her problems seemed so to burden her, I became more reluctant to tell her my minor problems. I didn't want to burden her with my troubles, so I would eagerly tell her all the happy things that happened because it always pleased her so.

For a child, the death of a parent can be both mystifying and terrifying. If this event should coincide with another mysterious and frightful occurrence, then the two in combination may have extraordinary repercussions.

One young women devoted her paper to two such events that occurred when she was ten years old: how she learned about sex and her father's death. The mother, she said, made sex into a dark secret, so she learned elsewhere, mostly from reading materials. She came to associate secrecy, danger, and sex with men, and all of these seemed to be entangled with her father's death. Sometimes young children interpret the father's dying as leaving them, producing suppressed anger. The young woman wrote:

When I was ten, my mother handed me five or six small booklets and told me to read them. It took me a long time to recover from the shock of learning about the role that fathers play in reproduction. It was unbelievable! For weeks I refused to admit that anything that vulgar could be real. I never told my mother that I thought her books were wrong. I just said that I understood everything. My mother and I never discussed sex, and I never asked her a sexual question.

My father died when I was ten, after which I became very quiet and shy around boys and men. It was as if I had lost faith in all of them because he had left me. I loved him very much, and because I was the firstborn, I got most of the attention. Boys my age terrified me—I'd walk blocks out of my way to avoid them. It still makes my heart pound wildly to have to pass a group of teenage boys. It wasn't until ninth grade that I finally began to make a desperate attempt to rejoin my age group. I made friends with the girl who became my best friend, and we went through darkest adolescence together.

My father had been a quiet, kind man. I can't tolerate men who scream and shout at women. My father's death caused me to idealize him and to think that only worthwhile boys acted like him. It also caused me to withdraw into a world where I spent too much time thinking about sex. Although I think about sex, I still can't bring myself to talk about it. All these factors have contributed to disruptions of my menstrual cycle.

To deny information to a child about something he feels he is entitled to know has unfortunate consequences. I have dealt with this in chapter 15 regarding sex information; it applies with equal force to information about death and divorce.

If the divorce of parents takes place when a child is too young to appreciate its legal aspects, there will come a day when he will want to know why the divorce occurred. To put him off by saying, "I'll explain it when you are older," may stimulate all kinds of erroneus fantasies about the missing parent in the mind of the child. The parent with custody may be the last person to be objective about the reasons for the divorce, but to be honest and forthright about one's biases is better than to evade issues and postpone questions. When the child becomes mature he will be better able to put the pieces together, including the biases, and he will give credit to the parent who was honest about his interpretation of distressing events.

In the discussion of human frailties, it is important to make a distinction between the worth of a person and his habits, addictions, and illnesses that (in the context of his family and economic circumstance) may account for harmful behavior. In the following case, a younger daughter wanted to know about the circumstances of her older sister's divorce and about the death of a younger brother who apparently had been institutionalized for most of his life. The deep-seated and life-long resentments against the parents who denied her request for such knowledge were exacerbated by the rebuffs she had received from her father when she sought affection from him.

When I was a child I can remember trying to give my father a kiss on the lips, a simple act of affection. My father thought this to be a terrible gesture for his little girl and told me never to do it again. The reason for this is still a mystery to me. My mother was the same way—I would get a hug but nothing more. I kept this inside me, and to this day, I have never let my parents know the hurt I felt and still feel.

The first day my parents brought me to college, my Dad shook my hand goodbye, and my mother reminded me to go to church. I really felt an emptiness that day and felt I was saying goodbye to strangers. A feeling of resentment, almost hostility, toward my parents overwhelmed me.

Family members may be separated physically from one another by death and divorce or, psychologically, by resentment and hostility. If physical separation continues, then the passage of time leads to psychological separation. Some life histories indicate multiple traumas from all sorts of fortuitous circumstances. Take the case of Sam, for example. When Sam was a little boy, he would hear voices threatening divorce coming from his parents' bedroom, and then he would run crying to his mother to beg her not to get a divorce. He would also hear loud arguments and see his mother coming out of the bedroom to sleep elsewhere. When he and his brother came home from school they would check to see if the suitcases were gone. When he was nine years old his mother was committed to a mental hospital, and his schoolmates taunted him about his crazy mother. When he was thirteen, his older brother died, and he had a feeling that his father wished that he had died instead. Sam was a severe problem in school and had several contacts with the police. When his mother came home from the mental hospital, she did not want to recognize him as her son. He then entered the army where he drank to excess and "used sex as a weapon to get back at women." Sam finally entered the university and secured treatment at the counseling center.

Sometimes the death of a parent is a blessing in disguise. In one family the death of alcoholic father prompted the following remark: "My family, whose emotional tone had been erratic while conflict raged between my parents, became stable after my father's death." This tragedy united a family that was swiftly falling apart.

In chapter 5 I dealt with the principle of psychosexual balance in families. In one case a young man introduced his family analysis by saying he was brought up in a henhouse. He went on to explain that his father had developed an incurable illness and had withdrawn to the home of his mother. The young boy was brought up by his mother, several aunts, and a grandmother. His life history revolved around his attempt to achieve manly autonomy, which he finally obtained by marrying at a young age against all the machinations of the women in the household. We can imagine that if his father had been healthy and adequate, the boy's life history would have been different.

Reconstituted Families

Reconstituted or blended families involve remarried persons who have children by previous marriages. Such families have certain special difficulties that other families do not have. As a rule, parents in reconstituted families have suffered from previous hurt or grief; some of them may feel inadequate because they failed in a previous marriage or were abandoned by a partner. The children, likewise, may have suffered from parental loss and love, or they may have so idealized the departed parent that any substitute parent would have to be a virtuoso of perfection to be acceptable. However, a child who is about to become a stepchild may have good reason to hate his natural parent so much that he is poised to project his hate onto any stepparent. If a child has had additional trauma in foster homes or in homes of relatives, he may become distrustful of all adult figures.

In addition to these unfortunate possibilities, two cultural myths handicap the reconstituted family. One myth is that of the cruel stepparent; the other is what Gerda Schulman has called the myth of instant love.[1] By this she means the cultural expectation that when stepparent and stepchild, almost strangers to each other, are brought together by marriage, they are to love each other instantly. Says Schulman, "No other relationship is burdened by such an expectation."

I am sure the reader has known of cases in which a woman, courted by a man with children, withheld her commitment to marry him until she succeeded in establishing some kind of rapport with his children. Such cases may be rare, but they indicate that some women, at least, anticipate the tasks of their future role. As premarital counseling seems appropriate for inexperienced youth, so might premarital consultation with a family counselor be appropriate for persons about to establish a reconstituted family.

I have several histories in which very sensible, stable, professional men with children, who had suffered the sudden and tragic loss of a wife, married women so rapacious, deceitful, and untrustworthy that they had to divorce them forthwith. To what extent does the sudden tragic loss of a fine spouse unhinge one's good judgment in finding another mate?

I think it would be helpful for partners contemplating a marriage that involves a blended family to chart their respective family constellations as outlined in chapter 5. They should indicate the dates of death, divorce, and remarriages on the line showing the time progression in the birth of the children. With the constellation charts, they will get a perspective on what the constellation will be like when their families are combined. Each could, for the benefit of the other, more clearly point out what dyads or triads have developed within their respective constellations and significant features in the personality development of each child. It would also be helpful to include in the chart several generations including the grandparents because, in some instances, the grandparents, along with uncles and aunts, have had charge of the children before or after the divorce and may play a continuing role.

If a woman with children married a bachelor, she will get some comfort from Duberman, who found that such men are better than either divorced men or widowers in developing good relationships with stepchildren.[2] A few of my cases seem to confirm this, although other investigators do not agree.

When a woman with children marries a bachelor, she should watch for one thing—namely, is he or was he so dependent on his mother that he is looking for a mother figure instead of a wife? If he is a strong character who has achieved independence and autonomy, then prospects for marriage could be favorable.

Most writers on the subject seem to agree that young children adapt quite readily to any reasonably good stepparent; teenagers, however, find such adjustment much more difficult. My materials support this generalization. I notice that children under twelve at the time their parent remarries use Mom or Dad when referring to the stepparent, while teenagers use *stepmother* or *stepfather*.

If the departed mother of teenage children was an excellent person, then the task of a new stepmother will be especially difficult; if the mother was inadequate, then by comparison the superior qualities of the stepmother will be advantageous. What are the superior qualities of a good stepmother? They may be the same qualities that make any woman a good mother, including a warm and healthy personality. I am inclined to feel, however, that the stepmother role requires extraordinary sensitivity and empathy. When the new stepmother moves into the home of her husband who has teenage daughters, then I think she should endeavor to find out what things in the house the children especially associated with their dead mother. Did they associate their mother's memory with her favorite chair, her favorite room? The stepmother might do well not to tamper with the chair or remodel the room, at least not right away. Including the children in discussion about disposing or altering anything associated with their mother could be revealing. Another point to consider: If the children observe that their new stepmother has made their father happier than before, they will appreciate that, but manifestations of affection for her new husband should be balanced by concern for his children lest they become jealous of her diverting their father's affection away from them. To put it another way, the daughters may feel that their closeness to the father is threatened by an intruder.

Difficulties arising between stepparents and stepchildren and between stepsiblings need not be exaggerated. I recall writing the case history of a new probationer years ago. The young man said that his father, a widower with six children, had married a widow with six children. Together they had six children, I blurted out, "How did you all get along?" "Just fine," he replied.

A blended family has complications arising from its structure; alcoholism further complicates the family process. In the midst of the stress of such a family, some of the children seem to bear up and become stronger while others weaken. The following analysis illustrates how the alcoholism of the father and the stepfather affected the writer of the story.

The mother was pregnant at the time of the first marriage; she was sixteen and the father was nineteen. Three daughters were born to this union. When the second daughter was seven, the mother divorced the father, presumably because of his excessive drinking.

The mother's second marriage was to a divorcé who had a son; from this union two children were born, a boy and a girl. The narrator and her older sister Bessie called the stepfather by his first name, Henry. She writes:

> Very soon after Henry moved in, he started criticizing us for the way Bessie and I behaved and the work we did. He was constantly finding more jobs for us to do, and his discipline was harsh. This, of course, alienated us right away. The feeling of intense hatred for him did not develop until we were older. I think we might have accepted him if he hadn't been such a fake and cold in his attitudes and actions.

The narrator then elaborated on Henry's excessive drinking, laziness, hypochondria, quarreling with the mother, and inability to communicate with any member of the whole family. Henry identified with his son, whom he favored and indulged, while he scapegoated his two older stepdaughters.

Concerning the marital relationship, the narrator wrote:

> My mom gets real upset when Henry comes home drunk and acts obnoxious. There's always a fight then. Communication between my parents is terrible. After writing this analysis, I realize how close I am to my mother and two sisters. I see how much they have helped me and I'm grateful for its. I look at my mother's marriages and feel sorry for her. I see too many characteristics I don't want in my own marriage. At home, so many dreams were crushed because my parents couldn't afford this or that. I got so sick of hearing this I could scream.

One might think that a girl whose father was alcoholic and whose step-father was both alcoholic and obnoxious would have negative feelings toward men. About her reaction to her natural father's death she said:

> What little I remember of my father is all good. He favored me over my older sister, and I loved all the attention he gave me. It made me feel like something special. He spent a great deal of time playing games with me, taking me for walks, and telling me stories from his imagination. I will always remember him as a kind and gentle person. When he died of acute alcoholism last year, I didn't want to go to the funeral service. I didn't want to see him in any other way than as the kind, gentle person I had known as a child. I think my father would have understood.

In my casework experience I often saw women downgrade their ex-husbands severely in front of their children. Such downgrading makes the children ill at ease when they are visiting the father; it will make them resent the mother and will impair the relationship with her. It also blurs in the mind of the child the distinction between father as a person and his bad characteristics as perceived by the mother. Another tendency of divorced women that should be discouraged is pressuring the child to tattle on his father's activities, especially those that concern his girlfriend or new wife. One daughter, visiting her divorced father, learned about his marriage and later about his new baby, but she did not tell her mother of these events because the mother was so bitter abut her ex-husband. When the mother finally learned of the marriage and the baby, she was very angry with her daughter.

We take it for granted that difficulties are due to the inadequacies of the stepfather when a divorced woman with children marries a single man. In one case the trouble was diagnosed by the daughters of such a woman as being centered in the behavior of the mother. This mother divorced her first husband when the daughters were ten and twelve. She remarried when the daughters were nineteen and twenty-one. The second husband had not been married before; he was described as a capable salesman with much responsibility and was rated very high on empathy and judgment. The mother was an energetic, capable professional who employed her harsh, loud voice in a domineering manner. The daughters came to be fond of their stepfather and respected him. They called him by his nickname Chuck.

The younger daughter described Chuck as ''the best man I have ever met.'' She pointed out that her mother assumed too many roles, making her uptight from role strain. The younger daughter wrote, ''My parents clash in communicating because she rarely gives Chuck a chance to voice his opinion, and when he does, my mom usually disagrees with him.'' Both daughters remonstrated with their mother quite forcefully to treat Chuck better. One said, ''I have learned so much from observing these little things that hurt Chuck that I'm learning how to be and not to be when I get married.''

A young woman recounts that, after her mother's divorce, they moved in with the maternal grandmother. After her mother's second marriage they moved to the house of her stepfather. After a second divorce, they moved back into the home of the grandmother where the girl had three adult women telling her how to behave. She wrote:

> I feel that my strange family situation—that of having three mothers and no father figure for so many years—has affected my attitude toward men. I distrust most of them to a great extent. However, I realize this isn't a healthy attitude, and I'm trying to overcome it.

Jealousy within the family can take place in several different triads involving three siblings, a child and both parents, or a parent and two children. Folk wisdom implies that reconstituted families have more jealousy and that the child is jealous of the stepparent's affection for his natural parent. It can happen in the other direction in which the stepparent is jealous of the spouse's affection for his or her child. This can also happen with biological children.

The saddest cases are those in which a mother and child desperately need the love and security of a spouse-stepfather but in which the latter makes the child an outcast. In the following history, the daughter's biological father operated a tavern, and his drinking made him so violent that his wife fled in terror to another state, hiding her whereabouts and suing for divorce. The daughter's physical and emotional plight was devastating, and she finally made her way to her mother's abode. By this time the mother had married the man who had helped her to escape from her situation at the tavern. When the daughter arrived at her mother's home, she had a violent argument with the new stepfather and had to go back to her father's house. Her sadness and loneliness were pathetic. We have no record of how guilty the mother felt.

Reference was made previously to the myth of instant love. When stepparent and stepchildren are suddenly brought together, what can be done to lay the basis of the development of a friendly rapport? One possibility is for the stepparent to be alert to give quiet recognition to his or her stepchildren according to their talents and accomplishments; this might be done first for the child who seems least friendly or for the one who is considered the most difficult. It might make a difference if compliments come first and corrections last. To compliment the most talented first may intensify the feelings of inadequacy in the one who has suffered previously from invidious comparisons. It might also be helpful to bolster the self-image of stepchildren by giving attention and recognition to their performances in their respective playground and school settings as mentioned in chapters 2 and 13. I think it is also helpful to take extra pains to develop and strengthen creative family rituals as described in chapter 12 because there is no substitute for family rituals to bring about a sense of family cohesion.

Alcoholism

The extent to which the use of alcohol has disrupted family life is incalculable. One sad narrative after another details the conflict, misery, and grief that families suffered from alcoholism. I collected fifty narratives in which the student had labeled one or both parents as alcoholics. The students did not always take pains to indicate all elements of family disorganization that might be related to alcohol addiction, but from their narratives I found that of these fifty families:

thirty-nine fathers were considered alcoholic.

seven mothers were considered alcoholic.

In four families, both parents were considered alcoholic.

In nineteen families, nervous breakdowns occurred.

In twenty-one families, divorces or threats of divorce occurred.

In twenty-four families, physical violence was reported.

In seven families, suicide was threatened.

In eighteen families crime or delinquency was reported.

In sixteen families with an alcoholic father, the mother was quite adequate.

In all these families, the husband-wife relationship was poor; the parent-child relationships ranged from fair to poor. The attitude of the children toward the addicted parent was influenced by whether or not the children had pleasant memories of that parent during childhood prior to the onset of the addiction. If the addiction was well advanced during infancy of the children, then they expressed hatred of him. As a rule, wives of alcoholics were either overburdened or inadequate. Most of them felt neglected by their husbands and were tense, nervous, and lonely. One became involved with wine and pills.

When a girl enters a forced marriage with an alcoholic psychopath, she will suffer from one crisis after another until she divorces him. One such man impregnated a sixteen-year-old girl; after marriage he took his family to live with his mother off and on. In three and a half years of married life, he lost numerous jobs because of his unreliability and moved from place to place; he wrecked four cars and disappeared for days at a time. He drank to excess, seduced every available woman whether married or single, and offered to pimp for his wife. In spite of the presence of two children, he forced his wife to work in a factory. He finally became so violent and so frightened his wife that she sued for divorce. In the face of severe obstacles, she completed her high school education and enrolled in the university.

What factors in our culture tend to foster chemical addictions that plunge so many families into crises? This is a complex problem, and I can only mention a few situations that have impressed me. Much has been said about individuals who resort to drink when confronted with stress or difficulty. Children with parents or grandparents who are alcoholic have, at close range, a human model in confrontation with irritation or a problem was followed by drinking. Film and television scenarios project this pattern for both heroes and villains. The association is so prevalent that the viewer looks for the bottle whenever the actor is nonplussed; if he misses the actor's negative setback; he will see it when the bottle appears. What this association of difficulty and liquor does to a generation of young Americans is a question still awaiting an answer.

One theme in the advertisement of nostrums is that one can safely overindulge because the magic pill will fast relieve all subsequent pain. It is no accident that, within U.S. families, the combination of pills and alcohol is so often a source of tragedy. When children in a pantrophic family hear their parents quietly discuss a difficult problem, they have a model of behavior in which there is no resort to drugs or alcohol but a cooperative resort to logical thinking. Television advertising of nostrums involves no logic but offers a silly image in which the ingestion of a pill suddenly alleviates the pain. The message advertising alcoholic beverages may or may not be silly and the image may be colorful and sexy, but the messages are similar—drink and you will be happy. Anyone who has ever dealt with criminals understands the association of criminality with liquor and drugs. One thing that impressed me was the failure of my clients to face up to their difficulties. Occasionally I found myself saying that, when a person runs away from his problem, the problem runs after him bigger than ever.

Another feature of associating pain or trouble with liquor and drugs is the affinity of both with violence. In the media it is a special kind of violence that seems to be not the outcome of circumstances but an end in itself—a violence divorced from consequences with no flow of blood, tears, funerals, grief, or loneliness, a shameful violence whose sole purpose is to sell nostrums or beverages that people ordinarily do not want, should not have, and cannot afford. Too much dramatic art in the United States, like news and politics, is but an adjunct to advertising that promotes chemical addictions and the destruction of families.

Social workers commonly hear, ". . . I didn't realize I'd married a drinker." The alcoholic and neoalcoholic are extraordinarily clever in hiding their habit when it is to their advantage. Sometimes a fond mother will exclaim that her dear son did not drink heavily until he married "that woman."

I wish now to reverse this sequence with a case involving a son and a daughter. The son wrote:

> In his youth and early marriage my father liked to drink, and on many occasions he drank to excess. No one had been able to reason with him on this matter before he was married. The communication of my parents and the empathy on the part of my mother in this crisis were most remarkable. Within two years after their marriage, my father had given up drinking and has not touched another drop of any kind of alcoholic beverage in the last twenty-five years. This was done without any help from marriage counselors or doctors.

The narrator neither attributed this happy turn of events to his mother nor did he say much about her good qualities. He talked about their attributes as a couple and the nature of their relationship. In short, he described a family that one would rate rather high on the pantrophic scale.

From the narrative and from the questionnaire on voice patterns, I concluded that this man perceived the following about the nature of his parents' marriage. To him, both parents had:

A high degree of empathy;

Excellent communication;

Well-modulated voices;

Similar interests in music, landscaping, and decorating the home;

Similar rural backgrounds;

High ratings for sense of humor, tact, and appreciation for and demonstration of affection;

Low ratings for conflict, admonition, interrogation pressure, and criticism;

No quarreling that the children were aware of.

The whole family derived much pleasure from family rituals. The mother was slightly more dominating than the father, but they were equal in argumentation.

The treatment for chemical addictions has made considerable strides in the past few decades.[3] What should family members do when one suffers from such addiction? The following narrative reveals how one daughter reacted when her mother became alcoholic and the father would take no initiative to provide treatment. The mother's father had died of alcoholism, and her sisters were heavy drinkers or alcoholic. The mother had grieved for the death of two of her young children; four children survived.

> I never remember really loving my mother when I was small. I also felt guilty when I didn't. I have very little memory of my childhood. I guess this is called repression. My parents overprotected us. We couldn't leave the yard unless we asked permission, which was seldom granted. Our home was father centered, and what he said was rule. So not only were we overprotected but also we were told everything we were to do and when we should do it. There was no freedom or choice. As a result I have become very self-conscious and lack self-confidence.

> My mother became alcoholic slowly as I was growing up. This partly accounts for my lack of friends. I was ashamed to bring them home. The house was scarcely ever cleaned, and when it was, it was done by my sister and me. My mother existed by laying on the davenport drinking (oftentimes secretly), watching the boob tube, and occasionally doing the cook-

ing and the wash. She rarely smiled and was hostile when things didn't go
her way. She constantly harped on Dad; she had him jump to every command. I hated my mother because of the changes occurring in my father.

My brother was born in the midst of this chaos. Today he is ten and very
confused and hyperactive. He is something of a scapegoat since my dad
yells at him for no reason at all, and my brother never comes close to my
mother. We finally admitted to ourselves that she was sick (alcoholic).

I took the first step to help my mother. I talked with our doctor and then
with my dad. Dad was afraid and left the whole thing in my hands. I made
all the appointments. The drying-out period was a special hell. I never want
to see another human being in such a state of utter hopelessness and
dependence.

My mother is well now. This has brought our family a little closer together,
but all the pieces don't quite fit yet. My mother is a whole new person I
never knew before. The old love is back for my mother, and the guilt is
erased. It used to be shocking to hear my mother laugh, but now it is frequent. I wish we had done this sooner.

The onset of alcoholic addiction in a family has a disturbing effect on
family dynamics. There seems to be a reassignment of distorted family
roles: one member may become the admired, courageous, efficient martyr
who holds the family together in spite of all difficulties. Others may include
the family clown, the scapegoat, the academic achiever, the rebel, the delinquent.

Alcoholism has been described as a primary, permanent, terminal
disease with a predictable course, but if we take into consideration the influence of several generations and the internal and external pressures on the
family, perhaps it should also be considered a family disease. This disease is
not often cured unless some family members take the initiative and
cooperate with outside therapeutic resources. Cooperation in the
therapeutic process finds expression in family therapeutic sessions plus participation in such organizations as Alcoholics Anonymous, Al-Anon, and
Operation Alateen. Most communities have specialized agencies for referral
or professional treatment of chemical addictions.

When alcoholism prevails in a family, that family is usually in a
dystrophic condition, but this condition is not synonymous with dystrophic
families since many bad families have no chemical addiction. The next
chapter contrasts the dystrophic families with those I consider pantrophic.

Notes

1. Gerda L. Schulman, "Myths that Intrude on the Adaptation of the
Stepfamily," *Social Casework* (1972), pp. 131–139. Reprinted in Gladys

Phelan, *Family Relationships* (Minneapolis: Burgess Publishing, 1979), pp. 211–219.

2. Lucile Duberman, *The Reconstituted Family: A Study of Remarried Couples and Their Children* (Chicago: Nelson-Hall, 1975), p. 56.

3. An excellent summary of the nature and treatment of chemical-dependecy disease is found in a brochure, by the Johnson Institute, "Alcoholism, A Treatable Disease," (10700 Memorial Highway, Minneapolis, MN. 55441).

19 Measuring Quality in Family Life

In the past, family researchers have assumed that there is a fundamental or dichotomous difference between broken and unbroken homes, intact and divorced homes, one-parent and two-parent families, and families with and without a delinquent child. From my experience, I believe that any research based upon the assumption that a mutually exclusive difference exists in such dichotomous categories is suspect. If we were to develop an instrument to measure the quality of family life, I think we should find considerable variance on both sides of the dividing line in any of these categories.

Failure to define and measure the quality of family life has resulted in fragmentation of the symptoms of poor family functioning into many pieces. Each fragment is investigated by different researchers; each fragment has its own special agency soliciting funds for its own special programs. These symptomatic fragments involve problems such as marital conflict, divorce, desertion, truancy, runaways, premarital pregnancy, drug and alcohol addiction, crime, delinquency, wife abuse, child abuse, psychosomatic disorders, nervous disorders, suicide, and sexual maladjustment. In pantrophic families we seldom have any of these; in any large group of dystrophic families we have them all. Since any one of these forms of personal disorganization operates in a faulty family system, why not set forth a blueprint for pantrophic family living and reshape our social structure to promote healthy family systems? This might be more effective than dealing with human debris after it has accumulated. Budgets for ameliorating these types of disorganizations at the local, state, and federal level constitute a tremendous societal burden. It would be cost-effective if we were to shape up social and economic programs to promote quality families.

The annual cost of crime is a crippling burden. Space does not permit speculation on the relationship between pantrophic families and community leadership or between dystrophic families and crime and delinquency. I disparage ideas that crime can be reduced or controlled by changing the law-enforcement process, probation, parole, or prison treatment. Crime can be reduced only by a constructive approach. Each society gets as much crime as it deserves, and ours deserves plenty. It is hard to conceive how the goals, values, and structure of our society could be altered to produce any more crime than we now have. If every child could be nurtured in a pantrophic family and given an opportunity to achieve independance from that family by an opportunity to earn a decent living with a decent mate, then crime might be reduced to that arising from institutional malfunctioning in the process of social change, which would be much better than what we have now. Space does not permit a discussion of the complexities of crime and the influence of class in defining crime.

It is difficult to promote something for which we have no measure; therefore, developing an instrument to measure the quality of family living is a must. With such an instrument we could appraise the quality of families and its relationship to social class, location, and other factors.

Lewis and his colleagues believed that the important finding from their research was that the degree of family competence (quality) "involved a large number of variables rather than a few very important ones."[1] My agreement with this is apparent from the many aspects of family life with which I have dealt in this book.

I mentioned in chapter 1 that most research therapists think in terms of categories such as healthy, unhealthy, optimal, or adequate. In my view, the boundaries between such categories are tenuous. Throughout the life cycle, families move up and down the scale of quality; this movement may go down abruptly in a crisis and come up again later. What we need is an instrument to measure family quality on a numerical scale from a plus, high-pantrophic, number to a minus, low-dystrophic, number. Such an instrument would be useful to any person whose family is good but who wants to make it better. If such a family member changes his behavior and improves his score, however slightly, he may be motivated to continue his efforts.

This leads to the question: Should the measuring instrument be administered only by experts or self-administered by family members? Many families object to being probed by outside experts. A recent article discusses the ethical dilemmas of such procedures.[2] A self-administered paper-and-pencil instrument would avoid the ethical problems of family probing. Separate questionnaires could be devised for each parent and for children over a certain age. Such devices were used during the 1940s and 1950s to measure success in marriage.[3] They were used by middle-class persons and university students. An instrument for measuring family quality need not be complicated.

In lieu of such an instrument, I offer contrasting indicators related to the quality of family life (table 19-1). From the analyses of hundreds of families, contrasts in behavior between pantrophic and dystrophic families emerge. I have tried to capture these differences by listing pantrophic patterns on the left and dystrophic on the right. If the reader recalls the material in this book suggested by these phrases and checks his own family on these items, he will be able to gauge whether his family rates low, medium, or high on the pantrophic or dystrophic side of the zero point.

Table 19–1
Contrasting Indicators Related to Quality of Family Life

Pantrophic	Dystrophic
Overall Family Characteristics	
Parents with adequate personalities	Parents with gross personality defects
Many satisfying family rituals	Rituals absent, few, or superficial
A *hestia* that is relaxed, cheerful, cohesive, promoting spontaneity and humor	A *hestia* that is tense, foreboding, depressing, rigid, isolating
Expectation that behavior conforms to religious, moral, ethical principles	Little or no reference to religious, moral, or ethical principles
Good balance in distribution of family resources among settings	Lopsided distribution of family resources among settings
Reasonable economic security	Poverty and economic uncertainty
Family integrated with kin and community	Family isolated from kin and community
Husband-Wife Relationships	
Good marital adjustment	Poor marital adjustment
Compliments with positive stroking	Negative stroking, indifference, rejection
Affectionate patterns openly displayed	Affectionate patterns absent or weak
Roles congruent, well allocated, flexible	Roles incongruent, conflicting, rigid
Good communication	Poor communication
Equalitarian patterns	Dominant-submissive, withdrawal patterns
Leveling with calm discussions	Decisions in limbo, silence, shouting
Cooperative patterns	Patterns of conflict, epithets, violence
Parent-Child Relationships	
No favoritism, no invidious comparisons, stress upon uniqueness of each child	Favoritism, scapegoating, invidious comparisons
Positive stroking evenly distributed	Negative stroking, indifference, ridicule
Parents promote independence of children	Parents stymie independence of children
Self-expression of children encouraged	Self-expression suppressed or ridiculed
Well-modulated voice patterns	Harsh and loud voice patterns
Adequate parent-child communication	Inadequate communication blocks self-revelation
Reciprocal trust and respect between parents and children	Reciprocal distrust and disrespect between parents and children
Interest in and recognition of children's activities	Little or no interest in or recognition of children's activities
Affectionate patterns openly displayed	No display of affection for children
Development of inner controls in children but setting limits	Discipline too lax or too strict, inconsistent, arbitrary, violent
Allocation of tasks for children	No training in task responsibilities
Peers of children welcomed	Peers of children not welcome, criticized
High visibility of children's settings	Low visibility of children's settings

Table 19-1 continued

Pantrophic	Dystrophic
Freedom granted to children for making choices compatible with maturity	Children restricted, indulged, overprotected, and overpossessed
Orientation of children for growth opportunities in the larger society	Negative orientation of children for growth opportunities in the larger society
Sexuality perceived as natural and wholesome	Sexuality perceived as secret, evil, dangerous
Parental solidarity in family leadership	Children play one parent against the other
Generational boundaries respected	Generational boundaries weak or violated

Sibling Relationships

Siblings proud of each other	Siblings jealous of each other
Siblings devoted and helpful to each other	Siblings hostile to each other
Childhood conflict is later displaced by cooperation	Childhood conflict persists throughout adolescence and adulthood

Certain items on the indicator list reflect similar patterns in the larger society. For example, two items on the dystrophic side deal with violence in the family; in the larger society we have violence in the streets, in the media, and in military operations.

The list of contrasting indicators of the quality of family life may be of value to a person who wishes to discover the strengths and weaknesses of his family. He may be encouraged by the strengths to work on the weaknesses. One's potential for improving his family may be related roughly to his education and to the mixture of nurturant and nonnurturant factors in his childhood.

It is possible, of course, for parents with meager education and limited resources to generate a pantrophic family, provided their own family backgrounds were healthy and secure. Table 19-2 contrasts the education of parents in fifty-six pantrophic families with those of fifty-six dystrophic families. The five pantrophic families for which we have no data had some kind of business, suggesting an adequate education. Narratives of the twenty dystrophic families with no education data indicate that the parents were immigrants or impoverished, from which we infer a limited education. Parents in pantrophic families had better nurturant and educational backgrounds.

Establishment of a pantrophic family requires that at least one parent is reasonably adequate as spouse and parent. The children may rally around the adequate parent to form a remarkably good family; and they, by freely assuming added responsibilities, may blossom into strong personalities. Any reader who feels discouraged because of inadequate parenting may

Table 19-2
Educational Levels of Pantrophic and Dystrophic Families

Educational Levels	Dystrophic	Pantrophic
Professional degrees of father	2	7
Both parents, college degrees	2	7
One parent, college degree	4	12
One or both parents college dropouts	8	0
Both parents, high school only	2	14
One parent, high school only	3	4
One or both parents, grade school only	15	7
No data on education of parents	20	5

take notice of students who came from incredibly terrible families and yet who succeeded in college. What has happened to these students after college I do not know, although a few of them have written to me later about family happiness.

To what extent can a person from a dystrophic family, by diligently analyzing his family, assuage the hate and guilt he has for his parents and establish a pantrophic family of his own? I can only report that hundreds of students from all kinds of families have testified to a variety of ways they have benefited from writing their family analyses. The worst thing a person with a deplorable background can do is to feel sorry for himself. I suggest he read *A New Guide to Rational Living* by Ellis and Harper.[4] One who has severe difficulty with relationships would do well to consult a family therapist.

Developing an easily applied instrument for appraising family quality to be widely used would reveal two things that persons on power and authority dimly appreciate: (1) the extreme differences in family quality in all groups and classes in our society and (2) a large number of families, who on the surface appear to function normally, whose members are writhing in pain, frustration, and sorrow.

I was surprised at the large number dystrophic families who remain intact in spite of incredible suffering. In one group of fifty-six such families, there were only thirteen reports of divorce at the time of writing. There were, however, twenty reports of fear or violence and twenty-seven reports of alcoholism.

Many heavy drinkers and alcoholics seem to be able to hold on to their jobs; hence, wives put up with drunken husbands for economic reasons until the children are out of school. One reason is that a mother whose health has been impaired by abuse, child rearing, and overwork has a dim view of her future life after divorce. Her chances of remarriage may be considered slight and her economic plight precarious. Although money available for the family is diminished by the purchase of liquor, it might be practically nil after divorce. Nothing is more discouraging for a parole officer than trying to collect support money from a lonely drunk living in a rooming house. Many a wife will not think of divorcing an alcoholic partner because she has happy memories of a previous period and does not wish to abandon a man who would be quite helpless by himself. The same may be true for a man whose wife is alcoholic. Improved facilities for treating alcoholism have given many spouses a constructive option.

In view of the many dystrophic families who continue intact, and of the number of divorced persons who remarry and do better in their second marriage, it would appear that divorce is not a good indicator of family stability. Various writers suggest that family stability is measured by the degree to which family relationships are broken by death, desertion, and divorce; the ability of a family to meet a crisis; and the quality of interpersonal relationships within the family.

One who has a pantrophic familiy does not need to worry about divorce or desertion, the ability to meet a crisis, or poor relationships. He has something more meaningful than mere stability—the joy and ecstasy of experiencing growth arising from high-quality living.

I have suggested that the widespread practice of measuring family quality would change the nature and direction of family research. I can think of no dependent variable more important than the quality of family life, and I can think of nothing more important to a society than the quality of its families. This new approach would, I think, change the nature of questions we have about families and society. Some writers are fond of posing the question: What is wrong with the family? This fatuous question implies that the family is some kind of animal that must be retrained. More-appropriate questions are: What is wrong with society that we do not have more families of high quality? What changes in social structure should be made to promote pantrophic families so that human resources in our society can be safeguarded and nurtured? Instruments for measuring quality in family living could be used to measure the effectiveness of various kinds of family therapy, enrichment programs, and family-life education programs. These instruments could save time for family counselors during initial meetings by pinpointing the perceptions of family members about family relationships. They would be useful in exploring the quality of family life in all segments of U.S. society to illustrate how such quality is related to social and economic conditions.

Notes

1. Jerry M. Lewis, W. Beavers, J. Gossett, and V.A. Phillips, *No Single Thread* (New York: Brunner/Masel, 1978).

2. Ralph Larosa, L. Bennett, and R. Gelles, "Ethical Dilemmas in Qualitative Family Research," *Journal of Marriage and the Family* (May 1981), pp. 303–313.

3. See Ernest Burgess and P. Wallen, *Engagement and Marriage* (Chicago: Lippincott, 1953).

4. Albert Ellis and R. Harper, *A New Guide to Rational Living* (North Hollywood: Wilshire Book Company, 1978).

20 Outlook for the Future

As goes the family, so goes the state. There is a symbiotic relationship between the two; each depends on the other. The society exists in a macro-system; the family in a microsystem. Both will find it advantageous to conserve their material and human resources.

Are the two essential functions of the family to replenish the population at zero population growth and to socialize each new generation? Sociologists view the latter function as simply inducting children into conventional social norms. This is not enough because the problems of the state are so numerous, complex, and dangerous that children must achieve beyond the conventional. They must develop their creative potential in all aspects of growth at an accelerated pace in order to supply the type of leadership the state now requires. Only pantrophic families can accomplish this mission. If this source of leadership proves to be insufficient, then we may expect the vacuum to be filled by leaders who have been steeled in the hardships of dystrophic families. Such leaders often are the first to forget their humble origins and to fawn on the rich and powerful to attain selfish and dangerous objectives.

Wise and compassionate leaders never attain positions of authority unless they have a voting constituency to put them in office. As economic conditions worsen, the number of dystrophic families increases and their members become so anxious, apathetic, and alienated that they fail to vote. Those who have the most to protect are in the best position to acquire more, participate more, and spend more energy to control it.

Occasionally, a politician whose family background gives him some compassion for underprivileged families acquires high political office. However, the system limits what he can do to promote pantrophic life. To date, the slight amelioration of wretched family life has arisen out of what little compassion the powerful may have for the less fortunate. Motives based on compassion are insufficient. Motivation for the affluent to lessen dystrophic aspects of family life and to promote pantrophic family life is rarely based on altruism but more often on self-interest. The family is the crucible that turns out personalities from worst to best. When the percentage of the former increases, our capacity to solve domestic and foreign problems is threatened. Investing in human resources that can be nurtured

357

only in pantrophic families is far more important than investing in capital equipment that demoralized human beings cannot operate well enough to compete in foreign markets. This brings to mind the leadership of our political and economic institutions in the early 1980s; our leaders neither view the family from any perspective at all nor have any thought of conserving our natural or human resources in the macro- or the microecosystem.

An observer from the societal perspective will be impressed with the alternation of war and depression in nearly every other decade during the past century, with the disarray and intermingling of our political and economic institutions, and with a third institutional structure that both have spawned and that engulfs them both—namely, the military-industrial complex. Our observer might conclude that these faulty institutions have produced a sick society that is incapable of creating the nurturant conditions in which pantrophic families can flourish. He may conclude that only a restructuring of the society can provide such conditions.

What happens to the U.S. family in the 1980s will depend on whether the conduct of our foreign policy gets us into another war and on whether the leadership of our political economy solves our economic problems. If there should be a nuclear war, then speculation about the future of the family is irrelevant. Those leaders who are feverishly stockpiling nuclear weapons are talking about a limited nuclear war, presumably limited to Central Europe—a prospect that obviously frightens the peoples of that area. Intellectuals scoff at the notion that limited use of nuclear weapons can be restricted in armed conflict. Whether this war is conventional, limited, or all-out nuclear, U.S. families will pay a terrible price. Even with a conventional war, heads of families will suffer from high taxes, high energy costs, and high inflation at a time when parents are separated from their young sons and young husbands and wives from each other.

Not since the Civil War has our land been disrupted by armies. In the next war, even without nuclear warheads, our land could be devastated by bombs and missiles, especially if one should strike a nuclear facility. Our nuclear scientists are worried. The plume of radioactive dust would travel downwind for a thousand miles or more and panic hundreds of thousands of families, not to mention the effects of radiation from the center of the explosion.

In preparation for the next war and during its course, many restraints on pollution and safeguards for consumers will be lifted. These trends will accentuate the decline of our standard of living and jeopardize the safety of the family. Perhaps more than in previous wars, if the next one occurs in the 1980s, we shall have a considerable percentage of draftees indulging in chemical addictions and permissive sexual patterns. We can expect these patterns to be accentuated during the course of the war so that veterans will be less marriageable on their return to wives, many of whom will be living

with in-laws as they did during and after World War II. The housing shortage after the next war will be even more acute because we shall have entered
it with a greater shortage than we had at the beginning of World War II. It
will be severer because of high interest rates, a high inflation rate and the
trend to converting apartment complexes into condominiums.

When the veterans return, after suffering physical and psychological
damage from the war and presumably with a greater incidence of chemical
addictions and sexually transmitted disease, just when they must grapple
with the problems of housing and jobs, we can expect the divorce rate to
peak again as it did in 1946 when it reached 18.2 per 1,000 existing marriages. Soon after, we may expect an increase in the number of blended
families and of children not living with their natural parents.

That war brings prosperity is a dangerous notion harbored by Americans. The next such prosperity will be a disaster. Circumstances prior to
World War II were quite different from those of today. In the 1930s we had
deflation, our capacity for industrial output was sound, and we had plenty
of domestic oil, natural gas, and mineral and timber resources. In the post-
war period we had a monopoly on nuclear power, led the world in auto production, and for several decades, rode high on an increasing standard of living. Now our automotive prosperity is in shambles, and taxes, inflation,
unemployment, crime, and interest rates are high. This is the worst time to
stumble into a war from the standpoints of our economy and the family.

Unemployed working-class persons who think that the next war will
give them nice jobs may find that their wages are frozen and their earnings
are quickly liquidated by high rents, interest, transportation costs, and
inflated prices for consumer goods and low-grade babysitters, not to mention the destruction of homes, hospitals, and factories from missiles and
conflagrations.

What about the families of the middle class whose future depends upon
the vagaries of war and depression? During this century, the lumber, railroad, mining, and oil barons have already taken the cream of those natural
resources that were easily available to form a class apart from the main-
stream of U.S. life. They have restructured corporate organizations to form
monopolies and near-monopolies that diminish competition and put the
squeeze on consumers. They have created powerful bureaucracies that fat-
ten on military contracts and have acquired such a potent relationship to the
political process that they can subsidize a defense candidate for Congress
versus a peace candidate twenty to one. The corporate side of the military
establishment is the only business that never worries about bankruptcy from
blunders or about prosecution for shortchanging and overcharging. The
military-industrial complex consists of two closely related bureaucracies:
one in the private sector, the other in the government sector. Engineers,
generals, and administrators move freely from one to the other; their inter-

ests and philosophy are one. The future of the U.S. family will be determined by whether or not its people can bring this bureaucracy to heel so that we can succeed in disarmament negotiations, ease international tensions, and proceed to convert from the production of weapons to consumer goods.

It seems that the conscious and subconscious processes in the minds of those in the military establishment really do not want a shooting war but a state of public apprehension that will permit the continuance of vast appropriations for lucrative military contracts. The current ballyhoo about peace through strength fits in with this idea. This bit of conventional wisdom has given us nothing but war through the centuries; but the propaganda that has distorted public opinion about defense makes it difficult to rise above conventional wisdom. It does not take much propaganda to keep the U.S. people on edge about the designs of the Soviets. If this state of affairs continues, it will be very risky for the peace of the world, and while it lasts, U.S. families will continue to suffer from the economic dislocations inherent in this situation. Since the production of military systems requires the least labor force for the money invested, we can expect that high rates of unemployment will continue, with a devastating effect on the family life of the working and middle classes.

The nonchalance of our political leaders toward the plight of the unemployed is astonishing. Unemployment of 5 or 6 percent is considered normal, but the consequences of this are much greater than 6 percent. For every father unemployed, four or five dependents and semidependents also suffer. When the unemployment rates rises up 10 percent or more, it is considered to be unfortunate but acceptable—that is, acceptable for the corporate monopolies—but there is little concern for what it does to the family life of the unemployed.

The high rate of unemployment of young men among blacks and other minorities is appalling. These youth cannot aspire to marriage and satisfactory family life; our present administration sees no connection between their frustrations in idleness and their violations of the mores and the criminal codes. Amir Menachen finds that, of the young men convicted of forcible rape in Philadelphia over a two-year period, 92 percent were unemployed.[1] I wager that if we could examine the work records of the other 8 percent we should find that the income from their jobs would not support a family.

The attitude of the affluent toward the unemployed is similar to that of the wife of a man who had been placed on probation for nonsupport. I asked her for an appraisal of her husband's conduct. She admitted he was not a drinker, lazy, or abusive, but she said, "He's no good, he hasn't got a job." When I said that many men were unemployed, she replied "But my neighbor's husband has a job." I said, "When 50 million men are rotated through 40 million jobs, 10 million will always be out of luck." Thus, the affluent are prone to think that any kind of job will suffice for the working-class breadwinner. Not so. In my experience, the quickest way to get a parolee back in prison is to give him a job he dislikes and for which he is unsuited. Jobs that are temporary, seasonal, subject to frequent layoffs, and dangerous should not be considered as employment. They should be considered as the postponement of trouble, and one cannot erect a pantrophic family on trouble. The presence of a suitable, well-paying, steady job does not guarantee a pantrophic family, but it is the only foundation on which one can build such a family.

The middle-class breadwinner also has problems on the job. Many of them work in huge bureaucracies, both public and private, where they may suffer from the influence of cliques, favoritism, frustration, and tension. Those in the public sector may go into a slow burn when a fellow employee (who was never inducted into a task role at home) shirks his work and the supervisor has not quite the courage to discipline him in the face of tenure, obstacles, or pressures from the outside.

How to stimulate and utilize effectively the creative potential of employees in a bureaucracy is in some ways similar to the problems of stimulating the creative potential of family members. The influx of employees from pantrophic families would improve the functioning of the bureaucracies; the influx of employees from dystrophic families would impair the bureacracies; and improved bureaucracies would improve the functioning of families.

Every nation is confronted with the problem of reducing unemployment and putting its people into constructive activities that would increase the standard of living. Many believe this cannot be done without changing the focus of societal goals and values. I believe that the future of the U.S. family, therefore, depends on the creativeness of our people in effecting social change in an orderly fashion in the area of political economy. I think we should restructure our society so that the control of our natural resources would be taken from the conglomerates and, by some democratic process, brought to serve human needs for all classes. This would set the stage for developing pantrophic families and for diminishing violence and the risk of war.

Whatever administration leads our nation into war will have a morale problem on its hands. In World War I, the soldiers thought they were fighting to curb German militarism and to make the world safe for democracy; in World War II, they were fighting against Hitler and all he stood for. The rationale for the next war has not yet been clearly defined. One possibility is to refurbish the slogan about curtailing the spread of communism, but the verbal rubbish we got from our leaders during the Vietnam fiasco may not be sufficient a second time around. Furthermore, Soviet influence (of dubious quality) has diminished to thirteen countries that are the most poverty stricken of all in the Third World. Another possible rationale for war is to protect our access to oil in the Middle East. Apparently we are to achieve this end by arming foreign potentates who have cozy connections with the international cartels and by using expeditionary forces. If we are to fight for oil, then the youth to be drafted for high-risk military expeditions might suggest that they will fight only if those who profit from the oil take their fair share of the risk. They might also say, since it will be a push-button war, that men in middle age would be just as useful as teenagers in the technical operation of military equipment. After all, it is only just, since the older men have already lived most of their lives, that young men should have a chance at living. Besides, the oldsters and not the youngsters are pushing the risks for war. The young might say that priority in the draft should be given to executives of the oil companies and to belligerent congressmen. We can imagine how father and son within the same family would anguish over the issue as to who should take the risk in fighting for oil or for maintaining our posture before the world as some benighted giant.

The belligerence of our foreign policy abroad and within our families at home reflects the violent nature of our society.[2] If war and preparation for war should depress unduly the material well-being of the middle class, then our society is ripe for charismatic charlatans who have political ambitions. If these persons should acquire ready access to the media without equal participation of more-level-headed politicians, we are in for the kind of trouble that festers in a milieu of violence. All this bodes ill for the family. Success in disarmament and the curtailment of U.S. militarism not only would provide more employment and education for youth but also would tend to curb violence in our society.

In addition to war, preparation for war, and economic dislocation is another factor: The rapid change in sexual attitudes and behavior that took place in the 1960s and 1970s has been called by some a sexual revolution. Whatever we call it, the direction of its progress has a bearing on the future of the family. In historical perspective, one might conceive of changes in sexual behavior as a huge pendulum that is now swinging in the direction of sexual permissiveness. This swing may slow down gradually and then somewhat reverse itself. (A few experts believe that such a reversal has already taken place.) What influences, if any, would accomplish this? Such influences, I think, will arise out of the life experience of men and women who have suffered from the aftermath of unfortunate sexual experience and who are concerned about the risk of greater sexual freedom to significant others. Students have been open in recounting the adulterous behavior of fathers and mothers. They do not like it. It makes them rebellious and disturbed. One young woman made it clear that, if her future husband should conduct himself as had her father, she would ditch him forthwith. This comment was made as she referred to all the suffering her mother had endured because of her father's philandering. My experience with students leads to the observation that, in looking to their future marriage and family, they want love and commitment on a long-term basis. This yen is consistent with their sexual experience with a series of boyfriends or girlfriends and with their experience in cohabitation. The realization of mismatching is reason enough to break a commitment either before or after marriage; the desire for permanence in a love relationship is strong. Even a Don Juan gets tired of dalliance and seeks a permanent partner. If we reach a point at which sexual behavior is far out of the boundaries of affection, then I think the family is in for trouble. Marriage often can stand an occasional affair and even a mistress, but not continuous philandering.

If the children of our country are given a chance, their irrepressible desire to develop their latent powers in a creative and constructive way should give us hope for the future. The first part of such a chance is growing up in a family wherein at least one parent can provide suitable nurturance and the kind of stimulation that impels children to develop their latent powers, not only within the family setting but also in the settings of the larger society. The other part is the opportunity to earn a living upon reaching their majority. This full chance is the non sequitur for satisfactory family life in our society.

An important aspect of the sexual revolution is not so much changes in the behavior of adults but changes in adolescents (ages 13 to 17), except that adult behaviors serve as models for youth. Recently, a great deal has been written about the personal and family disorganization taking place because of premarital pregnancies of young girls.[3] This has many facets: congenital disease, impaired health, wretched children, and wrecked families, careers, and lives, not to mention pragmatic costs. Youngsters permitted to fondle each other in private go through the sequence of activity from light petting to intercourse during a period of months. Reducing these tragic pregnancies requires only the prohibition of privacy for two sexes during the early teenage years, or at least until girls are physically mature. Some will say this cannot be done. Maybe so. If the Arabs could lock their women into harems for decades, surely we could lock youngsters out of outdoor theaters, parked cars, and bedrooms for the few years prior to physical maturity. Parents in pantrophic families have little difficulty in this regard. By socialization and supervision of youngsters of both sexes during the critical period, sexual risks are reduced. Reducing such risks in dystrophic homes is difficult; it is even more difficult when such families live in settings characterized by poverty and unemployment. Another handicap is the lack of culturally prescribed puberty, except for the Jewish community, and no uniformity or certainty as to when transition to adult status occurs.

In conclusion, a bright future for the U.S. family will obtain if we are able to curb violence in our society, develop a sane foreign policy, put our economy in order, stabilize population growth, improve the mate-selection process,[4] slow down the sexual revolution, popularize the model for a pantrophic family, and restructure our society so that our natural resources and wildlife are in harmony with our human resources. There is nothing wrong with the U.S. family that a decent society could not cure.

Notes

1. Amir Menachen, *Patterns of Forcible Rape* (Chicago: University of Chicago Press, 1971).

2. Murray A. Strauss and Gerald T. Hotaling, eds., *The Social Causes of Husband-Wife Violence,* (Minneapolis: University of Minnesota Press, 1980).

3. For an excellent discussion of premarital problems of young girls, see Ivan F. Nye and Martha B. Lamberts, "School-Age Parenthood," Extension Bulletin 0067 (Pullman: Washington State University, Cooperative Extension, 1980).

4. Gordon Shipman, "In My Opinion: The Role of Counseling in the Reform of Marriage and Divorce Procedures," *Family Coordinator* (October 1977), pp. 395–407.

Appendix A:
One of the Outlines
Used to Guide Students
in Writing
Family Analysis

I. Cultural and social background of parents: similarities and differences. You may condense some of this information on the attached form. (Circumstances of marriage of parents and early married life, nature of household, neighborhood, and relationships with relatives. Moving and economic advances and declines.) Do not elaborate on this portion unless it has an important bearing on your parent's marriage and your own development. Sometimes children are influenced greatly by grandparents.

II. Family configuration and interpersonal relationships. By using the family constellation form, indicate your position in the family constellation as well as the positions of each of your parents. In your family of orientation indicate age and sex differentials. Explain how these differences affected personality development. If pertinent, show how parallel positions between parent and child promoted understanding or favoritism. Note evidences of affection, cooperation, favoritism, hostility, dominance, submissiveness, rebellion, rejection, indifference, competition, withdrawal from competition, jealousy, and so forth. What effect did all this have on your present attitudes and behavior toward others?

III. Heterosocial behavior (dating and courtship)
   A. Psychosexual development. Earliest sex training: preparation for puberty, reaction to menarche or spermarche, misconceptions about reproduction, sexual anxieties, nature and source of learning experiences about reproduction, correction of misconceptions, development of attitudes toward opposite sex, and sexuality in general.
   B. Sociocultural behavior. Your role in peer groups in neighborhood and school. Dating and courtship experiences and how they affected your development either negatively or positively.
   C. Family influence on your courtship behavior. Effect of religion

365

and social class. Parental limits. Attitude of parents toward your dates. How did relationships with parents determine the type of person you were attracted to or repelled from? Source of image of ideal mate. Influence of other families or other persons.

IV. Your family as an interactional system
    A. Quality of communication between parents. Voice patterns and gestures. Degree of empathy, autonomy, judgment, creativity.
    B. Patterns of problem solving and decision making. Patterns of dominance, submissiveness, equality. Withdrawal patterns. Release of tensions. Manifestations of affection or hostility.
    C. Participation of children in family affairs. To what extent did parents value and accept ideas and opinions of children in family matters? Evaluate the quality of communication between parents and children, especially between each parent and self.
    D. Functioning of your family system in terms of role theory. Examine the congruence of conflict of social roles within family. Examine role changes in terms of complementarity, rigidity, flexibility.
    E. Family rituals. Evaluate the quality and number of family rituals and their impact on family cohesiveness. Appraise the emotional tone of the family.
    F. Family disorganization or solidarity. If your family became unstable, explain how the difficulties developed: alcoholism, conflict, divorce, and so on. Analyze what you can do in the future to help your family operate more effectively. If you cannot help the family as a whole, what can you do to help certain members who have special problems? How has the disorganization of your family affected you adversely or how has it benefited you? If you family is stable and successful, analyze the main elements that made it so.

V. Final appraisal. What patterns in your family of orientation will you wish to carry over to your family orientation? Which will you discard or modify? What are the main things you have learned by writing this analysis that you did not appreciate before? How will this analysis benefit you when you establish your own family or procreation?

VI. Alternate assignment. Those who do not wish to turn in the entire paper may submit what they have written under V and add a summary of what they have learned from writing the analysis. All complete papers will be read only by the instructor who may make appropriate comments and who will return the paper to the students.

Appendix B:
Toman's Family
Constellation

An analysis of the interrelation of children in the family structure and their unique characteristics due to position.

The Only Child:

1. Remains a child long after adulthood.
2. Wants to be the center of attention.
3. Will not mind making a fool of himself so long as he is the center of attention.
4. Takes all material things for granted.
5. Never ready for a peer relationship.
6. Knows better how to handle adults and gets his parents to help him.
7. Can attract followers and lead to the degree they identify with authority figures or with subject matters.
8. May identify with the parents of the same sex and take on their positional characteristics.

Twins

1. Will tend to have trouble separating and taking the step of getting married.
2. Tend to be glued together and stay attached to each other for life.

Oldest Brother of Brothers:

1. Is a leader.
2. Is a good worker.
3. Can accept authority of male superior, his boss.
4. Builds up property.
5. Is a tough guy with women; Tends to treat girls like younger brothers.
6. Plans for his children's future; Orderly disciplinarian.
7. Politically, believes in strong leadership, elites, dictatorships.

Youngest Brother of Brothers:

1. Is capricious and willful, but also annoys elders.

Walter Toman, *Family Constellation* (New York: Springer, 1981).

2. Is irregular worker.
3. Is not a good leader.
4. Can accept authority provided it is not too demonstrative.
5. Does not create or preserve property; squanders savings of others.
6. Is soft with women—a gentleman.
7. Has difficulty accepting children for they threaten his own status.
8. Politically, is against monarchy, dictatorships, or strong leadership.

Oldest Brother of Sisters:
1. Believes love is the most important of all concerns.
2. Is a good worker—as long as there are female colleagues or co-workers.
3. Best match would be youngest sister of brother(s).
4. Is not a gang man.
5. Is a ladies man; appreciates women; loves the favors of beautiful women; knows how to handle women; is attentive and understanding.
6. May acknowledge professional authority but bristles at unfounded authoritarian demand.
7. Is a good father.
8. Can accept children in any temporal order or sex.

Youngest Brother of Sister(s):
1. Expects women to love him, care for him, dote on him; is quite willing to let them do all these things for him without much regard for recompense.
2. Is much less competitive and reactive than youngest brother of brothers.
3. May procrastinate.
4. May do well in his work if there is little interference from others, especially men, and provided some motherly woman is around to look after his comfort.
5. Is not good in leadership position.
6. Wants to do or refuses to do whatever he likes.
7. Is not as ambitious as other men.
8. Nice with the ladies; knows how to flatter them.
9. Among peers, is more interested in women. They all want to help him.
10. Is in no hurry to have children; leaves his wife to care for them.
11. May be jealous of care and attention his wife gives to children.
12. Grants freedom and independence to children, but likes to have them help him.

Youngest Sister of Sister(s):
1. Likes adventure, entertainment, and change.
2. Is competitive with men and women.

3. Can seduce men better by her greater inclination to submit. Not as bossy as older sister of sisters or as motherly as oldest sister of brothers; thus, is successful with men, but may be too capricious, willful, competitive, or distractable.
4. Would not be a good boss or leader over others.
5. Best match is oldest brother of sister(s), middle brother, or only child.
6. Is vivacious, impulsive.
7. Overreacts when people try to manipulate her.
8. Loves to excell at work; craves praise.

Oldest Sister of Brothers:
1. Is a helper of men; they are important to her; is impelled to retain the one she has, in finding new ones, or winning back old ones.
2. Is liked by men; they tend to confide in her; she has an ear for them and is a good sport; does not compete with them as a man, but rather assists them as a big wise sister.
3. Knows how to handle a belligerant man; is usually tactful and unoffensive.
4. Best match is youngest brother of sisters; worst match is oldest brother of brothers.
5. Is good with children; loves them.
6. Is independent and strong; tends to treat men like little boys; does not compete with men, but may act as an umpire in their quarrels.

Youngest Sister of Brothers:
1. Can attract men better than other girls.
2. Is feminine, friendly, kind, sensitive, tactful, submissive but not subservient, devoted, a good companion of men.
3. Will not let a man go, even when he has serious faults and abuses her; will defend him against others.
4. At work, is an ideal employee, the best person to work under somebody's guidance.
5. Is an excellent secretary, especially to men.
6. Best match is oldest brother of sisters, middle brother with younger sister.
7. Among peers, ismore interested in men.
8. Can get what she wants from men; sometimes appears spoiled or extravagant; is not ambitious on her own; will do anything for the man she loves; is nice and charming, and men like her.

Oldest Sister of Sisters:
1. Can stand on her feet, take care of others, and boss them effectively.
2. Has a certainty and finality in what she says and the way she says it.

3. Pretends to be surer of herself than she really is.
4. May cut people short who know more about the subject.
5. Will be unhappy and angry if she cannot dominate.
6. At work, is responsible and competent, especially in a position of leadership.
7. Will tend to identify with her superior, especially if he is a man; better if he is much older and distinguished—a father figure.
8. Despises official female figures above her.
9. Is a self-righteous, consciencious queen, accepting orders only from her king father.
10. Is politically conservative.
11. Best match—youngest brother of sister(s), youngest brother of brothers, or middle brother having older sisters.
12. Is better prepared for contact with women.
13. Stays tied to her father more strongly.
14. Finds girlfriends more important than boyfriends.
15. Sees children as more important to her than her husband.

Key: 0 = Oldest   Y = Youngest   B = Brother   S = Sister

1. O.B. of B.
2. O.B. of S.
3. Y.B. of B.
4. Y.B. of S.

Bad Relationships:
O.B. of B.—O.S. of S.—Rank and sex conflict—0 points
Y.B. of B.—Y.S. of S.—Rank and sex conflict—0 points

Excellent Relationships:
O.B. of S.—Y.S. of B.—No conflict—3 points
Y.B. of S.—O.S. of B.—No conflict—3 points

Good Relationships:
O.B. of B.—Y.S. of B.—B Sex conflict—2 points
O.B. of S.—O.S. of B.—Rank conflict—2 points
O.B. of S.—Y.S. of S.—S Sex conflict—2 points
Y.B. of B.—O.S. of B.—B Sex conflict—2 points
Y.B. of S.—O.S. of S.—S Sex conflict—2 points
Y.B. of S.—Y.S. of B.—Rank conflict.2 points

Fair Relationships
O.B. of B.—O.S. of B.—Rank and B Sex conflict—1 point.
O.B. of S.—Y.S. of S.—B and S Sex conflict—1 point

Index

Index

About the Author

Gordon Shipman was a teaching Fellow at the University of Nebraska for one year and wrote his dissertation at Columbia University as a Carnegie Fellow in International Law. He received the Ph.D. in political science at the University of Wisconsin—Madison in 1932. He has worked as a state probation-parole agent in Wisconsin, taught at Shurtleff College, and then he taught criminology and marriage and the family at Milwaukee State College. In the mid-1950s, Dr. Shipman was appointed chairman of the Department of Sociology and Anthropology of the University of Wisconsin—Milwaukee, where he helped to organize the Wisconsin Family Life Association and became its first president. He has written for both popular and scholarly journals. In 1966 he was appointed chairman of the Department of Sociology and Anthropology at the University of Wisconsin—Stevens Point and taught there until his retirement in 1971. For three years after retirement he taught part-time.